JPA

£19-95

Contemporary Issues in Physical Education:
International Perspectives

D0530536

Ken Hardman and Ken Green (eds.)

CONTEMPORARY ISSUES IN PHYSICAL EDUCATION:
INTERNATIONAL PERSPECTIVES

Meyer & Meyer Sport

British Library Cataloguing in Publication Data
A catalogue record for this book is available from the British Library

Contemporary Issues in Physical Education: International Perspectives
Maidenhead: Meyer & Meyer Sport (UK) Ltd., 2011
ISBN 978-1-84126-312-0

© 2011 by Meyer & Meyer Sport (UK) Ltd.
Auckland, Beirut, Budapest, Cairo, Cape Town, Dubai, Indianapolis,
Kindberg, Maidenhead, Sydney, Olten, Singapore, Tehran, Toronto
Cover Design: Sabine Groten, Germany
Cover Photo: © fotolia/anson tsui
Member of the World
Sport Publishers' Association (WSPA)
www.w-s-p-a.org
Printed and bound by: Beltz Druckpartner GmbH & Co. KG, Germany
ISBN 978-1-84126-312-0
E-Mail: info@m-m-sports.com
www.m-m-sports.com

CONTENTS

DEDICATION

This book is dedicated to the memory of David McNair (1916-2010). For over 60 years David had a distinctive involvement in, and made invaluable contributions to, regional, national and international physical education-related activities. He had a profound influence on the lives and careers of many as well as on national and international developments in physical education both personally and through the many former students he mentored during his tenure-ship at the University of Manchester, UK. He was a worldwide renowned History of Physical Education scholar. At regional level, David was an active "servant" within the North Western Counties Physical Education Association (NWCPEA), an Association in which he variously served as Chairman, Secretary, Member of the Executive Committee and Research Group and Blackpool Easter School Principal. He was a prominent member of a NWCPEA group that conceived the idea of a new research-focused journal, the *Physical Education Review* (now the *European Physical Education Review*), the first issue of which was published in Spring, 1978 and, which subsequently became an internationally recognised "impact" journal. As NWCPEA Honorary President, his continuing interest in research was manifest in his support first for what has become an internationally significant text in the domain of physical education, *Physical Education. A Reader*, published by Meyer & Meyer in 1998 and now in its 3rd edition and secondly for this *Contemporary Issues in Physical Education* book. Those who knew, or were acquainted with David McNair, will also remember him for his sharp intellect, his quick wit, charismatic charm, confidence and assurance, comradeship, as an all round attractive personality who was an inspiration to all.

INTRODUCTION

KEN HARDMAN AND KEN GREEN

Physical education across the world represents a rich tapestry of accumulative influences and developments, which have evolved distinctively from individual and/or "local" institutional and, in some cases, externally imposed initiatives. These initiatives have variously shaped national systems either through assimilation or adaptation or colonial imposition. Taking these evolutionary developments into account, it is unsurprising that different and various forms of structures and practices are evident. Characteristically, diversity prevails but there are elements of congruence in concepts and practice. The congruence is seen in a presence largely grounded in the Aristotelian concept of "harmonious balance" and variously linked with an expanding range of instrumental outcomes to include an ascribed role in achieving broader educational objectives such as whole school improvement, community development and effecting personal behavioural and attitudinal change. The congruence is also seen in the advocacy of physical education as a source of positive developmental characteristics and healthy well-being from early childhood, through adolescence to elderly adulthood; that is, as a life-long process, epitomised in the notion of the "cradle to grave physically educated person". Within this process, physical education, as a school subject, is granted "broad brush" scope and potential. It is, therefore, in a relatively unique position with responsibility in some way and somehow addressing many contemporary issues with its perceived distinctive features and characteristics within formal education systems not offered by any other learning or school experience. Hence, at one level, physical education seems to hold a prime position within the school curriculum. Paradoxically, over the last two decades this position has been under threat with evidence of marginalisation, reductions in curriculum time allocation, inadequacies in resources (personnel, facilities and financial), a perception by many of physical education as a "non-cognitive" subject, inferior in status to other so-called academic subjects and by association, inferior status of physical education teachers. The paradox is mirrored on the one hand both in the growth of modular programmes in Higher Education Institutions that in a variety of ways relate to physical education and, since the publication of *Physical Education. A Reader* in 1998, which was intended as a core thematic and issues text primarily to meet the needs of those innovative programmes, with several additions to the physical education-related literature; on the other hand, the two decades have witnessed two worldwide, two continental (European) and several national surveys pointing to concerns about the situation of physical education in schools, a widespread rise in obesity amongst children and young people, especially in economically developed countries, a concomitant increase in sedentary lifestyles as well as a perceived increase in numbers of school pupils no longer seeing the significance of physical education as a school subject: the traditional content of physical education and extra-curricular activity structures and emphasis on competitive sport has little relevance to their life-style context! Furthermore, during the same period, there has been a plethora of inter-governmental, governmental and non-governmental initiatives, policies and advocacy commitments to improve access to, and provision of, physical education. Testimony to the array of actions has been ministerial Communiqués, Conclusions, Recommendations and Resolutions, and institutional Declaration and Commitment Statements and Manifestos etc. Collectively, the various advocacy statements and associated diverse developments in school physical education policies and practices across the world have raised hopes about a secure future for physical education; however these positive initiatives are juxtaposed with sufficient broadspread evidence to generate continuing disquiet and doubts about a sustainable future. Thus, one view would be that physical education is currently at a kind of directional cross-roads, where its hitherto largely indispensable position is arguably unsustainable and the inevitable question arises of "w(h)ither physical education?" (Hardman, 2010).

The essential orientation of this book is on the "whither" rather than the "wither". It consists of a collection of chapters prepared by European-based established experts and emerging scholars, who have made, or are now making, significant contributions to the present and future physical education debate. Whilst ostensibly there is a "European flavour" in some of the chapters, in that they draw from, or relate to, European-centric national or regional studies, the contemporary issues addressed in all chapters have international resonance. This is because the issues are generic in their topicality; they offer bases for comparative reflections and/or involve references to international aspects and dimensions of the various topics and themes under consideration.

From initial chapters presenting empirically-based information in the form of reality checks on the situation of physical education in schools in international and exemplar national contexts that respectively have had considerable international and national impacts on political and educational debate as well as policy re-orientation, the ensuing contributions provide insights into a broad spectrum of contemporary issues pertinent to physical education and related areas (such as physical activity education, physical fitness, and health and exercise science). Generally, these issues are variously linked to pedagogy, didactics, inclusion, multi-culturism, policy, institutional structural harmonisation, including qualification frameworks, multi- and cross-disciplinary curriculum developments, personal and professional competences, and career cultures and frames. More specifically, the issues addressed encompass: representative situational national case studies, which reveal policy and political features common elsewhere in the world; perceptions of physical education curricular influences on the constitution of physically educated pupils; the concept of inclusion when applied to pupils with social emotional and behavioural difficulties; modes of delivery that embrace modern approaches to physical education teaching in general, peer tutoring to support student learning in physical education and teaching games through understanding in particular; perceptions of "significant actors" in active lifestyle promotion in schools with some focus on quality, meaning and relevance of school physical education curricular experiences encompassing curriculum content that not only extends to widening its nature and scope to achieve aims and competences associated with schoolchildren's physical activity and its role in promoting fitness and reducing health risk behaviours and complementary discussion on physical education-physical activity policies but also introduces "back to the future" traditional or "folk" physical and/or sporting activities in line with a global resurgence of interest in such activity to stimulate young people's active participation in fostering physically educated persons in multi-cultural school settings; the post-1999 Bologna Declaration structural harmonisation of Higher Education in

Europe launching compatibility-seeking "Qualification Frameworks" including theoretical concepts and practical implementation of assessment, extended to include a more global dimension; Bologna Process reference points' core principles for universal application in the development of physical education teacher education curricula; professionalization and professionalism within physical education teaching as a career; and finally, the future of physical education in a context of social change. In essence, the contributions serve to form a compendium of contemporary issues, which both separately and collectively, should be of wide appeal and, which equally may be of special interest to under- and post-graduate students following academic and professional programmes in physical education and related areas and their tutors, physical education practitioners and professionals in schools and further and higher education institutions, sport pedagogues and other vested-interest professionals and academics.

The editors wish to thank all contributors for their commitment to this collaborative enterprise of preparing chapters, all of which are grounded in research-based evidence and are intended to inform discussion on physical education-related issues as well as to stimulate reflective thought and action. We also want to thank Thomas Stengel of Meyer and Meyer Verlag for his support in the realisation of the publication of this book. Finally, we acknowledge the encouragement of the North Western Counties Physical Education Association to build on its *Physical Education Reader* predecessor with a follow up complementary text on internationally pertinent, contemporary topical themes and so meet with the Association's aims of broadening knowledge and understanding of physical education, fostering critical academic activity, disseminating relevant information on physical education through provision of opportunities for experts to share their research experiences and promoting physical education to international levels.

REFERENCE

Hardman, K., (2010). *W(h)ither Physical Education?: The Future Ain't What It Used To Be!* Unpublished paper presented at the 5th Youth Sport Congress, Ljubljana, Slovenia, 2-4 December.

CHAPTER I

GLOBAL ISSUES IN THE SITUATION OF PHYSICAL EDUCATION IN SCHOOLS

KEN HARDMAN

INTRODUCTION

The first Physical Education World Summit held in Berlin in November 1999, which highlighted concerns about a perceived decline and/or marginalisation of physical education in schools in many countries of the world, culminated in an *Agenda for Action* that prompted an unprecedented expression of interest and a range of inter-governmental, governmental and non-governmental initiatives, policies and advocacy commitments to improve access to, and provision of physical education. Testimony to a subsequent array of actions and advocacy initiatives, were ministerial Communiqués, Conclusions, Recommendations and Resolutions, and institutional Declaration and Commitment Statements and Manifestos[1] etc. Collectively, the various initiatives raised hopes about a secure and sustainable future for physical education but evidence of a perceived gap between "hope and happening" (Lundgren, 1983) generated continuing disquiet about the situation of physical education (PE) in schools. The disquiet was instrumental in precipitating a second worldwide school PE situation survey that was conducted over a period of four years (2004-2008) and a European Parliament Project survey of the situation of physical education in the European Union (2006-2007). In focusing on selected issues in school PE, this chapter draws from the European Parliament Survey Report (Hardman, 2007) as well as the multi-source informed *Final Report* of the second worldwide Survey (Hardman & Marshall, 2009) and, wherever appropriate, from the post-world economic and financial crisis period developments.

THE SITUATION OF PHYSICAL EDUCATION IN SCHOOLS

Within general education systems, a majority (around 95%) of countries have either legal requirements for PE or it is generally practised in schools. Despite official commitment to entitlement of access to physical education in schools either through state legislation or as a matter of general practice, such provision is far from being assured, particularly in contexts of localised implementation of the curriculum. The international surveys

---

1 These include *inter alia*: MINEPS III, Punta del Este Declaration (3 December 1999); European Non-Governmental Sports Organisation (ENGSO) support (October, 2002); European Physical Education Association (EUPEA) Forum on *Quality Physical Education (October, 2002)*; UNESCO 'Round Table Meeting' *Communiqué* (January 2003); Council of Europe Committee of Ministers Recommendations (April 2003); Central Council for Physical Recreation (CCPR) *Declaration from the National Summit on Physical Education* (London, January, 2004); *Recommendations of the International Conference on Women's Sport for Peace and Development* (Kathmandu, Nepal, November, 2004); MINEPS IV *Athens Declaration* (December 2004); *The Bangkok Agenda for Actions on Physical Education and Sport in School* (November 2005); Second Physical Education World Summit's *Magglingen Commitment* (December 2005); Latin and Caribbean Summit of Physical Education Declaration (Havana City Cuba, April, 2006).

undertaken over the last decade infer that almost 79% of countries (in Europe 89%; in Asia and North America only 33%) adhere to implementation regulations and delivery. The global percentage figure, however, is distorted by comparatively smaller sample sizes' data from the Central/Latin America and Middle East regions and a high proportion of European nation's positive responses; they can, and do, differ between schools in many countries. Conversely, globally in 21% of countries, PE is not actually being implemented in accordance with legal obligations or expectations. This proportion rises to 33% in Central and Latin America and the Middle East, 40% in Africa, and 67% in Asia and North America; in Europe only 11% of countries allege a shortfall in implementation.

The "gap" between official policy and regulations and actual practice is geographically widespread. Pervasive factors contributing to the gap are seen in devolvement of responsibilities for curriculum implementation, loss of time allocation to other competing prioritised subjects, lower importance of school PE in general, lack of official assessment, financial constraints, diversion of resources elsewhere, inadequate material resources, deficiencies in numbers of qualified personnel and attitudes of significant individuals such as head teachers. Additionally, exemption from physical education classes, granted on presentation of a medical certificate, is only acknowledged by a few countries. Such exemption practice on medical grounds is recognisably widespread throughout the world, thus perhaps undermining its status within the curriculum. An issue here is that exemption is rarely sought from other subjects except, perhaps, for religious education classes in some countries.

Examples from across the world show disparities between state policy legal requirements and implementation with clear indications of non-compliance with regulations and especially so in countries where curriculum responsibility lies with education districts or individual schools and are, therefore, subject to local interpretations:

- Venezuela
  There is "a national policy (but) the government does not take care of it; there are laws but they are not followed" (PE Teacher).
- Finland
  "Legal status is the same, but in practice not. The freedom of curriculum planning at schools has led to situations where implementation of physical education is not done according to the regulations concerning the weekly lessons" (University Professor).
- Canada (Quebec)
  Schools have "autonomy to adapt to the needs of their settings. This autonomy has helped most schools but some use it to limit PE time to the minimum and act against the efforts to legitimize PE programs on the curriculum" (Rivard & Beaudoin, 2005, pp.154-155).

Physical education provision during compulsory schooling years varies across regions and countries according to age or year stage of attendance. Overall the average number of years during which PE is taught in schools is 12 (range 8-14) with a 73% cluster of 11 and 12 years. The start-end years' continuum and associated access to PE are significant for individual development and sustained participation in physical activity. The early years are important in development of basic motor skills and provision of opportunities for optimal development of physical capacities during the crucial years of growth and maturation; for later age school start, pre-school experiences might offer similar opportunities but often they are neither compulsory nor accessible to every child. The significance of school finishing age centres on tracking physical activity engagement from adolescence to adulthood. When access to PE programmes ends at an earlier age, pupils are vulnerable to disengaging from physical activity. Consequently they might not continue with it in later life and there may be insufficient time to embed habits for regular engagement throughout the full lifespan.

PHYSICAL EDUCATION CURRICULUM TIME ALLOCATION

The issue of time allocation is generally complicated not only by localised control of curricula but also by practices of offering options or electives, which provide opportunities for additional engagement in PE and/or school sport activity. Student "uptake" of such opportunities can vary within, and between, countries and not all take advantage of the extra provision. Whatever, the options/electives available may be included in curriculum time allocation indicated in some countries' survey responses and, hence, may not accurately represent the prescribed time allocation for all students in at least some schools in those countries where additional opportunities exist. However, data triangulation produces a scenario of policy prescription or guidelines not actually being implemented in practice for a variety of reasons as exemplified in Lithuania and Nigeria:

- **Lithuania**
  Even though there is a legal basis, "it is difficult to put regulations into practice; the School Boards decide PE hours (obligatory and supplementary); the 1995 Law on PE and Sports stipulated 3 lessons but only 26% achieve this in classes 1-4, moreover, 38.9% do not have a third lesson; fewer than 10% schools comply with the 1995 Act for 3 lessons" (Puisiene, Volbekiene, Kavaliauskas & Cikotiene, 2005, p.445).
- **Nigeria**
  "Theoretically, five weekly lessons... are recommended for elementary and secondary schools...Unfortunately, however, at neither level is the weekly workload really adhered to" (Salokun, 2005, p.501).

Over the years, surveys' findings have revealed variations in the amounts prescribed or expected time allocated to PE (and actually delivered). "Guaranteed" access does not equate with equal amounts of access as seen in variations in timetable allocation. The situation is exacerbated by curriculum time allocated to other subjects and in some countries is deteriorating where recent educational reforms have resulted in PE teaching time decreases as observed in geographically distanced countries in different socio-cultural and economic settings:

- **Ghana**
  "Numerous attempts have been made to reduce the number of periods... the local situation determines actual practice. The timetable slots exist on paper. However, about 30% of schools use them for other subjects areas or...as free periods" (Ammah & Kwaw, 2005, p.316).

- **Ireland**
  "PE is being squeezed out of the education system by more and more compulsory academic courses, which hold little benefit compared to PE" (PE Teacher).
- **Taiwan**
  "Mergence of PE with health education has led to the reduction in the teaching time of physical activities (and) the time allocated to PE (is) affected (by an increase in) the teaching time of English... and new subjects (e.g. computer and dialects) (have been) introduced into the curriculum" (PE Teacher).

Physical education has not escaped the continuing consequences of the global financial and economic crisis of 2008-2009. In the USA, for example, whilst Californian Governor Schwarzenegger has proposed trimming the state budget as he tries to cut billions from college "physical education classes leaving athletic programs... in doubt..." (Krupnick, 2009), and the Portland School Board "in an effort to reduce their budget by $19 million, is considering the elimination of a significant portion of physical education programs" (Aahperd, 2010).

The allocated amount of PE curriculum time can be determined from policy and/or curriculum documents but local levels of actual control of curriculum time allocation give rise to variations between schools and, therefore, difficulties in specifying definitive figures for a country or region. However, some general tendencies can be identified. During the primary school phase years, there is an average **100** minutes (in 2000, the average was **116** minutes) with a range of 30–250 minutes; in secondary schools, there is an average of **102** minutes (in 2000, it was **143** minutes) with a range of 30–250 minutes per week. There are some clearly discernible regional differences in time allocation: European Union countries **109** minutes (range of 30-240 minutes) with clusters around 60 and 90 minutes in primary/basic schools and **101** minutes (range 45-240 minutes) with a cluster around 90 minutes in secondary and high schools (notably, figures in 2000 were higher with an average of **121** minutes in primary schools and **117** minutes in secondary schools, thus representing a perceived reduction in curriculum time allocation in the period 2000-2007); Central and South America (including Caribbean countries) **73** minutes in primary schools and **87** minutes in secondary schools. There is a gradual "tailing off" in upper secondary (high) schools (post 16+ years) in several countries and optional courses become more evident (Hardman & Marshall, 2009).

PHYSICAL EDUCATION SUBJECT AND TEACHER STATUS

Legal and perceived actual status of PE and its teachers is a contentious issue. Data indicate that equal subject legal status is claimed in 76% of countries. Africa, where only 20% of countries indicate equal legal status of subjects, represents a marked contrast with Europe's 91%. Data indicate that across all regions except Europe, in practice PE is considered to have lower status than other subjects. Notably in the Middle East and North American regions, all countries/states indicate that PE's actual status is perceived to be lower than that of other school subjects. High proportions of perceived lower status of PE are also seen in Africa (80%), Asia (75%) and Central and Latin America (67%), whilst in Europe lower subject status is reported in less than one third (30%) of countries. There are widespread exemplars of PE's perceived lower status:

- **Brazil**

  "The discipline does not enjoy much prestige... in the formal education environment; ... lack of interest and monotonously repetitive classes (are) factors that contribute to this resistance" (Costa & Tubino, 2005, p.143).

- **Luxembourg**

  "Legally PE is part of the national curriculum. In practice, PE is perceived as not important; it is just playtime, time off from serious school subjects. In theory it has the same status but other subject teachers believe themselves more important, PE comes always after academic lessons. When teachers have problems to finish the programmes of French for example they cut PE lessons" (PE Teacher).

- **USA**

  "PE is not an academic subject, so it is inappropriate to have it as an academic subject'... 'We do not require students to go to the dentist, take showers, get more sleep, and eat balanced meals – we shouldn't require PE either" (Grossman, 2009).

Physical education's inferior status and lower value as a mere antidote to academic subjects are evident in parental pre-disposition to favouring academic subjects with time spent on physical education perceived as a threat to academic achievement and/or examination performance as testified by European observers:

- **France**

  "Unfortunately parents don't protest (when physical education lessons are cancelled) and it (physical education) is not considered as fundamental" (PE/Sport Teacher).

- **Germany**

  "There is absolutely no protest from parents, when PE lessons are cancelled. There is always a protest if lessons in e.g. maths, German, English, etc. are cancelled. Occasionally parents demand that PE lessons are 'converted' to maths etc." (PE Teacher)

- **Malta**

  "Head teachers give a lot of lip service, but when it comes to effective support this is virtually non-existent" (and) "even parents look at it as a waste of time" (PE Teacher).

Frequency of cancellation of lessons is one indicator of subject status. Evidence indicates that the low status and esteem of the subject are detrimental to its position: in many countries (44%), PE lessons are cancelled more often than other so-called academic subjects; 41% of countries indicate that PE is the same as all other subjects when it comes to cancellation; and 5% indicate PE is less likely to be cancelled than other subjects, with 10% indicating that it is never cancelled. Apart from its attributed low subject status as of little educational value etc., other reasons for the cancellation of PE include: government financial cuts; insufficient numbers of qualified PE teachers; adverse weather conditions; the use of the dedicated PE lesson space for examinations and preparation for examinations; concerts; ceremonial occasions such as celebratory prize giving; spiritual exercises as at Easter time; and use as dining areas.

Illustrations of lesson cancellation causal factors are encapsulated in the following quotations:

- Israel

  "Principals and school staff generally do not perceive PE as a valuable academic subject... PE classes are the first to be cancelled when there is a special project, performance, trip or other school event" (Harari, 2005, p.402).

- Scotland:

  "Our programme is adversely affected when we lose two-thirds of our indoor teaching area; ...the games hall is used for exams and prize giving which can disrupt PE programmes" (Scottish PE Teachers).

Table 1 shows that in 28% of countries PE teachers do not enjoy the same status as other subject teachers but there are regional differences. In Central and Latin America, Asia and Europe, over two-thirds indicate that the status is the same. However, in Africa, North America and the Middle East the situation is reversed and in a majority of countries, there are clear indications of lower status accorded to PE teachers when compared with other subject teachers.

Table 1.

Physical Education Teacher Status: Globally/Regionally (%)

Global/Region	Higher Status	Same Status	Lower Status
Global	-	72	28
Africa	-	40	60
Asia	-	67	33
Central/Latin America	-	67	33
Europe	-	85	15
Middle East	-	33	67
North America	-	25	75

This is a feature illustrated in several countries in different regional locations:

- Australia

  "Teachers of the academic curriculum continue to command higher status within the education profession" (Tinning, 2005, p.60).

- Ghana

  "Since PE is somewhat marginalised, its teachers do not enjoy the same respect as teachers of compulsory academic subjects...The status of most PE teachers leaves much to be desired. It is often argued that they lack professionalism in the way they go about their job" (Ammah & Kwaw, 2005, p.321).

- South Korea

  "PE teachers' pay/work is worse than their colleagues in other subjects. Physical educators earn the same salaries as other subject teachers. However, unlike (them) they perform multiple responsibilities alongside teaching, like coaching, counselling and running intramural sports activities... They are often not viewed as 'real' teachers, but as custodians who simply 'roll the ball out'" (Kang & You, 2005, p.581).

THE PHYSICAL EDUCATION CURRICULUM

Physical education is often advocated as a source of a plethora of positive developmental characteristics from early childhood, through adolescence to late teen-age and now, when it is perceived to be a lifelong process, throughout adulthood, epitomised in the notion of the "physically educated person". Over the past century and a half, there has been an ebb and flow among differing, sometimes contradicting, PE curriculum themes. A number of these themes are alluded to in the November 2007 European Parliament's *Resolution on the Role of Sport in Education* (2007/2086NI), in which PE, subsumed in sport, as a generic term, is linked with socio-cultural, educational and social values, psycho-social qualities, socialisation, inclusion, moral codes of behaviour, cognitive and physical development, healthy well-being, healthy diet and other benefits to be derived from engagement in regular physical activity. Implicit in the European Parliament *Resolution* is the view that PE has the propensity to make significant and distinctive contributions to children, schools and wider society: respect for the body, integrated development of mind and body, understanding of physical activity in health promotion, psycho-social development (self-esteem and self-confidence), social and cognitive development and academic achievement, socialisation and social (tolerance and respect for others, co-operation and cohesion, leadership, team spirit, antidote to anti-social behaviour) skills and aesthetic, spiritual, emotional and moral (fair play, character building) development, a panacea for resolution of the obesity epidemic, inactivity crisis and sedentary lifestyles, enhancement of quality of life etc. With educational reforms in some countries and responses to concepts of healthy well-being related to active life styles in sedentary lifestyle contexts, the role of PE is expanding to embrace achievement of broader educational objectives such as whole school improvement, community development and effecting personal behavioural and attitudinal change. New activities are being incorporated into some programmes (fitness-based activities such as aerobics and jazz gymnastics and popular culture "excitement" activities such as snow-boarding and in-line skating etc.). Also evident, is increasing attention devoted to quality physical education concepts and programmes. Ostensibly as a school subject, with such broad brush scope and potential, PE is in a relatively unique and indispensable position with some kind of responsibility in somehow addressing many contemporary issues with its perceived distinctive features within the educational process with characteristics not offered by any other learning or school experience. The alleged distinctive profile of PE with its unique characteristics is summed up in the November 2007 European Parliament's *Resolution on the Role of Sport in Education* (2007/2086NI). The preamble to the *Resolution* alludes to physical education as "the only school subject, which seeks to prepare children for a healthy lifestyle and focuses on their overall physical and mental development, as well as imparting important social values such as fairness, self-discipline, solidarity, team spirit, tolerance and fair play..." and together with sport is deemed to be "among the most important tools of social integration". Nonetheless, the various surveys' data, supported by the literature, intimate narrower scenarios of curricular aims and content across the world: provision reality challenges policy rhetoric!

Examination of the thematic aims of curricula suggests that PE is primarily concerned with development of motor skills and refinement of sport-specific skills (35% in primary schools and 33% in secondary schools respectively). This tendency is encapsulated in Australian and South Korean commentaries:

"In reality, most PE teachers (in Australia) still give preferential treatment to those outcomes related to *developing concepts and skills for physical* activity. Accordingly, social learning and fair play education, probably receive less explicit focus than motor skills, sports and fitness" (Tinning, 2005, p.58).

In South Korea "PE strongly focuses on sport skills rather than health promotion and the affective domain. Most physical educators still have a traditional perspective that the subject's basic role is to develop motor skills in a variety of sports" (Kang & You, 2005, p.583).

Aims linked to broader lifelong educational outcomes such as promotion of health-related fitness (17% of primary and 18% of secondary schools' curricula) and active lifestyles (12% and 14% of primary and secondary schools respectively) as well as recognition of PE's contributory role in personal and social (21% and 23% of primary and secondary schools' curricula respectively) but less so of moral (4% and 3% of primary and secondary schools' PE curricula respectively) development are apparent.

According to "official" documents, many countries arguably commit to a "broad and balanced" range of curricular activities' opportunities and at one level, this would appear to be reflected in practice with the range of different activities taught within many PE programmes (see Table 2).

Table 2.

Physical Education Curriculum Activities in Primary and Secondary Schools: Countries (%)

Activity Area	Primary Schools %	Secondary Schools
Team Games	96	91
Individual Games	77	84
Gymnastics	87	82
Dance	79	71
Swimming	66	66
Outdoor Adventure Activities	53	54
Track & Field Athletics	88	91
Other	38	49

However, analysis of international surveys' data challenges the actual extent to which breadth and balance are provided: Activity areas' time allocation across the world reveals how, in practice, competitive sport Activities such as Games and Track & Field Athletics dominate the physical activity experiences of pupils globally, thus echoing indications in the World-wide PE Survey I of an orientation to a performance sport discourse in which in both primary and secondary schools there is a predominantly Games (team and individual) orientation followed by Track and Field Athletics and Gymnastics. Together these three activity areas account for 77% and 79% of PE curriculum content in primary and secondary schools respectively. Collectively, swimming, dance and outdoor adventure activities are accorded only 18% of activity time allocation at primary level and only 13% at secondary level. Such orientation runs counter to societal trends outside of school and raises issues surrounding meaning and relevance to young people as well as quality issues of programmes provided.

The competitive sports scenario is typified in African and Oceanic region contexts:

- **Nigeria**
  "Emphasis in PE leans rather towards developing athletes for state, national and international competitions. So right from elementary school, competition and winning are the elements stressed in PE classes. The idea of participation in order to make new friends or develop sportsmanship and moral 'uprightness' is rather remote in the Nigerian context" (Salokun, 2005, p.507).
- **Tunisia**
  "Contents center much more on sport activities than on physical development or broad physical experiences (with) individual over team sports (favoured). The most frequently taught contents are gymnastics... track and field... and team sports..." (Zouabi, 2005, p.679)
- **Australia**
  "Most (PE classes) are oriented around sport(s). Teachers use HPE classes as practice sessions and/or selection opportunities for sporting events. In most HPE classes it is typical to see students playing volleyball, soccer, field hockey, tennis, rugby, netball, Australian Rules football and doing track and field" (Tinning, 2005, p.60).

The issue of relevance of PE curricula in a context of societal values' and norms' changes is becoming significant in an increasing number of countries. The scenario of a discrepancy between what the school offers and what the pupils are looking for is not untypical in many countries. An emerging theme in recent surveys is repeated teachers' and officials' references to pupils no longer seeing the significance of PE as a school subject: the traditional content of PE and/or sports activity has little relevance to their life-style context.

The overall situation is not only seen in content of curricula but also in extra-curricular activity structures and emphasis on school sport. In some countries, this situational orientation may be counter to, or not aligned with, the lifestyle needs and demands, trends and tendencies of young people in out-of-school settings. Collectively, the experiences acquired from unwilling engagement in competitive sport-related physical education are a "turn-off". It would appear that this goes beyond those who have traditionally been either put off by, or not enjoyed, PE. In some instances, there appears to be a much deeper rejection of PE as a legitimate school activity:

- **England**
  "PE lessons are the cause of our unhappiest school day memories...Nearly a third of people claimed it was the unhappiest experience of junior and secondary school – outranking exams, bullying, teachers and school dinners" (Editorial, Cricket Foundation Survey, 2009).
- **Tunisia**
  "Students seem to be decreasingly motivated to take part in SPE (Sport and Physical Education) in its current form. This is clearly expressed by the high number of students who stay away from PE lessons, and by the increasing number of dispensations" (Zouabi, 2005, p.674).

Media headlines in the USA and the UK draw attention to questionable quality in PE practice:

"So just how bad is your child's gym class? PE programs often poorly run, provide few health benefits". "Experts Dissatisfied With PE Classes" (The Associated Press, Jan. 17, 2005).

"Call for Scottish PE overhaul after damning report" (Ferguson, 2009).

There are numerous examples testifying to negative experiences and impacts, lack of commitment to teaching and pedagogical and didactical inadequacies in some countries. The failure of teachers to provide meaningful experiences is underpinned by individuals' commentaries on PE in schools:

- **Slovenia**
  "Inappropriate curriculum for PE in elementary and secondary school. Curriculum is not realistic and in many parts has nothing together with practice" (PE Teacher)
- **Scotland**
  A Scottish individual recounts his experience of spending his "teenage years dreading games, shivering on rugby fields and subject to all manner of rebuke for my ineptitude at the game from staff and schoolmates. In my final week at school I finally confronted my physical education teacher and challenged him as to why I'd been made to endure this torture. "Well son", he replied, "at least you know now that you can't play rugby, and that's what we call an education" (Anon, cited in Kay, 2005)
- **USA**
  "Our society seems to have forgotten that PE is a daily dose of physical and emotional torture. At least it was for kids like me, anyway... When I was in school, I'd have given anything - my two front teeth, my 'Dirty Dancing' cassette tape, absolutely anything - to get out of PE for a single day. But I was cursed with good health and strong bones and never had the requisite cast or set of crutches. Year after year I suffered through having to play the same games, like Run the Mile Even Though it's August and You Could Die of Heat Stroke, Lay on Your Back and Kick at a Giant Canvas Ball While Everyone Can See Down Your Shorts, and, my personal favorite, Hold Out Your Thigh to be Pinched by the Body-Fat Percentage Counter" (McGaughey, 2006).

PHYSICAL EDUCATION RESOURCES

a) Teaching Personnel

A majority of countries have generalist (71%) and/or specialist (67%) teachers for PE in primary schools, whereas in secondary schools, specialist teachers predominate (98%). Concerns, regarding inadequacies of teaching personnel for PE classes, and especially so in the primary school phase, are persistent. The following illustrations may not be typical within each country, but they do indicate some problematic issues, which are replicated in other countries.

- **Austria**
  "...In primary schools teachers are not trained well – they often just go for a week or do German or mathematics instead of PE" (PE Teacher).
- **Nepal**
  "Physical education teachers are not very well trained" (PE Lecturer).
- **Cyprus**
  "The subject of PE is taught by teachers with either no formal training in teaching PE or with little or no formal teaching" (Government Official).
- **South Africa**
  "The majority of teachers who have to present the PE section of life orientation is not qualified" (PE Teacher).

There are opportunities for In-service training (INSET) or continuing professional development (CPD) of teachers in 73% of countries (only 33% in Central and Latin America), but there are considerable variations in frequency and allocated time. Frequency varies from specified hours, through days to weeks. Complexity related to the number of years indicated is evident: they range from choice through nothing specifically designated, every year, every two years, every three years to every five years and beyond. Nonetheless, some patterns can be identified: nearly half (49%) of all countries surveyed indicate that INSET/CPD opportunities are required every year; almost a quarter (23%) indicate that INSET/CPD has to be undertaken every three years; and the remainder (28%) note it was greater than every two years. Duration of INSET/CPD also reveals differences in practice between countries: those with annual training range from 12 to 50 hours, from 3 to 25 days; biennial and triennial training courses of 4 weeks; and five years range from 15 days to 3 weeks or 100 hours over the five year period. Data conversion into hours as a common denominator, (on a 36 hour week and a 7 hour day basis), results in 15 variations of INSET/CPD hours per year, ranging from 7 to 180 hours, though 71% of responses were clustered at less than 1 week per year (<36 hours per week) of provision.

In some countries, inadequate promotional infrastructure, finance and school-imposed barriers can inhibit participation in INSET/CPD. A consistent feature of all questionnaire surveys informing the Final Report of PE Worldwide Survey II on the issue of further professional development of teachers involved in PE teaching is the prevalence of a widespread need for INSET/CPD and recognition in some countries that in-service and resource materials provision is minimal and are accompanied by a continuing decline in PE advisory/supervisory service numbers.

b) Facilities and Equipment

A pervasive feature of concern, and particularly so in economically underdeveloped countries, is quality and quantity of provision of facilities and equipment because level of provision can detrimentally affect quality of physical education programmes. Over a third (37%) of countries indicates relative dissatisfaction with the quality of facilities. It is not surprising to see that quality of facilities is generally regarded as lower in economically developing regions (Africa, 60%; Central/Latin America 67%; and Asia 59%). Nevertheless, in spite of the apparent shortfalls in quality and quantity of facilities, encouragingly these proportional figures compare more favourably with those reported in Worldwide Survey I. Worldwide, more than a third of countries regard equipment provision as "below average"/"inadequate". Regional data indicate that in the three regions (Africa, Asia, and Central/Latin America) there is a majority of countries with "below average"/"inadequate" provision. At best (32%) of countries surveyed, there is an indication that the quantity of facilities is sufficient. Collectively, 50% of countries indicate that the quantity provided is "limited"/"insufficient" with only 18% indicating "above average"/"excellent". Regionally, in Africa (66%), Asia (53%), Central/Latin America (87%) and Middle East (57%) a majority of countries regard facilities as "limited"/"insufficient". Only in North America is the quantity of facilities assessed as "sufficient" or "above average". Consistent with the quantity of facilities, data suggest that at best 35% of countries surveyed indicate that equipment is "sufficient", whilst collectively 43% indicate that supply of equipment is "limited"/"insufficient" compared with 22% indicating "extensive"/"above average"). Regionally, there is consistency with data on quantity of facilities: considerable shortages of equipment in Central/Latin America countries (78%); and substantial shortages in Africa (62%), the Middle East (57%) and Asia (53%). Only the North American region has a positive assessment of equipment supply. Problems of low/poor levels of maintenance of existing physical education PE sites are reported: Middle East 100%; Africa 83%; and Europe 63%.

PARTNERSHIP PATHWAYS

Within the PE environment, teacher networks exist at schools' level in most countries. Municipal, region/county and national levels networks are evident in around 70% of countries; less widespread are networks of PE/sport teachers, sports clubs and other outside school community providers. In some countries there are inadequate links between school PE and the community but in others there is co-operation between school PE/sport and sports organisations on a regular basis. However, many children are not made aware of, and how to negotiate, the multifarious pathways to out-of-school and beyond school opportunities. Voluntary links between school PE and sport and wider community physical activity are reported in only around 36% of countries and, in total, direct school-community links are indicated in only 51% of countries. As a French PE teacher observes, co-operation between school and outside school agencies is inadequate and/or insufficient in many countries: there is "not enough co-operation between schools and sport organisations". This teacher's observation is underlined by some 61% of countries indicating lack of links between school PE and the community.

In Africa (80%), but more significantly in North America, Central and Latin America and the Middle East, where no school-community links are indicated, there appears to be a dearth of formal links between school PE and the community. Only European countries (55%) (with Asia close behind) appear to have a greater proportion of existing effective partnership links.

CONCLUDING COMMENTS

Collectively, the post-1999 Berlin World PE Summit's action and advocacy developments were demonstrative of broad-spread political will and indicative of an international consensus that issues surrounding PE in schools deserve serious consideration in problem resolution. There is evidence to suggest that national and, where relevant, regional governments, have committed themselves through legislation to making provision for PE but some have been either slow or reticent in translating this into action through actual implementation and assurance of quality of delivery. Generally, the 2004-2008 "reality check" period reveals several areas of continuing concern:

- continuing deficiencies in curriculum time allocation and actual implementation as well as a failure to strictly apply legislation on school PE provision, subject status, material, human and financial resources
- relevance and quality of the PE curriculum, especially in countries where there is a sustained pre-disposition towards sports competition and performance-related activities dominated by Games, Gymnastics and Athletics
- considerable widespread inadequacies in facility and equipment supply, especially in economically developing (though not exclusively so) countries; a related issue in the facility-equipment concern is insufficient funding
- disquiet about teacher supply and quality embracing insufficiency in numbers and inadequacy of appropriately qualified PE/sport teachers
- whilst some improvements in inclusion (related to gender and disability) policy and practice can be identified since the Berlin Physical Education Summit, barriers to equal provision and access opportunities for all still remain
- insufficient and/or inadequate school-community co-ordination physical activity participation pathway links.

These and other concerns are summarily embraced by a central European physical education academic's statement:

"PE in (recent years) has gone through intensive development and many changes. In spite of attempts by PE professionals, PE teachers, pupils and parents still struggle, sometimes more, sometimes less successfully with a range of problems. Some of these are presented here: decreasing amount of compulsory PE; often decreasing quality of education; large PE class sizes and increasing pupils' behavioural problems; growing numbers of non-participating and 'excused' pupils from PE lessons; stagnating physical fitness and performance of youth; care of pupils with disability; inadequacies in provision and lack of PE facilities; increase in PE teachers' average age and low interest of young graduates to work in the field of PE; inadequate social and financial reward of PE teachers, low work ethic of PE teachers that results from insufficient evaluation of their work; low representation of PE teachers in schools' management positions; absence of monitoring of PE teaching – there is a limited number of inspectors; monitoring by school directors is non-existent; weak organisation (professional associations) of PE teachers; shortages in pre-graduate teachers' preparation; unfinished system of lifelong PE teachers' education; lack of financial resources for science (research) in the field of physical education and sport".

To a large extent these concerns are rather typical of former "socialist bloc" countries in central and eastern Europe, a region where in the early 1990s countries entered into a politico-ideological transition period typified by democratic freedom and idealism and in educational reforms by conceptual re-orientations based on ideas of humanism and liberalisation. Reactionary forces of conservatism inculcated over almost half a century of physical culture and sport embedded in centralist authoritarianism has contributed to slowing down the reformed policy into practice realisation processes.

Generally across the globe, positive developments and policy rhetoric are juxtaposed with adverse practice shortcomings and continuing threats to PE, as portrayed not only in the above summary statement but also in a UK magazine headline in a context of proposed reforms to the Primary School Curriculum in England by the then Labour Government: "Future of PE is at risk, claims afPE" (Cordell, 2009).

The specific concern about relevance and quality of the PE curriculum is largely embedded in the widespread practice in PE curricula to provide experiences, which merely serve to reinforce achievement-orientated competition performance sport. Arguably, this is a narrow and unjustifiable conception of the role of physical education. For many boys and girls, such programmes do not provide personally meaningful and socially relevant experiences and they limit participatory options rather than expand horizons; moreover, they are contrary to trends and tendencies in out-of-school settings amongst young people. In this context, it is unsurprising that pupil interest in PE declines throughout the school years and young people become less active in later school years. If PE to play a valued useful role in the promotion of active lifestyles with children moved from cyber space virtual reality games and/or the potato "couch" to participation in physical activity, it must move beyond interpretations of activity based upon performance criteria. The nature and quality of delivery of the school PE curriculum is fundamental to the future not only of the subject in schools but also to the future of active life-styles over the full life-span for the two are inextricably entwined. If physical educators want to make an impact on enhancing activity levels in order to improve health, then some current practices should be abandoned because they do not appear to work for many children. Additionally, radical changes to pedagogy would be required, especially when trying to meet challenges embedded in the rhetoric of meeting the individual needs of each child but all "need to acquire knowledge, understanding and behavioural skills to ensure physical activity becomes a regular part of their daily life" (Fairclough & Stratton, 2005). Engagement in PE needs to be relevant and meaningful to sustain regular and habitual participation in, and out of and beyond school. Associated PE curriculum developments need to be accompanied by improvements to raise the quality of teaching and learning processes as well as that of associated teacher educational preparation or training. Recent pedagogical and didactical developments have consequences for PE teacher education both at initial and in-service training levels.

With the knowledge that educational experiences have a propensity to facilitate and help enhancement of life-span welfare and well-being, PE should be focally involved with the process of personal fulfilment in the future. It is worth remembering, however, that it is not the activity, but the reason for taking part that sustains participation. PE's role in fostering such "partaking" should be regarded as an essential element of education and as indispensable for the upbringing and education of people. I would add that its role embraces the often overlooked intrinsic value of the "sheer joy of participation in physical/sporting activity".

Another issue relates to the attention devoted to increasing levels of obesity and the association with physical inactivity might appear to bode well for PE but this association may prove to be a mixed blessing because arguably there is a risk of ignoring many of the most beneficial outcomes of quality PE if the subject matter is reduced to simply being a means to countering the obesity problem. It is tempting for physical educators to see their subject matter as the solution to children's obesity but over the last couple of decades, PE has not prevented an increase in obesity levels. The PE profession alone cannot solve the complex problem of the obesity crisis. Inactive lifestyles and unhealthy diets issues ignored by families, communities, media, and some kind of legislation, mean that the best efforts of the physical education profession to turn the tide of obesity will not succeed. A school's role extends to encouraging young people to continue participation in physical activity, through the provision of links and co-ordinated opportunities for all young people at all levels and by developing partnerships with the wider community to extend and improve the opportunities available for them to remain physically active. Hence, there is a need for wider community-based partnerships. With less than two hours per week time allocation (in many countries, it is frequently less), PE cannot itself satisfy physical activity needs of young people or address activity shortfalls let alone achieve other significant outcomes. Bridges do need to be built, especially to stimulate young people to participate in physical activity during their leisure time. Many children are not made aware of, and how to negotiate, the multifarious pathways to out-of-school and beyond school opportunities.

To this end, goals will be better served by effective partnerships with shared responsibilities of all vested interested agencies and institutions involved in policies and their implementation. The principle of partnerships embracing multi-sectoral policies is an essential feature of the World Health Organisation's (2004) *Global strategy on diet, physical activity and health* policy framework as well as the European Parliament's 2007 *Resolution*. PE Teacher Education programmes should address these facilitation and intermediary roles of the physical education teacher. Thus, at the very least, their professional preparation should embrace familiarisation with pathways for participation in wider community multi-sector provision and the achievement of personal excellence.

Support is fundamental to the realisation of such ideals. It can be achieved through the collaborative, co-operative partnership approach involving other professionals and committed, dedicated and properly mentored volunteer individual and group enthusiasts. Personnel functioning in partner institutions should have appropriate skills and competences, which might be acquired through some special training.

In essence, the situation, especially in economically under-developed and developing regions, has changed little since the 1999 Berlin Physical Education Summit and it is clear that many children are being denied the opportunities that will transform their lives in too many schools in too many countries. Thus, the overall scenario is one of "mixed messages". As Maude de Boer-Buqiccio (2002) (the then Council of Europe Deputy Secretary General) observed at the *Informal Meeting of Ministers with responsibility for Sport* in Warsaw, "the crux of the issue is that there is too much of a gap between the promise and the reality" (p.2); policy and practice do not always add up!

The European Parliament's 2007 *Resolution* represents a significant political step forward in policy guidance in the domain of PE. Noteworthy is its call on Member States to consider, and implement, changes in the orientation of physical education as a subject, taking into account children's health and social needs and expectations, to make PE compulsory in primary and secondary schools with a guaranteed principle of at least three PE lessons per week, a principle, which is widely advocated including regional professional organisations such as EUPEA (Europe) and the National Association for Sport and Physical Education (NASPE) in the USA, and inter-governmental agencies such as the Council of Europe. It is an agenda, which UNESCO is also actively pursuing as it attempts to formulate quality physical education policy principles, which Member States can suitably adapt to "local" circumstances and conditions. With such inter-governmental commitments to policy principles and action advocacy, a secure and sustainable future for PE appears to be realisable (Hardman & Marshall, 2009). Nevertheless, maintenance of monitoring of developments in PE across the world is an imperative. The Council of Europe's 2003 *Recommendations*, the UNESCO "Round Table" *Communiqué* and the WHO *Global Strategy* have advocated regular reviews of the situation of PE each country. The Council of Europe referred to the introduction of provision for a pan-European survey on PE policies and practices every five years as a priority! (Bureau of the Committee for the Development of Sport, 2002a; 2002b; Council of Europe, Committee of Ministers, 2003). A "watching brief" mechanism is essential to gauge whether "promises" are being converted into "reality" and so contribute to countering potential threats and securing a safe future for PE in schools. Otherwise with the Council of Europe Deputy Secretary General's intimation of a gap between "promise" and "reality", there is a real danger that intergovernmental agencies' *Recommendations* and *Resolutions* will remain more "promise" than "reality" in too many countries across the world and compliance with international and national Charters will continue to remain compromised (Hardman & Marshall, 2005) just as responses to the various *Declaration* and *Commitment Statements* will remain as conceptual ideals (Hardman & Marshall, 2009).

REFERENCES

Aahperd (2010). *Portland PE Teachers Speak Out*. Accessed via www.aahperd.org/about/announcements/portlandpe.cfm 15/09.

Ammah, J.O.A.A., & Kwaw, N.P. (2005). Physical Education in Ghana. In U. Pühse & M. Gerber (Eds.). *International Comparison of Physical Education. Concept - Problems - Prospects*. Aachen, Meyer & Meyer Verlag. pp.311-327.

Anon, (2004) Dundee Courier, December; cited in Kay, W., (2005), *Physical Education – Quality: A quality experience for all pupils*. Paper presented at the National Summit on Physical Education, CCPR, London. Monday 24 January.

Bailey, C. (1975). Games, Winning and Education. *Cambridge Journal of Education, 5* (1).

Bailey, R. (2005). Evaluating the relationship between physical education, sport and social inclusion. *Education Review, 57*, (1), pp.71-90.

Bureau of the Committee for the Development of Sport (2002a). *Draft conclusions on improving physical education and sport for children and young people in all European countries*. MSL-IM16 (2002) 5 Rev.3. 16th Informal Meeting of European Sports Ministers, Warsaw, Poland, 12-13 September. Strasbourg, Council of Europe.

Bureau of the Committee for the Development of Sport (2002b). *Draft conclusions on improving physical education and sport for children and young people in all European countries*. Revised by the Drafting Group. MSL-IM16 (2002) 5 Rev.4. 16th Informal Meeting of European Sports Ministers, Warsaw, Poland, 12-13 September. Strasbourg, Council of Europe.

Cordell, L. (2009). Future of PE is at risk, claims afPE. *Future Fitness. Sport and Fitness for today's youth,* June. p.1.

Costa, V., & Tubino, M. (2005). Physical Education in Brazil. In U. Pühse & M. Gerber (Eds.). *International Comparison of Physical Education. Concept - Problems - Prospects*. Aachen, Meyer & Meyer Verlag. pp.135-149.

Council of Europe, Committee of Ministers (2003). *Recommendation Rec(2003)6 of the Committee of Ministers to member states on improving physical education and sport for children and young people in all European countries*. Strasbourg, Council of Europe, 30 April.

Dallermassl, K., & Stadler, R. (2008). Physical Education and Education through Sport in Austria. In G. Klein & K. Hardman. *Physical Education and Sport Education in the European Union*. Paris, Editions Rcvue EP.S. pp.42-54.

De Boer-Buqicchio, M. (2002). *Opening Address*. 16th Informal Meeting of the European Ministers responsible for Sport. Warsaw, 12 September.

Editorial (2009). Unhappy memories of PE lessons. *Future fitness. Sport and fitness for today's youth,* July. p.1.

European Commission (2007). European Parliament Resolution on the Role of Sport in Education. Strasbourg, 13 November.

Fairclough, S.J., & Stratton, G. (2005). Physical education makes you fit and healthy: physical education's contribution to young people's activity levels. *Health Education Research, 20* (1), pp.14-23.

Ferguson, M. (2009). Call for Scottish PE overhaul after damning report. *Future Fitness. Sport and Fitness for today's youth*, July. p.5.

Garrett, R. (2004). Negotiating a physical identity: girls, bodies and physical education. *Sport, Education and Society, 9* (2), pp.223-237.

Grossman,D. (2009). *Physical Education Requirements Reduced From Two to One.* http://media.www.yucomentator.com/media/storage/paper652/news/2009/04/02/Ne 07/07/2009

Harari, I. (2005). Physical Education in Israel. In U. Pühse & M. Gerber (Eds.). *International Comparison of Physical Education. Concept - Problems - Prospects.* Aachen, Meyer & Meyer Verlag. pp.400-416.

Hardman, K. (1997). Socialisation into Physical and Sporting Activity in International and Cross-cultural Perspective: Reflections on Past, Present and Future Concepts and Contexts. *Journal of Comparative Physical Education and Sport, 19*, pp.25-43.

Hardman, K. (2002). *European Physical Education/Sport Survey.* Report submitted to Committee for the Development of Sport (CDDS) Council of Europe, Strasbourg, February.

Hardman, K. (2007). *Current Situation and prospects for physical education in the European Union.* Directorate General Internal Policies of the Union, Policy Department Structural and Cohesion Policies, Culture and Education, IP/B/CULT/IC/2006/10. 12 February.

Hardman, K. (2008). The Situation of Physical Education in Schools: a European Perspective. *Human Movement, 9* (1), pp.1-14.

Hardman, K., & Marshall, J.J. (1999). *World-wide Survey of the State and Status of Physical Education in Schools.* Paper, World Physical Education Summit, Berlin, Germany, 3-5 November

Hardman, K., & Marshall, J.J. (2000). *World-wide survey of the state and status of school physical education, Final Report.* Manchester, University of Manchester.

Hardman, K., & Marshall, J.J. (2005). *Update on the State and Status of Physical Education Worldwide.* 2nd World Summit on Physical Education, Magglingen, Switzerland, 2-3 December.

Hardman, K., & Marshall, J.J. (2009). *World-wide Survey II of School Physical Education. Final Report.* Berlin, ICSSPE.

ICSSPE (2005). *Second Physical Education World Summit Commitment.* Magglingen, Switzerland, November.

Kang, S., & You, J. (2005). School Physical Education in South Korea. In U. Pühse & M. Gerber (Eds.). *International Comparison of Physical Education. Concept - Problems - Prospects.* Aachen, Meyer & Meyer Verlag. pp.572-587.

Kirk, D., Fitzgerald, H., Wang, J., & Biddle S. (2000). *Towards girl-friendly physical education: The Nike/YST Girls in Sport Partnership Project – final report.* Loughborough, Institute for Youth Sport.

Krupnick, M. (2009). *Governor proposes big cuts to college physical education.* Contra Costa Times, http://www.insidebayarea.com/sanmateocountytimes/localnews/ci_12452961 07/07/09

Lambert, R. (1973). The informal system. In: R. Brown, (Ed.), *Knowledge, education and cultural change.* London, Tavistock.

Lundgren, U. (1983). *Curriculum theory, between hope and happening: Text and Context.* Geelong, Deakin University.

Martens, R. (1993). Psychological perspectives. In: B.R. Cahill & A-J. Pearl, (Eds.), *Intensive participation in children's sports.* Champaign, IL, Human Kinetics, pp.9-18.

McGaughey, A. (2006). If only more physical education teachers took sit-out bribes. *Associated Press*, Friday, February 24.

McNab, T. (1999). The joy of exercise. *The Guardian*, Tuesday May 4.

Ontario Government (2010). *The Ontario Curriculum (Revised). Grades 1-8. Health and Physical Education,* January. www.edu.gov.on.ca

Ogilvie, C., & Tutko, T. (1871). Sports: if you want to build character, try something else. *Psychology Today*, October.

Puisiene, E., Volbekiene, V., Kavaliauskas, S., & Cikotiene, I. (2005). Physical Education in Lithuania. In U. Pühse & M. Gerber (Eds.). *International Comparison of Physical Education. Concept - Problems - Prospects*. Aachen, Meyer & Meyer Verlag. pp.440-459.

Rivard, M-C., & Beaudoin, C. (2005). Physical Education in Canada. In U. Pühse & M. Gerber (Eds.). *International Comparison of Physical Education. Concept - Problems - Prospects.* Aachen, Meyer & Meyer Verlag. pp.150-173.

Royal Thai Government/UNO (2005). *The Bangkok Agenda for Actions on Physical Education and Sport in School.* November.

Salokun, S.O. (2005). Physical Education in Nigeria. In U. Pühse & M. Gerber (Eds.). *International Comparison of Physical Education. Concept - Problems - Prospects.* Aachen, Meyer & Meyer Verlag. pp.497-511.

The Associated Press, Jan. 17, 2005.

Tinning, R. (2005). Physical Education in Australia: An Interpretative account. In U. Pühse & M. Gerber (Eds.). *International Comparison of Physical Education. Concept - Problems - Prospects.* Aachen, Meyer & Meyer Verlag. pp.52-65.

UNESCO (1978), *Charter for Physical Education and Sport.* Paris, UNESCO.

UNESCO (1999). *Declaration.* MINEPS IV, Punta del Este, Uruguay, 30 November-2 December.

UNESCO (2003). *'Round Table' Communiqué. The United Nations General Assembly Resolution 58/5.* Paris

UNESCO (2004). *Declaration of Athens - A Healthy Society Built on Athletic Spirit.* MINEPS IV, Athens, Greece, 6-8 December.

Wankel L.M., & Kreisel, S.J. (1985). Factors underlying enjoyment of youth sports: sport and age group comparisons. *Journal of Sport Psychology, 7,* pp.51-64.

World Health Organization (2004). *Global Strategy on Diet, Physical Activity and Health.* Geneva, WHO. 17 April.

Zouabi, M. (2005). Sport and Physical Education in Tunisia. In U. Pühse & M. Gerber (Eds.). *International Comparison of Physical Education. Concept - Problems - Prospects.* Aachen, Meyer & Meyer Verlag. pp.672-685.

CHAPTER 2

CLAIMS AND REALITY: AN EMPIRICAL STUDY ON THE SITUATION OF SCHOOL PHYSICAL EDUCATION IN GERMANY

WOLF-DIETRICH BRETTSCHNEIDER &
HANS PETER BRANDL-BREDENBECK

INTRODUCTION

School Physical Education in different countries of the world has to face numerous challenges with regard to its state and status in the educational setting. Several publications (Hardman, 2003; Hardman & Marshall, 2009; Klein & Hardman, 2008; Pühse & Gerber, 2006) on the current situation of physical education have expressed continuing perceived concerns. The content of this chapter draws from the first representative study of physical education and school sport in Germany (DSB, 2006). The aims of the study were to describe and analyze the situation in the context of the current debate on the future of physical education from different perspectives, that is, from pupils' and teachers' perspectives as well as those from parents' and school Principals'[1] perspectives. Before presenting the empirical study with its theoretical framework and design and highlighting selected findings, a few preliminary remarks, which deal with the importance and difficulty of conducting a survey on physical education, may help to better understand the background of the study.

THE IMPORTANCE OF CONDUCTING A STUDY ON SCHOOL PHYSICAL EDUCATION

Recently a number of meta-analyses have been undertaken to identify the multitude of factors, which may influence young people's physical activity and sport involvement. The typologies found, differ in terminology and complexity, but concur on the following correlates and determinants: physiological, psychological, socio-cultural and ecological (Biddle et. al., 2005; NICE, 2007; Sallis et al., 2000).

Physiological determinants include age, gender and ethnicity. Young people's physical activity and sport involvement is strongly influenced by these factors. International studies agree in the findings that physical activity decreases with age and boys are more physically active than girls. Most findings confirm that ethnicity is correlated with physical activity (Sallis et al., 2000). Psychological correlates of physical activity include self-efficacy and self-perception of one's physical fitness, motor ability and sport competence. Physical activity and sport involvement is positively associated with enjoyment, zest for life and a positive attitude toward physical activity. Conversely, low self-esteem and low

---

1 In some countries, the Principal is designated as "Head Teacher" or "School Director".

physical self-concept (physical fitness in boys and physical attractiveness in girls) correlate inversely with physical activity. When it comes to socio-cultural correlates, most studies agree that a family's socio-economic status and parental educational background strongly influence physical activity among children. Parental and peer support are positively associated with physical activity. The sport participation of the mother supports the daughter's sport involvement. For boys' level of physical activity, it is the father's interest that is influential. Ecological influences include accessibility to sport facilities and playgrounds as well as the availability and quality of equipment. Public transport to activities and safety on the way to the facilities are influential factors as well; these factors are valid for organized physical activities such as club or community based sport programmes as well as for informal activities in play spaces.

Physical education in schools is one of the most, if not the most important setting for physical activities among young people. As most schools across the world require physical education as part of the curriculum, school-based programmes ensure that many of the young generation are exposed to intervention, regardless of age, gender, ethnicity, social and cultural background. Most of the above–mentioned correlates associated with physical activity can be influenced by physical education teachers. Targeting interventions at the entire school population could avoid excluding children, who are at the bottom of the social ladder and usually not found to be participating in organized sport. Interventions directed to all school children could also avoid stigmatizing children with special needs, obese boys and girls and those with chronic diseases. School physical education interventions focus on creating and arranging situations to ensure all childrens' awareness of physical activity benefits. In conclusion, if the increase and improvement of young people's physical activity in all its variety of forms is part of the school focus, physical education and school sport have to be high on the agenda.

THE EDUCATIONAL SYSTEM IN GERMANY
AND ITS IMPLICATION FOR PHYSICAL EDUCATION

As school systems including their physical education curricula differ across countries, it is important to know the educational context of the school physical education study in Germany. Germany has a population of about 80 million people and is a Federal Republic with 16 States (Länder). One of the consequences of the federal system is the decentralization of administrative responsibilities with the implication that each State (Land) has exclusive responsibility in the field of education, including the school system as well as curriculum development and implementation. For young people aged 6-16 years, education is compulsory with a subsequent period of either three years of vocational training or three years Grammar school with a current gradual conversion to 12 years of schooling instead of 13 years being under way.

Regardless of Land and type of school, physical education as a school subject is part of the compulsory curriculum for all young people from grade 6 to the end of secondary education. Reviews and analyses of the current situation of physical education in Germany send mixed messages. On the one hand, there are concerns about curriculum time allocation with a reduction of physical education time in most Länder, lack of qualified physical education teachers in primary schools, status of physical education teachers and inadequacies in provision of facilities and equipment, whereas on the other hand, positive aspects of physical education such as physical education being placed on top of the pupils' favourite subjects' charts, its potential to promote health and fitness and enhance cognitive functioning, as well as its contribution to character development or to the school's corporate identity, are presented to the public (Brettschneider & Brandl-Bredenbeck, 2008).

Important questions arise in this context: When using the term "physical education" do we mean a school subject that is clearly demarcated or is the debate on an amorphous field characterized by a variance between programme aims, content and outcomes, according to the individual Land's policy? On a conceptual level, physical education curricula may vary in the different Länder. As any other school subject, physical education is a product and compromise of struggles and tensions between powerful social forces. In other words, the physical education curriculum is socially constructed and, therefore, presents itself with multiple and varied agendas. Despite all variations in specificity and scope allowing a wide range of experiences from limiting options to expanding horizons, a core can be identified in the different physical education concepts. It is safe to state that physical education is seen as that part of education, which aims through a balanced and coherent range of physical activities to contribute to the development of an individual's potential including growth and development, physical and psycho-social competencies. It provides young people with knowledge, skills and understanding, necessary to perform and enjoy a variety of physical activities and maintain physical fitness as part of a healthy lifestyle. Physical education is a springboard for involvement in sport, a source for communication with others and a platform for development and moral education.

This is a relatively broad concept leaving broad scope for specific interpretations of meanings and functions. A variety of learning experiences and subject matters might be selected to construct a programme. The concept contains elements that can be attributed to the concept of *Bildung* as well as those that can be attributed to "health promotion". *Bildung* is a term that dates back to the Age of Enlightenment. In its modern interpretation and with reference to physical education, it aims at the development of one's personality in all its dimensions – physical, cognitive, emotional and social. The individual is seen as an active producer of his/her development. *Bildung* also aims at enabling young people to experience the various human movement phenomena (play, games, sport and dance) and to enjoy its correlates such as play, competition and creation; it also aims at empowering people to critically observe and evaluate the development of current body and sport culture. To engage in sport is to value its various forms as ends in themselves. They are separate from the routine instrumental activities that we take up in our daily lives.

Physical education as sport technique, a concept on which some Länder still place some weight, can also be attributed to the above mentioned umbrella concept. This concept gained importance and became popular in the 1970s with competitive sport as well as "sport for all" moving into the domain of public attention. Physical education benefitted from this development in the former German Democratic Republic (GDR – East Germany) as well as in the former Federal Republic of Germany (FRG - West Germany). It lost its importance in the 1990s when educators claimed that physical education should not reflect the world of organized sport but rather criticize the darker sides of its development and instead, present multi-faceted movement culture with its educational potential as an alternative.

The overall concept is also open for physical education as health promotion or health optimizing physical education, which can be seen as magic words mantra used in the current debate on the justification of school physical education. The line of argument runs as follows: Young people in Europe become fatter and fatter, supposedly because they eat too much, spend too much "screen" time, fail to take enough exercise in their daily life and are less physically fit than any previous generation. The so-called "obesity crisis" is ubiquitous (Brettschneider & Naul, 2007). The reported prevalence rates are drawn upon as arguments for the importance and indispensability of school physical education, for it is the only setting, where all children (independent of talent, gender and social status) learn how to practise and enjoy various kinds of physical activity and how to benefit from them.

The question to be answered in our study is not whether physical education as *Bildung*, or as sport techniques or as health promotion or whether intrinsic or instrumental rationales can claim priority. Neither is it the question which concept might secure the future of physical education. The questions to be answered in an empirically grounded way are more down to earth. The findings serve as a basis on which theoretical concepts can be elaborated. The questions addressed are: (i) is what is expressed and explained at curriculum level reflected on a physical education practice level, particularly in terms of what physical education teachers do in the subject's name?; the question behind this question is whether it is really the curriculum that controls physical education teachers' teaching behaviour or is it physical education teachers' socialization into sport and into education?; (ii) what are the instigators and what are the barriers for quality physical education in the eyes of physical education teachers?; (iii) what about the workload and the stress physical education teachers have to cope with in daily lessons?; (iv) as the quality of physical education is also in the eyes of its beholders, how do pupils experience and evaluate the subject?; (v) how do significant others such as Principals and parents view physical education and its contribution in enhancing young people's well-being, in enriching the school's campus life and atmosphere, and in developing corporate identity?; and (vi) whether physical education teachers' qualifications and competencies and whether the time allocated to physical education and its learning and teaching environment allow realization of the goals expressed on the conceptual level of the physical education curriculum? Prior to answering some of these questions empirically, the theoretical framework of the Study is outlined.

BACKGROUND OF THE STUDY

It was the ambitious goals of the study a) to meet the methodological level and standards of international studies assessing young people's academic achievements and their learning environment (e.g. PISA, TIMMS, IGLU) and b) to consider the specificity of school physical education in the research programme.

The consequences for the research paradigm are two-fold:

1. Because of the complexity of the teaching/learning process and its outcomes, the theoretical framework underlying the study is not only focused on pupils, but also takes into consideration the socio-economic status and educational level of parents, the competencies of their teachers and the specific learning environment including facilities and equipment as well as the interventions that might have explicitly or implicitly been implemented in multiple settings such as school, sport clubs, community and other public places (refer figure1).

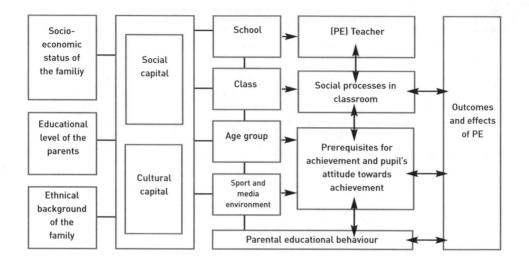

Figure 1. Theoretical Framework (according to Helmke & Weinert, 1997)

2. Consequences of the research concept are also reflected in the design of the quantitative study (accompanied by qualitative case studies). The stratified and randomized sample comprises 4th, 7th and 9th graders from various Länder and different types of schools in Germany (N=8863) as well as physical education teachers (N=1158), school Principals (N=191) and pupils' parents (4352). Survey data were gathered through questionnaires. Descriptive and analytical statistical procedures (e.g. regression analysis, MANOVA) were applied in the process of data analysis.

Different data sets can be distinguished. Beside the master-file, there are sub-files with aggregated data, the coding of which allows the linking of sub-files with their aggregated or individualized data as well as follow-up studies with a longitudinal design. This way physical education teachers' data, for instance, can be linked with their pupils' data and their Principals' data. Pupils' data can be linked to, and compared with, their parents' data. In addition to these unique opportunities, schools placed at the top or bottom can easily be identified and data analyzed. Qualitative in-depth interviews with pupils, teachers and Principals provide highly differentiated pictures of these schools and serve as empirically verified examples of good or bad practice (see fig.2).

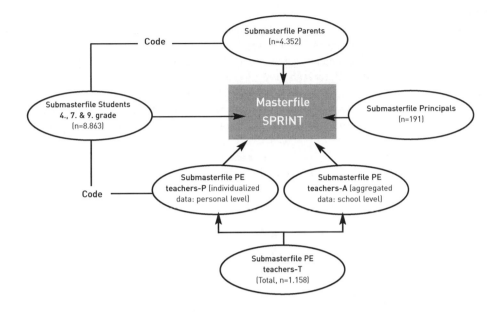

Figure 2. Structure of data set

PHYSICAL EDUCATION IN GERMANY:
SELECTED FINDINGS FROM THE NATION-WIDE "SPRINT" STUDY

The above-mentioned opportunities provided by the study design are currently being realized in a number of doctoral theses. In this chapter, reference is made to the first set of descriptive data, the publication of which has had, and continues to do so, a remarkable effect on political leaders and those institutions responsible for the developmental growth and education of the young generation in Germany. Without any doubt, present reform initiatives undertaken by the responsible respective administrations can be attributed to the publication of the first results of the SPRINT study. The selected findings reported here refer to the following issues: the conditions under which physical education takes place; pupils' assessment of physical education; effects of physical education; physical education teachers in the eyes of their pupils; and the social status of physical education teachers.

When it comes to the conditions under which physical education takes place attention has to be paid to at least three issues: curriculum time allocation; qualifications of physical education teachers; and availability and quality of facilities and equipment.

Time allocation to Physical Education
Ignoring minor variations, most schools in most Länder require physical education as part of their curricula. From grade 1 to grade 13 (i.e. 6–19 year olds) three "hours" per week (i.e. around 135 minutes) are compulsory. The overall statistical figures when comparing official curriculum requirements and pupils' information on the physical education classes

offered, show a remarkable discrepancy between requirement and reality across all Länder. With regard to adolescents attending secondary modern schools (*Hauptschule* – low track and *Realschule* - middle track) especially, notable differences between the demands of the curriculum and physical education lessons actually given can be observed (2 "hours" per week instead of three "hours" per week). This finding has to be seen in line with the fact that the young people attending the *Hauptschule* are also under-represented in their involvement and participation rate in sport clubs. Hence, physical education lessons would be essential in these schools to encourage socially under-privileged young people into engagement in sport, however, the opposite is the case. With variations between the individual Länder, the findings reveal that one in four physical education classes does not take place, reasons for which differ from school to school (see Table 1).

Table 1. Time Allocated to Physical Education: from Curriculum to Reality

	Baden-Württemberg		Bayern		North-Rhine Westphalia		Schleswig-Holstein	
Secondary Modern School (Lower track) Hauptschule	3 Curricul. ⇩ 2.67 Students	- 0.33	2+2 ⇩ 2.27	- 1.73	3 ⇩ 2	- 1.0	3 ⇩ 2	- 1.0
Secondary Modern School (Middle track) Realschule	3 Curricul. ⇩ 2.32 Students	- 0.68	2+2 ⇩ 2	- 2.0	3 ⇩ 2.1	- 0.9	3 ⇩ 2.5	- 0.5

Teachers' Qualifications

In order to teach physical education in schools, successful completion of a Physical Education Teacher Education programme and a relevant qualification according to the specific type of school are pre-requisites for all teachers. The responses to the question of who teaches physical education show that physical education teachers' qualifications differ from school type to school type. In Secondary Modern Schools/High Schools, almost all physical education teachers are highly qualified and meet the requirements. In schools mostly attended by children from families with limited educational aspirations and a lower socio-economic status, between 10 and 30 per cent of teachers teaching physical education classes do not have the formal qualification needed for teaching the subject. When it comes to primary schools (again varying from Land to Land), some 50% of the teachers (mostly female) teaching physical education are not formally qualified. Clearly, it takes more than just a formally certified qualification to determine a good or bad physical education teacher, but the consequences of lack of qualification and expertise are obvious, as two examples serve to illustrate: (i) a recent study (Kurz & Fritz, 2006) shows that almost one third of primary school children in Germany cannot be regarded as competent and safe swimmers; one of the main reasons for this deficiency is that classroom teachers (that is, teachers who have to teach physical education) simply do not have the expertise and competence to impart development of necessary skills and improve swimming techniques; and (ii) as there is a strong relationship between perceived competence and professional contentment, the high rate of those primary school teachers without formal certified qualification, who have to teach physical education, is not surprising; these teachers tend to be discontented because they feel incompetent (Oesterreich, 2005; 2006).

Facilities and Equipment

For the school as a setting and its teaching and learning environment, physical education teachers and their pupils agree that the facilities, apparatus and equipment meet the requirements for quality physical education, though a minority of both groups sees deficiencies for teaching innovative sporting activities such as roller-blading, climbing etc. Some primary school teachers complain about the loss of time spent on commuting between school and swimming baths (Breuer, 2006). Principals were asked to rate their sport facilities on a scale from 1 (=excellent) to 6 (=very bad) with regard to different aspects: the findings concerning availability (2.64), state of the building (3.04), apparatus (3.01), equipment (2.75), cleanliness (2.99), safety (2.85), locker (changing) rooms (3.12), hygiene (3.21), attractiveness (3.13) can be considered neither very positive nor very negative (DSB 2006).

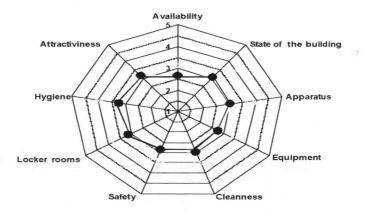

(1=excellent; 6=very bad)

Figure 3. Sport Facilities in Schools: Principals' Assessments

When compared with the Principals, teachers' and pupils' evaluation of the facilities reveals a similar tendency: notably, the judgement of both teacher and pupil groups with regard to attractiveness, cleanliness, size, state of the building, up-to-dateness, proximity, and sports equipment is almost identical.

Pupils' Assessment of PE

Most studies on the popularity of school subjects agree that physical education is ranked first in the charts. The reasons for this perceived popularity vary from "it's fun" through "health-improving" to "neither strenuous nor demanding". When compared with Mathematics or German, the scores for physical education are significantly higher, though they do decrease with age. The levels of importance attached to physical education lessons as well as to the evaluation of its quality are relevant aspects when justification of the subject in comparison with the other subjects is sought.

Almost two thirds of all pupils consider physical education lessons (with low differences between the genders) to be important, respectively very important. The level of importance of physical education decreases with age but even in grade 9 students assess it to be rather important; only 13% of pupils consider that physical education lessons are not important at all (DSB 2006). As Figure 4 indicates, the curves run parallel to each other, one explanation for which may be that the pupils' estimation becomes more realistic with age.

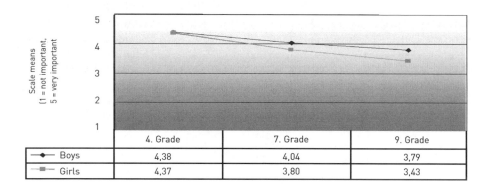

	4. Grade	7. Grade	9. Grade
Boys	4,38	4,04	3,79
Girls	4,37	3,80	3,43

Figure 4. Importance of Physical Education: Students' Perspective

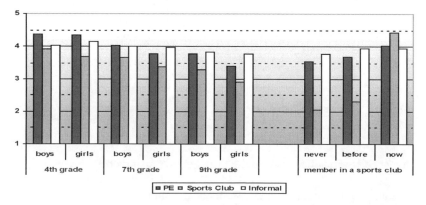

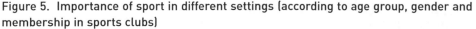

Figure 5. Importance of sport in different settings (according to age group, gender and membership in sports clubs)

Concerning the importance of school physical education, pupils, teachers, parents and Principals agree in confirming its high significance. Above all pupils, attach great importance to physical education, with boys scoring more positively than girls, decreasing with age in both groups and those being actively involved in organized sport outside school scoring highest. On attachment of importance of different settings, the findings show that the school is an ideal environment for popular physical activities. Amongst both genders, informal activities in play spaces are ranked highest, followed by physical education classes, which are more popular among boys and sport organized in clubs or communities.

Effects of PE

Young people's estimation of physical education (albeit decreasing in value with age) is not only emotionally determined because pupils clearly have specific expectations associated with school physical education. Schoolboys and girls want, and expect, a strong relationship between what they learn in school physical education classes and what they can apply in their sport involvement out of school. Figure 6 shows that there is a discrepancy between expectation and reality. Regardless of age, the children confirm that in physical education lessons they can make use of the skills and abilities acquired out of school. They see a possible transfer of the externally acquired competencies to school physical education. However, contrary to this view and strongly so with increasing age, they have doubts as to whether they can apply what they have learned in physical education classes to outside school sport-related leisure activities. They do not believe in the transfer of school physical education outcomes to either their organized or informal sport activities out of school. In other words, this can be interpreted as both boys and girls not being content with what is being offered in school physical education classes.

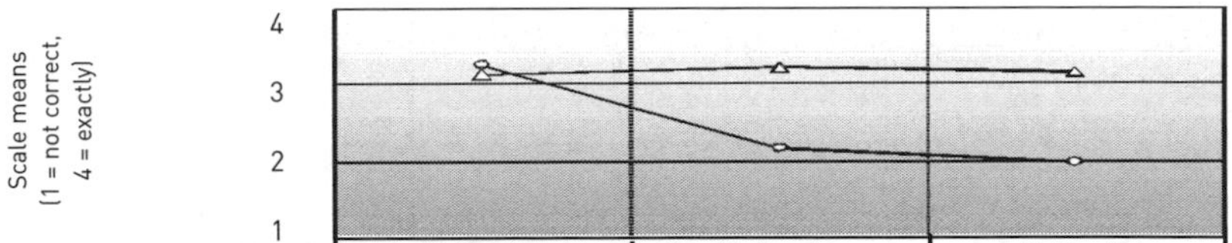 Scale means (1 = not correct, 4 = exactly)	4. Grade	7. Grade	9. Grade
Transfer leisure time – Physical Education	3,14	3,21	3,15
Transfer Physical Education – Leisure time	3,27	2,15	1,98

Figure 6. Transfer leisure time – Physical Education – Leisure (Students by Grade)

Nevertheless, school children are aware of the positive effects of physical education. When asked to assess their subjective well-being, findings clearly demonstrate physical education's contribution. Decreasing with age and with gender differences (boys score more positively than girls), school children estimate physical education's contribution to their well-being at a significantly higher level than any other subject or school in general (refer Figure 7.).

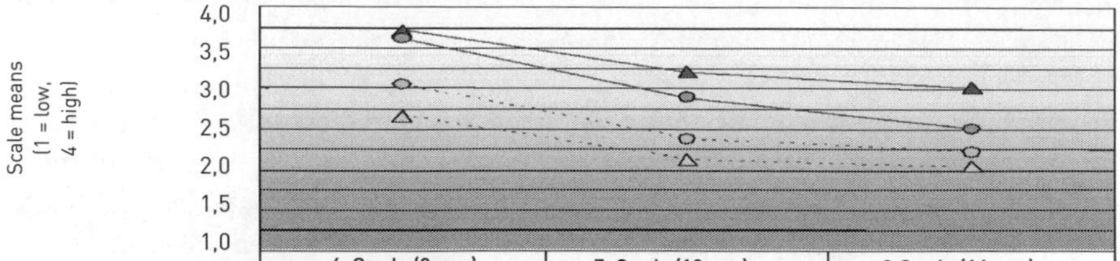

	4. Grade (9 yrs.)	7. Grade (12 yrs.)	9.Grade (14 yrs.)
▲ Boys PE	3,72	3,21	3,02
·-·▵·-· Boys School	2,67	2,13	2,04
⊙ Girls PE	3,62	2,89	2,51
·-·⊙·-· Girls School	3,05	2,38	2,22

Figure 7. Well-being in Physical Education Classes and in School

PE Teachers in the Eyes of their Pupils

The student vision of physical education teachers is markedly positive (see Figure 8): pupils appreciate their competence in the subject, their emotional and social commitment as well as their sports proficiency; moreover, they are perceived as being self-confident and friendly. Notably, physical education teachers receive a higher rating from their pupils than do any other subject teachers with regard to the scope and quality of their teaching skills as well as to their pedagogical concepts and social competence (Gerlach et al., 2006).

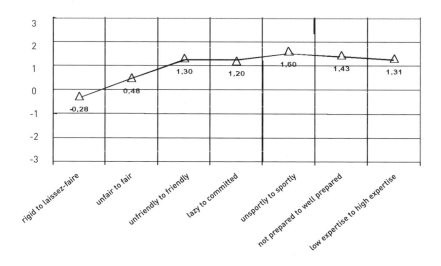

Figure 8. Physical Education Teachers: Pupils' Assessments

The data also reveal another important issue with regard to physical education teachers' age and the way they are seen by their pupils (Brandl-Bredenbeck, 2006). Independent of gender (of pupils and teachers) and independent of age of the pupils in nearly all dimensions, a noteworthy age effect of teachers can be observed (refer figures 9-11).

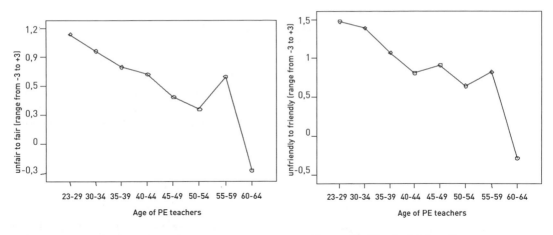

Figure 9. Physical Education Teachers: Pupils' Assessments on the Dimension "unfair to fair" in Relation to Age of Teacher

Figure 10. Physical Education Teachers: Pupils' Assessments on the Dimension "unfriendly to friendly" in relation to Age of Teacher

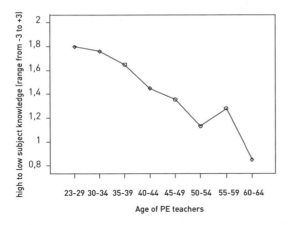

Figure 11. PE Teachers: Pupils' Assessments on the Dimension "high to low subject knowledge" in relation to Age of Teacher

Over the course of the professional career, the assessment level of the teachers by their pupils is gradually decreasing. There is only one exception and this is for the 55-59 years age group. At least two issues arise here: (i) the gradual decline with age may be interpreted as an indicator that there should be a stronger emphasis on programmes of career-long/continuing professional development (CPD); up to now in Germany, there has been no obligation for a teacher to attend any further training or continuing education once he/she is employed in the school system; and (ii) with regard to the age group 55-59 years, the data may be interpreted as an attempt by these teachers (who will have only a few more years to work before they retire) to initiate some changes in their own professional teaching and perhaps in their behaviour towards the pupils.

Social Status of PE Teachers

As to their social status, physical education teachers themselves, as well as the school Principals, do not see any difference from other teachers. With regard to the status of physical education teachers, 84% of the Principals do not see any differences from teachers of other subjects (see Figure 12). However, Principals appreciate the commitment of their physical education teachers and their contribution to the positive public image of the school. They emphasize physical education teachers' various contributions to school life. When it comes to the participation in on-the-job-training, physical education teachers rarely differ from their subjects' colleagues, with both groups not being very active.

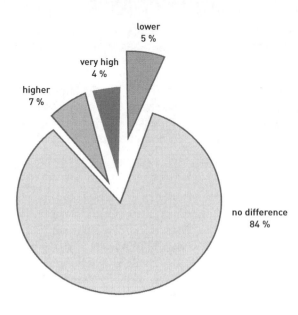

At first sight this scenario does not confirm the usual findings, which show physical education teachers having a kind of inferiority complex compared with other teachers. This might be explained by the German educational system demanding that all High School teachers have to study and teach two subjects.

Figure 12. Social Status of Physical Education Teachers compared with other Subject Teachers: Principals' Assessment

SUMMARY OF THE FINDINGS

The findings detailed above are based upon aggregated data of the sample. In other words, the findings are representative for the population in the selected Länder, regardless of whether their curricula focus on teaching and improving motor skills and physical abilities or tend to place emphasis on physical education's propensity to support and promote young people's development in all its dimensions: physical, cognitive, emotional, moral and social. Curricula differ not only in their major goals, but also in the activities offered in physical education classes. Some Länder have traditional activities such as track and field athletics, swimming and games as main courses on the menu and regard informal physical activities and elements of modern movement culture almost as a dessert to be avoided. Others put the non-codified sporting activities and the non-sportive elements of movement culture to the fore.

In this context, the SPRINT Study presents findings that should provide curriculum designers and lobbyists with cause for thought on the one hand, and enhance physical education teachers' self-esteem and confidence to a large degree on the other hand.

When comparing the pupils' estimation of physical education in the different Länder with their varying emphases on goals and contents, the Study's findings show no difference at all between them. Obviously it is not the curriculum with its goals and contents that controls physical education classes, rather it is the physical education teachers' socialization referring to sport as well as to education that really counts and not so much what is being expressed in curriculum. This is a finding that may be frustrating for some people and encouraging for others.

POLITICAL EFFECTS OF THE STUDY

This part of the chapter deals with the issue of the Study's public and significant vested-interest authorities reception of its findings and whether the findings have had any effect on them. The findings have been, and are still being, intensively debated both in the general public and in the scientific community. They were welcomed by sport organizations, which have been arguing for decades for a greater amount of time allocated to physical education in schools and they were highly appreciated by physical education teachers, who, through their subjective comments, confirmed the research findings.

The reaction of the authorities has been different and is demonstrated by three distinctive phases in the reception process:

Phase 1: Rejecting the findings and questioning the methodology of the Study;

Phase 2: Checking their own limited data, comparing them with the SPRINT data, gradually initiating reforms (with no official reference to the SPRINT study). Continuing education for physical education teachers in primary schools was variously introduced or increased in most Länder; more importance was placed on physical education in those school types that had been identified as being neglected. Competitions were initiated and prizes were awarded for best practice examples in school physical education.

Phase 3: Currently all minor and major curriculum reforms refer to the findings of the SPRINT study and use them as a basis for argument. In addition, the Study has aroused a greater interest in evaluating the outcomes of physical education.

A NATIONAL STUDY ON THE SITUATION OF PHYSICAL EDUCATION: LESSONS FOR THE INTERNATIONAL PERSPECTIVE

With regard to the numerous challenges physical education has to face and in an international perspective one final issue needs to be addressed. This issue is whether there are any consequences and if so, what the consequences are of the SPRINT-study that was designed and conducted in a specific national (German) context for an international audience.

When the debate on educational reforms reaches its climax one question is inevitable: which traditional subjects will remain in the school curriculum and which new subjects will replace the old ones? The answer is clear: those subjects will survive and become a safe and integral part of the new curriculum, which can refer to convincing arguments concerning the achievements of the subject and its contribution to the all-round education of young people. Repeating the old records and merely emphasizing that physical education is inevitable and claiming that physical education can promote social interaction, enhance cognitive functioning or support character building will not convince curriculum developers and political stakeholders, who ask for and seek robustly sound evidence. In this context another answer is clear, too: those arguments will be respected that can claim to be based on findings that are theory-grounded and guided as well as empirically proven, and tell us something about the effects of physical education.

A literature review analysis of studies characterized by those attributes will produce results that are not overly satisfactory. There will be hundreds, if not thousands, of descriptions of physical education teacher and student behaviour with variations of observation instruments; there will also be many studies on teachers' recognition and socialisation as well as interventions to improve teacher education. Furthermore, there is quantitative research on effective teaching skills and on daily routines of In-service teachers. Many of these studies would not pass methodological quality tests and many of them are classroom studies based on small samples and producing descriptive data without applying any statistical methods. Additionally there are numerous studies with an array of qualitative methods for data collection and analysis. These studies provide a deeper insight, but cannot claim to be evaluation studies. More recently, there have been some well designed intervention studies, the results of which are opening new horizons.

By way of a summary, representative surveys as well as research on the outcomes and effects of physical education programmes remain rare and modest in their findings. With regard to the SPRINT-study and its implications for the international discussion on physical education, several items are considered to be pertinent.

Studies are required that are representative and can claim methodological quality meaning that they are based on a theoretical framework and produce findings that have been statistically tested. Physical education studies should meet the qualitative standards of international assessment studies on pupils' academic achievements and they should provide data on outcomes and effects of physical education programmes. The findings of the empirical study focused on in this chapter reflect contextual deficiencies in physical education in Germany; they are deficiencies that are to be found in many countries where physical education features as part of the school curriculum. Above all, the deficiencies relate to the time allocated to physical education and the qualification of teachers responsible for physical education delivery in primary/elementary schools. The latter deficiency has particular resonance as one important formative basis for a lifelong engagement in sport-related activities and for an active healthy lifestyle is the distinctive contribution of quality physical education programmes in the primary phase of schooling. Apart from information on the time allocated to physical education and qualifications of physical education teachers and, in many economically developing countries, facility and equipment provision, studies should also deal with the daily class tasks and associated stresses and strains encountered and experienced by teachers responsible for physical education.

With respect to physical education's contribution to the learning environment, two issues seem to be important: (i) on the one hand, many physical education teachers arguably are held in high esteem not only because of their expertise concerning movement, sport, exercise and health, but also, and occasionally even more so, because of the emotional and social closeness physical education teachers provide and pupils are looking for; and (ii) on the other hand compared with other subjects, physical education's contribution to the ambience of the school and, therefore, to a positive learning atmosphere is unrivalled, regardless of the question as to whether this is due to the physical activity that is on offer or to the enjoyment that is experienced by the pupils.

The SPRINT-Study points to the necessity to pay more attention to discrimination based on gender and social background from which many pupils are suffering. As it stands, for girls and children from families that are placed at the bottom of the social ladder that are under-represented in sport and community clubs, physical education should be a setting in which social inequalities do not occur. Finally, with regard to performance and the mark or grade awarded to pupils in physical education classes, the findings of the SPRINT-Study show that pupils want to achieve and to compete and that they want to see their performance reflected in the marks/grades they obtain. Many pupils are seemingly not happy with their mark/grade; they have the impression that marks/grades in physical education, unlike marks/grades in other subjects, are unjust; moreover, transparency is missing. They see a discrepancy between the generally good marks/grades awarded by physical education teachers and the physical and motor deficits, which the same physical education teachers identify as main obstacles for quality physical education and consequently complain about. To a greater or lesser extent all of these items are indicative of some of the central concerns articulated by a range of inter-governmental and non-governmental international and national agencies and associations. The empirically-based Sprint Study in Germany offers a template for other national studies, which can be properly used to better inform political and policy-making decisions in the domain of physical education in schools.

REFERENCES

Biddle, S.J.H., Whitehead, S.H., O'Donovan, T.M., & Nevill, M.E. (2005). Correlates of participation in physical activity for adolescent girls: A systematic review of recent literature. *Journal of Physical Activity and Health, 2,* pp.423-434.

Brandl-Bredenbeck, H.P. (2006). Der/die Sportlehrer/in aus Sicht der Schüler/innen. In: W. Miethling & C. Krieger (Eds.), *Zum Umgang mit Vielfalt als sportpädagogische Herausforderung. Tagungsband der dvs-Sektion Sportpädagogik,* Hamburg, Czwalina, pp.221-225.

Brettschneider, W-D., & Brandl-Bredenbeck, H.P. (2008). Physical Education and Education through Sport in Germany. In: G. Klein & K. Hardman (Eds.), *Physical Education and Sport Education in European Union,* Paris, Edition Revue EPS, pp.145-161.

Brettschneider, W-D., & Naul, R. (Eds.) (2007). *Obesity in Europe. Young People's Physical Activity and Sedentary Lifestyles.* Frankfurt/Main, Peter Lang.

Breuer, C. (2006). Die Sportstättensituation. In: DSB (Eds.), *Die DSB-SPRINT-Studie. Eine Untersuchung zur Situation des Schulsports in Deutschland,* Aachen, Meyer & Meyer, pp. 53-75.

DSB (Deutscher Sportbund), (Eds.), (2006). *Die DSB-SPRINT-Studie. Eine Untersuchung zur Situation des Schulsports in Deutschland.* Aachen, Meyer & Meyer.

Gerlach, E., Kussin, U., Brandl-Bredenbeck, H.P., & Brettschneider, W–D. (2006). Der Sportunterricht aus Schülerperspektive. In: DSB (Eds.), *Die DSB-SPRINT-Studie. Eine Untersuchung zur Situation des Schulsports in Deutschland,* Aachen, Meyer & Meyer, pp.115-152.

Hardman, K. (Ed.), (2003): *Physical education: deconstruction and reconstruction - issues and directions.* Schorndorf, Hofmann.

Hardman, K., & Marshall, J.J. (2009). *Second world-wide survey of school physical education.* Berlin, International Council of Sport Science and Physical Education (ICSSPE).

Helmke, A., & Weinert, F.E. (1997). Bedingungsfaktoren schulischer Leistungen. In: F.E. Weinert (Ed.), *Psychologie des Unterrichts und der Schule,* Göttingen, Hogrefe, pp.71-176.

Klein, G., & Hardman, K. (Eds.), (2008). *Physical Education and Sport Education in European Union.* Paris, Edition Revue EPS.

Kurz, D., & Fritz, T. (2006). Die Schwimmfähigkeit der Elfjährigen. *Betrifft Sport 28*(6), pp.5-11.

NICE (National Institute for Health and Clinical Excellence), (2007). *Correlates of physical activity in children: A review of quantitative systematic reviews.* (http://www.children-on-the-move.ch/dateien/dokumentation/NICE_Promoting PhysicalActivityChildrenReview2QuantitativeCorrelates.pdf).

Oesterreich, C. (2005). Qualifikationen, Einstellungen und Belastungen von Sportlehrkräften. Erste Ergebnisse der SPRINT-Studie. *Sportunterricht, 54*(8), pp.236-242.

Oesterreich, C. (2006). Berufsbezogenes Erleben von Sportlehrkräften. In: W. Miethling & C. Krieger (Eds.), *Zum Umgang mit Vielfalt als sportpädagogische Herausforderung,* Hamburg, Czwalina, pp.226-229.

Pühse, U., & Gerber, M. (Eds.), (2006). *International Comparison of Physical Education: Concepts, Problems, Prospects.* Aachen, Meyer & Meyer.

Sallis, J.F., Prochaska, J.J., & Taylor W.C. (2000). A review of correlates of physical activity of children and adolescents. *Medicine and Science in Sports and Exercise, 32,* pp.963-975.

CHAPTER 3

THE IMPORTANCE OF RESEARCH-BASED EVIDENCE FOR POLITICAL DECISIONS ON PHYSICAL EDUCATION

MARJETA KOVAČ, GREGOR JURAK, GREGOR STARC AND JANKO STREL

INTRODUCTION

The formation of States, when politico-ideological traditions are being abandoned and replaced, is problematic for decision-making because the heterogeneity of values, ideology and politics of professionals is not firmly based. In such circumstances, public sector (education, health, social services etc.) solutions are accepted in line with the values of those in authority, thus granting the legitimacy of their implementation in practice. Education, in particular, is an area of special public interest with various political stake-holders building their own identity by personifying and affirming different professionally specific views on education as their personal views. Hence, solution resolution decisions in educational systems usually have a political as well as a professional dimension in the sense of research-based solutions.

The decision-making process concerned with key issues of the education profession is not always kept within the domain of the critical professional and/or scientific public. It is usually controlled by the governing political party, which legitimately has been granted the right to make decisions, albeit that these decisions can seriously hinder the development of an educational system, if exercised solely on the ruling party's authority without due regard to any carefully considered research-based arguments. Populist decisions on, and in, an educational system are especially questionable professionally.

The involvement of politicians in the education system has been observed in Slovenia in recent years. As the areas of education and sport fall under the same Ministry, political decisions have also extended to the sports field. Numerous declarations related to physical education (PE) and extra-curricular sport programmes for children and youth have not been actioned at time when the position and share of PE in the curriculum has deteriorated particularly during the last five years. Moreover, because of ill-conceived solutions (such as, for example, disbanding the institution that oversaw children and youth extra-curricular sport programmes and inadequate provision of financial resources for such programmes) formulated without consultation with experienced PE domain experts, the proportion of physically active young people in these programmes has decreased (Kolar, Jurak & Kovač, 2010).

In focusing on the Slovenian situation, this chapter highlights positive and negative effects of recent political decisions. On the basis of research data, it also contends that the planning of school and sport programmes should build on research evidence and experience, should be organisationally well-designed and should also receive financial support at local and national levels. In the current "high risk" society (Davis, 1999), it is important to act swiftly as soon as the negative influences of lifestyle changes on the health of children and youth become apparent (Ortega, Ruiz, Castillo & Sjostrom, 2008). However, remedial and/or preventative measures should be based on in-depth analyses of such changes and with consideration of the social environment.

RECENT CHANGES IN THE SLOVENIAN EDUCATIONAL SYSTEM

During the year 1991 an expansion of educational strategies occurred as new conceptual starting points of education were being prepared. The key starting point was the notion that in modern society a system of education should be based on the principles of democracy, autonomy and equal rights, principles set out in the *Universal Declaration of Human Rights* and in State legislation. Beside formal rights, the government also guarantees equity rights of every individual regardless of gender, social and cultural background, religion, nationality, physical and mental well-being etc. The transition from eight to nine years of compulsory education, the reinstatement of the "gymnasium" (i.e., secondary school) as a basic general secondary-school programme, emphasising the concept of choice and school autonomy, the introduction of the integration of children with up-graded inclusiveness, the increase of resources for education in the State budget, the preparation of new school legislation and the improvement of material conditions resulted in a reformation of the Slovenian school, representing an escape from uniformity of education and the development of various teaching strategies.

Such a perceived positive trend has also been observed in the area of PE. The beginning of the 1990s saw the gradual introduction of three 45-minute school PE lessons (instead of the previous two lessons) per week in all general (gymnasia) and technical four-year secondary schools. The numbers of students in PE classes were reduced from 32 to 20 in all secondary-schools with their own sport facilities. The number of PE lessons in primary schools has remained the same (three lessons per week in the first six years of schooling and two lessons in the last three years). The newly designed concept allowed school children to choose three elective subjects in the last three years of primary schooling. Among a hundred possible subjects, two of them were sport-related (with three one-year programmes – *Sport for Health, Optional Sport* and *Sport for Relaxation*) and Dance Activities (also with three one-year programmes: *Dance, Traditional and Modern Dances, and Folk Dances*). Approximately 70% of school children thus had an additional lesson per week beside the two compulsory physical education lessons; some of them (approximately 10%) chose two "hours" and received two additional PE lessons. As young people remain in formal education longer than previously, the majority of schoolchildren have more than 1200 hours of PE during their schooling.

In 1996, new school legislation gradually introduced over a two-year period novel, goal-oriented curricula for all levels of education. The legislation, however, did not ensure PE being taught by a specialist PE teacher in the first three years of primary school. Nonetheless, it did allow the possibility of joint teaching of PE by a "specialist" and an elementary school class ('generalist') teacher. Subsequent changes in university and further education resulted in an improved structure of teacher education. Thus, at present, more than two thirds of teachers who teach in primary schools and all teachers in secondary schools have a university degree. PE is the most popular school subject among young people, and parents attribute special significance to it for their children's future lives (Kovač, Jurak, Starc & Strel, 2007). Numerous new sport facilities have been built near schools and old ones have been renovated (Kolar et al., 2010). Well organised and free of charge extra-curricular sport programmes became available for young people and attracted a high proportion of the young population group.

In the period 2004-2008, some political decisions did not favour PE and sport programmes for children and youth. The number of PE lessons was reduced, inferior PE curricula were introduced and extra-curricular sport programmes were neglected. Collectively, when implemented, the decisions, grounded in questionable interventions, resulted in a number of negative consequences:

- During the first six years of schooling, children still have three lessons (135 minutes) of PE per week and two (90 minutes) in the last three years of primary school. With the changes ushered in by the 2005 *Law on Primary School*, the amount of elective subjects in the last three years of compulsory education was reduced from three to two lessons per week. Additionally, pupils can register their extra-curricular activities as an elective subject (e.g., music lessons, but not sport activity). Although among the elective subjects PE was still chosen by the highest proportion of children in the last three years of primary school, the percentage of children with three hours of PE in this most sensitive maturational period has been reduced from 70% to 50%.
- In 2005, the government started to accelerate change in the programmes of Technical and Vocational Secondary Schools by reducing the number of PE lessons from three to two or from two to one lesson per week, respectively. A similar intervention in general secondary schools (Gymnasia) was prevented in 2007, after strong protests from the National Association of Physical Education Teachers.
- The tightening in funding school programmes has resulted in smaller primary schools placing pupils from different years into one group for PE lessons, thereby achieving the prescribed norm of 20 pupils in the group. As a result, the social cohesion of the group has been disrupted and lessons in mixed-age groups have become significantly more demanding.
- Despite the regulation that a group can consist of 20 students for PE lessons in secondary schools, the majority of schools were allowed to form larger groups.
- Despite the legislation prescribing lower norms in cases of a class with "special needs" pupils, the number of pupils in a group has not been reduced in PE classes. This places more demands on the teacher, particularly when a pupil with special needs requires an individually adapted programme.
- Pupils with special needs are entitled to adaptation only if they have a special instruction certificate. The waiting time for a certificate is usually six months, during which time there is no entitlement to any adaptation. Despite the certificate, few pupils receive additional help in PE and in any case, PE teachers consider themselves inadequately trained for work with such pupils (Kovač, Sloan & Starc, 2008).
- In sports halls, equipment is not usually adapted to younger age categories' needs (Kolar et al., 2010).

- Some secondary schools still do not have their own sport facilities and PE lessons are held outside of school premises with consequent strains placed on the school timetable (Kolar et al., 2010), which, in some instances has caused increased absences of pupils from lessons (Kovač et al., 2007).
- It has been revealed that schools are ill-equipped with the information/communication technology needed for PE lessons (Jurak & Kovač, 2009). In order to introduce modern approaches to lessons that would better motivate young people, schools require (in particular) pulse and energy consumption monitors, video recording devices and laptop computers. Modern technology could markedly contribute to appropriate planning and realisation of tailor-made practices, as it can provide an objective picture of the intensity of practice and the progress of individuals. Additionally, it can be used as a good motivational tool for practice and can influence the development of aerobic fitness of young people in a more proficient way (Kovač et al., 2007).
- Extra-curricular sport programmes, which form a part of the national sport programme (school sport competitions, the *Golden Sun, Krpan,* and *Learn to Swim* sport programmes), are mostly organized by schools. After the politically motivated disbandment of the Slovenian Sports Office, which managed and co-ordinated these programmes until 2005, the organisation of these programmes has seriously deteriorated and participation in some programmes has fallen to less than half of previous numbers (Kolar et al., 2010).
- Despite a supposedly innovatively designed curriculum (including a number of aims, designed to justify the subject in a number of ways to satisfy a range of interests and beliefs), the teaching of PE in many schools is still based on a sporting model, which focuses largely on the acquisition and performance of skills centred around team games. Also, many teachers in Slovenia adapt, modify and re-create the National Curriculum for Physical Education to match their own interests (Kovač et al., 2008).
- Inadequacies in the realisation of PE lessons in the early years of education have been observed (Jurak & Kovač, 2009; Strel, Kovač & Jurak, 2007). Because of inadequate levels of knowledge, many PE teachers do not include modern approaches to programme content and its delivery. Some activities have also been excluded or reduced in scope because of the fear of potential injuries to children (Kovač et al., 2007). In secondary schools, the concept of elective choices has not lived up to expectations (Jurak & Kovač, 2009); the understanding of abilities and needs of children is particularly poor as well as the direction of programmes for the health, and the personal and social development, of children (Kovač et al., 2007).
- Lack of government funding has led to young people in secondary schools not being systematically offered extra-curricular sport programmes. This situation is exacerbated by voluntary sector organisations not providing specific extra-curricular sport programmes (Kolar et al., 2010).
- Primary schools do not offer extra-curricular sport programmes for children with special needs, although the curriculum prescribes them, nor are such programmes provided by the government or the voluntary sectors (Kolar et al., 2010).
- The changes in primary school and secondary school curricula in 2006 and 2007 were not based on any relevant teaching process evaluation studies (Jurak & Kovač, 2009). Additionally, major changes documented (Strel et al., 2007) in the physical fitness of young people in the last ten years have not been considered. Minimal changes were

made only on the declarative level of educational planning and its realisation, whereas the changes of conceptual starting points (orientation into health-related fitness, personal and social development) are not visible, although research findings suggest that they are needed.

- Since the 1999 Bologna Declaration and reform process of harmonization of study programmes, PE is no longer compulsory for students in Slovenian universities.

Academics and practitioners have been warning that changes were/are necessary, albeit they should be based on evaluation studies on the realisation of PE, one element of which is its re-conceptualisation (Hardman, 2005; Jurak & Kovač, 2009). Any re-conceptual change of programmes, however, should be accompanied by changing PE teachers' attitudes, many of whom have entered the profession because of their sporting interests, experiences and achievements, as opposed to any desire to be educators (Stidder & Hayes, 2006). To this end, the Faculty of Sport in the University of Ljubljana has separated PE teacher education programmes from other study programmes (Coaching, Sport Recreation and Kinesiology). Notwithstanding this reform development, the Government in 2008 acknowledged that the existing conceptual starting points of the entire system of education needed to be analysed. However, a Working Group, appointed by the Minister of Education and Sport, did not include a single PE expert.

ESSENTIAL DIFFERENCES BETWEEN RESEARCH-BASED AND POLITICAL DECISIONS IN PHYSICAL EDUCATION

A key issue in modern societies relates to major changes in all areas of living. Regarding the individual, lifestyle can be understood as a group of practices, activities, cultural orientations and desires, which are expressed in habits of dressing, eating, acting and popular areas for socialising with others. The problem of the rapidly changing lifestyles of children and youth is multi-layered, highly dynamic and complex, and the influences of a "hidden" supply of unhealthy habits (for which immediate action is required) are alarming (Brettschneider et al., 2004; Ortega et al., 2008). The profession is aware of the difficult position of PE worldwide (Hardman, 2005) as it cannot facilitate the major changes in the lifestyles of children and youth, neither by the volume nor the quality and variety of programmes on offer (Strel et al., 2007).

The need for physical activity is a primary need of human beings. It is a so-called modal need, i.e., the activity itself already represents a goal. The proportion of physical activity in everyday life is decreasing with many young people not recognising the positive effects of physical activity. Under the influence of a broad supply of other, mostly physically passive activities, they are less active in their free time (Brettschneider et al., 2004; Kovač et al., 2007; Strong et al., 2005). Consequently, the role of PE during childhood and maturation is important for the healthy development of children and youth (*European Parliament Resolution on the Role of Sport in Education*, 2007; Strong et al., 2005; Trudeau & Shephard, 2005). Nowadays, many experts agree that quality, structured and regular PE, grounded on research-based data, forms a significant sphere of activity that can counter the negative effects of today's sedentary life-styles, inappropriate eating habits of young generations (Brettschneider et al., 2004) and inadequate social competency (Trudeau & Shephard, 2005). Therefore, a key issue to be addressed by both educators and politicians is how to facilitate healthy, active life-styles. Often, politicians do not heed the warnings of researchers and practitioners and remain supportive of physical activity only on a declarative level: politicians declare necessary activity to be an optional extra and one that does not provide equal inclusion opportunities for all young people. Tensions can, and do, arise between proponents of responsibilities towards children and youth's well-being (development aspect) and finance providers (control aspect), because frequently there are allegedly insufficient public funds available for research-based problem resolutions. The present day emphasis on economics in society and short term benefits needs to be re-appraised and set in a long term context of values to be derived through quality active life-style promoting school PE programmes, which may lead to reduced expenditure on health- and various social-related etc. programmes (Colditz, 1999). PE practitioners and researchers agree that reappraising short term economically- (and politically-) based policies and encouraging longer term strategies designed to increase PE provision and to stimulate quality practices could significantly influence the lifestyles of Slovenian children and youth to such an extent that any alleged lack of finances should not be a limiting factor. Three illustrations of policy re-orientation are presented immediately below:

1. As the effects on children are the greatest during the pre-pubertal period (Gallahue & Ozmun, 1998) and the current realisation of PE lessons is not optimal (Kovač et al., 2007), higher quality PE should be provided in the early years of schooling.
2. PE is a subject with a mission and goals oriented to the healthy development of individuals (Trudeau & Shephard, 2005). As such, in line with the principles of equal rights and inclusion opportunities in education, there should be a guarantee that all young people experience the same number of PE lessons throughout the entire schooling period. This is particularly the case for young people aged 15 to 19, attending technical and vocational secondary-school programmes, as, at present in Slovenia, they only receive one or two PE lessons per week.
3. As schools cannot provide the recommended amount of daily physical activity for all children and youth within the compulsory curriculum (*European Parliament Resolution on the Role of Sport in Education*, 2007; Hardman, 2005), the amount of public finance for extra-curricular programmes needs to be increased. These programmes should be well organized with ensured free access to them and so help in increasing the amount of young people's daily physical activity regardless of social status.

1. THE URGE FOR HIGHER QUALITY PHYSICAL EDUCATION IN THE PRE-PUBERTAL PERIOD

At the time of entering compulsory schooling, children have achieved different levels of physical, intellectual, emotional and social development. The most favourable period for the development of a child's various motor abilities is between the ages of 6 and 12 (Gallahue & Ozmun, 1998); developmental aspects ignored during this period are difficult or impossible to compensate for later. Practitioners and researchers have been warning for a long time that children in this age period require at least an hour of quality physical exercise every day, provided by professionally competent teachers. Studies (Starc, Strel & Kovač, 2010; Strel et al., 2007) of the physical development of children aged 6-10 have revealed that the proportion of overweight and obese children in Slovenia has been increasing particularly in this age group (see Figure 1) and that the physical fitness of these children is decreasing, more so than amongst adolescent youth.

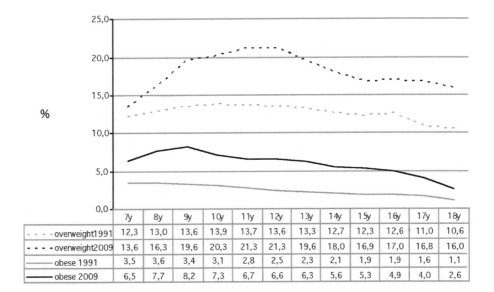

	7y	8y	9y	10y	11y	12y	13y	14y	15y	16y	17y	18y
- - - - overweight1991	12,3	13,0	13,6	13,9	13,7	13,6	13,3	12,7	12,3	12,6	11,0	10,6
- - - - overweight2009	13,6	16,3	19,6	20,3	21,3	21,3	19,6	18,0	16,9	17,0	16,8	16,0
.... obese 1991	3,5	3,6	3,4	3,1	2,8	2,5	2,3	2,1	1,9	1,9	1,6	1,1
—— obese 2009	6,5	7,7	8,2	7,3	6,7	6,6	6,3	5,6	5,3	4,9	4,0	2,6

Figure 1. Comparison of overweight and obese pupils in Slovenia by age (1991-2009)

As indicated earlier in the chapter, in the first six years of schooling, Slovenian children have three PE lessons (45 minutes each) per week and that legislation prescribes that all the subjects in the first three-year period are taught by elementary class teachers (educated at a Faculty of Education in a Higher Education Institution). In the fourth and fifth years, two or three subjects can be taught by a subject specialist (including PE). The only institution in Slovenia where PE teachers are educated is in the Faculty of Sport, University of Ljubljana. Although in the last twenty years over one fifth of such students (approximately 30 students per year) have specialised in teaching of children up to the age of 9, the new post-Bologna Declaration Study Programme has made this specialisation compulsory for all students. Notably, as mentioned earlier, current legislation does not allow PE teachers to teach PE independently in the first three years of primary school but rather they have to be accompanied by elementary school class teachers. Such joint teaching comes at a cost because schools are responsible for the necessary financial resources either through local municipalities, or parents or their own sources (Jurak et al., 2005).

Many primary schools understand the importance of everyday physical activity and some have been offering daily PE lessons since 1984. Jurak, Kovač and Strel (cited in Jurak et al., 2005) analysed the organisation of the PE curriculum in 21 schools that provide additional PE lessons and came to the following conclusions:

- Schools offer additional PE lessons by forming daily classes with enriched content; the pupils are taught by both elementary teachers and PE teachers. After the introduction of nine-year compulsory education, additional PE lessons are offered to all pupils who wish to engage in PE every day.
- The majority of schools offer such programmes between the first and fourth years of schooling.
- Parents give written consent for paying for the extra programme when enlisting children in school. If a child does not attend additional PE lessons, s/he stays in the classroom and the parents do not pay for the additional programme.
- Before the introduction of nine-year compulsory schooling, approximately 10% of Slovenian primary schools offered classes with additional PE lessons; since 2003, their number has decreased. Schools list financial rather than organisational problems as the main reasons for stopping these classes. They do not see a problem of social differentiation of children in the realisation of the programme.
- Although some schools stopped offering special classes with a greater number of PE lessons, they undertook other measures to raise the quality of lessons at school (e.g. joint teaching by PE education and elementary teachers in regular PE lessons in Years 1-4).
- Schools that have stopped such programmes, as well as those still offering them, consider daily PE to be a positive influence on the physical and social development of children; they share the opinion that the government and local municipalities should ensure an hour of physical education per day for all pupils.
- Sport activities courses such as swimming, skiing, skating are usually organised during school hours and less often after school or during the holidays and weekends. Schools do not consider that such practice interferes with delivery of other school subjects.
- Schools have offered various sports as part of additional PE lessons, as well as one week-long courses (e.g. swimming, trekking, alpine skiing and snow- boarding); most additional sport activities are carried out in Year 4.
- All the schools offering additional PE lessons have good facilities, usually with a large sport hall and outside tarmac or grass surfaces. Most of these schools also have small sport halls and other specialist sport facilities (track and field facilities, swimming pool, fitness room, dance hall etc.).
- The funding of additional PE lessons is accomplished in various ways. Some schools cover the costs of programmes entirely from resources received from local and government budgets, sponsors and their own resources, resulting in the programme being free of charge. Other schools also include contributions from parents, whereas some finance the extra programme entirely from parental contributions.
- The average contribution of parents for implementation of a daily programme of PE involving two teachers is € 11.40 per month, a figure believed by schools to be within the reach of all families. For parents, this is a much less expensive option to practice in clubs or private coaches' instruction. Moreover, time and transport costs accrue because parents do not have to transport children to afternoon practice.

The first study on pupils who participated in daily PE education classes was carried out twenty years ago (Novak, Petrovič, Tušak, & Kovač, 1990). More recently, this chapter's authors have examined the influence of the one-year programme on some morphological, motor, socio-demographic, psychological and micro-social dimensions of school children of both genders in first year of primary school. The findings are as follows:

- One year of practice, following a special, enriched programme, had a positive influence on all monitored dimensions of pupils of the experimental group (N=28). The pupils of three control groups comprising a simulated class of pupils with similar characteristics, a randomly chosen class from the same school and a randomly chosen class at another school (N=73) also progressed, albeit statistically less significantly. After one year, the experimental group pupils had statistically significantly thinner skin-folds than the other three groups; they also achieved better results in tests measuring various forms of strength (repetitive and static strength, strength endurance) and coordination of movement. Pupils from the class in the same school progressed more than pupils from the neighbouring school, indicating that organisation of work also had positive influence on other classes with a regular number of PE lessons.
- Pupils from all four groups had similar socio-demographic characteristics.
- There was no difference in the amount and type of free time activities among the pupils of all four groups.
- The academic record of pupils from the experimental group was better in comparison with pupils from the other groups. Notably, pupils from the experimental group missed more lessons than other pupils, something for which the research team found no explanation.
- After one year, statistically significant changes also occurred in the psychological variables. The experimental group had more favourable results in social self-esteem and body self-image, less hostile emotions towards parents; they were also more direct in emotional expression and more frequently expressed extra-punitive aggression (aggression directed towards the environment); members of the experimental group also more frequently attempted to solve problems instead of giving up.
- The results of the socio-metric tests revealed that the number of social connections desired and created was statistically significantly larger in the experimental group. The researchers concluded that PE in this class was an important factor in social openness.

Štihec and Kovač (1992) studied the effects of a three-month programme on a sample of 533 school children of both genders, aged 8 (+/- 0.5 years), who were divided into two experimental groups (EG1=75 boys and 47 girls; EG2=72 boys and 78 girls) and two control groups (CG1=74 boys and 52 girls; CG2=78 boys and 57 girls). The programme was carried out by PE teachers (EG1 and CG1) and elementary class teachers (EG2 and CG2). After eliminating the effects of the initial status, it was revealed that the special experimental programme with more demanding skills positively influenced both experimental groups. The group taught by the PE teacher made more progress. Particularly evident in this group were a decrease of skin-fold thickness and an increase of some body circumferences. The control groups that followed a regular PE programme also progressed, but statistically less so than the experimental groups; the progress was higher in the CG1 group taught by a PE teacher.

In a longitudinal study, Jurak, Kovač & Strel (2006) examined the effects of a larger number and quality managed PE lessons. The study included 328 schoolchildren, in Year 1 (age 7) in the year 2000. Over the following three years (2001–2003), all the SLOfit[1] system tests were carried out. Two groups of pupils from the same schools were formed: the experimental group (EG=81 boys and 76 girls) included children who had one daily PE lesson, and the lessons were delivered by PE and elementary teachers; the control group included pupils (CG=87 boys and 84 girls) with three PE lessons per week and who were taught by elementary teachers. The fact that both EG and CG came from the same school reduced the influence of conditions of individual schools for the realisation of PE lessons as well as the influence of the wider social environment on the results. The researchers found the following:

- Everyday activity had a positive influence on physical fitness (refer Figure 2). By eliminating the influence of different initial status, statistically significant differences between the experimental and control groups were noted in the motor tests (*obstacle course backwards, sit-ups* and *600 metre run*). Additionally, boys were statistically significantly different in *body weight*.

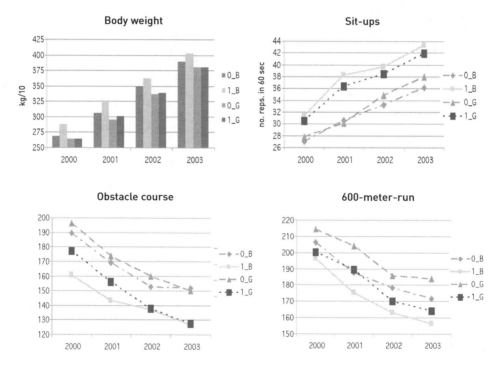

Groups: 0_B = boys in regular classes; 1_B = boys in classes with daily PE; 0_G = girls in regular classes; 1_G = girls in classes with daily PE

Figure 2. Trend of results in tests body weight, obstacle course backwards, sit ups and 600-metre run of schoolchildren with three physical education lessons and daily physical education from Year 1 to 4, according to gender.

1 SLOfit system monitors the physical fitness of Slovenian schoolchildren. Measurements are held every April during physical education lessons in all Slovenian schools and include about 95% of primary schoolchildren. The test battery consists of three anthropometrical and eight motor tests (Strel et al., 1997). Data have been systematically collected from 1986.

- The better progress of schoolchildren from the experimental group in the stated variables indicated that a larger number and better managed PE lessons have positive effects, particularly on the co-ordination of movement and muscular endurance, and on a more favourable morphological structure amongst boys, thus, confirming previous research (Novak et al., 1990; Štihec & Kovač, 1992).

The basic aim of the study *Impact of the Eight-year Educational Programme with Additional Sport Subjects on Selected Motor and Psycho-Social Dimensions and the Final Grade of Male and Female Pupils* carried out by Peternelj, Škof & Strel (2008) was to establish whether there are differences in selected motor, morphological and psycho-social dimensions in the final grade between groups of pupils attending a class with additional PE lessons for eight years and those attending a regular class, and which of the included variables contributed the most to these differences. The experiment was based on three generations of pupils (N=134), who were monitored throughout the period of attending primary school. Sixty-eight pupils attended the class with additional PE lessons (experimental group) and 66 were in the regular school programme (control group). The sample of variables consisted of selected tests of the pupils' morphological characteristics and motor abilities, grades in individual school subjects, values, attitudes to sport activities, motivational orientation in physical education and their social status. The findings revealed:

- At the end of schooling, the pupils in the experimental group had achieved better results in motor tests, had more favourable ratios of body dimensions (body composition) and higher final grades. Some of the differences in motor efficiency were caused by differences already established at the beginning of schooling.
- Statistically significant differences between the two groups were also discovered in individual parameters of the family social status and in some dimensions of attitudes to sport activities.
- No statistically significant differences were found for motivational orientation and values.
- The school programme with additional PE lessons has a different impact on female than on male pupils.
- The discriminate analysis confirmed the statistical significance of the differences between the groups. The largest and only visible correlation with the canonical discriminate function was seen in the variable of parents' education. It is evident that in a family environment where high levels of knowledge and education are perceived as values, parents show greater interest in, and care, for education and that their children develop healthy lifestyle habits.

Because of increased sedentariness, the proportion of overweight and obese children as well as in the decrease in physical and aerobic fitness, it is necessary for children, particularly in the pre-pubertal period, to have access to daily and quality managed PE (Dwyer, Sallis, Blizzard, Lazarus & Dean, 2001; Jurak, Kovač & Strel, 2006). Nowadays, this should not be provided as an optional extra, accessible only to those who can pay for it, but it is increasingly becoming a necessity for the healthy development of children. Due to the higher quality of PE education when taught by both PE and elementary teachers (Jurak, Kovač & Strel, 2006; Peternelj et al., 2008; Štihec & Kovač, 1992), it would be sensible to provide funding for such joint teaching, particularly as PE teachers have acquired competencies for working with the youngest children. At the same time, the training and education of elementary class teachers should be improved and efficient "In-service" teacher training should be provided, as research (Kovač et al., 2007) shows that elementary teachers do not feel sufficiently competent to teach PE.

2. UNEQUAL CARE FOR SECONDARY-SCHOOL STUDENTS

During the period of adolescence, when young people are at a crossroads of searching for their future path and the formation of their own identity, their motivation for participation in various activities changes. Public opinion research shows, particularly for younger age groups, that major values, once based on strong ideologies, are being replaced by values closer to the individual and personal experience. Their different interests, the supply of comfort via the click of the mouse and a virtual world without realistic problems lead young people into more passive spending of their free time (Brettschneider et al., 2004; Jurak, 2006; Jurak et al., 2003; Riddoch et al., 2004), most often in front of TV screens and play stations and on mobile telephones etc. "Screenagers" (the term was coined in 1997 by Douglas Rushkoff) feel comfortable only in virtual world in which they communicate only with the computer screen (Rushkoff, 2006), which prevents them from acquiring important social competencies – expressed by the term *cocooning* (Cocooning, 2010). Specific ways of spending free time at weekends for some young people usually include risky types of behaviour, such as smoking, drug use and drinking alcohol (Jurak, 2006).

For modern youth, physical activity has lost its primary value – enjoyment in movement. Activity, particularly sport, does not represent any challenge for adolescent young people today, because results require time and effort, as the effects of motor learning and achieving adequate fitness are possible only with a sufficient number of repetitions of specific motor patterns. Jurak et al. (2003) found that teenagers feel cramped by being included in the organised types of sport activity offered by schools and sport clubs. This represents "traditionalism" and "ideology", whereas they wish to practise in their own time. Certain sports in which young people participate mostly informally have become a part of the culture of teenage behaviour and dressing (skateboarding, snowboarding, mountain biking etc.).

It is acknowledged that physical fitness of youth has a correlation with the amount of free time they devote to sporting activities (Jurak et al., 2003). Recently, some major changes in the way Slovenian young people spend their free time have been observed. Boys are more physically active in their free time than girls; nevertheless, the amount of free-time physical activity gradually decreases with age in both genders (Jurak et al., 2003; Kovač et al., 2007). The proportion of secondary-school boys who do not participate in any sport activity during summer holidays rose from 10.6% in 1993 to 15.2% in 2004 (Strel et al., 2007). As a result, studying the lifestyles of young people has also become the subject of numerous research projects in Slovenia, indeed, in many other countries across the globe. Jurak (2006) found in a sample of 681 secondary school students of both genders that in Slovenia they can be divided in two extreme typical groups according to their lifestyle, which have, in relation to

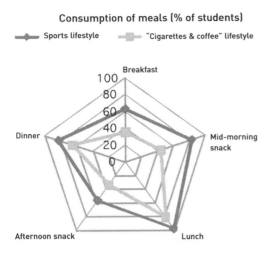

Consumption of meals (% of students)

the (un)healthy habits, been named the "coffee and cigarettes" and the "sport" lifestyles. The groups show statistically significant differences not only in free time sporting activity, regular smoking and alcohol drinking, academic results, educational level of their parents, but also in eating meals (see Figure 3) and self-evaluation of well-being (see Figure 4).

Figure 3. Eating meals in correlation with two typical lifestyles of secondary-school students

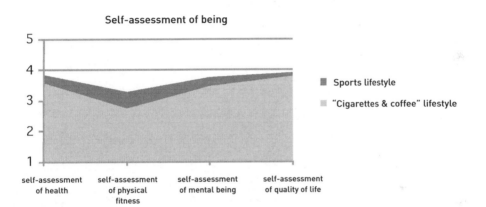

Figure 4. Differences in the evaluation of well being between the groups of secondary-school students with sport and "cigarettes & coffee" lifestyles

All secondary-school curricula state that the main purpose of PE is to positively influence the physical fitness of young people (and thus compensate the negative effects of modern life) and form positive attitudes towards a healthy lifestyle. The formation of positive attitudes towards physical activity represents an important step to actual participation in activity. PE offers young people a range of opportunities for personal growth and acquiring social competencies at a relatively unstable period of their lives.

At the starting point of curriculum changes, it was emphasised that the educational system in Slovenia should guarantee equal opportunities in education for all individuals and different social groups. Therefore, it is a paradox that students in secondary school education who follow different academic programmes have different amounts of PE lessons, as the need for physical activity is the same for all groups. Consequently, it would be legitimately reasonable to expect that in the subject intended to foster a healthy lifestyle, everyone be offered optimal developmental opportunities. Furthermore, in view of differences between young people, those in need of more motor encouragement should also have more PE lessons.

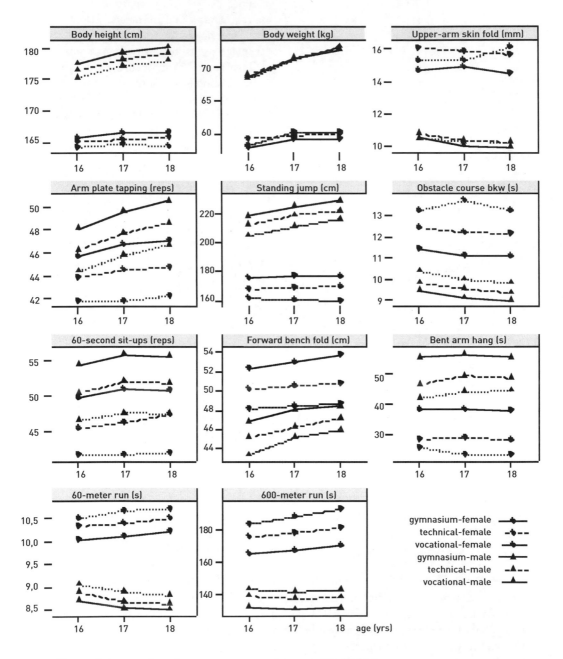

Figure 5. Interaction plots among secondary school students

Students from different secondary school programmes are dissimilar not only in the level of their achieved knowledge in primary school (Peček, Čuk & Lesar, 2006), but also in their physical fitness (Leskošek, Kovač & Strel, 2007; Westerståhl, Barnekow-Bergkvist & Jansson, 2005) and the socio-economic status of their families (Gabrijelčič Blenkuš, 2001; Jurak, 2006; Peček et al., 2006; Westerståhl et al., 2005). Young people from lower socio-economic status families with lower level educated parents are less physically active and participate in sport less often in their free time (Jurak, 2006; Jurak et al., 2003; La Torre et al., 2006).

A group of Slovenian researchers analysed differences in various characteristics between groups of students from different secondary school programmes according to their gender, age and the type of programmes they attend (Leskošek et al., 2007). Data from the SLOfit information system (Strel et al., 1997) were used to identify the status of their physical fitness. The study included 18,374 boys and 16,308 girls; 6,989 of the boys and 9,096 of the girls attended gymnasium programmes, 7,255 boys and 5,672 girls attended technical/professional programmes, while 4,130 boys and 1,540 girls attended vocational programmes. Amongst others, the findings featured in Figure 5 revealed: i) the type of programme differentiates boys and girls the most with the best results in all tests achieved by boys and girls in Gymnasia school programmes, followed by Technical Schools and the worst results achieved by boys and girls from Vocational Schools; ii) the differences are smaller amongst boys than girls; iii) the greatest difference between the types of programme – whilst controlling for age and gender – was observed in the results of sit-ups and arm-plate tapping tests; and iv) statistically significant differences were also observed in morphological differences, particularly in body height and the amount of body fat.

The researchers concluded that these differences may occur as a result of the students' different socio-economic environments. The less favourable morphological structure of students from vocational programmes is probably a result of their lower amount of physical activity and unsuitable eating habits. The results confirm the findings of other researchers suggesting that Vocational Schools' students have the worst nutritional habits (Gabrijelčič Blenkuš, 2001). The poorer physical fitness of Vocational schools' students is probably a result of the more infrequent free-time sport participation, the lower amount of school PE lessons as well as attitudes to sport activity, which serve as an indicator of a quality way of spending one's free time (Jurak et al., 2003).

One of the most important aspects in the formation of opinions towards an active lifestyle is knowledge and understanding of phenomena and events. The level of the cognitive knowledge that students possess can provide a sound foundation for changes in their behaviour, which may cause them to be more active. The physically active student is more likely to be academically motivated, alert and successful (Dwyer et al., 2001). As physical fitness and the frequency of physical activity of secondary-school students depend on the school programme undertaken, the differences between PE knowledge according to gender, secondary-school programme, year of study and the type of knowledge (conceptual knowledge about the benefits of physical activity and healthy lifestyle and specific knowledge of some sports) have been examined (Kovač et al., 2007). The sample of measured subjects included 771 students who attended three different secondary-school programmes in the 2004/2005 academic year. The findings suggested that: in a multivariate analysis of variance, all three main effects (programme, gender and year of study) showed significant simultaneous impact on both dependent variables (conceptual and specific knowledge); the programme of study had the highest impact (accounting for around 20% of the variance); and the impact of the gender of the measured subjects was about half as high, whereas the impact of the year of study was much lower. As a consequence, PE teachers will need to acquire special didactic competencies, particularly when teaching in Technical and Vocational Secondary Schools.

A systematic, structured PE process has important effects on the physical fitness of young people and their knowledge about healthy lifestyles. At the same time, it can serve as an important compensational tool to a one-sided vocational load. Hence, from the professional point of view, it is groundless to offer varying amounts of PE lessons to different groups. For many young people, particularly those attending Vocational Schools, PE represents their only physical activity (Jurak et al., 2003). Similarly, in adulthood, lower educated people with inferior socio-economic status are less physically active and are, as such, deprived of the important effects of physical activity on health. The appropriate physical activity can also effectively prevent the negative effects of their work stress, which are usually one-sided (most often also asymmetrical), often static and can in the long-term cause physical defects.

Limitations of the studies detailed above do not allow direct evaluation of the effects of reduced number of PE lessons. Any evaluation of such studies requires additional analysis. Since it is generally acknowledged that physical activity has several benefits that improve the health status and quality of life of adolescents, it is particularly important that governments do not increase the differences between the social groups with systemic measures. In the context of fairness (which a school purporting to offer equal opportunities should represent), the school system should neutralise some of the social inequalities among young people. Unfortunately, research shows that the differing number of physical education lessons in different educational programmes increases the differences between young people. Hence, some groups of young people are disadvantaged, and particularly so, those from deprived social environments, who are less physically active.

3. INADEQUACIES OF EXTRA-CURRICULAR SPORT ACTIVITIES

In Slovenia, there are attempts to apply the recommendations of various global organisations. One of the recommendations is that young people should be physically active at least for 60 minutes or more a day (Kristan, Cankar, Kovač & Praček, 1992) and consequently the National Programme of Sport (2000) emphasised that the physical activity of children and youth is a priority task of the government and the civic sector. Strong et al. (2005) recommend that aerobic exercise should dominate in the sport activity of children and that at least twice a week more attention should be placed on the development of strength and flexibility; in addition, activity should be pleasant and suitable to the developmental stage of children.

The civic sector in Slovenia offers numerous prepared sport programmes, which are based on research-based support starting points and form a part of the National Programme of Sport (2000): the *Golden Sun* programme for the youngest (aged 5 to 8); the *Krpan* programme for children aged 9 to 12; *Hurrah, free time* for out-of-school days; more than 70% of children aged 11 to 19 participate in the system of school sport competitions and many more also practice and compete in clubs (Kolar et al., 2010).

The analysis of the ten-year National Programme of Sport (2000) revealed that its implementation has been far from the declared statement of being a priority, especially in the area of sport of children and youth. Both the government and local municipalities have provided less than a quarter of planned finances (24.1%) for these programmes, whereas others received significantly more (e.g., top sport 113.1%; Figure 6) (Kolar et al., 2010).

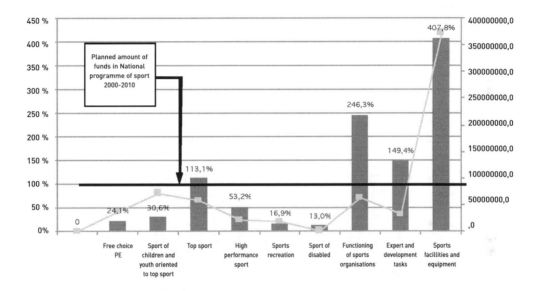

Figure 6. Public finances for various areas of the National Programme of Sport (2000), 2001-2008.

Public finances for the programmes of young, talented athletes reached only 30.65% of planned finances in period 2001–2008; nevertheless, the positive trend of funding young athletes resulted in a significant increase in their number: from 1.162 in 2001 to 2.277 in 2009 (Kolar et al., 2010).

Sport in Slovenia is financed from government and local municipalities in a 25%:75% ratio. The government has attempted to fulfil its role at least partially in the last ten years, whereas local governments have succeeded only to a small extent. They directed funding mainly into sport facilities and, despite the guidelines that sport for children and youth has a priority, also into elite sport. An analysis of funding, aimed at young people, has revealed that at the national level, 55.76% of planned finances has been spent on talented young athletes in comparison with 23.85% at the local level, whereas the amount of money spent on sport programmes of children with special needs at the national level was 37.93% in comparison to 3.22% of planned finances at the local level (Kolar et al., 2010).

It is of particular concern that the results analysed within the framework of the national SLOfit system (Strel et al., 1997), measuring the physical fitness of children and youth with eight motor tests and then calculating an average value of their motor efficiency (XT), revealed an increased proportion of those with an XT of 40 or less (5.5% of the population, who can be labelled as children and youth with reduced motor competency, many of them also having developmental problems). The proportion of such children among primary school boys nearly doubled between 1990 and 2008; similar results can be also seen for secondary school boys (Figure 7), whereas only a slight increase has been observed for primary and secondary school girls. The reasons are different: inclusion of children with special needs into regular school programmes, but mainly an increased number of overweight and obese children with reduced motor competency.

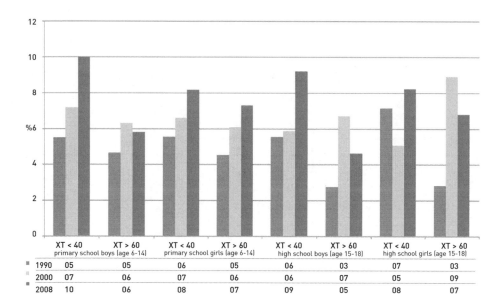

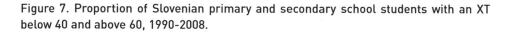

| | XT < 40 | XT > 60 | XT < 40 | XT > 60 | XT < 40 | XT > 60 | XT < 40 | XT > 60 |
	primary school boys (age 6-14)		primary school girls (age 6-14)		high school boys (age 15-18)		high school girls (age 15-18)	
1990	05	05	06	05	06	03	07	03
2000	07	06	07	06	06	07	05	09
2008	10	06	08	07	09	05	08	07

Figure 7. Proportion of Slovenian primary and secondary school students with an XT below 40 and above 60, 1990-2008.

In all the groups apart from the primary school girls, the proportion of those who can be labelled as extremely talented for sport (5% of the population with XT above 60) has decreased. Therefore, it is undoubtedly professionally unacceptable that, despite the increased proportion of children with difficulties in motor development, this group does not receive adequate professional attention, as there are almost no special programmes available for them. In addition, political decisions about the allocation of finances among sport programmes have almost completely neglected this group of young people (Kolar et al., 2010).

CONCLUSIONS

Historically, education and sport have invariably been linked with politics. Politicians can act on all social areas in an encouraging or discouraging way. Solutions proposed and implemented by politicians can be soundly based, although all too often they are a reflection of political expediency and/or aspirations, representing changes without any appropriate research/evidence-based support and they, which can have long-term negative effects.

In the period 1991-2004, from its formation as an independent State, various education and sport policies in Slovenia were positively oriented towards PE and extra-curricular sport activities of children and youth. Consequently, the quality of PE improved and a broad and well-organised system of extra-curricular sport programmes was established on a national level. Between 2004 and 2008, some opportunistic political decisions led to a reduction of the number of PE lessons for the first time in history and in the cut-back of sport programmes for children and youth.

Thus, the goals set out in official documents (Kristan et al., 1992; National Programme of Sport, 2000) were fulfilled on a strictly limited basis (Kolar et al., 2010; Jurak & Kovač, 2009). The influence of accelerating or decelerating policies can be observed in the quality and quantity of PE and the availability of sport for young people (Kolar et al., 2010), the ways of spending free time (Jurak et al., 2003), inappropriate eating habits (Gabrijelčič Blenkuš, 2001; Jurak, 2006) and subsequently also in the decline of physical and aerobic fitness of young people (Strel et al., 2007). Positive or negative measures introduced in the area of PE and sport activities usually have long-term positive or negative consequences, which are retrospectively evaluated through the historical context in the future. Undoubtedly, the Slovenian Government (indeed, governments across the globe have) should recognise the important role of PE and extra-curricular sport programmes in the formation of healthy lifestyles for children and youth as well as for the personal development and fulfilment of individuals.

The present situation demands immediate resolution attention. An evaluation of PE lessons, together with a re-appraisal of the curriculum to embrace the various needs of children and youth, are needed. Initial teacher training and continuing professional development courses should appraise trainee/experienced teachers of, and equip them with, latest pedagogical and didactical methods and skills including differentiation and individualisation of lessons, "new" activities, motivational techniques, inclusion issues with particular attention devoted to children and youth with special needs, and use of ICT etc. In the processes of seeking to enhance the relevance and quality of school PE and assisting in fostering healthy active life-styles, politicians and policy-makers should also introduce measures to ensure: (i) daily PE provision and joint teaching (PE teacher and elementary class teacher) in the first five years of education; (ii) at least three hours of PE for all secondary school students; and (iii) increased financial support for, and accessibility to, extra-curricular programmes, which are offered by the public sector. As shown in this chapter, the research evidence on the benefits of regular engagement in physical/sporting activity engendered through quality school PE programmes, and which are professionally delivered, is demonstrably overwhelming. Policy-making and -taking decisions affecting PE need to be informed by research and good practice and not solely made on economic grounds and political expediency. This is the case not only in Slovenia but in countries worldwide.

REFERENCES

Brettschneider, W., Naul, R., Armstrong, N., Diniz, J., Froberg, K., Laakso, L., et al. (2004). *Study on young people's lifestyle and sedentariness and the role of sport in the context of education and as a means of restoring the balance. Final Report.* Paderborn, EC, Directorate-General for Education and Culture, Unit Sport.

Cocooning (2010). In *Merriam-Webster Online Dictionary.* Retrieved July 2, 2010, from: http://www.merriam-webster.com/dictionary/cocooning.

Colditz, G. (1999). Economic costs of obesity and inactivity. *Medicine and Science in Sports and Exercise, 31*(11), pp.663–667.

Davis, N.J. (1999). *Youth Crisis: Growing Up in the High-Risk Society.* Westport, CT, Praeger Publisher.

Dwyer, T., Sallis, J.F., Blizzard, L., Lazarus, R., & Dean, K. (2001). Relation of academic performance to physical activity and fitness in children. *Pediatric Exercise Science, 13,* pp.225–238.

European Parliament Resolution on the Role of Sport in Education, November 13, 2007 (2007/2086(INI)). Retrieved January 10, 2008, from: http://www.europarl.europa.eu/oeil/DownloadSP.do?id=14182&num_rep=7012&language=en

Gabrijelčič Blenkuš, M. (2001). Nekatere prehranjevalne navade ljubljanskih srednješolcev s poudarkom na razliki med spoloma. [Some nutritional habits of secondary-school students in Ljubljana with an emphasis on differences between genders] *Zdravstveno varstvo, 40*(Suppl.), pp.135–143.

Gallahue, D.L., & Ozmun, J. (1998). *Understanding Motor Development: Infants, Children, Adolescents, Adults.* Boston, McGraw-Hill.

Hardman, K. (2005). Trends in physical education and society: challenges for the physical education profession. In: D. Milanović and F. Prot (Eds.), *Proceedings, 4th International Scientific Conference on Kinesiology.* Zagreb, Faculty of Kinesiology, pp.9–17.

Jurak, G. (2006). Sports vs. the "cigarettes & coffee" lifestyle of Slovenian high-school students. *Anthropological Notebooks, 12*(2), pp.79–95.

Jurak, G., & Kovač, M. (2009). Ali kurikularne spremembe dohajajo spremembe v življenjskih slogih otrok? [Do curricular changes keep up with changes in lifestyle of children?] *Sodobna pedagogika, 60*(1), pp.318–333.

Jurak, G., Kovač, M., & Strel, J. (2006). Impact of the additional physical education lessons programme on the physical and motor development of 7-10 year old children. *Kinesiology, 38*(2), pp.105–115.

Jurak, G., Kovač, M., Strel, J., Majerič, M., Starc, G., Filipčič, T., et al. (2003). *Sports activities of Slovenian children and young people during their summer holidays.* Ljubljana, University of Ljubljana, Faculty of Sport.

Jurak, G., Kovač, M., Strel, J., Starc, G., Žagar, D., Cecić Erpič, S., et al. (2005). *Športno nadarjeni otroci in mladina v slovenskem šolskem sistemu.* [Sports talented children and youth in Slovenian educational system] Koper, Annales, Univerza na Primorskem, Znanstveno-raziskovalno središče Koper.

Kolar, E., Jurak, G., & Kovač, M. (Eds.) (2010). *Analiza nacionalnega programa športa v Republiki Sloveniji 2000–2010.* [An analysis of national programme of sport in Slovenia 2000–2010] Ljubljana, Zveza za šport otrok in mladine Slovenije.

Kovač, M., Jurak, G., Starc, G., & Strel, J. (2007). *Šport in življenjski slogi slovenskih otrok in mladine.* [Sport and lifestyles of Slovenian children and youth] Ljubljana, Fakulteta za šport, Inštitut za kineziologijo, Zveza društev športnih pedagogov Slovenije.

Kovač M., Sloan, S. & Starc, G. (2008). Competencies in physical education teaching: Slovenian teachers' view and future perspectives. *European Physical Education Review, 14*(3), pp.299-323.

Kristan, S., Cankar, A., Kovač, M., & Praček, T. (1992). *Guidelines of physical education in schools.* Ljubljana, Zavod RS za solstvo in sport.

La Torre, G., Masala, D., De Vito, E., Langiano, E., Capelli, G., Ricciardi, W., & PHASES collaborative group (2006). Extra-curricular physical activity and socio-economic status in Italian adolescents. *BMC Public Health.* Retrieved October 21, 2006, from: http://www.pubmedcentral.nih.gov/articlerender.fcgi?artid=1431521.

Leskošek, B., Kovač, M., & Strel, J. (2007). A Comparison of the Physical Characteristics and Motor Abilities of Boys and Girls Attending Different High-school Programmes. *Acta Universitatis Carolinae Kinanthropologica, 42*(2), pp.85-101.

National programme of Sport in Republic Slovenia (2000). Ljubljana, Ministry of Education and Sport, Slovenian Sports Office.

Novak, D., Petravić,K., Tušak, M., & Kovač, M. (1990). *Športni razred z motoricnega, socialno-demografskega, psihološkega in mikrosociološkega vidika.* [Sports class from the motor, socio-demographic, psychological and microsocial aspect] Ljubljana: Inštitut za kineziologijo.

Ortega, F.B., Ruiz, J.R., Castillo, M.J., & Sjostrom, M. (2008). Physical fitness in childhood and adolescence: a powerful marker of health. *International Journal of Obesity, 32*(1), pp. 1-11.

Peček, M., Čuk, I., & Lesar, M. (2006). Šola in ohranjanje družbene razslojenosti – učni uspeh in vpis osnovnošolcev na srednje šole glede na izobrazbo staršev. [School and maintaining of social strata – academic results and the entering of primary school students into secondary schools according to the education of parents]. *Sodobna pedagogika, 1*, pp.10-34.

Peternelj, B., Škof, B., & Strel, J. (2008). Differences between Slovenian pupils attending sport class and those attending a regular school programme. *International Journal of Physical Education, 45*(3), pp.144-151.

Riddoch, C.J., Andersen, L.B., Wedderkopp, N., Harro, M., Klasson-Heggebo, L., Sardinha, L.B., et al. (2004). Physical activity levels and patterns of 9- and 15-year old European children. *Medicine & Science in Sports & Exercise, 36*, pp.86-92.

Rushkoff, D. (2006). *Screenagers.* Cresskill, NJ, Hampton Press.

Starc, G., Strel, J., & Kovač, M. (2010). *Telesni in gibalni razvoj slovenskih otrok in mladine v stevilkah. Solsko leto 2007/08.* [Physical and motor development of Slovenian children and youth in figures. 2007/08 academic year] Ljubljana, Fakulteta za sport.

Stidder, G., & Hayes, S. (2006). A longitudinal study of physical education teachers' experiences on school placements in the south-east of England (1994–2004). *European Physical Education Review, 12*(2), pp.313–333.

Strel, J., Kovač, M., & Jurak, G. (2007). Physical and motor development, sport activities and lifestyles of Slovenian children and youth – changes in the last few decades. In: W-D. Brettschneider & R. Naul (Eds.), *Obesity in Europe: young people's physical activity and sedentary lifestyles.* Sport Sciences International, vol. 4. Frankfurt am Main, Peter Lang, pp.243–264.

Strel, J., Ambrozic, F., Kondric, M., Kovač, M., Leskošek, B., Štihec, J., et al. (1997). *Sports Educational Chart.* Ljubljana, Ministry of Education and Sport.

Strong, W.B., Malina, R.M., Blimke, C.J., Daniels, S.R., Dishman, R.K., Gutin, B., et al. (2005). Evidence-based physical activity for school-age youth. *Journal of Pediatrics, 146,* pp.732–737.

Štihec, J., & Kovač, M. (1992). The influence of an experimental programme of physical education on the development of some morphologic and motor dimensions of 8 year old pupils. *Kinesiologia Slovenica, 1*(1), pp.71–74.

Trudeau, F., & Shephard, R.J. (2005). Contribution of school programmes to physical activity levels and attitudes in children and adults. *Sports Medicine, 35,* pp.89–105.

Westerståhl, M., Barnekow-Bergkvist, M., & Jansson, E. (2005). Low physical activity among adolescents in practical education. Scandinavian *Journal of Medicine & Science in Sports, 15*(5), pp.287–297.

CHAPTER 4
A PHYSICALLY EDUCATED PERSON
RICHARD FISHER, ROSE MARIE REPOND AND JOSÉ DINIZ

INTRODUCTION

For more than thirty years there have been concerns worldwide about the situation of physical education (PE) in schools. Pühse and Gerber's (2005) international review of the subject highlighted the ground lost since the 1970s and 1980s, which they claim amounts to some 15-20% of curriculum time . This loss of time has been accompanied by problems such as the priviliging of other supposedly more important subjects, lack of equipment, unsatisfactory infrastructure and for primary schools in particular an almost universal shortage of appropriately qualified teachers. There has been no shortage of effort by professional PE associations in many countries to raise awareness of these issues and their international counterparts have been equally vociferous in pressing the needs of the subject and its valuable contribution to what we might refer to as a well educated person. For example, professional associations in Europe combined in 1990 to form the European Physical Education Association (EUPEA) with the express purpose of protecting and promoting PE. However, progress has generally been slow even though Klein (2003) pointed out that the threats were recognised as long ago as 1976 in the International Conference of Ministers and Senior Officials for Physical Education (MINEPS 1) in Paris.

By the turn of the century, PE was clearly registering on the agenda of international and particularly European region governmental and non-governmental institutions, testimony to which were initiatives such as the first World Summit for PE held in 1999 in Berlin under the auspicies of the International Council of Sport Science and Physical Education (Hardman & Marshall, 2000). By the time of the second World Summit a decade later (Hardman & Marshall 2009) the European Union had decreed 2004 as the Year of Sport Education and further impetus was gained from the United Nation's Year of Physical Education and Sport in 2005. In addition an entire chapter of the European Union Physical Activity Guidelines (2008) was devoted to physical education showing a firm EU interest in the subject in terms of its mission and social role. Nevertheless, whilst there has been some demonstrable progress in a number of countries, arguably the subject is: "in a position of permanent tension between the unmet humanist commitments of politicians and the compensation strategies developed by non-governmental organizations" (Klein, 2003, p 424).

Furthermore, a number of studies in Europe support the related idea that PE is in something of a paradoxical situation in that whereas there is widespread evidence of the need for physical activity for children and young people, the provision available has been decreasing (Klein 2003; Hardman 2005). Indeed, The European Commission's *White Paper on Sport* (2007) emphasises the importance of an allocation of sufficient time for quality physical education at schools and for reinforced links between educational and sporting institutions, so that children and young people can have sufficient access to physical activity inside and outside school.

However, as time goes on and more evidence is assembled it is clear that the situation has at least stabilised in a number of countries and Green (2008) observes that we may well be looking at a continuum for PE ranging from positive through stability to negative. Interestingly Green also comments that when attempting to ascertain the situation of PE there are a variety of perspectives flowing from different "voices" associated with the subject, such as teachers, politicians, parents etc. There are, therefore, a number of mixed messages about the health and strength of the subject and caution is advisable when summarising the situation across countries, in the case of this chapter, in Europe. PE could be considered as relatively consistent across European countries having at its core such things as a quest for movement literacy, well-being, maintaining the body, self-esteem and socialization etc. However, more realistically PE can be conceived as a forum for confrontation of different concepts and that there is not one PE but many and ultimately what the student learns is highly dependent on what the teacher wants to teach, and on the teacher's concept of his discipline and of its social utility (Delignières & Garsault, 2004). Fisher (2004) summarised several comparative models in a diagramatic version of the way that policy is interpreted and reinterpreted as it moves through different levels of the education system (Figure 1).

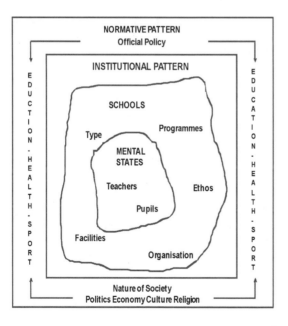

Figure 1: The Policy Practice Network (Source: Fisher, 2004)

The progress of official policy and curricula from what a State intends to how schools decide to implement it and then what teachers choose to deliver has been described by Penny and Evans (1999) as a "tortuous network". The various layers of this process are represented here and give some indication of the potential for re-interpreting official policy, to which we can add the influence of other significant players in the policy game, such as sport, health and parents. We need to understand better the centre of Figure 1, comparing formal pedagogical beliefs and the associated political arguments with what actually happens. This involves understanding teachers' beliefs about what PE should be and what constitutes a physically educated student based on their priorities, as well as the extent to which they believe it is achieved and what they think students have learned.

The need for a well formed view of a what physically educated person might look like has emerged in recent years as an important issue in the justification of the subject in schools and has affected the request for more resources to deliver it. At least one European Minister of Education listened to the team preparing a new PE curriculum and requesting more resources and asked what students had learned in the approximately 1,000 hours of PE they had received during compulsory schooling years (based on an average of 3 physical education lessons per week for around 10-11 years). Effectively, the question is asking what does a physically educated person look like at the end of what has to be said is a substantial amount of teaching and learning time.

This chapter explores the idea of a physically educated person through the findings of a EUPEA survey involving over 2,000 teachers in 20 countries – what they believe is a physically educated person and the extent to which it might be achieved.

BACKGROUND AND CONTEXT

Principles

Klein (2006) provides a useful starting point in terms of conceptualising a physically educated young person who might be seen to be:

- A responsible, competent and independent citizen;
- Educated in the fields of physical activities and sports;
- Responsible for his/her physical activity and his health;
- Respectful of partners and opponents;
- Capable of finding information, making decisions and becoming involved in physical activities and sport appropriate to his/her personal interests and capacities.

According to Meirieu (2009), this implies that the teacher needs to lead the students to "learn to learn by learning" by meeting three key objectives: having a project, implementing the intellectual operation required by the associated objectives ("structural invariants") and using the personal methods that are most efficient for oneself ("subject variables"). In other words, a physically educated student:

- Has a life plan that is both physically and intellectually active;
- Uses skills and knowledge to meet his/her objectives in different environments;
- Employs the most effective personal strategies based on the knowledge of self and lifestyle.

In order to scope and refine the notion of a physically educated person, it is necessary to secure a set of appropriate aims and outcomes, essentially a framework to prepare and deliver the appropriate programmes. For the purposes of the EUPEA survey a set of aims was prepared in focus groups at a EUPEA forum and refined later by a small group of experts, who took into account published work on PE in Europe (e.g. Hardman, 2005; Pühse & Gerber, 2005), as well as in official EU texts. In addition to creating the base of the study, the process used is noteworthy in that it evolved from a consensus view across European national professional associations about aims and outcomes in a European context. The group also took account of research in specific national contexts such as the Sprint study in Germany (Brettschneider et al, 2006) and pre-pilot-tested their work with PE teachers in their own countries.

This was followed by a pilot study in 2007, in which 13 national associations participated and responded to a questionnaire based on the following issues:
- The fit between the official aims and the reality experienced by teachers
- The pertinence of the aims proposed
- A description of the learning outcomes that teachers sought for their students
- An assessment of the extent to which they are achieved.

This work formed the basis of the main study, which is outlined below and which provides a guide to what professionals "on the ground" believe is a physically educated person.

THE EUPEA STUDY

Based on the work above, and in view of the various contexts involved, 13 aims deemed to be appropriate in a range of European countries were agreed by the members of EUPEA together with a set of outcomes for each aim. These were developed into a questionnaire that also contained basic biographical data on the teachers and their professional training as well as essential information on the school and its location. The thrust of the study as outlined in the introduction to the questionnaire was "to provide a definition of a physically well educated youth at the end of the period of compulsory education, from the point of view of physical education teachers in schools".

The idea was that a study of this kind could be used as a reference point for PE at school and through looking at three key areas it should be possible to make a contribution to the profession as follows by:

- Proposing a plan through curriculum mapping using the 13 proposed aims;
- Making comparisons between teachers in terms of priorities adopted for those aims in specific curricula;
- Testing perceived student progress against teachers' constructs of what was actually achieved. According to Scallon (2007, p. 102) this challenge is two-fold: "first, situations must be designed (and then) tools for judgment must be developed", which is an interesting issue when we see differences in ranking between the skills perceived as most important by teachers and the skills best acquired by the students;
- Confirming what might be termed a consensus table of contents.

In essence this was a "bottom up" field study involving an online questionnaire that was translated into 14 languages and cross-checked by teachers and national associations. The final questionnaire with all the instructions and response details can be seen on the EUPEA website (www.eupea.com) and could be completed by teachers in primary or secondary schools. In essence teachers had to undertake the following:

- Complete essential biographical data about themselves and information about their school;
- Rank the 13 aims in terms of importance to them;
- Rank the outcomes associated with each aim;
- Classify the learning outcomes in terms of student achievement, scaled 1 – not achieved, 2 – achieved, 3- mastered;
- Using a classification of subject content areas, indicate which areas were important in their programme.

The background data and contextual information were as follows:

Teachers - 50% of the teachers had teaching experience between 7 and 25 years, 16% from 4 to 6 years and 19% from 25 to 35 years. The remainder had either less than 4 years experience or more than 35 years. The majority of the teachers had four years of higher education (338 out of 726) or five years (302 out of 726). Only nine of the 20 countries had any physical education teachers with only two years of higher education (29 out of 726 total respondents) and 12 countries had physical education teachers with three years of education (54 out of 726 respondents). In terms of whether teachers also taught a second subject - 21.5% did so, while 78.5% specialised in PE. The Netherlands (90%), France (95%) and Portugal (74%) have a majority of single subject teachers but working in aother area is not ruled out. Sweden (60%), Switzerland (65%) and Finland (80%) on the other hand show a strong tendency for physical education teachers who teach a second subject.

Countries - Teachers from 20 European countries responded to the questionnaire as follows: United Kingdom (25), Ireland (1), Belgium (19), the Netherlands (64), Italy (9), Sweden (41), Denmark (11), Norway (1), Finland (50), Slovakia (2), Poland (88), Austria (6), Germany (1), Switzerland (32) (partially in French), France (269), Luxembourg (25), Romania (1), Portugal (73), Spain (1), Czech Republic (10).

Schools - The instructional setting is often considered to be a factor that affects learning and general environment was considered in this study. Some 32.5% of the schools were in a rural setting, 40.3% from urban areas and 27.7% from cities.

OBERVATIONS ON THE STUDY

The PE teachers' responses can be considered to comprise a view of their curriculum since they indicate aims, content and projected learning outcomes. The subsequent transition from teaching to the teacher's perception of the extent to which the skills, knowledge and understanding acquired by students have been realised through these learning outcomes adds a student-centred dimension. It does not of course convey what the pupils themselves believe, which is extremely important but could not be included in this study. In summary, this research provides a perspective on three levels of teaching and learning:

- A European consensus view of the aims of PE, some of which might be considered as generic to education as a whole, and their relative importance as perceived by teachers;
- The learning expected and considered a priority;
- The learning achieved most successfully by the students.

The findings of this study should be read with some caution since accessing treachers' responses is useful but does not provide a full picture of what is actually a quite complex situation. Even so it is a window on the current position of PE across Europe and it represents the voice of those who actually do the job. In addition, there are always risks in cross-cultural research as the cultural contexts are open to different interpretation and it was impossible to obtain uniform numbers across the countries involved. Furthermore, the questionnaire was translated into 14 languages so there was always a danger of variation across the sets of questionnaire. However, detailed attention was accorded to these matters and EUPEA members oversaw the process in each country with central guidance and co-ordination from the co-ordinating team. Consequently, notwithstanding these potentially problematic issues, the study's findings offer a contribution to understanding what teachers in Europe believe constitutes a physically educated person. The following sections deal with the various parts of the study.

a) The Aims of Physical Education

The backbone of the study was 13 purposes of physical education, representing generic and specific aims and following the process outlined above these were agreed and presented as follows:

1.   To encourage the adoption of active and healthy lifestyles
2.   To develop a feeling of personal wellbeing/wellness
3.   To inculcate a sense of important values in sport (fair play, solidarity...)
4.   To ensure safe practices in physical education
5.   To develop a broad repertoire of movement competence
6.   To develop an appreciation of cross curricular links in relation to physical education
7.   To promote an appreciation of the social and cultural significance of sport physical activity
8.   To develop the ability to evaluate own and others performance
9.   To develop a sense of leadership and the ability to organise others
10.   Appreciate what means to be fit and/or healthy
11.   To develop the capacity to apply and develop skills in specific activity contents (sport, dance ...)
12.   To contribute to the development of a sense of citizenship
13.   To provide opportunities for all pupils to learn and achieve, regardless of ability, gender or social and cultural background

The 13 aims were ranked by the teachers and the results are listed in Table 1; the highest ranked aim was given a score of 13 and the lowest ranked aim was given 1, with joint rankings sharing the two positional scores.

As indicated above, caution is urged in the interpretation of these results, for example an individual country might not have included one or two of these aims in the nation specific analysis. However, all countries agreed that they were a reasonable representation of what PE in Europe is about and in that context some interesting patterns occur. The classification of the aims made by the teachers demonstrates something of a separation between broader pedagogical and educational considerations that characterise the 5

Table 1: Ranking of Aims by Physical Education Teachers

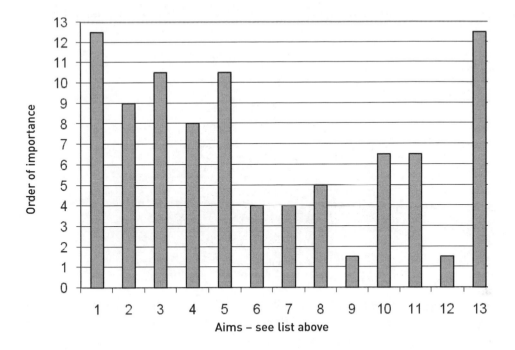

most popular choices (1,2,3,5, and 13) to the generally more specific or social skill oriented nature of the bottom 5 (6,7,8,9, and 12). As far as the most popular aims are concerned, the dominance of the health agenda in PE as identified by Penny (2008) is evident in the high ranking given to Aims 1 and 2. Equity of provision (Aim 12) was one of the first to be identified in the preliminary discussions about what should be included and it was no surprise that it was ranked joint highest. The importance of ensuring a sound platform for future participation in as many activities as possible is evident in the high ranking of Aim 5 and in practice is evident in the increasing emphasis in recent years on developing multi-skills, especially in the earlier years of schooling (Morley, 2009). Interestingly, whilst a traditional sport oriented curriculum appears to be prevalent as indicated above, the cultural and sporting heritage of the nation (Aim 7) is ranked lowest. It is also worth noting that several of the qualities valued by official curricula, such as developing leadership and being a good citizen, do not figure highly. Also the application of skills to specific contexts is ranked rather low, as is Aim 10, which was the functional partner to the highly ranked aim on active lifestyles.

b) The Outcomes

The pattern of teachers' responses to the outcomes under each aim is presented below in the rank order for the 13 aims. In each table the rank order of importance of the outcome (1 being most important, then 2 etc.) is the mode from across all the teachers' responses. The figures showing whether teachers felt they were achieved or not is the overall rank order of their ratings of each outcome from being mastered (1) to not achieved (3).

Table 2: Aim 1 (Rank 1=)

Aim	Learning Outcomes	Rank order	Achieved by Students
To encourage the adoption of active and healthy lifestyles	1. Choose a variety of activities to participate in or out of the curriculum	3	1
	2. Undertake exercise on a regular basis	2	2
	3. Make active choices in his/her daily life	4	3
	4. Have a balanced and active lifestyle with good habits	1	4

Establishing a balanced and active life is a priority for close to 50% of teachers, although they clearly believe that the outome reached most successfully by the students relates to choosing a variety of activities, whether they are part of the curriculum or extra-curricular. This suggests that while the teachers prioritise a broader educational thrust they believe students focus on the more immediate matter of choosing activities and what they want to participate in. Indeed a pattern begins to emerge that suggests that the more that the desired outcomes are close to actual student practices, the more they are achieved, from the teacher's point of view. The more the outcome projected by the teachers concerns behaviour, the less the perceived outcome corresponds to the intentions of the teachers. Semantics might indicate that action verbs (choose, participate) represent more specifically the activity of the assessable, more evaluable work of students while terms like "have" and "possess" are hard to identify in the field.

Table 3: Aim 13 (Rank 1=)

Aim	Learning Outcomes	Rank order	Achieved by Students
To provide opportunities for all pupils to learn and achieve, regardless of ability, gender or social and cultural background	1. Appreciate the needs of other pupils in PE and help them where appropriate	2	2
	2. Work effectively with pupils from social and cultural backgrounds different to their own	3	1
	3. Recognise their own needs and how to seek help to improve	1	3

The teacher's priorities are fairly evenly split between focusing on encouraging students to reflect on their own learning and encouraging a collaborative approach to learning by assisting others in their learning. On the other hand, in relation to perceived student achievement of learning outcomes, the second outcome is ranked a little higher than the others. Whilst this is not easy to explain, the overall pattern clearly offers a nice balance between individual and shared co-operative learning experiences.

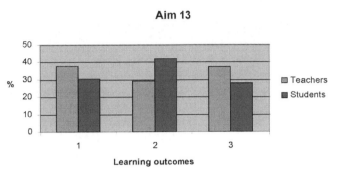

Table 4: Aim 3 (Rank 3=)

Aim	Learning Outcomes	Rank order	Achieved by Students
To inculcate a sense of important values in sport (fair play, solidarity, etc)	1. Participate in activities non-aggressively	3	1
	2. Make a contribution to group challenges and work as part of a team	1	2
	3. Accept winning and losing with the right attitude	2	2
	4. Accept the decisions of leaders	4	4

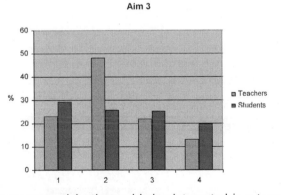

Teachers believe that group participation and being integrated in a team is clearly the most important outcome with close to 50% seeing group behaviour as their priority, indeed in some countries, Spain for example, the group is a core focus of PE. Interestingly, behaving appropriately towards other students through winning and losing properly and not being aggressive was more important than accepting decisions by officials and teachers also felt that this was the outcome achieved least by students.

Table 5: Aim 5 (Rank 3=)

Aim	Learning Outcomes	Rank order	Achieved by Students
To develop a broad repertoire of movement competence	1. Demonstrate the ability to undertake a diverse range of activities	1	1
	2. develop more advanced levels of movement relevant to their own capabilities	3	3
	3. Demonstrate a good range of fundamental skills	2	2
	4. Accept/attempt new challenges/skills	4	4

Aim 5

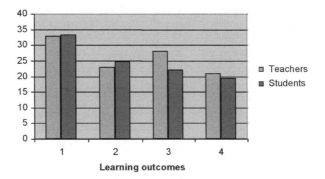

A belief in a broad and balanced curriculum is reflected in the ranking of outcome 1 as the most important, the ability to undertake a diverse range of activities. The learning outcomes targeted by the PE teachers and the students' level of mastery come together, indicating again the importance of matching outcomes to the activity to be mastered. The same pattern is apparent in the second and third outcomes where demonstrating and developing one's movement competence can be clearly identified and the desired learning outcomes and perceived achievement are practically identical.

Table 6: Aim 2 (Rank 5)

Aim	Learning Outcomes	Rank order	Achieved by Students
To develop a feeling of personal well-being/wellness	1. Learn to manage personal stress	4	4
	2. Accept his/her own capabilities and work within those parameters	1	2
	3. Demonstrate a sense of confidence to develop new skills	3	3

Aim 2

Once again teachers' educational ambitions are close to the perceived level of successful achievement. Realising and accepting personal boundaries was seen to be the most important, closely followed by developing confidence and being motivated. Developing a form of self-confidence combined with a sense of self-awareness, working with one's own means is clearly important for teachers. It is not possible in this overall picture to sift out the effects by age of the pupils and it was not the intention to do so but it would be a useful next stage. In the main, teachers felt that students tended to stay motivated with the means at their disposal and the abilities they have developed. These outcomes support the ongoing pattern that where action is involved, teachers' priorities are close to their perception of students' actual achievements. Clearly outcome 1 was not seen as particularly important and is an interesting indication of the gap between official representatives of the profession and the teaching cohort in general.

Table 7: Aim 4 (Rank 6)

Aim	Learning Outcomes	Rank order	Achieved by Students
To ensure safe practices in physical education	1. Demonstrate the ability to set out and use equipment in a safe way	3	1
	2. Exercise safely within his/her abilities and experience	1	2
	3. Understand the impact of the environment on participation in physical activity	0	4
	4. Be aware of the safety of others	2	3

Aim 4

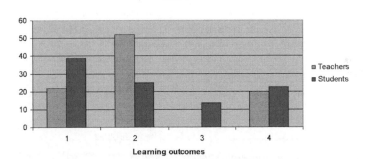

Learning outcomes

None of the teachers considered the understanding of the impact of physical activity on the environment to be worthy of interest, even though some countries had felt quite strongly about this matter. However, 13% of the students were perceived to have acquired this knowledge, either during PE classes or in general. Safe participation was a major issue during the focus group discussions and unsurprisingly it emerged as the principal learning outcome for teachers, although there was clearly a belief that there was some way to go in students achieving this outcome. The value of having the knowledge and ability to organise a safe environment in respect of equipment and being careful of others is quite well demonstrated in that teachers felt it applied so some 60% of students when outcomes 1 and 4 are combined.

Table 8: Aim 6 (Rank 6)

Aim	Learning Outcomes	Rank order	Achieved by Students
To develop an appreciation of cross-curricula links in relation to physical education	1. Be aware of the relevance of links with other areas of the curriculum – nutrition for example	2	1
	2. Understand the importance of physical education in wider curriculum initiatives, citizenship for example	1	2

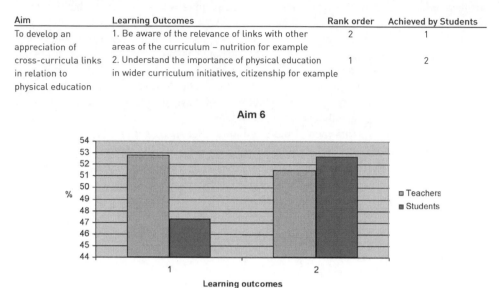

This outcome involves grasping the subject in a broader context and the learning outcomes projected by the PE teachers offer an interesting balance. Ostensibly, teachers feel that students have grasped the broader concept of how PE can contribute to social ideals such as being a good citizen. In this context, it is reasonable to assume the inclusion of such things as appreciating core values in competing properly, something that has long been promoted by politicians and has some substance in studies reporting decreases in youth crime where efforts are made to offer a broad package of sporting activities, such as in the first summer of sport for young people in the London Borough of Newham in 2005 where police reported a reduction in youth crime. There appears to be far less conviction regarding the extent to which students appreciate links with other subjects. This could be viewed as an area worthy of further interest in view of Penney's (2008) suggestion that in looking to the future, PE should view itself as a "connective specialism" as part of its educational raison d'être. Furthermore, Wild (2009) demonstrated the impact that cross-curricular work can have on motivating students and securing a richer set of outcomes both for them and indeed, their teachers. Clearly though it has to be acknowledged that there are issues about how this knowledge was evaluated and the basis for these observations, although it is an interesting topic.

Table 9: Aim 10 (Rank 7=)

Aim	Learning Outcomes	Rank order	Achieved by Students
Appreciate what means to be fit and/or healthy	1. Appreciate what it means to be fit and/or healthy	2	1
	2. Evaluate their health and fitness status	3	3
	3. Demonstrate an understanding of how to exercise properly to achieve health and fitness objectives	1	2

Proper form, exercise and mastering of a training regime are considered roughly equal in importance. Perhaps the relative lack of perceived achievement for outcome 3 is related to the greater complexity of interpreting knowledge in an activity context as opposed to having a general appreciation of what is required.

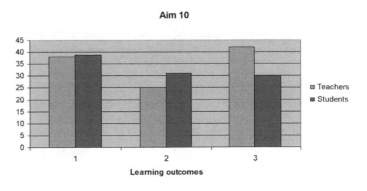

Table 10: Aim 11 (Rank 7=)

Aim	Learning Outcomes	Rank order	Achieved by Students
To develop the capacity to apply and develop skills in specific activity contents (sport, dance, etc)	1.Develop a range of skills in specific activities	1	2
	2. Apply these skills in specific activities	2	3
	3. Understand the rules governing specific activities	3	1

The teachers' objective of developing in students a repertoire of abilities in different activities was the most important priority and it was felt that it was largely achieved. In fact for close to 35% of PE teachers, students acquire specific skill repertoires during PE. On the other hand it is interesting that the rules governing these activities do not seem to be particularly important for teachers, although the students still succeed and possibly use their background outside school to build this knowledge. The extent to which teachers might, indeed should, make this obvious link with external clubs and experiences a formal part of their portfolio cannot be deduced from these data. Teachers observe also that the logic of the activity and its functioning seem to interest the students, who probably see in this the utility of their practice.

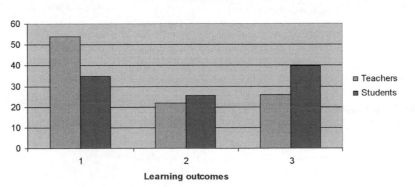

Table 11: Aim 8 (Rank 9)

Aim	Learning Outcomes	Rank order	Achieved by Students
To develop the ability to evaluate own and others performance	1. Evaluate and comment upon their own and others progress in a variety of activities	1	1
	2. Evaluate performance and suggest improvements	2	2

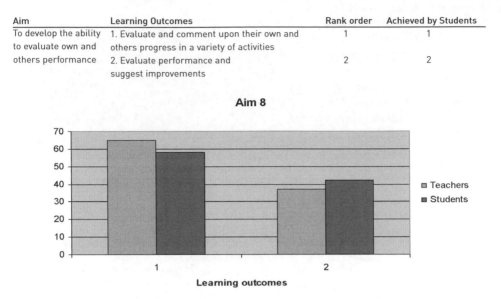

Developing students' knowledge and ability to evaluate their own progress and that of others is regarded as very important: it both confirms the strongly held views of the focus groups and sits well with one of Klein's (2006) proposed core components of a physically educated person. Teachers indicate that students acquire these evaluative tools, which is encouraging given the importance in many European curricula on encouraging personal reflection and learning to learn as a form of future proofing for students ongoing participation patterns.

The evidence in these outcomes appears to confirm the evolving pattern concerning the nature of those outcomes that appear to be more readily achieved. In this case they do not involve direct engagement rather a reflection on an engagement but as such it is in tune with the general thrust of what emerged in previous outcomes.

Table 12: Aim 7 (Rank 11=)

Aim	Learning Outcomes	Rank order	Achieved by Students
To promote an appreciation of the social and cultural significance of sport and physical activity	1. To appreciate the social and economic effects of sport and physical activity opportunities	2	2
	2. Show an awareness of the local and national sporting and physical activity environment and how to respond to it	3	3
	3. Demonstrate a knowledge and appreciation of the national sporting heritage	4	5
	4. Understand the social and historical roots of different sports	5	3
	5. Have an appreciation of the opportunities presented by the environment as an important resource for physical activity	1	1

Aim 7

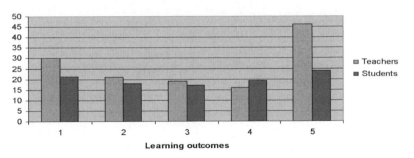

Learning outcomes

The importance and understanding of the setting in a holistic, or at least an ecological approach to physical activity, was a priority for close to 50% of the teachers and is no surprise given the general social agenda regarding the environment im many countries. The effects of this learning in terms of student engagement is mixed with around 25% students being perceived to buy in to this outcome . It also seems that the awareness of the utility of physical activity and sports in the social and economic environment is somewhat apparent for more than 20% of students. This outcome was rated near the bottom by teachers and the issue of participation in extra-curricular activities, sports and community programmes is worthy of further attention.

Table 13: Aim 9 (Rank 12=)

Aim	Learning Outcomes	Rank order	Achieved by Students
To develop a sense of leadership and the ability to organise others	1. Adopt a leadership role, for example officiating or judging	1	1
	2. Plan and organize group activities	3	3
	3. Provide support and motivation to their peers	2	2

Developing leadership skills and the ability to organise are ranked joint bottom of the aims for this group of teachers. Within this context, accepting the responsibility for supporting one's peers is considered a priority and is perceived as having been taken up by the students. This reflects a common theme in curricula across Europe and can be seen as part of the social orientation of the subject. A joint enterprise between teachers and students would appear to be in place and once again an outcome that targets the activity itself and the evaluation is direct, immediate, observable and seen as more readily achievable.

Aim 9

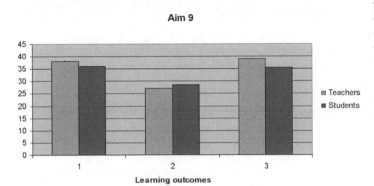

Learning outcomes

Table 14: Aim 12 (Rank 12=)

Aim	Learning Outcomes	Rank order	Achieved by Students
To contribute to the development of a sense a citizenship	1. Demonstrate a responsible behaviour in physical education and school sport	1	1
	2. Make a contribution to the life of the school and the local community	3	3
	3. Promote these values within the school and the local community	2	2

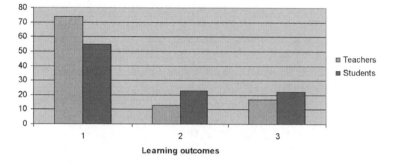

Responsible behaviour, contribution to the social life of the school and promotion of the values attributed to sports in general, physical activity and to physical education in particular are also rated at the bottom of the teachers' aims. However, teachers do emphasise that students should display a sense of personal responsibility and it is felt that just over 50% of them meet this objective. Contributing to community life is not deemed a priority for PE teachers, although it seems that they feel that a number of students absorb this message and in spite of this lack of interest from staff just over 20% of students are involved in the functioning of the school. Given that the first of Klein's (2006) suggested components of a physically educated person is about being a responsible citizen and that many schools across Europe would espouse a mission that supports such a thing it is worthy of note that PE teachers place it so low in their priorities. It may simply arise from PE teachers focusing more on their own immediate frontline priorities and the factors that support it, or perhaps there is a deeper issue about the place of PE in the school structure and the extent to which teachers see themselves, or are seen to be, somewhat separate from the mainstream of school activity.

THE CONTENT OF PHYSICAL EDUCATION IN EUROPE

The EUPEA focus groups discussed the possible content areas for a PE curriculum and assembled a representative list of what those areas might be. Of course it has the advantage of European-wide endorsement by professional associations but at the same time we must acknowledge the different nature of curricula in, for example, the Nordic countries with their strong emphasis on health and the environment and the UK with its focus on a student driven curricula and personal portfolios. Nevertheless, the areas identified are as follows (in number order only):

1. Dance activities
2. Striking and fielding games
3. Invasion games
4. Net and wall games
5. Gymnastic activities
6. Swimming activities and water safety
7. Athletic activities
8. Combat sports
9. Outdoor and adventurous activities
10. Personal development activities

For pragmatic reasons this part of the analysis focuses on the responses of the 5 countries with the highest number of responses and the general pattern is as shown in Table 13.

Table 15: Rank Order of Categories of Content Areas (Mode)

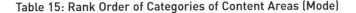

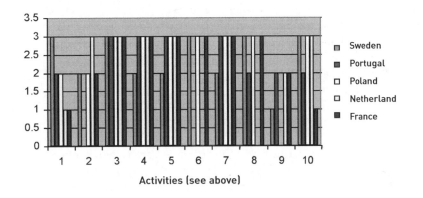

It is axiomatic that, to realise the overall objective of a physically educated person the content of the curriculum selected by teachers should facilitate that intention. It was not possible in this exercise to conduct an analysis of facilities and resources and we must accept that whilst these are important factors this study was about what teachers believe and try to do; the impact of such things as infrastructure is acknowledged but not covered here.

There are some clear national differences in approach, which is only to be expected but overall the curriculum areas considered to be most important are invasion games, net and wall games, gymnastic activities, swimming activities and personal development. With the exception of personal development, which is about such things as adopting an active lifestyle or individual exercise and activity practices, it is unsurprising to see a fairly traditional curriculum. In comparison it can be seen that areas such as dance, striking/fielding, outdoor and adventure and combat sports are ranked as less important. Certain content areas are ranked as priorities in all five countries: invasion games receive unanimous support, net and wall games (only Sweden does not rank these as priority activities) and athletics. Sweden placed a priority on activities considered necessary for survival, which is a national consideration in view of the environmental conditions. In particular they focused on orienteering as an outdoor activity, dance as a social *survival* skill and swimming in accordance with the prevalence of lakes in the environment. In some countries, there is a complete absence of swimming in the curriculum, notably Portugal, and teachers in the Netherlands in this study placed no priority on swimming, although certain PE teachers reported swimming lessons, either extra-curricular or integrated in the curriculum. There are frequently a number of issues surrounding swimming, which may be a lack of infrastructure in the local community or as in some other countries, the UK for example, timetable constraints, health and safety requirements or simply the cost of it. Whatever the reason it is an issue of concern in a number of countries.

In addition to identifying content areas, teachers were asked to identify activities within each area as exemplification of actual practice. The responses showed that the most common physical activities were volleyball (60%), endurance running (58%), basketball (53%), floorwork in gymnastics (48%), swimming (42%), orienteering (35%) and, as part of personal development - stretching (33%). The activities more specific to each country sometimes come together quite precisely as in Sweden for example, where dance, outdoor activities, swimming and water safety complement the exercises and training intended for maintaining and developing health. Portugal appeared to be more focused on major ball games, basic training and gymnastics. The Polish responses did not place any priority on outdoor and adventurous activities which, given the geographical nature of the country, would appear to be largely a curricular rather than environmental decision. In any case, there are many examples of this type of activity adapted for urban environments, such as parkour.

One of the main issues that arises from viewing content areas in the light of stated aims is whether they fit the priority objectives that teachers themselves profess to hold. A great deal of caution is necessary here because there is a danger of assuming too much from the data available. However, in as far as the pattern confirms issues raised elsewhere (e.g. Pühse & Gerber, 2005; Hardman & Marshall, 2000, 2009), it is a contribution to some of the key debates. For example, for the 5th aim (To develop a broad repertoire of movement competence) the teachers give top rating to "demonstrate the ability to undertake a diverse range of activities" but they appear to remain rather traditional in their activities with the laudable addition of personal development activities.

REVISITING THE CONCEPT OF A PHYSICALLY EDUCATED PERSON

Having identified an initial concept of a physically educated person (Klein, 2006; Meirieu, 2009) a preliminary view of what what that might mean in practice has now been advanced. The core principles that emerge from this exercise include important messages about developing personal and social responsibility in relation to seeking out and following active lifestyle opportunities on the basis of personal interests and capabilities. This is contextualised by the the idea of acting responsibly and respecting others as well as having some fundamental knowedge and experience about physical activity and sport. In addition there is planning to cope effectively with different environments and adopting appropriate strategies as the circumstances require. When looking at what teachers believe to be important and the extent to which that meshes with these general concepts and their view of priorities for learning outcomest are what might be considered as pieces to be added to a complex jigsaw.

The aims and learning outcomes prioritised by teachers demonstrate that the important factors for them are: the adoption of a balanced and active life with good habits; learners being able to recognise their needs and the needs of others; helping others by participating in, and contributing to, the success of the group; demonstrating ability in a range of physical activities and sports; and accepting one's limits and possibilities and acting appropriately. As such, they appear to touch base with central parts of the concept of a physically educated person. To have this balanced life, it is obvious to the teachers that a broad repertoire of abilities is essential and that the choice of activities, as well as the environment and the way they are performed, will be determining factors. The evidence also shows that teachers perceive that students do in fact participate in many physical activities and sports inside and outside of the curriculum (aim 1), co-operate with other students of different social and cultural backgrounds (aim 13), participate in activities while following the rules (aim 3), and they seem to be motivated to participate (aim 2).

However, while it is clear that purposes such as these are considered important in most of the countries involved, others are viewed less favourably. Those aims concerned with developing important social skills such as a sense of leadership, the ability to organise, or more broadly to develop a sense of citizenship are often the lowest priorities for teachers. Consequently, at least some of the broader strategic ideas on the concept of a physically educated person outlined above, ones that often seem to be at the heart education, do not appear to be picked up so strongly at an operational level. Furthermore, since links with other subjects are not viewed as important by teachers there is an additional sense of separation from the main educational agenda. In the thinking of the teachers it would appear from the responses that students demonstrating their acquisition of knowledge and skills is important and because evidence can be provided more clearly in practice, there is greater congruence between aims and learning outcomes that relate directly or indirectly to actual engagement. This would seem to suggest something of a distinction between broader personal and social aims on the one hand and skill learning learning and mastery of physical activities and sports on the other. However, this is a tentative suggestion and is a pattern that would have to be tested through plotting a reference grid for this work and testing it against others such as that advanced by Freis et al (2009).

Inevitably, there are differences across cultures in spite of general agreement as to what the package of aims and outcomes might be and a brief selection of the analysis of the five countries above (Portugal, France, Netherlands, Poland and Sweden) confirms the influence of culture, tradition and sporting heritage. It is possible, therefore, to derive some indication of a more differentiated image of the emhases evident in the different curricula on the basis of what these teachers believe within the context of their schools' programmes. Providing opportunities for all pupils to learn and achieve regardless of ability, gender or social and cultural background was strongly supported by all countries. There are differences, though, with Portugal, the Netherlands and Poland rating by more than 50% the aim to "appreciate the needs of other pupils in PE and help them where appropriate," while France gave top rating to the ability "to work effectively with pupils from social and cultural backgrounds different to their own" (53%), which is interesting in the light of the recent national debate about a multi-cultural society. As for students' learning outcomes, France and Portugal returned virtually identical results (48.9% and 50.8%) for students actually working with others from different backgrounds while the Netherlands and Poland gave equal ratings to the students' assessment of the needs of other students and actually working with them.

One would expect that an appreciation of the social and cultural significance of sport and physical activity (Aim 7) would throw up different cultural patterns and in fact for the Swedish, Portuguese and Dutch teachers around 60% felt this to be the most important. An appreciation of the opportunities afforded by the environment as an important resource for physical activity was very evident in Sweden and the connection with nature and the environment is considered essential for the practice of physical activity in and out of school, indeed for survival. For France the environmental context and students' evaluation of it are important (39%), while demonstrating knowledge and appreciation of the national sporting heritage follows close behind with 31%. The Netherlands considered the aim related to sporting heritage as less important (27%), while Poland, Portugal and Sweden rate it even lower (between 1% and 7%). Poland is the only country that accords a high rating to appreciating the social and economic effects of sport and physical activity opportunities, which may reflect the country's relatively new status as a member of the European Union.

In conclusion, whilst this chapter is only a contribution to understanding a European perspective of a physically educated person, it has the advantage of being rooted in the practice of the profession and as such it is a worm's eye view from the floor as it were. It is clear that as far as teachers are concerned the profile of a physically well educated young person includes being:
- a responsible citizen who is able to choose suitable activities, to follow good practice and to respect and help others;
- a person who is knowledgeable about physical activitity and sport with a good repertoire of skills and abilities;
- somebody who can be responsible for their own health and adopting an active lifestyle and be capable of evaluating their own progress and that of others.

There are numerous reasons for optimism in the perspectives of these teachers but unsurpringly the issues created by the process of translating policy into practice are also evident and of course the scope of this study could not deal with what teachers actually do and what students' think about it.

Note: The EUPEA project received valuable assistance and advice from Gilles Klein (University of Toulouse) and extensive management support from the Faculty of Human Motricity at the Technical University of Lisbon.

REFERENCES

Brettschneider, W.D., Prohl, R., Breuer, C., Rittner, V., Heim, R., Schmidt, W., & Altenberger, H. (2006). *DSB SPRINT-studie: eine Untersuchung zur Situation des Schulsports in Deutschland* (DSB SPRINT study: a research project regarding the situation of physical education and schoolsport in Germany). Aachen, Meyer & Meyer Verlag.

Commission of the European Communities (2007). *White Paper on Sport*, Brussels, COM (2007) 391 Final.

Delignières, D., & Garsault, C. (2004). *Libres propos sur l'Education Physique*. Paris, Editions Revue EPS.

European Union (2008). *European Union Physical Activity Guidelines: Recommended Policy Actions in Support of Health-Enhancing Physical Activity.* Approved by the EU Working Group "Sport & Health" at its meeting on September 25 and confirmed by EU Member State Sport Ministers at their meeting in Biarritz, November 27-28.

Fries, A-V., Baumberger, J., & Egloff, B. (2009). *Zum Auftrag des Fachs Sport in der Volksschule*. PH Zürich, BASPO.

Fisher, R.J. (2004). Physical Education: Current Trends and Future Perspectives. Presentation, *World Sport for All Congress*, Rome, November 11–14.

Green, K. (2008). *Understanding Physical Education.* London, Sage.

Hardman, K. (2005). Global Vision of the Situations, Trends and Issues of Sport and Physical Education in Schools. Paper presented at the *International Conference on Sport and Physical Education*, Bangkok, Thailand, October 30–November 2.

Hardman, K., & Marshall, J.J. (2000). *World-wide survey of the state and status of school physical education: the final report to the International Olympic Committee*, Manchester, University of Manchester.

Hardman, K., & Marshall, J.J. (2009). *Second World-Wide Survey of School Physical Education*, Berlin, International Council of Sport Science and Physical Education.

Klein, G. (2003). Une affaire de discipline. L'éducation physique en France et en Europe (1970-2000), *Editions Revue EPS*, 65.

Klein, G. (2006). *A Physically Educated Person*, Presentation to the European Physical Education Association Annual Forum, London, St Mary's University College, October 19-22.

Meirieu, P. (2009). *Lettre aux grandes personnes sur les enfants d'aujourd'hui*, Paris, Editions Revue EPS.

Morley, D. (2009). Multi-skills: Contexts and Constraints. *Physical Education Matters*, 4(3), pp.19-23.

Penney, D. (2008). Playing a political game and playing for position. Policy and curriculum development in health and physical education, *European Physical Education Review*, 14(1), pp.33-39.

Penney, D., & Evans, J. (1999). *Policy, politics and practice in physical education and sport*, London, E&FN Spon.

Puhse, U., & Gerber, M. (Eds.), (2005). *International Comparison of Physical Education: Concepts-Problems-Prospects*, Oxford, Meyer and Meyer Sport (UK) Ltd.

Scallon, G. (2007). *L'évaluation des apprentissages dans une approche par compétences*, Bruxelles, de Boeck: Pédagogie en développement.

Wild, A. (2009). Implementation of the new Secondary Curriculum, *Physical Education Matters*, 4(3), pp.15-18.

CHAPTER 5

INCLUSION: ISSUES OF SOCIAL, EMOTIONAL AND BEHAVIOURAL DIFFICULTIES IN PHYSICAL EDUCATION
RICHARD MEDCALF

INTRODUCTION

Within the context of school curriculum physical education, the content of this chapter highlights particular issues relating to the concept of inclusion, when applied to children and young people who are deemed to experience Social, Emotional and Behavioural Difficulties (SEBD). It discusses how these issues are circumscribed when enacted within multi-faceted and complex educational environments such as physical education (PE). The inter-actional nature of such environments causes a wide spectrum of polarised experiences that are a product of the visible manifestation of "need" which participation can evoke. The varying contexts, in meeting individual and diverse learning needs, are testament to the complexities inherent in ensuring that the rights of all pupils are accommodated. The rights of the child are both many and varied. For the purpose of this chapter, the foremost right of all learners is that of being included in an equitable experience of PE.

There is a general consensus that in providing effective learning opportunities for all pupils, and consequently including all learners in inclusively orientated learning environments, pro-active strategies and mechanisms that support children and young people to succeed are necessary. Booth and Ainscow (2002) contend that schools should concern themselves with increasing both the participation, and the broad educational achievements, of all students. These are clear moral and ethical foregrounds to the provision of equitable educational opportunities, which allow all pupils to progress irrespective of their relative abilities.

It is worth noting here the important differences between what is commonly termed "integration" (whereby the child fits into a pre-disposed system), and "inclusion" (whereby the system itself is adapted to suit the child). Despite the clarity of this distinction, "inclusion" itself is a term more difficult to define. The term is widely understood to mean different things to different people, and consequently is a challenge to define in any succinct way. Broadly speaking, Ainscow and Cesar (2006) describe the over-arching necessity in "working together to address barriers to education experienced by some learners ... within a particular context" (p.233). However, they go further by highlighting a typology of five different ways in which inclusion could be defined (see Ainscow, Booth, Dyson, Farrell, Frankham, Gallannaugh, Howes and Smith, 2006). The variance in how this term is interpreted, and the subjective nature of inclusiveness itself, are complications that are more adequately described by Ainscow and Cesar (2006).

There are clear philosophical justifications for the proliferation of inclusive practices in education. In contemporary research, these justifications are most commonly underpinned by internationally recognised policy documents such as the *Convention on the Rights of a Child* (United Nations, 1989). Another landmark publication is the *Salamanca Statement* on inclusive education (United Nations Educational Scientific and Cultural Organisation, 1994), which outlines guidelines in principles, policy and practice in special needs education, re-affirming the right and commitment to education for all, in schools of "inclusive orientation". These are further grounded by the commitments made by education curricula (at a national level). The legislative drive for an inclusive ethos in the English National Curriculum for Physical Education (NCPE) is also substantiated by research, which has resulted in a critical mass of papers that offer weight and credibility to the fundamental argument of the aforementioned rights of the child. In meeting these rights, there is the need for PE to provide effective and positive learning opportunities that reflect a differentiated level of support in regards to the fundamental movement skills of participants, especially so as "... Students learn in different ways ... and enter physical education with different levels of movement experience. This precipitates different learner needs and aspirations" (Byra, 2006, p.449).

The subsequent potential for PE to "include", and the ease to which it is possible for it to "exclude", is testimony to the common variance in affinity towards the subject. The importance of particular cultures, policies and practices of inclusion are further exacerbated in a number of ways, when learning in a physical context, through NCPE.

INCLUSION IN PHYSICAL EDUCATION

Values generally related to the ethical principles of fairness and honesty have long been internal, built in, logically constitutive features of the games and sports, which feature prominently in the familiar PE curriculum (Reid, 1997). As such, rather than an emphasis on the benefits resulting from participation in PE, the subject is seen by many as having value in its own right (Whitehead, 2000). The definition provided by Bailey (2006) is adopted in this chapter: it describes PE as "that area of the school curriculum concerned with developing students' physical competence and confidence, and their ability to use these to perform in a range of activities" (p.397).

Despite the often overlooked and sometimes marginalised position of PE in schools(Hardman and Marshall, 2009), the subject is one that is often advocated as being a source of many positive developmental characteristics through adolescence. As a statutory "core", principal or generally practised subject in many countries across the world, it offers a niche within curriculum time in which multiple personal, physical and social qualities can develop if complimented by teaching, learning environments, and lesson content, which the individual finds facilitative to his or her long term development.

> "PE helps pupils develop personally and socially. They work as individuals, in groups and in teams, developing concepts of fairness and of personal and social responsibility. They take on different roles and responsibilities, including leadership, coaching and officiating. Through the range of experiences that PE offers, they learn how to be effective in competitive, creative and challenging situations" (Qualifications and Curriculum Authority, 2007b, p.189).

Within the wider curriculum, there have long been claims of the multiple discourses at play in PE and, more specifically, the breadth of learning that it is invariably claimed that the subject develops, or is concerned to develop, in pupils (Penney, 2000). PE is one of few curriculum subjects, whose inherent motives, structures, pedagogies and content lend themselves to the opportunity for a holistic and developmental programme of activities, which go some way in fostering a range of positive attributes. Physical education lends itself to the development of physical skills, team building, character development, responsibility, creativity and imagination. Without claiming too much in the name of PE, there remains an important role for the subject to play in providing young people with a holistic knowledge, understanding, and social skills to ensure physical activity (of some kind) becomes a regular aspect of their daily life (Fairclough and Stratton, 2005).

Kay (2003) highlights the long term aims of participation including not only continued engagement in activities throughout life, but also now with an appreciation of a wide variety of considered, holistic and interdisciplinary benefits. The effects of PE are no longer seen as being merely part of the relatively short lived curriculum for children of school age. Its unique contribution to lifelong learning and education has been acknowledged by Doll-Tepper (2005), who spoke of the indispensable role of PE in the education process. It is also appreciated more widely as playing an important role in achieving broader educational objectives such as whole school improvement, community development and effecting personal behavioural and attitudinal change among pupils (Houlihan and Green, 2006).

The contested nature and purpose of PE is often dominated by wider educational and philosophical agendas. Historically, the inclusion of PE as a curriculum subject has been justified on the basis of broad and diverse goals of physical, social, and moral development (Sallis and McKenzie, 1991). These are goals to which many other subjects cannot lay claim. Despite the relatively active characteristics of other practical subjects, including drama and the arts for example, active participation in PE involves learning that is unique to the physical domain. The distinctive nature of PE has been postulated, therefore, to result in a range of outcomes that are not seen as being inherently possible in other curriculum subjects. Children and young people experiencing PE are encouraged, by the nature of the subject, to potentially engage in acts that are physical and often co-operative by design. The propensity of PE to produce profound affective gains in individuals has, as such, been widely researched. Researchers have recognised PE as a site that is well suited to the promotion of young people's social development (Lawson, 1999). Miller et al (1997) cited how responsibility and co-operation were key features of their socio-moral programme through PE. Moore (2002) has built upon this further by discussing how PE has the potential to develop personal qualities such as self-esteem, self-confidence, empathy, and compassion.

The subject is in a relatively distinct position, from which it can assume a level of responsibility to in some way address many issues in the life of a school. As such, the specificities of PE, in regards to its place within curricula in comparison with other subjects, are worthy of interrogation in relation to the affects upon children and young people. These varied effects should be considered as being dependent upon the characteristics of the learner, in context, and independence to the situational environment of their class. The implementation of pedagogies, which seek to plan for the full and active participation inlearning is vital in this regard. The uniqueness of this co-creation of experience means that there are also particular barriers to inclusion, within a subject of relative uniqueness in the curricula of PE.

Vickerman et al (2003) highlight four key principles when contextualising issues of inclusion to NCPE. They argue for entitlement, accessibility, integration, and integrity as being the cornerstones of inclusive practice in the subject. These are only possible because of the breadth of learning that can take place within PE. According to Penney (2002), such breadth is seen in "extending the range of skills, knowledge and understanding that are incorporated in descriptions of learning in physical education extends the potential for the subject to be inclusive of the varied educational needs, abilities and interests of all pupils" (p.124).

In providing opportunities, which cater for the needs of all pupils, irrespective of their practical ability or competencies, it is an expectation that PE can provide positive and inclusive outcomes through active participation and engagement. Such opportunities to experience success in learning are possible regardless of gender, race, ethnicity, cognitive aptitude or physical ability. Moreover, an educational provision that meets the needs of all pupils is widely expected to meet the needs of those deemed to experience a special educational need.

SPECIAL EDUCATIONAL NEEDS AND INCLUSION IN PHYSICAL EDUCATION

Prior to discussion of the specificities of the SEBD category within Special Educational Needs (SEN), it is worth acknowledging that, more broadly, there is legislation in a growing number of countries that supports the fundamental right to an inclusive education for all pupils with any form of SEN (Vickerman et al., 2003). In England and Wales, there is an excess of such legislative and non-statutory guidance, which has pursued this agenda. The Green Paper on *Excellence for All* (Department for Education and Employment, 1997), *The Special Educational Needs and Disability Act* (Department for Education and Skills, 2001a), *The Special Educational Needs Code of Practice* (Department for Education and Skills, 2001b), and, in relation to PE, the *Planning for Inclusion* statement within the National Curriculum (Qualifications and Curriculum Authority, 2007a), have each contributed in the most recent past. The issues, which surround students with SEN in the National Curriculum, have, hence, received noticeable recent attention within both academia and in policy. Whilst it is not the task of this chapter to provide an overview of the historical developments within this field, Smith (2004) indicates that the aforementioned contemporary developments are part of a process that "can be traced back as far as the mid-1800s", and points to the "long term social process'" in his conceptualisation of current PE provision for pupils with SEN (p.40).

The definition for Special Educational Needs used in the DfES (2001b) *Code of Practice*, is actually that contained within the *Education Act* (Department for Education and Employment, 1996). This describes a child having SEN if he (or she) "has a learning difficulty which calls for special educational provision to be made for him" (or her) (section 312). Despite remaining current in the main, this definition has been somewhat supplemented first by the introduction of *The Special Educational Needs and Disability Act* (Department for Education and Skills, 2001a), and, more recently, by Department for Children, Schools and Families (2008) guidance. The consistent feature of such guidance is that children and young people, who are deemed to experience a special educational need, do so as they are faced with particular barriers to learning and participation.

Despite this, localised interpretations of ideological statements, and subsequent national policies, are notoriously challenging to benchmark. In the UK, the decentralised nature of SEN assessment has been legislated through documents, which discuss the requirement for such a delivery of these principles to take place at a local level (Department for Education and Employment, 1996). The SEN Green Paper *Excellence for all Children* (Department for Education and Employment, 1997) drew attention to the regional dimension in SEN provision, which led to variation amongst the quality and nature of the provision being offered. It has been shown that such disparities continue to occur in regards to prevalence and support for SEN (Mooney, Statham, Brady, Lewis, Gill, Henshall, Willmott, Owen and Evans, 2010). Such a localised emphasis serves to perpetuate the differences between the extents to which pupils are included in relation to matters of their education.

Inclusive PE for pupils with SEN is concerned with a recognition of the philosophical basis of inclusion, as well as a commitment and desire to support its implementation through both the execution of policy and a desire to change practice (Vickerman et al., 2003, p.50). This point serves as a reminder that central to all processes occurring in their classrooms are the pedagogic and didactic behaviours of educators. Consequently, the role of the physical educator as a facilitator to these processes must, of course, not be forgotten. The great ranges of difficulty, which can attest to the label of SEN, are most regularly spoken about within PE, alongside literature discussing inclusive practice. In meeting any inclusion statements in PE curricula, "teachers need to actively review the pedagogical practices in order to ensure they meet ... requirements to facilitate entitlement and accessibility to inclusive activities for all pupils, including those with SEN" (Vickerman, 2007, p.58).

Studies have highlighted how PE teachers have, in the past, recognised the pragmatic and conceptual difficulties that such inclusion can pose (Robertson, Childs and Marsen, 2000). This can be seen as a reflection of what Smith and Green (2004) describe as the long established disposition of a "pre-eminence of a sporting ideology in (PE teachers) views" (p.605). In this regard, Morley et al (2005) discussed how PE teachers conceptualised the subject as one which is significantly different from other subject areas. Their research highlighted the perceived difficulties in teaching children with behavioural difficulties more so than other manifestations of SEN.

As mentioned previously, PE has the potential to make significant contributions to the education and development of all children and young people in many ways, most of which are not reproducible through other areas of the curriculum, or through other sporting or physical activities (Bailey and Dismore, 2004). In this regard, Wright and Sugden (1999) note how, for all pupils, but especially those with SEN, "physical education is not simply education of the physical, but also involves education through the physical of other naturally developing attributes such as language, cognition, socialisation, and emotions" (p.16). The subject's ability to offer such contributions is, nevertheless, mediated by the wider social cultures that can manifest themselves in curriculum PE. Arguably, in countries where emphasis is "placed upon sport and team games within the PE curriculum (it) appears to do rather more to exclude, than include, some pupils from particular learning situations in PE" (Smith, 2004, p.51). These experiences are, hence, heavily framed by individuals' special educational needs, or lack thereof.

The claimed and/or perceived benefits of active participation in PE are reconciled by individuals' reciprocity to the subject. Their affinity will undoubtedly be affected by the provisions made to address the additional needs of individuals who either excel, or experience difficulty, with the physical and visible nature of participation. These issues highlight the difficulties in what Smith and Thomas (2006b) perceive as being the diametrically opposed policies of inclusion in its broadest sense, alongside the emphasis within physical education on raising standards of practical achievement. There is a clear dichotomy between an ethos of performance, (borne out of a concentration on physical abilities and measures), and a desired inclusive philosophy. The corollary of such a culture is described by Morley, Bailey, Tan and Cooke (2005) as being the inherent "conflict" within PE, which seeks to promote equity and excellence simultaneously.

Such contradictions are potentially magnified through "needs" that are physical in nature. In turn, the challenges facing inclusive discussions in PE are most often spoken about within the remit of a physical need. Coates and Vickerman (2008) re-affirm that the majority of research that examines the PE perspectives of children with SEN do so from the perspective of a physical disability, and "as such may not prove representative of the full sphere of special educational needs" (p.170). Studies (e.g. Kristen, Patriksson and Fridlund, 2002; Fitzgerald, 2005; and Goodwin, 2007) of those with such physical difficulties reveal a range of contrasting experiences, including a spectrum of feelings from difference and estrangement, self doubt, acceptance, discrimination, to the enjoyment gained from socialising whilst strengthening their physique. However, when considering issues of inclusion in PE, it is important not to solely focus on the subject as a physical domain. Despite providing a foundation upon which to contrast experiences, these worthy additions to the field pay little direct contribution to the potentially very different experiences of those with SEBD.

Research has neglected recognition of the distinctive subset of SEN, which is SEBD. The relative importance of this lack of attention is exacerbated in that Smith and Thomas (2006) (2006a) highlight the fact that, actually, teachers often find it especially difficult to include pupils who have social, emotional and behavioural difficulties. The neglect of other sub-sets of SEN, namely SEBD in this instance results in a paucity of research that references the potential differences that these varying subsets can evoke.

SEBD AND PHYSICAL EDUCATION

When research has, in the past, acknowledged both SEN and PE, it has commonly discussed the two fields from the perspectives of those with a physical disability of some kind. As such, it has neglected to devote a proportionate amount of time to pupils who have some form of SEBD experience PE. The specific category of educational need, which carries the label of SEBD, is worthy of distinction from others, in that their experiences in PE are often manifestly different from those more commonly reported.

There are very few definitions of SEBD used in relation to, and alongside, the published criteria for the clinical diagnosis of other similar conditions that often occur in parallel to it. It is an umbrella term used to describe complex and often persistent difficulties and, as such, there are a great number of issues that can contribute to the ascription of the term and its use in school. As behaviour is defined within the context of social grouping, establishing both the existence and identification of "difficult behaviour" or "emotional disorder" is fraught with problems (Wearmouth and Connors, 2004). In the same way that the concept can be viewed from a number of theoretical and conceptual perspectives (Ayers, Clarke and Murray, 2000), for some, the root cause of their problem may have sociological undertones, some may have psychological undertones, and on the other hand, some conditions may manifest as a result of a biological base.

The definition most often used in England and Wales is still that featured in *Circular 9/94*, where children deemed to be showing signs of a social, emotional or behavioural difficulty are described as "lying on the continuum between behaviour which challenges teachers but is within normal, albeit unacceptable, bounds and that which is indicative of serious mental illness" (Department for Education and Employment/Department of Health, 1994, p.7). This goes on to state that their problems are clearer and greater than sporadic naughtiness or moodiness and yet not so great as to be classed as mental illness. As with the aforementioned definition of SEN that is being applied in this chapter, the DCSF guidance (2008) has also, in part, superseded the DfEE circular in relation to SEBD.

The term SEBD implies a sub-group of those with SEN, whose needs can be assessed and met with special educational provision (Travell, 1999). It has allowed policy makers and practitioners to "bracket" pupils who require special provision but do not suffer sensory-motor impairments or learning disabilities – referring to such pupils without unduly anchoring their SEN in psycho-pathology (Jones, 2003). There is no evidence to suggest that the different emotional and behavioural manifestations that are given the SEBD label are related to form a single condition, and it would be wrong to assume that there is any kind of homogeneity in what is placed under the broad and crude heading of SEBD (Cooper, 1999a). Despite this, the challenging nature of their externalising behaviours is a common feature of the difficulties that they portray. Commonplace within this is the manifestation of behaviours, which are socially constructed as being inappropriate.

For these definitions and conceptualisations to apply, there is a common acknowledgement that their difficulties should be persistent, frequent, severe emotional or behavioural problems occurring within or across particular settings (Ayers and Prytys, 2002). Since the 1970s, increasing recognition has been given to the argument that SEBD is best seen in interactive terms; that a child's SEBD should be seen as the product of unsuitable environments as well as problems of individual pathology; and that it marked a growing acceptance of the idea that the environment was the key to SEBD and disaffection in general. The most common category of need is when such personal and environmental characteristics combine.

The concept of SEBD attempts to come to grips with the perception that behaviour, which does not meet diagnostic criteria, sometimes poses serious problems at school (Jones, 2003). Alongside the behavioural tendencies, which many children with SEBD share, it remains important to appreciate that more often than not these children's needs are multi-faceted. They are most likely labelled with diverse and often co-morbid problems that are underpinned by their behavioural difficulties. With this in mind, the experiences of those deemed to portray signs of SEBD are unsurprisingly varied and multi-faceted.

The aetiology of SEBD is diverse and multiple due to the wide-ranging behaviours, which can be deemed as being classified under its umbrella. As such, Cole, Daniels and Visser (2003) describe the vague and incompleteness of available national and local data, which describe the SEBD sub-group of SEN in the United Kingdom. This recognises the chronic difficulties in calculating precise figures given both the differing weightings attributed to the aforementioned biological, social, educational, psychological, or cultural explanations, and the different perspectives of professionals working across and within different agencies cited previously.

Statistics, which clearly report SEN prevalence and severity, are widely accessible. Those of a similar credibility that recognise SEBD specifically are less commonly available and detailed. This, in part, is a result of the multiplicity of causative factors that contribute to the relative trends of SEBD prevalence within different demographics of society.

"Research shows that the prevalence of such difficulties varies according to sex, age, health and domicile. Rates are likely to be greater in inner cities; socially deprived families (for which a narrow notion of social class is not a good proxy); boys rather than girls, children with other learning, health or developmental difficulties; adolescents as opposed to younger children; and, amongst young children, those with delayed language development. While many children cope well with adverse circumstances and events, higher rates of emotional and behavioural difficulty are also likely to feature where there is or has been parental discord or divorce; mental health problems in other family members; neglect; or significant parental coldness or irritability towards the child" (Social, Emotional and Behavioural Difficulties Association, 2006, p.2).

Due to the wide ranging number of symptoms and conditions, which can be classed as being under the umbrella of SEBD, citing a collection of causes and/or possible antecedents is a wide ranging and extensive task. There have been shown to be a number of factors that pre-dispose children to develop certain difficulties, precipitating factors that then trigger the onset of difficulties and perpetuating factors that maintain these difficulties over time and across contexts (Ayers and Prytys, 2002). These include, amongst others, the impact of family structures, parental and family difficulties, and stressors such as separation, bereavement, and abuse. Other more personal pre-cursors can include low self esteem and self-efficacy, learned helplessness, and difficulties during developmental pathways. For these reasons, it is commonly seen that adolescence is the period when difficulties of a social, behavioural and emotional nature are most likely to occur.

Children and young people with a social, emotional or behavioural difficulty exhibit a complex array of problem behaviours in school settings, and they subsequently experience notable difficulties in learning (Cooper, 1999b). The time children spend on task in instructionally effective and productive classrooms is naturally reduced when behaviours of a disruptive nature are present. Nelson et al (2003) highlighted the severity and frequency of typical behaviours exhibited by children with emotional and behavioural disorders and found that twice as many students could be classed as exhibiting "externalising" behaviours (delinquent or aggressive) than "internalising" (withdrawn, anxious or social problems). Negative behaviours are regularly a derivative of children with an element of SEBD and hence, strategies, which seek to alleviate these, are often sought. Consequently, it could be postulated that the ways in which they experience curriculum PE, and in particular the way in which such a population react to these experiences, would differ to those of a generic cohort of students.

Children and young people with SEBD are, without assuming any element of homogeneity, pupils who tend to have difficulties in maintaining the behaviours that are deemed appropriate by their school. The type and extent of these difficulties differs markedly, and the realities that are faced by those given the label of SEBD vary hugely. In acknowledging the difference that the label invokes, the variance in realities, alongside the aforementioned variance in localised provision for SEN, results in disparities of inclusive practices, which affect their participation in PE.

In addition to any interpretations that are familiar to children and young people more generally, the potentially distinct and varied meanings that ground the PE experiences of a population of young people with SEBD, requires sufficient understanding and recognition. PE appears to meet some of the needs of those with SEBD, securing their motivation and concentration, and creating relevant and appropriately challenging educational experiences. Such benefits should be preceded by a recognition of the fact that practical, physical and expressive creative experiences are an important constituent when educating children with SEBD (Cole and Visser, 1998). The subsequent ways in which those perceived to experience SEBD perceive PE to affect them could have ramifications when planning for, and implementing, a curriculum that best suits their needs and desires.

PARTICIPATORY VOICE

The study of inclusive issues in PE is often, more recently, studied from the perspective of participatory student voice. This chapter is grounded in the outcomes of a series of case studies of such kind. These studies involved three phases of design that sought to understand the construction of participants' experiences in PE. A process of familiarisation was followed by two stages of a twelve week cycle that involved both local sensitisation, and thorough case study methods. By spending time embedded in schools, the intention was to become conversant with the particular idiosyncrasies and conventions evident in departments of physical education. The goal of this time was to attempt to grasp an understanding of the nuances, the language, and the interpersonal intricacies likely to be experienced by case study participants. Pseudonyms are used in all cases.

For a number of the boys, the physical elements of PE were its defining feature. Daniel for example spoke of this physicality in a number of ways. He described it both as a characteristic of the subject, which resulted in an increase in his obstructive behavioural tendencies, and also as something that led to a perceived task mastery that was often not possible elsewhere in his curriculum. These views were shared by a number of the more practically proficient and physically larger boys, including Tom and Paul. When they discussed with me the varying sports in which they participated during NCPE, they each placed a high regard on theirs, and others, practical abilities. Seemingly irrespective of the lesson content, they each approached lessons with an aim to demonstrate their performance capabilities. In contrast, for some participants who were not so practically able, including Jack for example, the physical nature of PE was attributed to causing some of the difficulties that he faced in forming friendships with his peers. In this case, he instead gained enjoyment through the act of having contact with the ball. He was someone who, like many of the other cases in this study, placed a high regard on being central to the passage of play.

In achieving some extent of control over their behaviours, in lessons in which they were proficient and predominantly active, the boys recognised PE as having an effect upon their behavioural and cognitive states. The conscious use of PE as a tool that would help them to manage their behaviours was something that participants spoke of in a number of ways. Ben, for example, perceived that the energy expelled during his time in PE resulted in an effect that was akin to escapism from situations that would more commonly cause him difficulties. Consequently, on occasions, the opportunities in PE to demonstrate exaggerated behaviours without the interference of other demands resulted in participants maintaining appropriate behaviours more so than in other lessons. For some, such as Paul, these opportunities were perceived as being acted upon within his own terms. Irrespective of the requirement of him, this perceived control over a situation, in apparently choosing when and when not to participate, resulted in more suitable actions when under direction from his teachers. This perceived control was something that, as with other aspects of their behaviours, the boys spoke of as being important in the eyes of their peers.

The opportunities to work alongside peers, and to share common goals within their teams, were seen as a trait of PE that had a number of recognisable implications. James spoke at length about the social nature of participation, and the subsequent importance of being given opportunities to be actively involved in tasks in conjunction with his peers. As well as giving opportunities to work co-operatively with others, these situations were also seen by some, including Paul and Ben, as a time in which they could directly and favourably compare themselves to others through cementing their relative practical abilities within their group. When not perceived as being competent in this regard, a number of the boys (including, and especially, Daniel) would behave in ways that were seen as potentially threatening to others. His time in PE directly affected the relations that he had with his peers in all other subjects. Most of the boys appeared to be seen by their peers as the ones who would "muck about", in each of their respective classes. PE offered an environment in which this prophecy seemed to commonly occur. In practical learning environments that rewarded effort and ability with increased physical freedoms, these behavioural tendencies appeared to manifest themselves more frequently. Ben highlighted his perceived need for space and freedom, which was given to him in some elements of PE. Furthermore, James recognised PE as a time that could alleviate his boredom through the virtues of movement that he himself could determine. For Tom, the inability to control the impulses, which were resultant upon boredom elsewhere, were not an issue within his PE lessons. Rather, such impulses instead resulted in potentially disruptive behaviours that were a product of the temptations which he perceived to face.

The boys recognised that PE had inherent characteristics that defined it as being a subject that, to them, and for different reasons, was unlike the majority of others in their curriculum. In contrast to the aims of their curricula, their motivation to participate appeared to be one that was framed in the desire, (and in some cases need), for a removal from the static learning environments found in other classrooms. Although widely seen as a subject requiring little or no cognitive effort, and a source of escapism from the rigour of learning elsewhere, they did highlight a number of elements to their involvement that were more than simply an avoidance of other subjects.

PE was shown, in the experiences of participants, to provide worthwhile and challenging opportunities to learn. The boys spoke of how it provided opportunities to be seen as competent in something, and, dependent upon their perception of competence, as such appeared to be sympathetic to their understandable desire for achievable tasks. For some, this prospect meant that the PE lesson was the only such occasion in their school day when they could achieve successes that were comparable with their peers. The nature of other curriculum subjects, which were perceived as privileging only academic attributes, potentially marginalised some of the academic and behavioural traits of the boys in this study. In contrast, elements of PE were on occasion deemed by participants as being more accessible and well suited to their strengths and needs.

The varying nature of responses from both between each case study participant, and from within each case itself, has demonstrated that PE provokes complex and changeable reactions that appear to be a product of a number of factors. It has been shown that boys with SEBD had varying reactions to participation in the subject. These polemic experiences ranged from, for example, a positive cathartic type remedial response, to examples of aggressive reactions that were explained as being incited by virtue of the physicality of the subject. The nature of these varying reactions, and the specificities of the factors that each participant deemed as being contributory to their experience of PE, are potentially issues that have relatively unique resonance to those who are deemed to have SEBD.

Concluding Comments
The difficulty of the concept of SEBD itself, the absence of a prescriptive model or definition for inclusion, and in light of the continued debate regarding the nature and purposes of physical education, this chapter has sought to highlight issues regarding the

changeable and highly individual nature of inclusive practice in NCPE. The inclusion of such children and young people, within an environment that is practical in nature, is both a moral and pedagogic matter worthy of interrogation. The resources to support learning and participation in PE are demonstrably different to those found elsewhere in their provision. In creating space for positive experiences to occur, the subject has a responsibility to include all learners so that they can engage with participation at their most appropriate skill level. Hence, enabling choices which are facilitative to the individual needs of all learners requires recognition of the changeable landscape of PE.

The environment in which the child is asked to learn and behave is a critical factor to consider, when discussing the causes of, and responses to, their school experiences. This is particularly magnified in PE, where the rhetoric and policies of inclusive education are intersected with the intrinsic physicality of the environment. The subsequent embodied responses are most likely to be a product of socially constructed perceptions of the subject, which have developed over time. The polarised nature of such experiences, and the variance in experience and perception of PE, are befitting of the overarching effect of context when educated through the physical domain (Eldar, 2008).

Participation (and experience) has been shown by previous literature to be circumscribed in a variety of ways by gender, social class, and the school (Smith, Thurston, Lamb and Green, 2007). Furthermore, people's actions and participation in PE are both enabled and constrained by the complex networks of inter-dependent people in schools (Smith et al., 2007). Factors that contribute to experiences and task adherence are multiple and inter-related to such extent that exhaustive description and differentiation is complex (Medcalf, Marshall and Rhoden, 2006). It is impossible to state, to any firm degree of conclusion, the relative importance of such inter-dependencies. It is one of, or a combination of, PE's curricular structures, lesson content, didactic practices, and the environmental structures inherent and consistent in any PE class, which contribute in some way to the varying perceptions of inclusive practice in PE.

In reflecting upon what Ainscow, Howes, Farrell and Frankham (2003) highlight as the importance of "learning from difference" in the development of inclusive practice, there is worth in recognising that perceptions of (and experiences in) PE are circumscribed by an individual's differing past experiences. Consequently, participation has a number of contrasting effects, from which we should learn. Florian (2005) suggests that "... Special and inclusive education are stuck in the dilemma of difference ... new understandings about how to respond to those who experience difficulties in learning are needed" (p.97). These differences cannot be delineated by label, location, pedagogy or activity. It is only by allowing time and opportunities for truly inclusive practice, that it is possible to appreciate the complex precursors and wide ranging variables which contribute to the experiences of children and young people. The dissimilarities inherent in experiences of inclusion attest to both the variance of difficulties, which are ascribed to characterise SEBD, as well as the dynamic nature of participation in PE. Physical educationalists should consider such variance, and the subsequent inconsistencies in their pupils' experiences, to be a matter of the individualities that define social, emotional and behavioural difficulties.

REFERENCES

Ainscow, M., Booth, T., Dyson, A., Farrell, P., Frankham, J., Gallannaugh, F., Howes, A., & Smith, R. (2006). *Improving schools, developing inclusion*. London, Routledge.

Ainscow, M., & Cesar, M. (2006). Inclusive education ten years after Salamanca: Setting the agenda. *European Journal of Psychology in Education, 21* (3), pp.231-238.

Ainscow, M., Howes, A., Farrell, P., & Frankham, J. (2003). Making sense of the development of inclusive practices. *European Journal of Special Needs Education, 18* (2), pp. 227-242.

Ayers, H., Clarke, D., & Murray, A. (2000). *Perspectives on Behaviour: a Practical Guide to Effective Interventions for Teachers*. London, David Fulton.

Ayers, H., & Prytys, C. (2002). *An A to Z Practical Guide to Emotional and Behavioural Difficulties*. London, David Fulton Publishers.

Bailey, R. (2006). Physical education and sport in schools: a review of benefits and outcomes. *Journal of School Health, 76* (8), pp.397-401.

Bailey, R., & Dismore, H. (2004). SpinEd. The role of physical education and sport in education; Project Report. 4th International Conference of Ministers and Senior Officials responsible for Physical Education and Sport (MINEPS IV), Athens, Greece.

Booth, T., & Ainscow, M. (2002). *Index for inclusion: developing learning and participation in schools (second edition)*. Bristol, Centre for Studies on Inclusive Education.

Byra, M. (2006). Teaching styles and inclusive pedagogies. In: D. Kirk, D. Macdonald & M. O'Sullivan, (Eds.), *Handbook of Physical Education*. London, Sage, pp.449-466.

Coates, J., & Vickerman, P. (2008). Let the children have their say: a review of children with special educational needs experiences of physical education. *Support for Learning, 23* (4), pp.168-175.

Cole, T., Daniels, H., & Visser, J. (2003). Patterns of Provision for pupils with behavioural difficulties in England; a study of government statistics and behaviour support plan data. *Oxford Review of Education, 29* (2), pp.187-205.

Cole, T., & Visser, J. (1998). How should the 'effectiveness' of schools for pupils with EBD be assessed? *Emotional and Behavioural Difficulties, 3* (1), pp.37-43.

Cooper, P. (1999a). Changing perceptions of EBD: maladjustment, EBD and beyond. *Emotional and Behavioural Difficulties, 4* (1), pp.3-11.

Cooper, P. (1999b). Introduction: What do we mean by emotional and behavioural difficulties? In: P. Cooper (Ed.), *Understanding and Supporting Children with Emotional and Behavioural Difficulties*. London, Jessica Kingsley, pp.9-13.

Department for Children Schools and Families (2008). *The Education of Children and Young People with Behavioural, Emotional and Social Difficulties as a Special Educational Need*. London, HMSO.

Department for Education and Employment (1996). *The Education Act*. London, HMSO.

Department for Education and Employment (1997). *Excellence for All Children: Meeting Special Educational Needs*. London, HMSO.

Department for Education and Employment/Department of Health (1994). *Circular 9/94 The Education of Children with Emotional and Behavioural Difficulties*. London, DfEE / DOH.

Department for Education and Skills (2001a). *Special Educational Needs and Disability Act*. London, HMSO.

Department for Education and Skills (2001b). *Special Educational Needs: Code of Practice*. London, HMSO.

Doll-Tepper, G. (2005). The UK in the world of physical education. *National Summit on Physical Education*. London.

Eldar, E. (2008). Educating through the physical - behavioural interpretation. *Physical Education and Sport Pedagogy, 13* (3), pp.215-229.

Fairclough, S. J., & Stratton, G. (2005). Physical education makes you fit and healthy: physical educations contribution to young peoples activity levels. *Health Education Research, 20* (1), pp.14-23.

Fitzgerald, H. (2005). Still feeling like a spare piece of luggage? Embodied experiences of (dis)ability in physical education and school sport. *Physical Education and Sport Pedagogy, 10* (1), pp.41-59.

Florian, L. (2005). 'Inclusion', 'special needs' and the search for new understandings. *Support for Learning, 20* (2), pp.96-98.

Goodwin, L.J. (2007). *The inclusion of children with physical disabilities in physical education.* PhD Thesis, University of Surrey.

Hardman, K., & Marshall, J.J. (2009). *Second World-wide Survey of School Physical Education.* Berlin, ICSSPE.

Houlihan, B., & Green, M. (2006). The changing status of school sport and physical education: explaining policy change. *Sport, Education and Society, 11* (1), pp.73-92.

Jones, R.A. (2003). The construction of emotional and behavioural difficulties. *Educational Psychology in Practice, 19* (2), pp.147-157.

Kay, W. (2003). Physical education R.I.P? *British Journal of Teaching Physical Education, 34* (4), pp.6-9.

Kristen, L., Patriksson, G., & Fridlund, B. (2002). Conceptions of children and adolescents with physical disabilities about the participation in a sports programme. *European Physical Education Review, 8* (2), pp.139-156.

Lawson, H.A. (1999). Education for social responsibility: preconditions in retrospect and prospect. *Quest, 51* (2), pp.116-149.

Medcalf, R., Marshall, J.J., & Rhoden, C. (2006). Exploring the relationship between physical education and enhancing behaviour in pupils with emotional behavioural difficulties. *Support for Learning, 21* (4), pp.169-174.

Miller, S. C., Bredemeier, B.J.L., & Shields, D.L.L. (1997). Sociomoral education through physical education with at risk children. *Quest, 49* (1), pp.114-129.

Mooney, A., Statham, J., Brady, L-M., Lewis, J., Gill, C., Henshall, A., Willmott, N., Owen, C., & Evans, K. (2010). *Special Educational Needs and Disability: Understanding Local Variation in Prevalence, Service Provision and Support (Extended Summary).* London, DCSF.

Moore, G. (2002). In our hands: the future is in the hands of those who give our young people hope and reason to live. *British Journal of Teaching in Physical Education, 30* (2), pp.26-27.

Morley, D., Bailey, R., Tan, J., & Cooke, B. (2005). Inclusive physical education: teachers' views of including pupils with special educational needs and/or disabilities in physical education. *European Physical Education Review, 11* (1), pp.84-107.

Nelson, J. R., Babyak, A., Gonzalez, J., & Benner, G.J. (2003). An investigation of the types of problem behaviours exhibited by K-12 students with emotional or behavioural disorders in public school settings. *Behavioural Disorders, 28* (4), pp.348-359.

Penney, D. (2000). Physical education, sporting excellence and educational excellence. *European Physical Education Review, 6* (2), pp.135-150.

Penney, D. (2002). Equality, equity and inclusion in physical education and school sport. In: A. Laker (Ed.), *The Sociology of Sport and Physical Education: An Introductory Reader.* Abingdon, Routledge, pp.110-128.

Qualifications and Curriculum Authority (2007a). *National Curriculum for Physical Education; Planning For Inclusion.* London, Qualifications and Curriculum Authority.

Qualifications and Curriculum Authority (2007b). *Physical Education; programme of study for key stage 3 and attainment target.* London, Qualifications and Curriculum Authority.

Reid, A. (1997). Value pluralism and physical education. *European Physical Education Review, 3* (1), pp.6-20.

Robertson, C., Childs, C., & Marsen, E. (2000). Equality and the inclusion of pupils with special educational needs in physical education. In: S. Capel & S. Piotrowski (Eds.), *Issues in Physical Education.* Abingdon, RoutledgeFalmer, pp.47-63.

Sallis, J.F., & McKenzie, T.L. (1991). Physical education's role in public health. *Research Quarterly for Exercise and Sport, 62* (2), pp.124-137.

Smith, A. (2004). The inclusion of pupils with special educational needs in secondary school physical education. *Physical Education and Sport Pedagogy, 9* (1), pp.37-54.

Smith, A., & Green, K. (2004). Including pupils with special educational needs in secondary school physical education: a sociological analysis of teachers views. *British Journal of Sociology of Education, 25* (5), pp.593-607.

Smith, A., & Thomas, N. (2006a). Including pupils with special educational needs and disabilities in national curriculum physical education: a brief review. *European Journal of Special Needs Education, 21* (1), pp.69-83.

Smith, A., & Thomas, N. (2006b). Inclusion, special educational needs, disability and physical education. In: K. Green & K. Hardman (Eds.), *Physical Education: Essential Issues.* London, Sage, pp.220-237.

Smith, A., Thurston, M., Lamb, K., & Green, K. (2007). Young people's participation in national curriculum physical education: a study of 15-16 year olds in north-west England and north-east Wales. *European Physical Education Review, 13* (2), pp.165-194.

Social, Emotional and Behavioural Difficulties Association (2006). *Definitions - SEBD and its overlap with disruptive and anti-social behaviour, mental health difficulties and ADHD.* Penrith, SEBDA.

Travell, C. (1999). Emotional and behavioural difficulties: perspectives on perspectives. In: J. Visser & S. Rayner (Eds.), *Emotional and Behavioural Difficulties: A Reader.* Staffordshire, QEd, pp.7-15.

United Nations (1989). *Convention on the rights of the child* [Online]. Available from http://www.unicef.org/crc/index_30177.html [Accessed 15th September 2006].

United Nations Educational Scientific and Cultural Organisation (1994). *The Salamanca Statement and Framework for Action on Special Needs Education* [Online]. Available from http://www.unesco.org/education/pdf/SALAMA_E.PDF [Accessed 15th September 2006].

Vickerman, P. (2007). *Teaching Physical Education to Children with Special Educational Needs.* Oxon, Routledge.

Vickerman, P., Hayes, S., & Whetherly, A. (2003). Special educational needs and the national curriculum physical education. In: S. Hayes & G. Stidder (Eds.), *Equity and Inclusion in Physical Education and Sport; Contemporary issues for teachers, trainees and practitioners.* London, Routledge, pp.47-64.

Wearmouth, J., & Connors, B. (2004). Understanding student behaviour in schools. In: J. Wearmouth, R.C. Richmond, T. Glynn & M. Berryman (Eds.), *Understanding Pupil Behaviour in Schools; a Diversity of Approaches.* London, David Fulton, pp.1-15.

Whitehead, M. (2000). Aims as an issue in physical education. In: S. Capel & S. Piotrowski (Eds.), *Issues in Physical Education.* Oxon, Routledge Falmer, pp.7-21.

Wright, H., & Sugden, D. (1999). *Physical Education for All; Developing Physical Education in the Curriculum for Pupils with Special Educational Needs.* London, David Fulton Publishers.

CHAPTER 6
TRANSITION FROM TRADITIONAL TO MODERN APPROACHES TO TEACHING PHYSICAL EDUCATION
MICHAL BRONIKOWSKI

INTRODUCTION

Education is more than learning about facts, information and skills; it is also about learning the things identified by a society as essentially desirable and relevant for living in a particular community and culture. The society's culture either confirms (through sustainability) the values of what is learned or rejects those that contradict the traditional values. Thus, there is social and cultural pressure to initiate young members of a society into some aspects of social life by providing them with selected, educationally valuable backgrounds but not with all the information pertaining to all aspects of life.

In the case of Physical Education (PE), this process depends on the "discipline's capacity and pedagogical responsibility to work on, effect changes in, develop and enhance the body's intelligent capacities for movement and expression in physical culture" (Evans 2009, p.169). Evans uses the term physical culture to refer to the variety of play[1], sport, adventure, dance and other leisure physical activities that help define the social fabric of local and national communities. I would extend it and say that physical culture today needs to be seen in a broader cultural context as a well-recognized part of life; it is concerned with developing natural, biologically-inherited, potential along cultural pathways while at the same time creating certain attitudes towards particular values concerning the domain of physical, social and moral aspects, in order to maintain health and well-being.

Over eight decades ago, Buckingham and MacLatchy (1925) commented that in education "we had tended to turn our attention from the teaching of facts or mere subject-matter to education through the formulation of desirable habits and the creation of worthy attitudes and ideals" (p.320). In some countries, physical educators ostensibly have not noticed what direction the education of other subjects took years ago. More recently, McBride and Cleland (1998) observed that "critical thinking in physical education (CT-PE), defined as reflective thinking that is used to make reasonable and defensible decisions about movement, is the idea whose time has come" (p.43). The authors argue for more social and cognitive processing in physical education, meaning employing more indirect teaching strategies in order to develop appropriate attitudes and habits. But teaching strategy is not everything. The issue is whether physical education can (re)create world-wide values in physical, moral and social domains and modernize its means to remain a valuable and valued "partner" in school curricula in societies, which increasingly have become more multi-cultural.

---

1 Play in this sense means a form of physical, playful activity, and a very first variety of game and sport. It refers to a range of spontaneous, voluntary, frivolous and non-serious activity. Some plays exhibits no goals or rules and is considered to be "unstructured" in the literature. For more information on play see Garvey, C. (1999). *Play.* Cambridge, MA, Harvard University Press.

Since we want quality and open-minded, inner-directed people as an outcome effect of an educational process, we have to pay less attention to scores/marks/grades, and at the same time accept that the outcomes might be less predictable in quantitative measures, trusting that any difference will be visible in a qualitative sense and more so with the process of time. But as such, the effectiveness of teaching becomes more difficult to evaluate and maybe even less comfortable for the whole educational system. Since there are no real traditions in using qualitative evaluation tools for assessing progress in physical education, there are not overly many that would be universal enough to fit all teaching/learning conditions. However, we need to remember that, in school physical education today, both forms of measuring outcomes are equally required and valuable, providing they can be balanced and positioned within the positive, overall development of a holistic person.

It is perhaps here where PE has to some extent lost its pace and touch with the changing educational environment. Moreover, the reported problems (see, for example, Hardman, 2009) currently faced by PE are a cause for re-consideration of its purpose, aims and contents. Therefore, in order to move forwards, physical educators should first look backwards for the arguments, which erstwhile contributed to the right for legitimization of physical education as an obligatory part of school curricula, and then re-examine those arguments to unravel the cause(s) for the problems being experienced now in PE in countries across the world. One of the potential problems, which might have brought PE to its present situation, has been the inexplicable attraction to a content-related approach in curricula with its concomitant drive for predictable outcomes, mentioned earlier. As evaluation tended to relate more to measurable outcomes of the learning process, it was easier to direct teachers' attentions towards motor-performance criteria. The "sportification" of most spheres of life (and a score/marks/grade orientation) has also played its role in this process, which in turn, has generated more attention to the biological aspects of human development and hence, leaving pedagogical aspects behind.

The emphasis on physical training with links to readiness for military action was visible until the 1960s in some British Commonwealth countries (McGeorge, 1992) or even later as in former Socialist "bloc" countries, where even in the 1970s and 1980s, educational imperatives came from the State authorities (Lipoński 1999). In such forms of PE, progress could only be achieved through a certain level of technical perfection of the teaching patterns and styles leading to the development of motor capacities. At the time, the teaching became simplified in the sense of pedagogical influence, turning itself more into a training process, rather than a truly educational one. Even today we can track traces of such a way of thinking in PE curricula in some countries, though over time in some of them, there has been a switch in the area of physical education to more contextual, daily activities with interests of young people taken into account in curriculum planning.

COMPARISONS IN DEVELOPMENT OF NATIONAL PHYSICAL EDUCATION CURRICULA

The comparative contexts referred to in this section combine to demonstrate how differently physical education as a school subject is perceived accordingly to social, cultural and educational backgrounds of a particular society. Naul (2003) argues that "the process of international assimilation of the three traditional basic European concepts of physical education (namely *Lingian Swedish gymnastics*, the *German Turnen movement and English sport games and plays*) have been melted and modified in different European education systems. In the 1960s and 1970s across Western Europe, physical education, associated with the motor, social and cognitive domains of curriculum development, was frequently linked with a set of five major physical activity areas: gymnastics, sports (including athletics), games, swimming and outdoor activities. These five areas of activity were also evident in the traditional concept of physical education related to three domains identified as development of motor abilities and technical skills, learning psychosocial attitudes and moral values and virtues" (pp.40-41).

Previously, Crum (1994) had presented an alternative version of those concepts in their historical context, when he asserted that early

"*biologically-oriented training of the physical concept* objectives were formulated in terms of training of anatomical and physiological variables, whereas in the *pedagogical concept* those were formulated in terms of general personal development. Recently the *personalist movement education concept* has been linked with objectives formulated in terms of the realisation of personal movement competence and identity, while in the *conformist socialisation concept*, aims are formulated in terms of physical fitness and technical and tactical capacities needed for participation in traditional sport disciplines. Lately *critical-constructive movement socialisation* has been introduced as a concept in which objectives are formulated in terms of the techno-motor, socio-motor and reflective competences that are needed for a personally and socially satisfying, life-long participation in movement culture" (p.522).

But no matter how good theoretical frameworks are, the change in teaching requires a shift in thinking by those who design curricula. Although generally, PE aims at the balanced development of holistic and autonomous individuals who are able to take care of their body and health, this remains more wishful thinking as reality demonstrates otherwise in many countries. In Greece, for example, in the 2003 Curriculum Document (ΦΕΚ 304, /t'Β/2003), the overall "aim of the physical education in Elementary and Junior High school is to assist the pupils' physical, affective and cognitive development and their smooth and successful integration in society" (p.4281). The Document later places "special emphasis... on the improvement of pupils' physical skills and health through exercise" (p.4283) with strands divided into: i) psychomotor; ii) affective; and iii) cognitive domains.

In Poland, where the definitions and theoretical frameworks of PE should have shifted the attention of PE teachers from the body to the mind many years ago, the school process does not sustain either. Although Demel (1973) advocated that the whole process should begin with, and progress, cognitive development in the direction of increasing bodily awareness in caring for the body, practice in schools has not kept abreast with change. Even recently in the new PE curriculum (Podstawa Programowa, 2009), general aims emphasize participation and health-care, yet content is still oriented to physical fitness and its diagnosis in the very first strand. In the 2009 reform of education in Poland, general aims of education embrace development of responsibility, respect, self-esteem and creativeness leading to a higher level of personal culture. It is the role of the school head-teacher to provide pupils with challenging situations and the appropriate conditions for fulfilment of curricular aims and objectives. In the case of PE, this particularly concerns the following: a) participation in physical culture activity both during and after leaving school; b) initiating and cooperating in promotion of physical activity; c) selecting life time sports and activities; and d) developing a health-related life style. Contents and more detailed information on what and how to teach are framed into strands: i) diagnosis of physical fitness and physical development; ii) health training; iii) leisure sports and recreation; iv) safe physical activity and personal hygiene; v) sport; and vi) dance. The dissonance between the general aims of education, which tend to be more socially-bound and those specific for PE, which still reflect a reasonable interest in the body and its performance-related outcomes is readily apparent. Notwithstanding this situation, a shift from traditional motor-related teaching towards a more pupil-centred, pedagogical approach can be observed. In the new physical education curriculum in Poland, a new organizational system has also been introduced. From the previous system of four 45 minutes classes per week, two classes of 45 minutes of obligatory PE lessons are now interwoven into the school time-table, but two additional lessons can either be included in the school daily time-table or arranged as extra-curricular (facultative) activities. Pupils themselves may choose (from an offer of activities provided by the school) what sports they would like to engage in during a particular semester. The idea behind this change was to activate young people and cater for their broad interests, thus providing them with opportunities for doing what they are happy to do and, therefore, maintain some motivation and long-term interest in physical activity. Only time will show whether or not this will be enough to encourage young people back into physical activity.

In England, in the new curricula, the four strands of PE were defined as follows: i) acquire and develop skills; ii) select and apply skills, tactics and compositional ideas; iii) evaluate and improve performance; and iv) acquire knowledge and understanding of fitness and health. These strands are indicative of changes in thinking about physical education and school sport. However, Sellers and Palmer (2008) commenting on the latest changes in the English physical education national curriculum allege that at Key Stage 3 (ages 11-14), the section on aims, which may be understood as an attempt to justify the subject and its place within a curriculum, is nothing more than just a set of wishes or dreams, rather more dogmatic in form and sense than truly educational. All the statements included in that section are directly linked to physical activity and some are even intended to influence other, more cross-curricular matters, such as for example "analyse the situation and make decisions" or "they develop the ability to use tactics, strategies and compositional ideas" (QCA, 2007, p.187). However, they rarely move beyond the "physical" side of activity.

In comparison, in the late 1990s New Zealand PE curriculum, the strands included: i) personal health and physical development; ii) relationship with other people; iii) movement concepts and motor skills; and iv) healthy communities and environments. The aims of the PE and health curriculum were formulated to: a) develop the knowledge, understanding, skills and attitudes needed to maintain and enhance personal health and physical development; b) develop motor skills through movement, acquire knowledge and understanding about movement, and develop positive attitudes towards physical activity; c) develop understanding, skills and attitudes that enhance interactions and relationships with other people; and d) participate in creating healthy communities and environments by taking responsible and critical action (Health and Physical Education in the New Zealand Curriculum, 1999). The New Zealand example reveals a clear visibility in holistic development, at least at the level of curriculum design.

In Asia, the situation is more complex. PE is perceived as a low priority subject and is seen as one that does not contribute to a country's economy. Priority is accorded to subjects that lead to jobs (and economic growth) more directly. De Vries (2009) observes that 60% of the physical education and sports programmes in Asian schools suffer from insufficient resources and deprived conditions and the subject is seen more as play rather than as a serious subject, mainly because Asia does not have a strong sports culture (with only 20% of the people engaged in sports and physical activity for up to three times a week in most Asian countries). Evolution of PE programmes is also retarded by political factors, as most of the important decisions on physical education and sports are made by government officials, with no academic or professional qualifications in the discipline. Furthermore, the centralized and bureaucratic system of education in most Asian countries is not an enabling environment for innovative ideas and efforts. Nonetheless, there are signs of change: there seems to be better integration of PE lessons and lifestyles, making the connection clearer for the pupils; current pedagogical concepts of teaching PE also attempt to transmit more knowledge-based lessons and include more indigenous activities and sports in the curricula (hitherto traditionally dominated by Olympic-originated sports); more emphasis on equal participation opportunities for girls (also in high performance sports); and the provision of areas designated to physical leisure activity (De Vries, 2009).

BRIDGING THE PAST AND THE FUTURE

Since the introduction of national curricula in many countries, sport in general and PE in particular, as subjects have been separated into two categories. The structure of a lesson (warm up, main part with new tasks introduced, cool down) with its clear orientation on pedagogical and health-related objectives serves to preclude PE from being a mere sport session in the same way as non-structured educational activities of play prevent sport from becoming a PE lesson. Therefore, the role of a teacher/coach has changed/is changing as well. In the main, a sport coach's role is to lead his/her pupils to a certain level of competency in the area of a specific sport, focusing on skills and technique, whereas a PE teacher should concentrate on the overall holistic development of motor (motor development), cognitive (moral, social and intellectual development) and behavioural patterns (attitudes and habits). However, along with introducing changes in the curriculum, the mode of professional conduct needs to change as well. It is up to teachers and coaches to be open to new technologies and innovative ways of teaching/coaching. In teaching, Lortie (1975) found openness to innovatory practices was problematic in so far as teachers tend to be conservative and treat new ideas and innovations with some scepticism. Many teachers teach in the way that they were taught themselves, and remain unaffected by the four or five years of teacher education training they undertake. Butler (1996) intimated that teachers believe they are open to experiment with new methods and activities but fear that pupils may lose out. An issue here is whether they consider it a risk for the pupils or for the teachers themselves?

In England, Lipsitt (2008) reported that teacher union leaders alleged that teachers were fearful of straying from the national curriculum and in many cases were no longer able to design lessons themselves. This situation highlights why there may be difficulties with introduction of new sports, or even new forms of movement activities derived from culturally and socially different origins. It is a feature that can be seen across the teaching profession in England. In research by Ha et. al (2008), it was found that experienced teachers show a strong commitment to their career, while novice teachers feel insecure about undertaking their professional role under the circumstances of the uncertainties of reform. This finding confirms earlier research (Rovengo, 1994), which noted the characteristic fear of curricular changes, expressed mostly by novice teachers who, bound by legal and administrative constraints, tend to confine the teaching process to the so-called "safety curricular zone of defensive teaching", that is, lowering course requirements and reducing teaching contents to a minimum. Very often the students are strictly supervised, and the teacher's real concern consists mostly of maintaining discipline in a class. Quite different outcomes can be achieved if inventiveness and creativity are expected from the teacher and the students. Therefore, two questions arise here: i) what direction should PE take in the future?; and ii) how can teaching of health be involved in the regular curricula of PE to emphasize the dual conception of a body, which exists in nature, though it remains under the influence of society and culture?

It can safely be argued that the teacher of today usually worries about covering the national curriculum and when this is combined with strong administrative expectations stressed by the school authorities (for example, head teachers, PE department heads) it makes the process of teaching/learning even less attractive for all parties involved. This may lead to a development of an autocratic teaching approach, which would involve direct instructions given to pupils with no margin for deviation. The opposite, indirect (democratic) approach, would allow pupils to become involved in the decision-making process, but this may demand more preparation prior to the lesson and extensive creative thinking during the lesson. Nevertheless, the use of any of the two teaching approaches could be beneficial to the pupils (at least for maintaining the discipline in a class) as long as the pupils understand that the person "in charge" is the teacher but the benefits are mutual. The issue though is how this is to be achieved.

The way lesson content is delivered depends on numerous circumstances, which vary in different national, local and even school settings according to factors such as learning stage, gender, the teaching models used, teachers' personal pedagogical skills and preferences, and the educational experience of the pupils taught. All of these factors need to be taken into account when planning long-term content and delivery strategy in education settings. However, it seems that the lower the teaching level and age of the pupils, the higher the percentage of direct methods to be used is advisable, as they could lay a solid foundation for exploration of one's own talents through discovery and guided teaching strategies at later stages of education. In the upper years of schooling, more problem-based learning, larger blocks of material and more intellectual freedom need to be given to the pupils for engagement retention and to allow them to discover and create the "story of their body". This leaves some room for innovative teaching, regardless of the teaching concept chosen. The question of supervision and the presence of the teacher is another area for consideration (i.e., should supervision be tight, highly monitored, or loose and based on trust and responsibility?). Certainly, supervision influences the quality of engagement, the pace, as well as the emotional involvement of the parties, as pupils usually perceive the teacher as the authority. The main issue, however, is whether they are convinced that they can do what they are asked to do by themselves. This is more about building up a sense of self-confidence through self-responsibility models such as Hellison's (2003) *Teaching Responsibility Through Physical Activity* model. The potential outcome of this process is the feeling of enjoyment when pupils produce something on their own (or within their groups). The teacher's role is to coordinate, stimulate, encourage and give hints to the pupils to facilitate positive solutions. This can be achieved through, for example, the use of a guided-discovery teaching style, remembering that sometimes more than one solution is possible, and leaving them space for verification of their solutions is also a plausibly acceptable idea. Even when solution resolution is not achieved, the issue is one that is still about their work and their efforts – challenging creativity competence, albeit on occasion, and in some cases, it is important to remember that the teacher's assistance and supervision may be necessary. Pupils should be also informed before task setting about any necessary safety precautions in case of unexpected hazards that may arise; for example, over excitement, "messing" around of those who are disinterested or waiting for equipment or those not "on task" can be potential threats or risk factors.

National curricula do not necessarily limit the contents or teaching strategies to those included in "official" documents and, indeed, there may be several paths leading to achievement of the same objectives. With more skilful, pedagogically autonomous and experienced teachers, they may differ within teaching units and even from lesson to lesson, as a progressive lesson plan is required for each lesson to cater for different levels of performance skills etc. If pupils find a technique too easy then the teacher has the scope to increase the complexity or, for example, have them increase the speed in which a particular task is being carried out, thus, contributing to continuity and progression of the various or specific skills sought. Therefore, the lesson needs to be seen and considered within the curriculum as a whole, both on its own, and also as a part of a larger scheme of the overall educational process and this is where the teacher has to find out what links can be made cross-curricular-wise with other subjects and how they can include cultural, social and moral aspects to develop pupils' wide-ranging life-skills through multi-points of focus. If pupils lack motivation, the solution may come from converting their daily interests, likes and routines into theme-based tasks of physical activity.

With regard to the interests of young people nowadays, many are attracted to the Internet, play stations and television programmes. Rather than being seen in opposition to physical education, these media forms could be used to "gain some territory" and seek inspiration for the educational ideas in "the magical box with a silver screen". Lines (2007) asserts that "media viewing and physical activity patterns provide an insight into how these young people value these activities within the broader context of their everyday life" (p.355). If these themes could be converted into educational tasks and introduced into school settings, there could be new-found levels of motivation. Potentially, this would be a valuable and attractive tool in combating pupils' sedentary habits. Computer companies observing social changes in daily living routines of youths have already spotted an opportunity to capture more "clients" with a novel idea based on an attractive sporting device: they have reacted quickly to this change by launching Wii-Fit and other Wii health-related computer games. There is no reason why PE should be left behind.

Nevertheless, this is easier said than done. There are numerous examples of good practice and there are excellent teachers working at "the front lines" in schools and it is not my intention to underestimate or ignore them. Indeed, my aim is precisely the opposite. However, when Penney and Chandler (2000) ask what is the future for PE, I can respond by saying that the answer depends on how quickly and attractively it can adjust its aims and contents to future social needs. Content, design of task and class management, teaching styles and methods, lesson pacing and pupils' level of motivation and processing are all important issues, but even in research it has to be borne in mind that it is not about finding a "silver bullet" teaching method in physical education, rather, it comes down to a question of the philosophy behind the teaching/learning process of the whole schooling environment.

Some arguments for justification of today's PE programmes in school curricula may arise again when looking back at traditional, universal humanistic values such as respect for others and their efforts, respect for social values and norms (rules), respect for cultural, religious and physical differences as well as respect for one's right to peace, love, compassion and self-perfection, all of which can potentially be fostered by physical education more than by other subjects. In 2004, the American National Association for Physical Education (NASPE) reported on a meta-analysis review of aims and standards in national curricula in over 50 countries in which outcomes of PE and sport can be seen in terms of children's development in five domains: physical, lifestyle, affective, social and cognitive. Nevertheless, during the last decade, the most frequent arguments for inclusion of PE in school curricula emanate from the health-related area.

The idea is nothing new, as Harris (2009) reminds us: "... Health once again became an important objective of the physical education curriculum in the early 1980s, and since then there has been a well documented and active interest by many physical educators in promoting health-related physical activity in schools in the UK" (p.83). Whether this will be enough for young adolescents to associate health with life-long physical activity developed into regular habits of active life style remains to be seen. The association of PE with health as well as the health-related gains and life-time long benefits are sometimes taken for granted by some physical education teachers. Kleiner (2007) claims that "physical education teachers often try to achieve health promotion with content from sport disciplines (e.g. games, athletics, hiking, biking, badminton or swimming) that are also part of the curricula" (p.77). But as mentioned earlier, reality is far removed from theory. Others argue (e.g. Penney & Evans, 1997) that the inclusion of health-related education into PE, especially at the beginning when it first started to appear in the (English) national curriculum, could cause some confusion in objectives and lead to marginalization in more general terms (Harris, 1995). Increasingly, PE teachers are including health promotion in their teaching routine, thereby moving away from a sport education model towards a movement-didactic model, and with recently incorporating health education models into schools, PE has broadened the area of influences and its means. It is now truly an education of physical culture, which in Kirk's (1997) terms can be understood as education to a range of discourses concerned with the maintenance, representation and regulation of the body through institutionalised forms of physical activity, and which, in my view, needs to be more culturally and socio-morally bound.

A crucial consideration is whether present day PE is able to deal with the challenges it faces, which ostensibly now seem to be beyond its capacity. It is important that the subject and its practitioners keep apace with more attractive, socially fashionable behaviours in the domain of recreation and leisure (certainly with less physically demanding ones like watching TV, playing computer games, and exploring the Internet). Perhaps Siedentop's *Sport Education* or Bunker and Thorpe's *Teaching Games for Understanding* models may prove to be successful, especially with their respective relatively new concepts. But perhaps also some hints could come from young people's attraction to the media and environment. Whilst watching sport on TV rather than actively engaging in it cannot be justified, PE can draw inspiration from the environmental and socio-cultural changes for increasing its cross-curricular links. Through arranging tasks into health-related activities based on the ideas taken directly from new sources of global influence (i.e., the media), PE can try and influence the motivation of the youngest to assist in increasing awareness of their health and health benefits to be derived from active participation. Maybe, in these especially culturally sensitive times, physical education should turn towards models more concerned with gender, sexuality and subjectivity, with more extensive use of dance and other forms of physical, yet artistic expressions (Gard, 2009), and helping young people discover "their body" in a social context? The *Health(a)ware* modular programme described below offers such a model.

A HEALTHY FUTURE FOR PHYSICAL EDUCATION

The growing prevalence of health-related problems in youth and elderly phases of life (Mota et al. 2002; Barkey et al. 2003; Vouri 2004) calls for more attention to be devoted to the education of young children. Gard and Wright (2009) indicate that risk becomes increasingly prominent and difficult to manage, as understanding and body image is a social construction and this is a society, which decides what is acceptable and what is not. They go on to comment that

> "it may be better for physical educators to say nothing about obesity, exercise and health, rather than singing the praises of slimness and vigorous exercise and condemning the evils of fat and sedentary life. Failing this, we implore physical educators to look underneath the surface of the discipline's cherished beliefs.

While the terror of finding nothing is ever present, we believe that a renewed focus on less instrumental and more child-centred approaches to physical activity, and the sheer pleasure of using one's body, may indeed be a liberating experience for all" (p.364).

Therefore, in order to meet the interests of pupils in the future, PE should involve itself in the main stream of providing skills enabling sustainability, beyond physicality. However, changing teaching schemas may in themselves be insufficient to increase the attraction of education and it may be necessary to consider changing the way of thinking of the teaching profession in general. Ennis (1996) suggests a way to overcome the perceived current crisis in physical education is coherence and clarity of training of prospective PE teachers, i.e. a clearly defined model of the PE teacher constituting the basis in formulation of educational goals and tasks. Previously, Fullan (1982) had proposed that the establishment of a new educational model, which allows the implementation of challenges ahead of the teacher and the pupil, should involve educational changes in three areas: curriculum basis – teaching syllabi and materials; teaching/learning process; and attitudes and beliefs of the educational community (academic centres). However, reality indicates that the least complex seems to be planning and developing teaching materials; much more difficult is changing the attitudes and pedagogical routines of the teachers themselves. In a research project concerned with changing the mentality of school youth and developing regular habitual physical activity, Johns et al. (2001) encountered these difficulties. Their thoroughly planned school programme, embracing the implementation of an increased, monitored level of physical activity, failed to produce the desired effects. The discrepancy between the theoretical assumptions of the project and capabilities and reluctance of teachers to implement the goals of the modified and challenging programme turned out to be too broad. No positive changes in the teachers' or students' attitudes and beliefs were obtained. It is possible that the level of involvement of teachers in the early stages of the project was insufficient; moreover, the teachers had no opportunity to assess the real possibilities of implementation of the planned changes. A presumably good theoretical framework was too difficult (or too remote from the school reality) to be put into practice. It is also possible that one of the drawbacks of the project was caused by neglect of the interests of pupils who were perceived as objects rather than subjects of the educational process.

Changing this situation would require changing the teaching routine and modernizing contents. It would also require, according to Young (1998),

"higher learning skills developed by providing: the context of criticism (in which it will challenge the theory and out-side school reality), the context of discovery (in which new concepts are developed and used) and the context of practical application (in which new ideas are tried out in the real world)" p.154).

A more reasonable proposition could be stimulating for all parties involved and perhaps could be achieved through the four-module *Health(a)ware* model. In 2006, a *Health(a)ware* model comprising a four-module approach to PE and health was introduced through a

European Union project team. The European project, *Health(a)ware – an experienced-based learning and teaching approach for physical and health education* [Health(a)ware - 28737-CP-1-2006-1-DE-Comenius-C2, www.health-a-ware.eu], was funded by the European Commission's Socrates-Comenius Programme to enable experimental health and physical education teaching within, and across, school courses. The model was developed with the idea of creating a platform for health(a)ware pan-European Physical and Health Education and was created by a joint working group of representatives of German, Austrian, Czech Republic, Norwegian, Polish and Spanish universities.

The *Health(a)ware* model represents a new way of dealing with physical and health education specific contexts. Although perhaps it does not provide all the answers to the problems, it does open up an opportunity for communication with young people through providing situations based on creating opportunities for self-expression of one's own ideas, and through allowing some time for reflection upon the ideas of the others. It also suggests how one can try to use the surrounding resources of the (constantly changing) social environment for educational purposes. Through four modules of *Body and Bodies, Body and Time, Body and Measure* and *Body and Environment*, the model proposes a new experience-based approach to these segments of curricula that relate to healthy life styles of the young adolescents. Firmly established was that the pupils and their interaction with the environment remained at the centre of interest in this approach.

The four-module model is a combination of theme-based and experienced-based approaches to physical and health education. The idea of the development of health awareness is implemented in four thematic groups:

- *Body & Bodies* – focusing on the individual functioning in wider social communities (including family), within a framework of changing social relations and integration, inter-cultural and aesthetical differences in physical activity
- *Body & Time* – concerning the transience of human life and historical aspects of health in terms of social, psychological and physical human capabilities of using physical activity to improve the quality of various aspects of daily life
- *Body & Measures* – focusing on experiencing physical (somatic and motor) changes in human capabilities in everyday situations (covering distances, lifting weights, reaction times), as well as developing self-control and self-evaluation and discovering one's own range of movements
- *Body & Environment* – concerning aspects of physical activity in changing environmental conditions to suit the individual in pursuit of pastimes' activities, experience of urban and rural environment and its influence on one's life style.

The model introduces (in some countries re-introduces) the idea of cross-curricular teaching, some practical illustrations of which are included in the next section. Although cross-curricular teaching of knowledge and skills may help pupils in the process of lifelong learning, it should be noted that the project does not cover all areas, objectives and tasks of physical education and health. Thus, it may better serve as a complementary model of teaching rather than the "ultimate" model. However, it can safely be said that it is the beginning of a new way of thinking about physical and health education. The idea itself though is not enough and it needs people who aware of new developments and who would develop the appropriate skills (educational tools) necessary for their implementation. Really needed in PE today are skilful, pedagogically aware, educators.

CROSSING THE BOUNDARIES OF THE GYM
INTO A REAL CROSS-SUBJECT TEACHING

Lines (2007) wonders

> "how then can [media] be used by PE practitioners to aid pupils in their "project of self', in supporting young people's new motivations and challenges arising from their engagement in media sport; and in developing the critical responses of young people to media images and messages?" (p.361).

Below are some examples of cross-curricular thinking in planning physical activities based on new ways of thinking (directed more towards social than physical skills), which have been inspired by observation that social interests of youths are changing. Additionally, some proposals are presented, which are related to the potential fields of interests of today's youth that have been designed to show how television programmes can be turned into motivating tasks and used in the process of physical education and health teaching thus making it more attractive and closer to their day-to-day interests.

Activity 1. **How far can I/you go? (a case of pursuit of excellence principle teaching – a 50m challenge).**
Instead of a teacher telling the pupils the distance to run (e.g. 50 metres) and clocking the time (presumably 8 seconds), the teacher asks the pupils to set the distance they think they are able to run within the 8 second time limit. For some it might be the same distance of 50 metres but others will try to challenge themselves and set it further; others will slowly develop their self-confidence and will increase the distance with caution. This concept of exercise can be adapted for use in any activity and the challenge may involve two or more participants. The first partner sets the distance for another one (with a change of roles after each task). In this way the pupils are able to discover their potential and thus, develop self-esteem and confidence, but also in a paired setting they are faced with public assessment of their potential (what do others think of me?)

Activity 2. **Crossing the river (a case of co-operation principle teaching).**
If the teacher wants this activity to be competitive then the pupils are split into groups of 4, 5 or 6 (depending on the size of the class) and each group is given 2 mats; a line of cones is placed around 15 metres apart from each other to act as markers. The pupils must work together to cross from one line of cones (river bank) to the other one (the opposite bank) without touching the ground, by placing one mat on the floor and standing on it whilst they manoeuvre the second mat to repeat until they reach the cones placed in front of them. Alternate rules could be applied such as only being able to touch the mat with one foot etc. This activity could also be an example of developing the whole-class' (or team) collective working skills. In such a case, the whole group is placed on one bench

and another bench is placed 3 meters away. The objective of the activity is to cross from one bench to another using only two pieces of solid, wooden planks each of 2 metres in length (the idea is that the distance apart is over 2 meters). The whole group has to work out how to cross all members of the team to the other side.

As mentioned previously in this chapter, school subjects should explore new territories, use new methods and interweave real-life situations and topics into their curricula. The following are examples of games invented on the basis of TV programmes and quizzes widely watched by young people today.

Activity 3. **Golden Balls (a case of trust and partnership teaching).**
The idea of activity is based around the idea of the British TV quiz *Golden Balls*, where contestants compete for prize money if they can agree to "share" or try to "steal". The teacher gives each pupil a card with two signs on it. It will be "+" on one side and "−" on the other. The idea of the activity is to promote co-operation. When a task is given (e.g., a number of exercises to be done), each pupil can decide whether to share it with their partner (when both of them show each other "+" side of the card), they do the number of repetitions asked; but they may also make their partner do the task on his/her own and doubled (when one of them shows the other one "−" side of the card). However, when two of them show each other "−", the task triples for each of them.

Activity 4. **Auctions – Who will give more/less? (a case of dealing with challenges teaching).**
The idea of this activity is built around popular auctions. The teacher challenges pupils by running an open auction on who is going to do more squats in 60 seconds (or more than 30), or who is going to run 1000 metres in less than 4 minutes. The pupils with the best offer receive an extra reward, mark, if they can meet with their offer. Additionally, the teacher can introduce a role for those who break the time set in the auction to receive a similar award. Through this exercise, pupils have a chance to volunteer and later stand for what they have committed to, learning self-responsibility for their own commitment to endeavour.

Activity 5. **Divided (a case of team working and learning to be responsible for others, supporting).**
This activity, developed around the concept of the TV quiz *Divided*, relies on reaching a common agreement on the answer to questions posed by three people involved. The sooner agreement is reached, the more money the three participants can win. However, if they are unable to agree, they lose the money. The teacher divides the class into groups of three. Each group is set a task. It may be a number of exercises to be performed by the group (a number of repetitions of a technical skill in volleyball, basketball or football, a time limit for a lap of running a relay, etc.), but it is up to the members of the group to decide how many repetitions (or time limits) will have to be completed by each individual member to successfully achieve the number (or distance) that was designated to the group. So, by judging their individual abilities and skills against the others in the group, everyone has to contribute a share to the end effect. This can obviously be used for other forms of tasks such as health-related information gathering/presenting. If the team fails to reach an agreement, every team member has to perform double the amount assigned.

CONCLUSION

In the future, civilization, technology and employment opportunities will require skills as well as qualifications that today some may not even think of. Preparation for this must come through education. Therefore, the way in which pupils are taught in schools now needs to change with the times as many young people currently are lacking in positive attitude and social skills (flexibility, adaptability, inter-changeability of skills, punctuality, responsibility, own initiative, creativity as well as citizenship, self-management or communication skills) required in modern society. To respond to the changing environment, children need to learn elementary universal skills rather than detailed knowledge and they need to develop aptitudes enabling them to create those skills throughout their whole life span. Simultaneously, it is also important that all children should be able to take part in physical activity organized in school-based settings that fosters fun and enjoyment, without promoting embarrassment, eroding confidence and self-esteem etc. related to their lack of technical ability.

In the teaching/learning process, a choice of content, use of a range of resources, variety of activities and teaching approaches needs to be employed more effectively and extensively than hitherto. However, it should be remembered that too many changes can make pupils (who are used to "traditional" teaching) feel uncomfortable and incapable of accomplishing the task. This may influence the progression of acquiring a skill or skills and eventually break down the structure of a process. A structured framework gives the pupil a sense of security and guidance, which provides physical and mental support. However, this does not challenge monotonous routines, which, when coupled with poor quality (i.e. unattractive content delivered in a command teaching style), results in children dropping out of after-school physical activity. The *Health(a)ware* model of teaching PE and health contents, introduced in this chapter, emphasizes the inter-action of the individual with the existing environment. At the same time, it does not lead to a revolution of the whole system.

Modern PE needs to be placed in a wider, holistic educational perspective. It should be "flexible" in combining the best practices of the past with the best practice and initiatives of the present (though, created on firm foundations) and, it needs to prepare students for the life's challenges ahead in dynamically changing social and cultural conditions. Such education should be placed within a proper socio-educational context allowing for specific historical conditions and should play a crucial role in promoting one's independence in gaining knowledge and skills and ensuring a proper context for attaining values of social co-existence and co-operation.

Finally,

> "physical education teachers cannot ignore the impact that this (media, especially television) can and does have, and should consider ways of working in partnership with both the products of the media sports as well as the media professionals to promote their subject disciplines. However, in an already increasing curriculum agenda it is acknowledged that this should not be seen as another area of work but rather integrated within already existing curricular programmes of study and

core strands of learning. Additionally, these ideas have the potential to draw on cross-curricular links and promote sport and physical education through other subject areas" (Lines, 2007, p.361).

Lines' ideas concurs with the threads of thinking expressed in this chapter, looking, as it does, for inspiration in daily routines and interests to motivate young people to engage in life-long physical activity; and so should we.

REFERENCES:

Bailey R. (2009). Physical Education and Sport in Schools. A review of benefits and outcomes. In: R. Bailey & D. Kirk (Eds.), *The Routledge Physical Education Reader.* London, Routledge. pp.29-38.

Barkey C., Rockett H., Gillman M., & Colditz G. (2003). One-year changes in activity and in inactivity among 10-to 15-year old boys and girls: relationship to change in body mass index. *Paediatrics, 111*(4), pp.836-843.

Buckingham B.R., & MacLatchy J. (1925). Direct versus indirect teaching. *Educational Research Bulletin, 4*(15), pp.320-322.

Butler J. (1996). Teacher responses to teaching games for understanding. Journal of Physical Education, *Recreation and Dance, 67*(9), pp.17-20.

Crum B. (1994). A critical review of competing physical education concepts. In: J. Mester (Ed). *Sport Science in Europe. Current and Future Perspectives.* Aachen, Meyer & Meyer, pp.516-533.

Demel M. (1973). *Szkice krytyczne o kulturze fizycznej* (Critical reflection in physical culture). Warszaw, Sport i Turystyka.

De Vries, LA. (2008). Overview of recent innovative practices in Physical Education and Sport in Asia. In: C. Haddad, Lay-Cheng Tan (Eds.), *Innovative Practices in Physical Education and Sport in Asia,* UNESCO, Bangkok, pp.1-19.

Ennis C.D. (1996). Curriculum Theory of Sport Pedagogy. *International Journal of Physical Education, XXXIII*(3), pp.92-97.

Evans J. (2009). Making a difference? Education and 'ability' in Physical Education. In: R. Bailey & D. Kirk (Eds.). *The Routledge Physical Education Reader.* London, Routledge, pp.169-181.

Εφηγεριζ τηζ Κυβερνησεωζ τηζ Ελληνκηζ Δημοκραταζ (ΦΕΚ), Τευχοζ 2°, Αρ. Φυλλου 304/13.03.2003.

Fullan M. (1982). *The meaning of educational change.* Toronto, OISE Press.

Gard M. (2009). Being someone else: using dance in anti-oppressive teaching. In: R. Bailey & D. Kirk (Eds.), *The Routledge Physical Education Reader.* London, Routledge, pp.255-269.

Gard M., & Wright J. (2009). Managing uncertainty: obesity discourses and physical education in a risk of society. In: R. Bailey & D. Kirk (Eds.). *The Routledge Physical Education Reader.* London, Routledge, pp.353-365.

Ha S.A., Wong A.C., Sum R.K., & Chan D.W. (2008). Understanding teacher's will and capacity to accomplish physical education curriculum reform: the implications for teacher development. *Sport, Education, Society, 13*(1), pp.77-95.

Hardman K. (2009). A review of the global situation of physical education in schools. *International Journal of Physical Education, XLVI*(3), 3rd Quarter, pp.2-21.

Harris J. (1995). Physical Education. A Picture of Health? *British Journal of Physical Education, 26*(4), pp.25-32.

Harris J. (2009). Health-related exercise and physical education. In: R. Bailey & D. Kirk (Eds.), *The Routledge Physical Education Reader*. London, Routledge. pp.83-102.

Hellison D., (2003). *Teaching responsibility through physical activity.* Champaign, Il, Human Kinetics, 2003.

Johns D.P., Ha A.S.C., & Macfarlane D.J. (2001). Raising activity levels: A Multidimensional Analysis of Curriculum Change. *Sport, Education and Society, 6*(2), pp.199-210.

Kleiner K. (2007). To promote health means to arrange multiple tasks – a basic didactic of health promotion. *Acta Universitatis Carolinae, Kinanthropologica, 43*(2), pp.71-86.

Kirk D. (1997). Schooling bodies for new times: the reform of school physical education in high modernity. In: J-M. Fernandez-Balboa (Ed.), *Critical Postmodernism in Human Movement, Physical Education and Sport*. Albany, New York, Suny Press, pp.403-406.

Lines G. (2007). The impact of media sport events on the active participation of young people and some implications for PE pedagogy. *Sport, Education and Society, 12* (4), pp.349-366.

Lipoński W. (1999). Sport in the Slavic World before Communism: Cultural traditions and national functions. *The European Sport History Review. Sport in Europe. Politics, Class Gender*, 1, pp.203-249.

Lipsitt A. (2008). National Curriculum Constraints Teachers and Pupils. *The Guardian* – www.guardian.co.uk/education/2008/jun/11/schools.uk4. (accessed 8.05.2009)

Lortie D. (1975). *The school teacher.* Chicago, University of Chicago Press.

McBride R.E., & Cleland F., (1998). Critical thinking in Physical Education. Putting the theory where is belongs: in the gymnasium. *Journal of Physical Education, Recreation and Dance, 69*(7), pp.42-46.

McGeorge C. (1992). The moral curriculum: forming the Kiwi character. In: G.McCulloch (Ed.), *The school curriculum in New Zealand: History, theory, policy and practice*. Palmerston North, Dunmore Press, pp.40-56.

Ministry of Education (1999), *Health and Physical Education in the New Zealand Curriculum*. (1999). Wellington, Learning Media.

Mota J., Santos P., Guerra S., Ribeiro J.C., & Duarte J. (2002). Difference of daily physical activity levels of children according to body mass index. *Pediatric Exercise Science, 14,* pp.442-452.

National Association for Physical Education. *Physical Activity for Children: A Statement of Guidelines for Children Aged 5–12. 2nd ed.* Reston, Va: NASPE 2004.

Naul R. (2003). Concepts of physical education in Europe, In: K. Hardman (Ed.), *Physical Education: Deconstruction and Reconstruction – Issues and Directions.* Schorndorf, Verlag Karl Hofmann, pp.35-52.

Penney D., & Chandler T. (2000). Physical Education: What future? *Sport, Education and Society, 5*(1), pp.71-87.

Penney D., & Evans J. (1997). Naming the game. Discourse and domination in physical education and sport in England and Wales. *European Physical Education Review, 3*(1), pp.21-32.

Ministerstwo Edukacji Narodowej (2009). *Podstawa Programowa z komentarzami. Wychowanie Fizyczne i Edukacja dla Bezpieczefstwa.* Ministerstwo Edukacji Narodowej, Warszawa.

QCA (2007). Physical Education programme of study for Key 3 and attainment target. Qualifications and Curriculum Authority, HMSO, London [online]. Available at: http://curriculum.qca.uk.uploads/QCA-07-3342-p PE KS3 tcm8-407.pdf. (accessed 15.05.2009).

Rovegno I. (1994). Teaching within a curricular zone of safety: school culture and the situated nature of student teachers' pedagogical content knowledge. *Research Quarterly for Exercise and Sport, 65*(3), pp.269-279.

Sellers V., & Palmer C. (2008). Aims and dreams. A sideways look at the Physical Education programme of study for Key Stage 3 and attainment target QCA National Curriculum document (2007). *Journal of Qualitative Research in Sport Studies, 2*(2), pp.191-217.

Young, M.F.D. (1998). *The curriculum of the Future: From the "New Sociology of Education" to a Critical Theory of Learning.* London, Falmer Press.

Vouri I. (2004). Physical inactivity is a cause and physical activity is a remedy for major public health problems. *Kinesiology, 36*(2), pp.123-153.

CHAPTER 7

TEACHING GAMES FOR UNDERSTANDING: AN INCLUSIVE TEACHING MODEL

RUAN JONES AND ED COPE

INTRODUCTION

On the 20th October 2010, George Osborne, the UK Government's Chancellor of the Exchequer, revealed the Comprehensive Spending Review (CSR) aimed at tackling the United Kingdom's £83 billion deficit. Of this, £162 million of public funding for the 450 School Sports Partnerships[1], which are presently in place is to be withdrawn as from April 2011. On average, this means that at least two hours of additional Physical Education (PE) will be lost every week compared with the provision currently in place. Consequently, time and resources will become a precious commodity as the "purse strings begin to tighten". Undoubtedly, there is much anxiety among the school and sporting communities about the adverse effect that this may have on the type of physical educational experience as well as the participation rate in general; whether this is the case and the extent to which this is affected obviously remains to be seen. Nonetheless, with the funding cuts that have been expressed it is presumed that "something will have to give" and that the *status quo* in relation to PE and school sport cannot be sustained. It is anticipated that innumerable stakeholders who value the subject of PE, and defend its inherent and instrumental worth, will view these cuts with increasing disquiet, and with good reason: on the face of it the cuts offer a bleak foreseeable future. As funding streams begin to dry up and the ubiquitous, and welcome, visits of the School Sports Coordinator (SSCo) lessen, increased scrutiny will fall upon the quality of the teaching and the students' learning experience. The axiom: "Physician heal thyself" will echo around PE departments.

Notwithstanding the advent of the revised National Curriculum for Physical Education (NCPE) and its student-centric heart, recent studies continue to illustrate the pre-dominance of motor competence and skill acquisition in PE – particularly through the medium of games (Capel & Blair, 2007). Games, we would argue, will continue to hold court over the PE landscape in England, and indeed, more widely within Western cultures (it is a cultural and historical legacy). Nevertheless, there is a responsibility to teach and learn about games within an environment that provides genuine, personal and meaningful movement experiences to young people.

Within this chapter, we attempt to offer a perspective, which can foster development of learners' knowledge, skills and understanding within a meaningful context, regardless of the resources, time and funding available. It is not our intention to discuss the effects the

---

1 School Sports Partnerships (SSP's) are families of secondary and primary schools that work together to enhance the quality of sporting opportunities, through the curriculum, Out of School Hours Learning, inter-school competitions and school to club links. The School Sports Partnership Initiative is one work strand of the Government's Physical Education and Sport Strategy for Young People (PESSYP) document (2008).

"Spending Review" will have on PE in the UK, but rather our purpose is to discuss the potential that teaching games in a manner that is more conducive to the learner (Kidman, 2001), can have on facilitating an enduring quality PE experience. Therefore, the aim of the chapter is to provide an overview of a "Teaching Games for Understanding" approach as an alternative practice in teaching Games.

LESSONS FROM HISTORY

The Teaching Games for Understanding (TGfU) approach was developed in England during the mid-1980s as a response to the prevailing teaching model of the time, commonly referred to as the "Skill-based approach" (Capel & Piotrowski, 2000). The "traditional" model to games teaching follows a series of highly structured lessons relying heavily on the teaching of skills and techniques. It is concerned primarily with the development of control and combination experiences through refining and mastering tasks, which lead toward skilfulness. The intention is that once skills have been mastered, the student will then be in a position to transfer these skills into game situations. Butler and McCahan (2005) argue that the technical model developed under the influence of curriculum reformist, Ralph Tyler, in the 1940's. Tyler advocated the need for teachers to develop specific objectives for their courses, develop activities and programmes to reach those objectives, and then prepare tests to determine if the goals had been reached, since the predominant aim of the technical model is performance.

Most PE teachers came through their formative years inculcated with a technique led approach, and once qualified as teachers sustained the use of the model to help students master the techniques required for games (Butler & McCahan, 2005). Specifically, Butler & McCahan (2005) affirm that this model remains the norm for a majority of the adult generation and significantly, the technical model has been found to be the prevailing teaching method used by PE practitioners today (Butler, 2006; Capel and Blair, 2007; Metzler, 2005).

The technical model, however, has been considerably criticised for its lack of creativity and learner empowerment (Butler & McCahan, 2005; Capel & Piotrowski, 2000), and researchers have advocated the need to call upon physical educators to re-examine the way games are taught and to find out ways to enhance the PE curriculum (Werner & Almond, 1990). The architects of TGfU, Dave Bunker and Rod Thorpe, were alarmed at the inability of young people to make appropriate decisions within games, chiefly, because of the non-situated way that they were taught skills necessary for the particular game. In 1986, Thorpe and Bunker and another Loughborough University, UK colleague, Len Almond, compiled a highly influential collection of works entitled: *Rethinking Games Teaching* that identified and discussed the current state of games education in schools and a number of associated issues including teacher education and strategies for progress. In an article originally published in 1982, Bunker and Thorpe identified the following concerns they held of graduate PE practitioners and, what could be interpreted as their legacy, within secondary schools in England:

- A large percentage of children achieving little success because of the emphasis on performance, i.e. "doing"

- The majority of school leavers "knowing" very little about games
- The production of supposedly "skilful" players who in fact possess inflexible techniques and poor decision making capacity
- The development of teacher/coach dependent performers
- The failure to develop "thinking" spectators and "knowing" administrators at a time when games (and sport) are an important form of entertainment in the leisure industry
- They contended that this was especially concerning since games were (and still are) the staple of the PE curriculum, but significantly, games naturally present problems that need solving and, therefore, require players to think – that is, knowing "why" (Bunker & Thorpe, 1982; 1986).

At this juncture it is, perhaps, prudent to emphasise that concerns regarding the teaching of games in England did not materialise in 1982; indeed Thorpe and Bunker acknowledge the contribution of influential figures (e.g. Wade, Worthington and Wigmore), who challenged students to consider the merits of small-sided and conditioned games in the particular games discourse when they were students at Loughborough University.. They also express their gratitude to the earlier work of Mauldon and Redfern (1969) and their consideration of games in primary education. Thus any historical review of the games for understanding (GfU) rationale (and we are deliberate in the use of this specific phraseology, as opposed to the formalised TGfU), an "historical eye" should be cast on their work at the dawn of the 1970s.

Mauldon and Redfern (1969) baulked at the practice of games teaching in primary schools during the 1960s and their expressions of dissent held much resonance with those of Bunker and Thorpe thirteen years later. In common with Bunker and Thorpe's later observations in secondary education, they noted that games concern "... the direct transmission of adult inventions (or possible simplified versions of these), [and consists] of little more than the acquisition of highly specialised techniques..." (Mauldon & Redfern, 1969, p.1). Hence, although there was recognition that small-sided games ("...simplified versions of [adult games]...") played a part in games education during this era, they were seen to merely serve technical development and expertise and not that of the tactical awareness of the learner. Furthermore, Mauldon and Redfern (1969) posited the social-psychological underpinnings of a GfU approach that Bunker and Thorpe favoured: "... To engage in what is essentially a play situation is always attractive and exciting, and the unpredictable nature of many games is a characteristic to which children readily respond" (p.1). They were able to clarify that it was the "playful" and problem-solving nature of games that should provide central tenets of games teaching. They alluded to the holistic nature of games (physical, intellectual and social, and moral) and stressed the importance of creativity and invention in overcoming problems that games provide. They also proposed and articulated, but did not formalise, several procedures that teachers could follow that allowed for experimentation or games invention; one of which is outlined below:

1. The game – known or invented
2. Suspension of game as problems arise or weaknesses become evident
3. Problem-solving: problems are selected for investigation; students with teacher facilitation, decide which aspects of the game require attention, and problem-solving experiments carried out

4. Discovery phase: discoveries shared and solutions examined
5. Techniques involved are practiced
6. Resumption of game with emphasis on aspects that attention had been drawn to.

This plan, as it is referred to, of which there were three in Mauldon and Redfern's original text, provides a prominent reference to the original six-step curriculum model of TGfU (Bunker & Thorpe, 1982) with its emphasis on "the learner" or "child" and his/her developmental needs that are taken into account at every stage of the procedural model (see Figure 1).

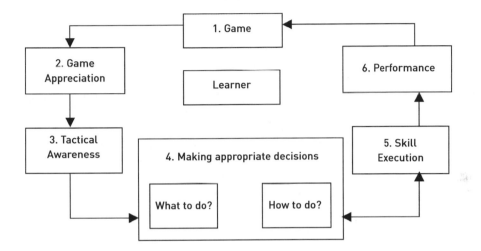

Figure 1: The original TGfU model.

1. The Game Form – modified to meet the developmental needs of the learner; this may include modification to playing area, number of players or equipment.
2. Game Appreciation: an understanding, but also note the word "appreciation" more than understanding – affective terminology that connotes an attachment of value – not just in how rules/conditions shape the way the game is played but also in the rituals, traditions and history of the game (Metzler, 2005); for example, ultimate and self-officiating (a responsibility on the part of participants to negotiate appropriate rules and respect these rules accordingly).
3. Tactical awareness: a presentation, or an increasing awareness of the tactical problems posed by the game – in essence what are the problems that prevent a successful outcome?
4. Making appropriate decisions: what decisions must students make in order to overcome the identified problem?; what to do (tactical awareness) and how (response selection and skill execution)
5. Skill execution: how to execute specific skills and/or actual movements *within* the context of the game and the learner; in other words the skill was relative to the desired outcome of the game and to that of the learner's perception of the appropriate response – not a teacher's idealised technique.
6. Performance: proficient game play (skill, tactical awareness *and affective sensibility*) is based upon specific criteria (learning outcomes, unit objectives, standards, etc).

Noteworthy are the similarities between the two conceptualisations of games-centred teaching and their foregrounding of the game or game-form; however, whereas Mauldon and Redfern in 1969, "... (stopped) short of making proposals for a "game-centred approach" (Bunker & Thorpe, 1986, p.25), the TGfU concept became institutionalised with Len Almond's invaluable contribution. Almond's knowledge of curriculum development was to be a factor in the instigation of action research with practising PE teachers at this time (Almond, 1986), and this made it distinct from the work of Mauldon and Redfern. The *South Australia PE Bulletin* in 1984 (cited in Thorpe & Bunker, 1986) clarified this distinction: "the idea of progressing from tactics to skills, or from 'why?' to 'how?' rather than vice versa, is not new, but its organisation and application has not previously been made coherent".

In addition to their conception of GfU, Mauldon and Redfern also proposed a rudimentary classification of games activities (net, batting, and running) several years before Len Almond articulated his classification that is recognised and commonly utilised today (net/wall, striking/fielding, invasion and target). What this classification system achieved was that it helped the learner as well as the teacher appreciate games conceptually rather than as discrete and abstract. Consequently, invasion games such as football and hockey, for example, provided the student with similar tactical problems to be overcome; a solution arrived at in one may allow for transfer to the other, provided the game classification was mutual. This idea also provides the basis of the four key pedagogical principles (Thorpe & Bunker, 1989) embedded within the TGfU model: *Sampling; Game representation; Exaggeration; and Tactical complexity.*

Sampling concerns the teacher constructing scenarios whereby the learner understands how tactical solutions, skills and rules can be transferred between conceptually similar games categories, such as exploiting the wings (width) in invasion games to outwit opponents.

Representation involves the introduction or development of mini or small-sided games that "represent" the tactical structure of the advanced form of the game (for example short tennis, pop lacrosse).

Exaggeration concerns the reinforcement of various playing conditions, facilitated by secondary rule changes (half court badminton necessitates the importance of the drop or overhead clear for example).

Tactical complexity involves matching the game to the developmental level of the learner, and increasing the complexity of the game when the learner is ready – when each problem encountered is resolved. Naturally, these principles do not occur in isolation, and it is evident how they could be combined in preparation and the execution of games teaching.

TGFU: A HOLISTIC MODEL

What constituted accepted games teaching and practice during the 1960s, 1970s and 1980s has been outlined, yet the skill-based *status quo* continues to endure into the current millennium if present findings are to be taken seriously (Capel & Blair, 2007;

Capel, Hayes, Katene & Velija, 2009). The complex and contending psycho-social, political and philosophical theories for the enduring popularity of the skill-based approach within PE are taken account of later in this chapter; needless to say, the rationale and continued appeal of the skill-based approach in games teaching is reflective of the broader debate that rages within PE itself over its very philosophical justification.

We have already alluded to the influence of Tyler's advocacy of a technical model during the 1940s; this received further credence during the 1960s when PE as a subject gained university status, and by inference, a relative degree of academic respectability within the walls of higher learning. With this newfound status, so Bunker & Thorpe (1986) claim, came a desire to rationalise PE according to increasingly scientific parameters:

> "The problem with Skill Acquisition courses, at least in England was that the desire for experimental stringency meant that skills studied were rarely in a sport context. Add to this the desire to measure and evaluate our work objectively and the well-recognised fact that isolated techniques are so much easier to quantify than other aspects of games and it is easy to see how the Physical Educator was pulled toward the technical side of games" (pp.26-27).

Advantages of this approach were that organisation, structure and content could be easily monitored, and naturally discrete movement patterns measured more easily. The disadvantages were of rigid, inflexible, technique–oriented teachers. At a deeper and more philosophical level of course a profound paradox had been fashioned: as PE has became increasingly "academicised" (Green, 2008; Kretchmar, 2005), it reinforced the liberal philosophical view as espoused by Richard Peters (1966), for example, that PE, and explicitly games, was merely a case of knowing "how" or "knack" and required no rational thought or understanding (procedural knowledge). Hence, the desire for measurement, stringency and objectification had the undesirable effect of seriously diminishing the cognitive process (declarative knowledge) from teaching games. By way of contrast, TGfU and its global iterations (e.g. den Duyn, 1997; Griffin, Mitchell & Oslin, 1997) has been reconceptualised within the last decade as a holistic *teaching and learning* model (Holt, Strean & Bengoechea, 2002; Kirk & MacPhail, 2002; Metzler, 2005).

Metzler (2005) theorises TGfU as a comprehensive model aligning environment, outcome, activity and duration, teaching strategy, assessment procedure, and teacher philosophy *inter alia*; furthermore, he asserts the requirement of domain specific knowledge, specifically, the psychomotor (doing), cognitive (thinking) and affective (feeling) domains of learning. Kirk & MacPhail (2002) give consideration to the situated nature of TGfU and discuss how the learner interacts and engages within authentic communities of practice, first as a "learning apprentice", then gradually advancing towards the centre of the learning community, consequently shaping behaviour and constructing new bodies of knowledge. Holt et al. (2002) proposed the integration of Thorpe's four pedagogical principles as essential in effective utilisation of the model; they also provided a necessary advocation of further research of the learner's experience within the affective domain of learning, and the mediating role of TGfU.

Research that has been undertaken to elucidate the relative strengths of the TGfU approach has, however, tended to focus mainly on cognitive and psycho-motor learning outcomes, with a limited but *budding* consideration of the affective domain of learning in published TGfU literature.

PSYCHO-MOTOR DEVELOPMENT

If PE teachers were to be asked to list the skills required in order to be an effective games player, the majority would identify psycho-motor skills such as kicking, throwing, control and tackling at the top of that list. On the other hand, there might be a number of teachers who cite decision-making, teamwork and problem solving as key determinants of an effective games player. However, the "proof is often in the pudding" as to whether these teachers develop in their students what they claim. By this we mean the approach teachers take to structuring lessons determines what skills the students can potentially develop (Butler, 2006). The following section presents two different approaches teachers take when delivering physical education lessons.

Approach 1: The teacher starts every lesson with a physiologically based warm up before proceeding into an unopposed isolated technique practice. The lesson then moves into a progressive opposed technical practice (1v1 progressing into 2v2), however, each student is prescribed the same content. The lesson will finish with a game with the aim for the students to demonstrate what they had previously been practising in the lesson.

Approach 2: The teacher starts the lesson by outlining what the aims of the lesson are. This will be incorporated in the warm up, which will be closely aligned to other parts of the lesson. The teacher will then set up a small-sided or conditioned game with questioning being the predominant pedagogical strategy used. Different groups will be given different problems to solve based on their development needs. The lesson will move into a more recognised game format, with the focus on transferring the skills learned.

Approach 1 is an example of a "traditional" approach to teaching games, whereby the learners have the opportunity to continuously practise the same "technique" over and over until it has been grooved. This rationalistic approach suggests that all learners are at the same developmental level and, hence, should be subjected to the same content. Through recent work in learner development (Bailey, Collins, Ford, Macnamara, Toms & Pearce, 2010), we know that this is not the case, and that individual needs should be at the forefront of planning, delivery and reflection. Approach 2 is a humanistic approach (see Lombardo, 1987) to teaching, where personal enjoyment and the inherent pleasure that comes from participating are facilitated. It is, therefore, about a whole range of skills being developed, (i.e. psycho-motor, cognitive or affective) as opposed to just a specific set of skills.

It is appropriate at this point to state what we actually mean by a skill, as we are not referring to technique here. We have deliberately used the term "technique" over "skill" in the examples above; as we believe skill is the learner's ability to combine complex techniques with effective tactical strategies (Gubacs-Collins, 2007). As such, we suggest that skilfulness cannot be achieved through the traditional approach to teaching games and so, psycho-motor skills are most appropriately developed through games based approaches.

Drawing on the work of Rovegno, Nevett, Brock and Barbiaz (2001), the techniques of passing and catching are relational (MacPhail, Kirk & Griffin, 2008): there is reliance upon someone making the catch, in order for a pass to be deemed successful. Therefore, it could be suggested that psycho-motor skills cannot be developed out of a game-based context, as technique-based practices do not prepare learners for the dynamism of games (MacPhail, *et al.*, 2008). By a game-based context, we are not implying this has to be a replication of a specific sport, but rather something, which is developmentally appropriate for the learner being taught. In other words, it must match the needs of the learner within the learning environment (Abraham & Collins, 2009). Nor are we intimating that psycho-motor skill development needs only to be developed in games categorised as "invasion" – the need to use game-based practices to develop psycho-motor skills in net/wall, striking and fielding and target games are just as applicable. For example in tennis, practising a forehand shot *ex situ* is refining technique, but it is not developing the psycho-motor skills required for game play. Therefore, teaching practitioners must be aware of what it is that they want the learners to develop, and how this can be achieved in an attempt to move away from the stereotypical notion that psycho-motor skills are best developed out of context.

COGNITIVE DEVELOPMENT

Turner and Martinek (1995) reported that the delivery of skill-based practice in PE and coaching sessions were common, whereby the drill is presented followed by a game at the end. This approach, known as direct instruction, weighs heavily towards the teacher giving lots of feedback, demonstration and instruction to guide the learner through the motor skill process (Rikard, Boswell & Boni, 1993). This leads to the learner becoming reliant upon the teacher and not acquiring the problem-solving and decision-making skills, which enable them to think critically for themselves (Schmidt & Wrisberg, 2004). Furthermore, this method of teaching is characterized by the teacher being the primary decision maker (Lyle, 2002), giving the learners little or no responsibility for their own learning. An example of this can be taken from the sports coaching literature. One of the most predominant pedagogical teacher behaviours associated with a TGfU approach is the ability to employ divergent questioning in order to develop effective decision-making and problem-solving skills (McNeill, Fry, Wright, Tan & Rossi, 2008). However, research into coach behaviours by Smith and Cushion (2006) found that questioning only made up 2.29% of their total behaviours, as opposed to instruction, which made up 24.26% of coaches' total behaviours. Because the ideology of direct instruction is that it is largely technique-based (Turner & Martinek, 1992), it has been proposed that learner understanding of how these skills should be applied in a game situation has been lacking (Rink, French & Tjeerdsma, 1996). As such, a learner fails to develop declarative (understanding why) and procedural (understanding of doing) knowledge, leading to a lack of effectiveness in any decision made (Abraham & Orr, in press).

It has been implied that to develop a cognitive understanding, a situational perspective should be embraced by physical educators and coaches (Kirk & Macdonald, 1998). This means that learning is social and involves interaction between the learners and others (Kirk & Macdonald, 1998). TGfU has the potential to be embraced within the situational perspective of learning due to an alignment in pedagogical principles (Griffin, Brooker & Patton, 2005). Furthermore, through the medium of teaching games, critical thinking skills can be developed and applied in situation (Daniel & Bergman-Drewe, 1998). Although there is a grey area over what critical thinking includes (Daniel & Bergman-Drewe, 1998), we concur with Ennis (1993), who asserts that critical thinking is thinking reflectively, leading to a decision to be made on to what to believe or do and may develop. By no means is this an all encompassing view of what critical thinking is, but rather a starting point in understanding the effect it can have. Certainly in a PE context, having critical thinking skills is advantageous given the direct link between the quality of the decision made by the learner and the performance outcome (Abraham & Collins, 2009). Thus, the development of cognitive skills is best achieved within a context that is most closely aligned within the one in which they are expected to be used, in this instance PE games.

Since the initialisation of the first TGfU curriculum model (Bunker & Thorpe, 1982), there has been growing support within the literature to further research this approach to learning (e.g. Butler, 2006; Griffin, Mitchell & Oslin, 1997; Macphail *et al.*, 2008). It has been proposed that TGfU involves the learner in meaningful practice (Butler, 2006), to which Turner & Martinek (1995) refer as giving the learner the opportunity to understand when, and where a skill should be performed in a game. Moreover, through game play, learners have the opportunity to reflect on their decision-making capabilities (Griffin, *et al*, 2005) in an authentic setting. Additionally, TGfU promotes the learning of game-based skills that can be transferred from one conceptually similar game to another (Hubbell, Lambert & Hayes, 2007).

AFFECTIVE DEVELOPMENT

There persists a degree of perceived imprecision or uncertainty about the exact meaning of affect (Pope, 2005), and the inability to provide an exact definition of "affect" is illustrated throughout social psychological literature. Tellegen (1989, cited in Russ, 1993) asserts that emotion and mood are sub-domains of affect; while Moore & Isen (1990) make reference to the generic and all encompassing nature of affect (what Forgas (2000) calls a feeling state) distinct from the intense, focused and disrupting nature of emotions (for example, disgust, anger, pleasure). Beane, meanwhile, in his 1990 multi-disciplinary work on the subject, details the relationship between affect, cognition and the social environment, while articulating the belief that affect is also founded on a range of dimensions including beliefs, aspirations, attitudes and appreciations, individually and collectively.

There is also an increasing body of social psychological empirical evidence illustrating a bi-directional relationship between cognition and affect (Forgas, 2008). The literature views cognition, in the first instance, as an affective antecedent, described, paradoxically perhaps, by Forgas (2008) as "emotional rules" (p.96), but also as a cognitive consequence (affect "infusing" cognitive processes). Intuitively, it is easier to rationalise the latter premise that a positive *or negative* affective climate can determine how we think and the subsequent quality of the decision-making process. Nevertheless, in conceptualising and operationalising TGfU, we need to consider evidence from social psychology, especially when Bunker and Thorpe's initial model emanated from the fundamental desire to engage young people affectively.

Naturally, these attempts to clarify the nature of the affective domain, particularly the relational social and cognitive components, hold particular resonance if we consider Kirk and MacPhail's (2002) idea of TGfU as a situated learning model and its emphasis on the social construction of knowledge. Ultimately it is necessary to reconsider the relationship between affective and cognitive components therein (see Figure 2).

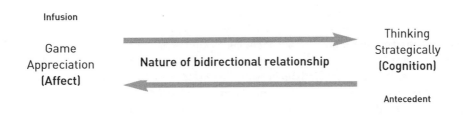

Infusion

Game Appreciation (Affect)   **Nature of bidirectional relationship**   Thinking Strategically (Cognition)

Antecedent

Figure 2: A reconsideration of the relationship between affect and cognition within the TGfU model.

From a general PE and sport perspective, albeit from a limited empirical base, young people consistently associate principal reasons for participation in terms of fun and enjoyment (Dyson, 2006; Smith & Parr, 2007). Therefore, the inference from these and other studies is that fun and enjoyment are defined as positive affective responses by young people, and, more saliently, intrinsic determinants of participation (Pope, 2005).

We have already noted the relatively overlooked reception (Holt et al., 2002) that affect has received within the TGfU research domain, and at this juncture, we think it sensible to consider some of the reasons why, "...it has...escaped the tentacles of most researchers" (Pope, 2006, p.21). In the first instance, its ambiguity: its collection of moods, emotions, attitudes and values ensures that affect is difficult to define. This also means that affording some form of measure, irrespective of the physical educational setting, to such a subjective phenomenon is problematic to say the least (Rink, 2006). Rink also proposes that there is a taken-for-granted sentiment within PE, in relation to affect: affective outcomes are implicit within the teaching and learning process, a natural by-product of the act, if you like. Beane (1990) goes further by asserting that affective outcomes *should* be explicit within an educational environment.[2] Notwithstanding, the ambiguous nature of

2 The National Standards for Physical Education (NASPE, 2004) identify two explicit affective goals: Standard 5: Exhibits responsible personal and social behaviour that respects self and others in physical activity settings Standard 6: Values physical activity for health, enjoyment, challenge, self-expression, and/or social interaction

affect, there is renewed theoretical (Jones & Cope, 2010; Kretchmar, 2005; Light, 2005; Pope, 2005; 2006), and empirical interest (Georgakis & Light, 2009; Mandigo, Holt, Anderson & Sheppard, 2008) in TGfU's courtship of the affective domain, and how the TGfU model, or similar conceptualisations, may enhance intrinsic motivation and values, but also, more deeply personal, subjective and experiential states including "joy" (Light, 2003) and "delight" (Kretchmar, 2005).

The subjective and deeply personal feelings that emotions can elicit in young people have long been emphasised as significant in meaningful movement experiences – including PE (Arnold, 1979); nonetheless, empirical literature is scarce, and more commonplace are the philosophical treatises or articles set within this context. This contention is central to Kretchmar's discussion (2005) reminding the reader how deeply personal and subjective movement can be to an individual, and that PE often excludes this notion in favour of measurement, objectivity and accountability. He contends that TGfU, subject to other appropriate and positive motivational conditions being present[3], may facilitate higher order emotional affective states – namely "delight". Furthermore, Kretchmar (2005) rationalises the importance of the affective domain with regards to understanding and learning, the paucity of related empirical literature, and the reluctance of the PE profession to engage wholeheartedly with the subjective from a teaching, learning and research perspective.

Georgakis & Light's (2009) research article is a valuable companion piece to Kretchmar's "delightful" discussion on TGfU, because it provides a valuable insight into alternative and little used research methodologies in allowing the "student voice" to be heard. Using Kratwohl & Anderson's revised affective taxonomy (2001, cited in Georgakis & Light, 2009) as a theoretical framework for the study, Georgakis and Light's primary data source consisted of year 6 students' drawings collected during a cricket unit taught through the medium of *Games Sense*. These drawings were subsequently used as stimuli for semi-structured interviews on the student affective experience. In the concluding paragraphs of the study, the authors argue that the drawings embody to some degree, residual value, feelings and attitudes from the completed unit of work.

Such emerging approaches to inquiry within the domain of games-centred pedagogies may contribute to our understanding of personal meaning in movement, especially the apparent dizzying affective highs that Kretchmar makes reference to. Indeed, contemporary human movement and PE scholars (Brown, 2008; Kretchmar, 2005) are becoming increasingly vocal in calling for a return to Arnold's *Education in Movement* conception of PE (1979); in essence the intrinsic value of the movement activity from the perspective of the moving agent in refashioning the subject. Ultimately, "meaningful" PE curricula, as espoused by curriculum designers should first take account of what "meaningful" PE is, as experienced and interpreted by the recipient.

Jones & Cope (2010), echoing Pope (2005) and Kretchmar (2005), bemoan the scant regard held for the affective domain from an English perspective, and proceed to discuss

---

3 These motivational conditions have echoes of a Self-Determined (SD) motivational PE climate. See Hagger & Chatzisarantis (2007) for a comprehensive volume of chapters that explores SD theory within sport, exercise and PE settings.

how seemingly, abstract and elementary game forms can be used to generate discussion of creative and intuitive solutions to problems. Critically they return to an often-overlooked aspect of the original Bunker and Thorpe model for their starting point – *Game Appreciation*. As they seek to clarify

".... 'appreciation' is not merely a process of understanding (cognition)...; it is *affective* because it intonates a degree of attached value, whereas understanding does not. The implication being, that, certain game behaviours will more likely be altered if students see value in it" (Jones & Cope, 2010, p.18).

We considered the adage expounded by Dave Bunker at a guest workshop in 2009, extremely prescient in facilitating student expression: "... It is more about what I don't say, than what I do". In other words, students trial the value and meaning of boundaries/conditions and rules through structured play often with unexpected, intuitive or apparently creative solutions: for example, students feigning capture in *prisoners*; the notion of self-sacrifice in *prisoner ball* (Jones & Cope, 2010). These socially constructed solutions are then discussed within the context of the game form and rule modifications are negotiated accordingly.

In a similar vein, some of Rovegno's (2010) most recent published work revisits *Game Appreciation*; she strongly advocates greater attention to this phase of the TGfU model in developing an array of related thinking and social (some, that we would interpret as affective) skills. Despite the fact that Rovegno's discussion is focused at the elementary school age level, we consider the *actual* teaching of *Game Appreciation*, equally important beyond this age group; naturally the game evolves, following the pedagogical principles that Thorpe & Bunker (1989) propose. Nevertheless, the cognitive and social/affective skills, for example: "Critical thinking" through to, "Valuing diversity and respecting difference" (Rovegno, 2010, p.225) are universal conditions of a holistic education irrespective of the maturational/developmental level of a young person, especially if knowledge is considered to be socially constructed.

A HYBRID INSTRUCTIONAL MODEL

In recent years, there has been a movement in the research towards combining curriculum models with similar pedagogical principles. In this section, using a combined TGfU and cooperative learning (CL) approach is discussed with the rationale being that learners are exposed to a more holistic learning environment whereby a broader range of skills are developed (Jones & Turner, 2006). It is due to our experience of using these two approaches as a hybrid instructional model (HIM) that they are used to provide examples of how a HIM can be of benefit in PE curricula. In line with the revised English National Curriculum (NC) which promotes "greater flexibility" in order to more appropriately meet the needs of individual learners, a HIM for teaching games allows a curriculum to be delivered, which does this (Metzler, 2005).

In a CL curriculum learners are required to work together, which in game-based activities, developing skills of teamwork would be of benefit (Putnam, 1998). Requiring learners to work together promotes an open-mindedness to evolve and this encourages more time to be taken when considering the options to take to benefit the decision made. This way a breadth first approach to problem solving can be taken whereby a number of options are considered before choosing which solution is most appropriate (Abraham & Collins, 2009). Just like TGfU, for CL to be authentically delivered, the role of the teacher moves from that to facilitator, allowing the learners to take more responsibility for their own learning and more opportunities to seek answers to problems set (Wright, 2004). One such way that this can be achieved is through "scaffolding" learning, which has been cited as an effective way to increase independent problem-solving by conditioning games to make them more developmentally appropriate (Wright, McNeill & Fry, 2009).

As well as cognitive and social skills being developed due to working as part of a co-operative team, learners also develop affective skills of inherent enjoyment (Kretchmar, 2005), developing philosophies and beliefs about PE that serve to motivate learners to remain physically active. Drawing on the work of Butler (2006) who confirms that, if a learner is only subjected to one aspect of performance (e.g. technical fundamentals), then all the leaner can expect to develop is this aspect. By choosing to adopt a HIM the possibilities for learner development are endless given the holistic skills, which have the potential to be developed.

USING TGFU IN EVERYDAY PRACTICE: RESISTANCE

The holistic set of skills that can be developed as a consequence of teaching using a TGfU approach would suggest that every teaching practitioner would adopt it in their practice. Since the emergence of the TGfU approach to teaching sport-related games, and in this time the significant advancement in research and awareness as a "legitmate" teaching approach (Griffin, et al., 2005), it has not yet been acknowledged by teaching practitioners and pedagogues alike in PE lessons (Light, 2004). Why is it that not every teacher uses this approach in their practice, given the suggested benefits it can bring to a learners development? The following section aims to answer this question by proposing why the TGfU approach (or similar approaches) is not being embraced.

Although nearly 30 years have passed since the initialisation of the TGfU approach (Bunker & Thorpe, 1982), there still remains resistance to this conceptual-based model for games, teaching and learning (Griffin, et al., 2005). This section explores why TGfU has met such resistance, and what can be done to change the approach teachers adopt when teaching games.

It has been suggested that teachers teach the way that they were taught (Butler, 2005) and knowing that GfU did not really become "commercialised" until it was adopted by Bunker and Thorpe in the early 1980s and re-conceptualised as TGfU, a large proportion of teachers today will have been taught by teachers using a "traditional" approach. Given our stance that learning is socially and culturally constructed (Kirk & Macdonald, 1998), we agree with the notion that beliefs are formed as a consequence of interaction with people in a particular context (Macdonald, Kirk, Metzler, Nilges, Schempp & Wright, 2002). Therefore, the experiences of the teacher will have shaped their beliefs and assumptions about how to teach PE (Templin, Sparkes, Grant & Schempp, 1994).

Brookfield (1995) suggests there are three levels of assumptions: paradigmatic, prescriptive and causal. In the case of a teacher's approach to teaching, this would be categorised as a paradigmatic assumption as it underpins a teacher's practice (Strean, Senecal, Howlett & Burgess, 1997). Assumptions at this level are the most difficult to uncover and change, and even once made explicit they require a large amount of evidence to bring about change (Strean, *et al.*, 1997). These paradigmatic assumptions are never going to be changed unless the teacher engages in constant reflection at a critical level so as to unearth these underlying beliefs (Hume, 2009). As a result, a teacher will continue to teach as he/she believes best to do so, unless challenged to understand practice from more than just one perspective (Loughran, 2002); this currently being a "traditional" approach to games teaching.

At a more philosophical level, the assumptions an individual holds is guided by the values and beliefs this individual holds, which in turn shape the way the individual acts. In other words, how we think is a consequence of our values and beliefs and our values and beliefs dictate how we think. There is agreement in the literature that values and belief systems are drawn predominantly from inter-actions, which are socially constructed (Fernandez-Balboa & Muros, 2006). Two of the leading theoretical perspectives offered that attempt to explain the effect that "life history" has had on belief systems are Bourdieu's notion of *habitus*, and Lawson's theory of occupational socialisation.

Bourdieu (1990) defined *habitus* as "the basis from which lifestyles are generated" (p.127). The theory of *habitus* relates to the generalised set of actions that many people do (Fernandez-Balboa & Muros, 2006) and, therefore, explains conformity to the "stereotypically" held view that PE is about the development of physical fitness, acquisition of relevant motor skills and participation in physical activity in order to be regarded as a "physically literate" learner (Doherty & Brennan, 2008). Through this discourse, teachers learn to behave and obey; a feature which is representative of their predecessors (Bourdieu, 1990).

According to Lawson's notion of "occupational socialisation", what a teacher learns, as well as when, how and where are integral to understanding a teacher's values and beliefs (Lawson, 1988). More specifically, Lawson affirms it is the stages of acculturation, professional socialisation and organisational socialisation, which determine teacher's inherent beliefs. Dependent on the experiences of a teacher at the different stages, most notably acculturation (Curtner-Smith, 1999), a direct link will emerge between the underpinning processes and the outcomes of teacher behaviour.

As such, epistemological positions that are held, dictate the outcome of an action (Grix, 2002). Epistemology refers to an individual's beliefs about how knowledge is constructed and learning is achieved (Schommer, 1990). Therefore, whether conscious of it, every individual has an epistemological viewpoint. Depending on what this is, it will affect the way in which a teacher teaches. For example, if teachers believe knowledge to be simple, fixed and passed down from authority (Schommer-Aikins, Mau, Brookhart & Hutter, 2000) then they will teach from a more "traditional" teacher-centred behaviourist perspective. Alternatively, if teachers view knowledge as complex, tentative and rational (Schommer, 1990), then they will teach from a more "games"-centred, learner-centred constructivist perspective.

Even if a teacher's epistemological viewpoint is that TGfU or similar constructivist teaching approaches are most appropriate for developing effective games players, this does not necessarily mean that this approach will suffice. When implementing any instructional model, in order for it to be reflective of this, certain pedagogical strategies need to be considered. Dyson, Griffin and Hastie (2004, pp.235-236) suggested these to be:

1. The teacher is the facilitator
2. Students are active learners
3. Students work in small groups and modified games
4. Learning activities are authentic and developmentally appropriate
5. Learning activities are interesting and challenging
6. Students are held accountable

As such, to be able to adopt this approach to teaching is something that cannot be done at a "flick of a switch", but requires large amounts of practice and understanding to be able to teach in this way (Putnam, 1998). The expectancy placed particularly on newly qualified teachers to instantaneously be able to teach in this way appears unrealistic and unattainable. Nonetheless, attempts to use this approach should not be discouraged, but rather embraced by physical educators.

USING TGFU IN EVERYDAY PRACTICE: CHANGE

Teachers who have been subjected to a history of traditional, teacher-centred teaching will continue to teach in this way unless they are explicitly challenged to address their practice (Little, 1993). Alternatively, for those teachers whose philosophy of teaching is centred on constructivist pedagogies like TGfU, but because of external influences their ability to teach in this manner is negatively impacted upon would suggest that there is very little they can do to prevent resistance. We suggest that through professional development, teachers beliefs can be changed, as well as the beliefs of the learners whom the teachers are responsible for teaching, and the members of the organisation, which play an influential role in dictating how the teacher teaches.

At present there is some agreement in the literature about ineffective practice in professional development for teachers (Sinelnikov, 2009). In order for learners' conceptions of teaching to change from being told to being asked, requires an alignment of teaching approaches across the educational spectrum (i.e. from primary years through to higher education). Professional development opportunities can help in achieving this as teacher and teacher educators beliefs about what constitutes quality learning can be explored, challenged and changed to better meet the needs of PE learners. Therefore, open-mindedness needs to evolve, which moves away from teacher and teacher educators feeling criticized to the point where they are unwilling to accept change, to a more empathetic viewpoint, which considers the interchangeable needs of the teacher, the learner and teaching context (Cote, Young, North & Duffy, 2007). By doing this, the process becomes one of educational purpose as opposed to an inspection of practice.

CONCLUDING THOUGHTS

It was never our intention to provide a complete historical and philosophical critique of TGfU, in addition to the myriad of contemporary issues related to its utilisation and interpretation; rather it was to provide a brief overview of how and why TGfU, as a conceptual instructional approach to PE teaching, has come to the attention of the PE fraternity, or not as the chapter has served to illustrate. We also contend that there are avenues of research yet to be fully explored with respect to TGfU that shed light on its rich and diverse characteristics. Nonetheless, as an approach to teaching games in schools, its potential is still left largely untapped. The terms "common practice" and "TGfU" uttered in the same breath remain a pipe dream on playing fields and sports halls the length and breadth of the United Kingdom and elsewhere given some of the reasons discussed in this chapter.

If PE is to move forward, it has to recognise the diverse needs of individuals entering school education. As a subject discipline, it can no longer be justified by its relationship to the sciences (Singleton, 2009) and the techno-rationalistic approach that has dominated the subject for decades (Tinning, 1991). If PE is to meet the physical, cognitive and affective needs of the learner, it is our belief that the subject moves beyond the current skill based approach, and within the context of our discussion in this chapter, teaching games. Rather, we contend that through the medium of TGfU approach, games teaching can physically educate learners in the purest and most holistic sense. If the aim of PE is to provide a connection, a degree of engagement with a physical activity, that a young person may pursue into post-compulsory education, an instructional approach such as TGfU may provide an answer.

REFERENCES

Abraham, A., & Orr, C. (in press). Improving skilled performance through effective coaching. In: D. Collins, H. Richards, & A. Button, (Eds.), *Psychology for Physical Performance*. Kidlington, Elsevier.

Arnold, P.J. (1979). *Meaning in Movement, Sport & Physical Education*. London, Heinemann.

Bailey, R., Collins, D., Ford, P., MacNamara, A., Toms, M., & Pearce, G. (2010). *Participant Development in Sport*. Leeds, Sports Coach UK.

Beane, J.A. (1990). *Affect in the curriculum: toward democracy, dignity and diversity*. Columbia, Teachers College Press.

Bourdieu, P. (1990). *The logic of practice*. Cambridge, Polity Press.

Brookfield, S.D. (1995). *Becoming a critically reflective teacher*. San Francisco, Jossey-Boss.

Brown, T.D. (2008). Movement and meaning-making in physical education. *ACHPER Healthy Lifestyles Journal, 55*, pp.5-9.

Bunker, D., & Thorpe, R. (1982). A model for the teaching of games in secondary school. *Bulletin of Physical Education, 10*, pp.9-16.

Bunker, D., & Thorpe, R. (1986). Is there a need to reflect on our games teaching? In: R. Thorpe, D. Bunker & L. Almond (Eds.), *Rethinking games teaching*. Loughborough, England, University of Technology, Department of Physical Education and Sport Science. pp.25-34.

Butler, J.I. (2006). Curriculum constructions of ability: enhancing learning through Teaching Games for Understanding (TGFU) as a curriculum based model. *Sport, Education and Society, 11*, pp.243-258.

Butler, J.I., & McCahan, B.J. (2005). Teaching Games for Understanding as a Curriculum Model. In: L.L. Griffin & J.I. Butler (Eds.), *Teaching Games for Understanding: Theory, Research and Practice* Champaign, IL: Human Kinetics. pp.33-54.

Capel, S., & Blair, R. (2007). Making physical education relevant: Increasing the impact of initial teacher education. *London Review of Education, 5*, pp.15-34.

Capel, S., Hayes, S., Katene, W., & Velija, P. (2009). The development of knowledge for teaching physical education in secondary schools over the course of a PGCE year. *European Journal of Teacher Education, 32*, pp.51-62.

Capel, S., & Piotrowski, S. (2000). *Issues in Physical Education.* London, Routledge Falmer.

Cote, J., Young, B., North, J., & Duffy, P. (2007). Towards a Definition of Excellence in Sport Coaching. *International Journal of Coaching Science, 1*, pp.3-17.

Curtner-Smith, M.D. (1999). The more Things Change the More They Stay the Same: Factors Influencing Teachers Interpretations and Delivery of National Curriculum Physical Education. *Sport, Education and Society, 4*, pp.75-97.

Daniel, M. F., & Bergman- Drewe, S. (1998). Higher-order thinking, philosophy, and teacher education in physical education. *Quest, 50*, pp.33-58.

den Duyn, N. (1997). *Games Sense: developing thinking players.* Canberra, Australian Sports Commission.

Doherty, J., & Brennan, P. (2008). *Physical Education and development 3-11: a guide for teachers.* London, Routledge.

Dyson, B. (2006). Students' perspectives of physical education. In: D. Kirk, D. Macdonald & M. O'Sullivan (Eds.), *The Handbook of Physical Education.* London, Sage, pp.326-46.

Dyson, B., Griffin, L., & Hastie, P. (2004). Sport Education, Tactical Games and Cooperative Learning: Theoretical and Pedagogical Considerations. *Quest, 56,* pp.226-241.

Ennis, R. (1993). Critical thinking assessment. *Theory into Practice, 32*, pp.179-186.

Fernandez-Balboa, J-M., & Muros, B. (2006). The Hegemonic Triumvirate-Ideologies, Discouses, and Habitus in Sport and Physical Education: Implications and Suggestions. *National Association for Kinesiology and Physical Education in Higher Education, 58*, pp.197-221.

Forgas, J.P. (2000). *Feeling and Thinking: The Role of Affect in Social Cognition.* Cambridge, Cambridge University Press.

Forgas, J.P. (2008). Affect and Cognition. *Perspectives on Psychological Science, 3*, pp.94-101.

Georgakis, S., & Light, R. (2009). Visual data collection methods for research on the affective dimensions of children's personal experiences of PE. *ACHPER Healthy Lifestyles Journal, 56,* pp.23-27.

Green, K. (2008) *Understanding Physical Education.* London, Sage.

Griffin, L.L., Brooker, R., & Patton, K. (2005). Working towards legitimacy: two decades of Teaching Games for Understanding. *Physical Education and Sport Pedagogy, 10,* pp.213-223.

Griffin, L.L., Mitchell, S.A., & Oslin, J.L. (1997). *Teaching Sports Concepts and Skills: A tactical games approach.* Champaign, IL, Human Kinetics.

Grix, J. (2002). Introducing Students to the Generic Terminology of Social Research. *Politics, 22*(3), pp.175-186.

Gubacs-Collins, K. (2007). Implementing a tactical approach through action research. *Physical Education and Sport Pedagogy, 12*, pp.105-126.

Holt, N.L., Strean, W.B., & Bengoechea, E.G. (2002). Expanding the Teaching Games for Understanding Model: New Avenues for Future Research and Practice. *Journal of Teaching in Physical Education, 21*, pp.162-176.

Hubball, H., Lambert., J., & Hayes, S. (2007). Theory to Practice: Using the Games for Understanding Approach in the Teaching of Invasion Games. *Physical and Health Education, 73*(4), pp.14-20.

Hume, A. (2009). Promoting higher levels of reflective writing in student journals. *Higher Education Research and Development, 28*, pp.247-260.

Jones, R., & Cope, E. (2010). Thinking (and feeling) outside the box. *Physical Education Matters, 5*, pp.16-19.

Jones, R.L., & Turner, P. (2006). Teaching coaches to coach holistically: can problem based learning (PBL) help? *Physical Education and Sport Pedagogy, 11*, pp.181-202.

Kidman, L. (2001). *Developing decision makers: an empowerment approach to coaching.* Christchurch, Innovative Print Communications.

Kirk, D., & Macdonald, D. (1998). Situated Learning in Physical Education. *Journal of Teaching in Physical Education, 17*, pp.376-287.

Kirk, D., & MacPhail, A. (2002). Teaching games for understanding and situated learning: Rethinking the Bunker-Thorpe model. *Journal of Teaching in Physical Education, 17*, pp.376-387.

Kretchmar, R.S. (2005). Teaching Games for Understanding and the Delights of Human Activity. In L.L. Griffin & J.I. Butler (Eds.), *Teaching Games for Understanding: Theory, Research & Practice*. Champaign, IL, Human Kinetics. pp.199-212.

Lawson, H.A. (1988). Occupational Socialisation, Cultural Studies, and the Physical Education Curriculum. *Journal of Teaching in Physical Education, 7*, pp.265-288.

Light, R. (2003). The Joy of Learning: Emotion, Cognition and Learning in Games through TGfU. *New Zealand Journal of Physical Education, 36*, pp.94-108.

Light, R. (2004). Australian coaches' experiences of game sense: opportunities and challenges. *Physical Education and Sport Pedagogy, 9*, pp.115–132.

Light, R. (2005). Introduction: An international perspective on Teaching Games for Understanding. *Physical Education and Sport Pedagogy, 10*, pp.211-212.

Little, J.W. (1993). Teachers Professional Development in a Climate of Educational Reform. *Educational Education and Policy Analysis, 15*, pp.129-151.

Lombardo, B.J. (1987). *The humanistic coach: from theory to practice.* Springfield, USA, Thomas.

Loughran, J.J. (2002). Effective Reflective Practice: In Search of Meaning in Learning about Teaching. *Journal of Teacher Education, 53*, pp.33-43.

Lyle, J. (2002) *Sports Coaching Concepts: A Framework for Coaches' Behaviour.* London, Routledge.

Macdonald, D., Kirk, D., Metzler, M., Nilges, L.M., Schempp, D. & Wright, J. (2002). It's All Very Well, in Theory: Theoretical Perspectives and their Applications in Contemporary Pedagogical Research. *Quest, 54*, pp.133-156.

MacPhail, A., Kirk, D., & Griffin, L. (2008). Throwing and Catching as Relational Skills in Game Play: Situated Learning in a Modified Game Unit. *Journal of Teaching Physical Education, 27*, pp.100-115.

Mandigo, J., Holt, N., Anderson, A., & Sheppard, J. (2008). Children's motivational experiences following autonomy-supportive games lessons. *European Physical Education Review, 14*(3), pp.407-425.

Mauldon, E., & Redfern, H.B. (1969). *Games Teaching: A New Approach for the Primary School.* London, Macdonald & Evans.

McNeill, M.C., Fry, J.M., Wright, S.C., Tan, C.W.K., & Rossi, T. (2008). Structuring time and questioning to achieve tactical awareness in games lessons. *Physical Education and Sport Pedagogy, 13*(3), pp.231-249.

Metzler, M.W. (2005). *Instructional models for physical education.* Scottsdale, AR, Holcomb Hathaway.

Moore, B., & Isen, A. (1990). *Affect and social behaviour.* Cambridge, Cambridge University Press.

Peters, R.S. (1966). *Ethics and Education.* London, Allen and Unwin.

Pope, C.C. (2005). Once more with feeling: affect and playing with the TGfU model. *Physical Education and Sport Pedagogy, 10*(3), pp.271-286.

Pope, C.C. (2006). Affect in New Zealand junior sport: the forgotten dynamic. *Change: Transformation in Education, 9*, pp.17-24.

Putnam, J. (1998). *Cooperative learning and strategies for inclusion: Celebrating diversity in the classroom (2nd ed.)* Baltimore, MD, Brookes.

Rikard, G., Boswell, L., & Boni, B. (1993). Teacher effectiveness in using direct instruction for student skill acquisition. *Physical Educator, 50*, pp.194-200.

Rink, J.E. (2006). *Teaching Physical Education for Learning* (5th Ed.). New York, McGraw-Hill.

Rink, J.E., French, K.E., & Tjeerdsma, B.L. (1996). Foundations and issues for teaching games and sport, *Journal of Teaching in Physical Education, 15*, pp.399–417.

Rovegno, I. (2010). A Model for TGfU in Elementary-School Physical Education. In: J.I. Butler & L.L. Griffin (Eds.), *More Teaching Games for Understanding: Moving Globally* Champaign, IL, Human Kinetics. pp. 209-230.

Rovegno, I., Nevett, M., & Barbiarz, M. (2001). Learning and teaching invasion-game tactics in 4th grade: Introduction and theoretical perspective. *Journal of Teaching in Physical Education, 20*, pp.353-369.

Russ, S.W. (1993). *Affect and Creativity: The Role of Affect and Play in the Creative Process.* New Jersey, Lawrence Erlbaum Associates.

Schmidt, R.A., & Wrisberg, C.A. (2004). *Motor Learning and Performance: A problem- based learning approach.* (3rd Ed). Champaign, IL, Human Kinetics.

Schommer, M. (1990). Effects of beliefs about the nature of knowledge on comprehension. *Journal of Educational Psychology, 82*, pp.498-504.

Schommer-Aikins, M., Mau, W-C., Brockhart., & Hutter, R. (2000). Understanding Middle Students Beliefs about Knowledge and Learning Using a Multidimensional Paradigm. *The Journal of Educational Research, 94*, pp.120-127.

Sinelnikov, O.A. (2009). Sport Education for Teachers: Professional Development When Introducing a Novel Curriculum Model. *European Physical Education Review, 15*(1), pp.91-114.

Singleton, E. (2009). *From Command to Constructivism: Canadian Secondary Physical Education Curriculum and Teaching Games for Understanding. Curriculum Inquiry, 39*, pp.321-342.

Smith, M., & Cushion, C.J. (2006). An investigation of the in-game behaviours of professional, top-level youth soccer coaches. *Journal of Sport Sciences, 24*, pp.255-266.

Smith, A., & Parr, M. (2007). Young people's views on the nature and purposes of physical education: a sociological analysis. *Sport, Education and Society, 12*, pp.37-58.

Strean, W.B., Senecal, K.L., Howlett, S.G., & Burgess, J.M. (1997). X's and O's and What the Coach Knows: Improving Team Strategy through Critical Thinking. *The Sport Psychologist, 11*, pp.243-256.

Templin, T. J., Sparkes, A., Grant, B., & Schmepp, P. (1994). Matching the Self: the Paradoxical Case and Life History of a Late Career Teacher/Coach. *Journal of Teaching in Physical Education, 15*, pp.274-294.

Thorpe, R. & Bunker, D. (1989). A changing focus in games teaching. In: L. Almond (Ed.), T*he Place of Physical Education in Schools.* London, Kogan Page. pp.42-71.

Tinning, R. (1991). Teacher education pedagogy: Dominant discourses and the process of problem setting. *Journal of Teaching in Physical Education, 11*, pp.1–20.

Turner, A.P., & Martinek, T.J. (1992). A comparative analysis of two models for teaching games (technique approach and game-centred (tactical focus) approach). *International Journal of Physical Education, 29*, pp.15-31.

Turner, A., & Martinek, T.J. (1995). Teaching for Understanding: a Model for Improving Decision Making During Game Play. *Quest, 47*, pp.44-63.

Werner, P., & Almond, L. (1990). Models of Games Education. *Journal of Physical Education, Recreation and Dance, 61*, pp.23-27.

Wright, J. (2004). Critical inquiry and problem-solving in physical education. In J. Wright., D. Macdonald., & L. Burrows (Eds), *Critical Inquiry and Problem-Solving in Physical Education* (pp 3- 16). Routledge, London.

Wright, S., McNeill., & Fry, J.M. (2009). The tactical approach to teaching games from teaching, learning and mentoring perspectives. *Sport, Education and Society, 14*, pp.223-244.

Ability

On the individual level, peer tutoring was found to be equally effective for low-skilled students as well as higher-skilled students (Johnson & Ward, 2001). On the dyadic level, a substantial body of evidence supports the use of peer teaching structures with students having motor and cognitive delays (Houston-Wilson, Dunn, van der Mars & McCubbin, 1997). DePaepe (1985) found that students with moderate developmental disabilities who were paired with fifth-grade peer tutors from the regular student population spent more time in *Active Learning Time in Physical Education* (ALT-PE), regardless of whether the peer tutors were trained or not.

The influence of peer skill level has been investigated in several studies on dyadic practice in the physical domain, but the findings have been largely inconsistent (McCullagh & Weiss, 2001). Several types of peer models have been discriminated in research. On the one hand, it was demonstrated that viewing a skilled model entailed higher self-efficacy and better motor performance (Lirgg & Feltz, 1991) than viewing an unskilled model. An unskilled model, however, could be seen as a "learning model", which in some studies was shown to lead to better performance than a correct model (McCullagh & Caird, 1990). Other studies reported that both learning models and correct models led to similar levels of performances (McCullagh & Meyer, 1997). On the other hand, a parallel concept emerging from social-psychological literature introduced the issue of mastery versus coping models (Schunk, Hanson & Cox, 1987). Mastery models demonstrate errorless performance and verbalize confidence, whereas coping models show gradual improvement in performance and progressively more positive statements. In general, coping models are considered to be peers. Research demonstrated that peer coping and mastery models yielded better performance, higher self-efficacy, and lower fear in swimming than the control group (d'Arripe, et al., 2002). Coping models (i.e., peer models), however, had a stronger effect on self-efficacy than mastery models (Weiss, McCullagh, Smith & Berlant, 1998); d'Arripe-Longueville, Fleurance & Winnykamen (1995) found that, for learning the forward somersault, a better representation and retention of the skill was found in asymmetrical dyads (i.e., higher-skilled peer with a lower-skilled peer) than in symmetrical dyads. In addition, higher-skilled tutors produced the best results for males, whereas both higher-skilled and average-skilled tutors produced similar effects for females.

Lou et al. (1996) reported that high-ability students learn equally well when they are paired with an equally high-ability partner or a low-ability partner. On the contrary, low-ability students improve the most when cooperating with a high-ability student. Webb (1992) suggested the appearance of an "expert-novice relationship" when a high-ability student co-operates with a low-ability student. The expert is believed to learn by analyzing the novice, giving feedback, and demonstrating, whereas the novice learns by asking relevant questions, receiving appropriate feedback, and observing a skilled model. Average-ability students, on the other hand, are believed to learn best with equally competent partners (Lou, Abrami, Spence, Poulsen, Chambers & d'Appolonia, 1996). The absence of an "expert-novice relationship" was put forward to support this statement.

Prior knowledge

Students might have prior knowledge about the learning task, about how to use the learning tools (i.e., task cards), and in tutoring behaviour. Often, prior knowledge is labelled as pre-training in literature. Research investigating the effect of prior knowledge on tool use and the learning task is limited in physical education peer tutoring. In reading education, more experienced students with higher prior knowledge in the domain of reading comprehension had a higher perception of competence and, therefore, often fostered learning better (Dochy & Alexander, 1995). For tutoring, Houston-Wilson et al. (1997) found better learning gains in students tutored by trained as against untrained tutors. Normally developing students were paired with students having disabilities, requiring more need for tutor training. When implemented, teachers typically taught students tutoring behaviours such as feedback or coding of assessments (Ward & Lee, 2001). In their review on tutor learning, Roscoe and Chi (2007) found equal learning gains for trained versus untrained tutors. Later on, it was claimed that it is not the amount of tutor training that influences learning, but the kind of training they receive (Topping, 2005). Training tutors to use constructivist strategies of learning has been shown to lead to impressive gains (King, Staffieri & Adelgais, 1998).

Relatedness with partner

The degree of relatedness with the partner (i.e., friend versus non-acquaintance) is influential for social interactions, and as a consequence for learning outcomes. Byra and Marks (1993) found that learners gave more specific feedback to partners, whom they identified as friends, and that learners felt more comfortable receiving feedback from friends than from non-acquaintances. Subsequent research reported that self-selection is the most appropriate pairing technique for peer tutoring (Ernst & Byra, 1998; Mosston & Ashworth, 2002).

MEDIUM

The medium in peer tutoring settings refers to a source of information. This medium can be the teacher, a peer, but also tools like task cards, and dynamic media such as animations, inter-active software, or a combination of the previously mentioned. This chapter only focuses on task cards. Task cards generally combine a picture of the skill with verbal instruction about how to perform the skill, and based on the definition by Mayer (2005), they are considered as multi-media instructional tools. Next to their implementation for appropriating new skills, task cards are also used to enhance task execution quality, provide instructions on task execution quantity, stimulate task oriented behaviour, and to manage the learning setting. Considering task execution quality, simple instructions by means of text and pictures can be presented. They can provide prompts, critical cues and directions to be followed by the students during practice (Lee & Ward, 2002). Considering task execution quantity, task cards can explain the number of exercises or trials to be performed (Block, Oberweiser & Bain, 1995). In enhancing task oriented behaviour, they can be used as checklists for peers to assess each other's performance or as a cognition support in organizing, supporting, and augmenting thinking (Iserbyt, Elen & Behets, 2009; Iserbyt, Madou, Vergauwen & Behets, in press; Pea, 1994; Salomon, Perkins & Globerson, 1991; Ward & Ward, 1996). In their roles as instructional, managerial or feedback tools, task cards have shown beneficial influence as powerful learning tools in the social domain (Dyson & Rubin, 2003; Pea, 1994). Dyson (2002) argued that task cards help to hold students accountable for learning motor skills, a key element of co-operative learning that is often missing. As a consequence, task card use has the potential to decrease social "loafing" (Johnson & Johnson, 1999), encourage inter-action between the both learners (Ernst & Byra, 1998), increase student participation and responsibility and lead to conceptual gains (Cohen, 1994). In his co-operative learning study, Barrett (2005) used task cards during practice time and to facilitate peer assessment during an 18-lesson handball unit. Johnson and Ward (2001) implemented task cards during a 20-lesson striking unit.

Learners rely on task cards to adopt the given task, and in some cases they are even the only source of information. Understanding how people learn from them is, therefore, significant to facilitate learning by an effective design and implementation in daily practice. The following section explains the cognitive theory in multi-media learning and its importance for task card use.

Cognitive theory in multi-media learning

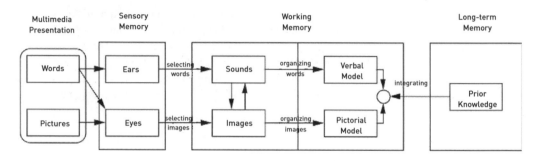

Figure 2. Cognitive theory in multi-media learning (Mayer, 2005)

Mayer's (2005) cognitive theory in multi-media learning explains how people learn from multi-media (see Figure 2). The basic hypothesis is that multi-media instructional messages that are designed in the light of how the human mind works are more likely to lead to meaningful learning than those that are not. This cognitive theory is based on three cognitive science assumptions of learning: (1) the human information processing system includes dual channels for visual/pictorial and auditory/verbal processing (i.e., dual-channels assumption); (2) every channel has a limited capacity for information processing (i.e., limited capacity assumption); and (3) active learning entails carrying out three cognitive processes during learning (i.e., active processing assumption), namely selecting relevant words/images, organizing the selected words/images into a coherent representation, and integrating the pictorial and verbal representations with prior knowledge. Learning occurs by altering long-term memory, which is only possible through inter-action with the working memory. Since this working memory is limited in processing capacities, it is significant to take this limitation into account when designing multi-media intended for learning. Based on this cognitive theory, the following research-based principles listed immediately below can be taken into account for effective task card design (Mayer, 2005).

Combine words and pictures (Multi-media). According to the multi-media principle, learners learn more deeply from words and pictures than from words alone. When both words and pictures are presented, students have the opportunity to construct verbal and pictorial mental models and to build connections between them.

Integrate words and pictures on the task cards (Spatial contiguity). The spatial contiguity principle states that when designing instruction, including multi-media instruction, it is important that corresponding words and pictures are presented nearer rather than further from each other on the task cards. When this is not the case, there is risk for a so-called "split-attention effect". A split-attention effect is detrimental for learning and occurs when learners are forced to divide their attention between, and mentally integrate, multiple sources of information. Instead, materials should be formatted so that disparate sources of information are physically (and temporally) integrated. This obviates the learner to engage in mental integration, fostering learning.

Connect corresponding words and pictures (Signalling). Signalling means that people learn more deeply from a multi-media message when cues are added that highlight the organization of the essential material. For example, important aspects in the picture can be connected by means of arrows to the appropriate written instruction.

Exclude extraneous material (Coherence). The coherence principle claims that people learn more deeply from a multi-media message when extraneous material is excluded rather than included. Distracting background, unnecessary pictures and/or signs, wrong use of colours, duplicate information, low-quality (e.g., blurred) pictures and so forth are examples of extraneous material. The implementation of this material does not contribute to the achievement of the instructional objective, and impedes learning.

Use a conversational style (Personalization). This principle states that people learn more deeply when the words in a multi-media presentation are in a conversational style rather than in a formal style.

As described above, the cognitive theory in multi-media learning provides empirically-based guidelines that help to facilitate learning by developing an appropriate instructional design for task cards. A potential challenge when learning from these tools is that the processing demands may exceed the processing capacity of the cognitive system (i.e. working memory), a situation called cognitive overload. Therefore, the relationship between cognitive demands imposed by the learning environment and the desired learning outcomes should be carefully examined (Moreno & Mayer, 2007). Teachers need to keep in mind that before learners faced with novel material can organize and incorporate it, they need to process it using a limited working memory. This characteristic of human cognitive architecture has implications for the design of instruction (Mayer, 2005). While intrinsic load is generally believed to be immutable, instructional designers can manipulate extraneous and germane load (Moreno and Mayer, 2007). In general, it is suggested that learning is facilitated when extraneous load is reduced and germane load promoted. Reducing extraneous cognitive load frees working memory capacity and so may permit an increase in germane cognitive load (Sweller, 2005). By developing task cards according to multi-media research, extraneous load is reduced and learning fostered. Figure 3. below shows an example of a task card from the area of Basic Life Support, designed with the application of multi-media research principles.

INSTRUCTION

According to cognitive load theory (Sweller, 2005) and the cognitive theory of multi-media learning (Mayer, 2005), there are three kinds of cognitive processing that can contribute to cognitive load: intrinsic (or essential) processing, extraneous processing, and germane (or generative) processing (DeLeeuw & Mayer, 2008). Each load refers to the load imposed on working memory during instruction. Intrinsic processing occurs when the learner engages in cognitive processing that is essential for comprehending the presented information. Accordingly, intrinsic load is related to the difficulty of the task and cannot be altered by the instructor or the instructional tools. Extraneous processing occurs when the learner engages in cognitive processing that does not support the learning objective. The load resulting from extraneous processing, called extraneous load, is increased by poor lay out such as presenting printed words on one page and corresponding pictures on another page. Consequently, extraneous load is related to the design of the instructional materials (introduced in the previous section). Germane processing refers to the processing, construction, and automation of information. By germane processing, the learner engages in deep cognitive processing such as mentally organizing the words and pictures and relating it to prior knowledge. Cognitive load theory is of particular importance for the provision of instruction. In peer tutoring, instruction can relate to the learning task and/or organizational aspects.

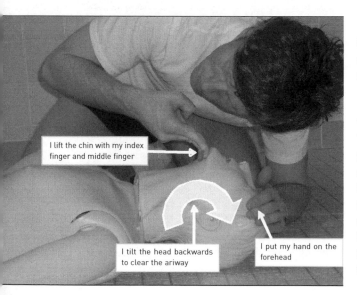

Figure 3. Basic Life Support task card designed with the application of multimedia principles

Task instruction

Task instruction specifically relates to the task to be learned and encompasses information on technical task execution quality, amount of trials, managerial aspects of time etc. Task instruction in physical education goes beyond the scope of this chapter, and is, therefore, not discussed.

Organizational instruction

Organizational instruction (i.e., guidance) generally comprises co-operating features. This type of instruction structures the peer tutoring setting and is of significant importance for the effectiveness of the model. Taking into account information processing theories, such as cognitive load theory and the cognitive theory in multi-media learning, questions concerning the organisation of peer tutoring settings spontaneously arise. Some educational researchers encourage settings in which students work together in groups with no, or minimal, guidance. It was argued that students learn best in a non- or minimally-guided environment where they have to discover or construct knowledge for themselves (Jonassen, 1991; Schmidt, 2000). Advocates of this non- or minimal-guidance approach argue that instructional guidance might interfere with the natural learning processes and learning styles of learners and consequently negatively affect learning outcomes. In addition, they consider learning to be idiosyncratic and, hence, a common instructional format or strategy might be ineffective to enhance individual learning (Steffe & Gale, 1995). On the other hand, an increasing amount of research reveals learning settings with no or minimal guidance to be inferior to guided methods of instruction in helping students learn and transfer (see Kirschner, Sweller & Clark, 2006; Mayer, 2004). This has been explained by arguing that learning environments with no or minimal guidance do not consider human cognitive architecture although it is of prime importance (Kirschner et al., 2006). Research on human cognitive architecture describes long-term memory as the dominant structure in human cognition. It contains a large amount of information that is central to all our cognitive activities. Learning implies the alteration of this long-term memory, which requires inter-action with working memory. Working memory is the cognitive structure in which conscious processing occurs. It is severely limited in capacity and duration as explained by cognitive information processing theories (Chandler & Sweller, 1991). Instructional procedures with no or minimal guidance, then, are argued to overload the working memory. By using working memory to search for problem solutions, less capacity is available for information-processing and learning activities (Kirschner et al., 2006). Thus, it has been stated that providing direct instructional guidance on concepts and (co-operating) procedures to learners with limited prior knowledge in any subject matter is more effective than asking these learners to discover these procedures on their own (Mayer, 2004).

Extrapolating the above mentioned issues to peer tutoring, adequate organisation is worth investigating. Research in cooperative learning suggests that only when structure (i.e., guidance) is implemented so that students understand how they should work together, cooperation and learning are maximized (Johnson & Johnson, 1994). Extending this statement to reciprocal peer tutoring, two main guidance variables affect the structure of this setting: role definition and role switching. Consequently, organizational instruction (i.e., guidance) indirectly addresses co-operating between learners. Next to role switching and role definition, peer assessment is commonly employed during peer learning. These three guidance variables are discussed below.

Role switching

According to Cohen, (1994) role switching fosters a reciprocal exchange in which the output of the observer becomes the input of the doer. Student partners can work in their roles for a specific amount of time or a set number of turns depending on the skill to be learned (Block et al., 1995; Mosston & Ashworth, 2002). This role switching is considered to be an important factor in explaining learning gains in general education settings. Previous research argued that reciprocal roles are intended to promote mutuality in the tutoring process and provide equivalent opportunities for partners to engage in various cognitive and meta-cognitive activities (King, 1998; Mosston & Ashworth, 2002). Implementing role switching ensures equal practice times as a doer and observer, resulting in equal opportunities for giving feedback and practising (Mosston & Ashworth, 2002). In contrast, without role switching, peers have to decide themselves when to switch roles. This could be problematic for peers who are not able to distribute the given practice time according to their individual learning needs and learning pace. One study directly addressing the effect of role switching for learning *Basic Life Support* (Iserbyt, Elen & Behets, 2010) found significantly higher percentages of correct chest compressions immediately after learning with students switching roles compared with a control. At retention test, however, this effect disappeared.

Role definition
Clearly defining roles of observer and doer creates a positive inter-dependence between partners, which means that partners rely on each other to complete the task (Cohen, 1994). This positive inter-dependence is considered to be an essential element of cooperative learning outcomes (Putnam, 1998). It helps to prevent social "loafing" (Johnson & Johnson, 1999), encourages interaction between the observer and doer (Ernst & Byra, 1998), increases student participation and responsibility and leads to conceptual gains (Cohen, 1994). Also, role taking helps to distribute the cognitive load between the two partners by allowing each partner to focus on one particular type of cognitive process to be used (King, 1998). Block and colleagues (1995) stated that roles of doer and observer should be clearly defined. The doer knows exactly what he/she should be working on while the observer knows exactly what components of a skill to look at and what kind of feedback that should be given. Also Dyson (2002) found that roles should be taught explicitly to enhance social and motor learning. In his cooperative learning study, he implemented the role of coach (i.e., observer) and held the student responsible for providing the doer with feedback. In doing so, a sense of respect was developed between learners. Literature investigating the impact of role definition found no significant improvement of learning compared with a control group receiving no role definition (Iserbyt et al., 2010). This finding should be interpreted with caution, since this study had significant limitations. First, the study was conducted with university Kinesiology students, familiar with learning psycho-motor skills in small groups. Second, these students were free to choose a partner with whom they preferred to work. This influences social interactions between partners, and possibly triggers cooperation and learning more compared with partners who are not familiar with one another.

Without guidance on role switching and role definition, partners are free to organize the learning environment themselves. This implies that they need to agree on a large amount of decisions like how to use the task cards (e.g., read silently or aloud; use as instructional and/or feedback tool; etc.), how to practise, when to switch practice turns, and what to do when not practising. Maybe this mutual decision-making in order to organize a peer tutoring setting poses a higher cognitive load on the learners' working memory compared with receiving explicit guidance on how to co-operate. In addition to this self-organization of the learning environment, partners also have to focus on learning the skill. From this point of view, it is suggested that receiving explicit guidance on how to organize a peer tutoring setting with task cards reduces cognitive load and allows learners to focus more on the content to be learned. As a consequence, more space in working memory is available for learning through interaction with the long term memory, resulting in better skill retention. This reasoning is in line with previous research where it was argued that peer tutoring settings can be effective on condition that the organization is adequate (Topping & Ehly, 2001).

From a social constructivist perspective on learning, teaching and learning are highly social activities. Inter-actions with teachers, peers and learning materials like task cards could influence the cognitive and affective development of learners (King, 1998). When learners perform intellectual activities, they dynamically interact with the learning environment, which could support improved performance. Defining how to use the learning tools and how to interact with the partner by means of defining clear roles, might, as a consequence, be advantageous in enhancing learning outcomes. The importance of instructing students how to use learning tools has previously been stressed for learning cardio-pulmonary resuscitation performance in a class-wide peer tutoring setting (Ward & Ward, 1996). It was found that *Basic Life Support* performance increased when student pairs were instructed how to use a task analysis checklist to assist each other and to give feedback. Previous research also indicated that clearly defining roles is beneficial for student learning (Block et al., 1995; Dyson, 2002). In subsequent research by Iserbyt et al. (2010), the isolated implementation of role definition as an instructional guidance variable was not beneficial for learning outcomes. Only when role switching as well as role definition were implemented, was student skill retention enhanced.

Peer-assessment

At present, scholars recommend that students become key participants in the assessment process by tracking their own progress (Marzano, 2006). This implies a greater use of peer and self-assessment, which should be implemented in the instructional process (Shepard, 2001). Although the use of peer assessment is recommended in the psycho-motor domain (Johnson, 2004), research documenting its effect on learning psycho-motor skills is lacking (Hay, 2006). This is in contrast with the interest that this topic has been given in general education research. Similar to self-assessment, research on peer assessment in physical education has been largely focused on the practice of assessment, and less on its impact on student learning (Hay, 2006). Butler and Hodge (2001) implemented peer assessment during a softball unit for an ethnically diverse group of high school students; they concluded that peer assessment enhanced feedback, increased thrust, and that providing feedback was an important behaviour during class. Other research (Richard, Gotbout, Tousignant & Grehaigne, 1999) found that, although very time-intensive and requiring constant prompting, teachers viewed peer assessment favourably in their class.

PEER TUTORING PROCESS

Students enter peer tutoring settings with cognitions through which they view events (Solmon, 2006). These cognitions affect learner behaviour and comprise perceptions about their own and their partner's ability, perceptions of instruction, motivational factors, conceptions about the task to be learned, conceptions related to the environment, prior experiences and so forth. These cognitions can be considered as outcomes from peer tutoring, but also as mediating variables affecting peer tutoring. It is clear that research in learner cognition is very complex, and most data are obtained through self-reports (see Solmon, 2006). As indicated by the arrows in Figure 4, personal cognitions and behaviours are in constant inter-action. These inter-actions are present within the learner himself, and between both learners. For example, a low-confident student enters a peer tutoring setting for learning a motor skill. After some successful trials and positively formulated feedback from a peer, however, this student's feeling of competence and self-confidence might be increased. This in turn affects motor activity (e.g. amount of trials performed) during future learning. On the behavioural level, inter-action between learners is bi-directional as well. For example, if learners have 10 minutes to learn a skill in pairs of doer and helper, then the longer learner A acts as a doer, the less learner B can act as a doer. Between cognitions of learners, to date research documents no proof of inter-actions. Finally, behaviour of learner A influences the cognitions of learner B. By working together with a peer, learners develop cognitions about their partner. Although these cognitions can be based on prior experiences, they are easily subject to change during tutoring as well.

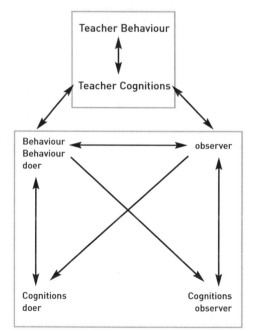

Figure 4. The peer tutoring process in the field of physical education

Teacher behaviour

The implementation of peer tutoring with task cards requires a conceptual shift in teacher functioning (Fullan, 1999), resulting in altered planning, management, and instruction (Dyson & Rubin, 2003). Consequently, this instructional model sometimes obliges teachers to operate outside their comfort zones, with possible negative consequences such as discomfort and anxiety. These could lead to the inability or unwillingness of teachers to delegate responsibility to students (Cohen, 1994). Similarly, little is known about teacher behaviour in student-centred settings and about their influence on practice time and quality of practice. Previous research compared teacher behaviour in student-centred learning with task cards to teacher-centred instruction during a 7-week intervention for learning tennis game play. *Active Learning Time in Physical Education* (ALT-PE) and (collective) instruction were explored (Iserbyt et al., in press). Six different teacher behaviour variables were coded: (1) intervention type - instruction or feedback; (2) intervention target - a sub-group of students or an individual; (3) initiative for intervention taken by the student (or sub-group) or the teacher; (4) intonation of the intervention - notifying or interrogative; (5) contents of the intervention - technique, tactics, regulations, social behaviour, encouragement, annoying behaviour, and a miscellaneous category; and (6) the presence or absence of demonstrations during the teacher interventions. Behavioural analysis revealed that the teacher provided significantly more instruction and less feedback in the student-centred setting compared with the teacher-centred condition. The initial adaptation process for student-centred learning was the main reason for the higher amount of instruction moments. In the first lesson, the teacher often simply repeated the instruction on the task cards to an entire sub-group or a single student. In addition, more instruction moments do not necessarily result in longer instruction as the collective instruction moments in the teacher-centred group were always significantly longer. The lower technical feedback rate in the student-centred condition was due to the regulations on teacher behaviour prescribed in the methodology. Teacher feedback was only allowed by guiding the tutoring student with the help card. All other feedback was delivered equally in both conditions.

Task card implementation and student-centred learning demand serious adaptations for both teacher and students. The teacher needs to adapt to new management and instructional models consistent with teaching using task cards and the students must become less dependent on the teacher and more dependent on the task cards. The higher amount of sub-group re-instruction of task card content in the student-centred group reveals this.

Student behaviour
The study by Iserbyt et al. (in press) implementing tennis game play during student-centred learning encoded student behaviour using a two level structure. Level one denoted the actual function of the student: player or coach. Level two concerned the task orientation of the student. It distinguished three variables: (i) task oriented behaviour; (ii) non-functional behaviour; and (iii) disturbing behaviour. Student behaviour was classified as task-oriented if the expected behaviour was executed at the right time and place, otherwise the behaviour was labelled "non-functional". If classmates showed disturbing behaviour, it was qualified "disturbing". Task-oriented and non-functional behaviour was distinguished for both players and helpers during the four lesson weeks. Results indicated that disturbing behaviour was (almost) completely absent in all lessons. More task-oriented behaviour than non-functional behaviour in each lesson was found. An inter-action effect between condition and role was found, showing more task-oriented and less non-functional behaviour in players compared with helpers in all lessons. Although playing tennis provoked more student attention than the helping tasks did, raw helper scores on task orientation were high and definitely showed a beneficial impact of task cards on students' functional behaviour. Besides the impact on quality and quantity of instruction, this influence on task orientation and motivation for tutors in a peer mediated environment is an issue worth considering when using task cards in student-centred learning environments.

In explaining the effectiveness of peer tutoring, researchers have stressed the importance of behaviour and verbal interactions during learning. Mosston and Ashworth (2002) argued that reciprocal peer tutoring promotes natural learning situations and opportunities for students to socialize among peers, and actively engage in learning through problem solving. In general education, studies have used specific tutorial arrangements, tutor-tutee roles and tutorial procedures to promote success in tutoring (e.g., Fantuzzo, Riggio, Connelly & Dimeff, 1989; Person & Graesser, 1999). These tutorial structures influence how partners in a tutoring pair interact with each other and that interaction in turn influences learning. In peer tutoring, students primarily interact with each other and the learning tools (i.e., task cards). Consequently, improved inter-action with peer and task cards should enhance learning outcomes.

Research on the effect of tutorial structures on student behaviour is almost non-existent. Iserbyt (2010) analysed student behaviour and inter-actions in four different tutoring settings for learning *Basic Life Support* with task cards. Settings differed in the implementation of tutorial structures: role switching, role definition, both role switching and role definition, and a control group without tutorial arrangements. Several behaviours were defined based on co-operating features. These behaviours generally comprised: (a) individual behaviours, such as help seeking and observing; and (b) inter-active behaviours like instructing, giving feedback, asking for help, motor performance and assessment strategies. The frequency and total percentage of time these behaviours occurred were analyzed and linked to the learning outcomes. Particular attention was paid to the control group in this study, where no guidance was implemented. This group provided data of the learning process not previously recorded when two people are assigned to learn a psycho-motor task like *Basic Life Support* in 20 minutes with task cards as learning tools, and without any guidance on the co-operation procedure. It was found that in this group, the frequency and percentage of time spent on help seeking activities (e.g., reading the task cards individually in silence) was significantly higher compared with the most guided setting. Although it should be acknowledged that help seeking is not necessarily negative as behaviour, it might become detrimental for learning when it occupies too much working memory. Without guidance, students spend a lot of time trying to make sense of the information they receive, thereby, placing high demands on their working memory. In addition, from a social constructivist perspective, it can be argued that in order to facilitate learning, verbal interactions are recommended. While seeking help, no verbal inter-actions took place.

When receiving guidance on role switching and role definition, learners divided their learning time in motor time-on-task (30%), instructing their partner (15%), task-oriented observing (15%), cognitive assessment (10%), cognitive-motor assessment (10%), irrelevant behaviour (8%), help seeking (i.e., reading the task cards in silence) (4%), and giving unsolicited feedback based on task card content (3%). Cognitive assessment implies verbally rehearsing the task, discussing critical steps, interrogating and so forth. Cognitive-motor assessment on the other hand includes cognitive assessment with additional motor practice. Results also showed that students receiving guidance on role switching and role definition had a significant lower frequency but a significant higher total percentage of motor activity. It seems that instructional guidance comprising role switching and role definition is beneficial for increasing motor learning time in peer tutoring. Also, with guidance on role switching and role definition, significantly less irrelevant questions are asked and more time is spent giving instructions. This could indicate that with more adequate guidance, students are more focused on the task to be learned, and have a better understanding on how the learning setting works. Previous observational research in cooperative learning from Gillies (2003) indicated that children in structured, guided groups provided more solicited and unsolicited explanations than their counterparts in the unstructured, unguided groups. For giving adequate instructions and feedback, the helper should consult the task cards. Therefore, defining roles linked to the use of task cards could enhance learning for both helper and doer because of the improved inter-action between peers and task cards. This inter-action with the learning environment is crucial for learning according to social constructivist learning theories.

Gender effects in behaviours and verbal interactions have previously been described in educational psychology. Charlesworth and Dzur (1987) stated that girls generally exhibit more sensitivity to their partner than do boys and prefer to engage in teaching and learning activities or sharing (e.g., instructing). Boys, on the other hand, are more ego-oriented and prefer to direct their energy to the individual acquisition of knowledge (e.g., motor time-on-task). In physical eduaction, d'Arripe-Longueville et al. (1995) reported that boys trained more and consequently performed better than girls, who in turn adopted higher learning goals and gave more verbal instructions. Further research is recommended on this matter.

PEER TUTORING OUTCOMES

Peer tutoring outcomes encompass a broad range of competencies. Depending on the educational objective, peer tutoring can address motor, cognitive, social, and affective goals. Several studies have supported the contribution of peer learning for social, cognitive and motor learning (Barrett, 2000; Johnson, Bjorkland & Krotee, 1984). Ward and Lee (2005) stated that most studies in peer tutoring assessed psycho-motor goals. Additionally, peer tutoring has been demonstrated to be an effective model for social and cognitive learning (Olson, 1990). The effect of peer tutoring on affective outcomes has been investigated in a limited amount of studies. In general, these studies assessed affective constructs such as self-esteem and self-efficacy by means of psycho-metric inventories, interviews or surveys. Ernst and Byra (1998) found that working with a peer was a positive experience and enhanced social interactions among students.

Physical education curricula necessitate teachers to address motor as well as social goals in everyday practice. The pursuit and achievement of social goals aim at teaching students meaningful social skills, applicable in their future life and work environment, and promoting lifelong learning. In the teacher-centred model of instruction, where the teacher autonomously takes all content, managerial, and instructional decisions, little space is left for emphasizing social goals. Therefore, student-centred settings like reciprocal peer tutoring with task cards are often put forward as instructional models capable of addressing both these academic and social goals.

CONCLUSION

In this chapter, a research model for peer tutoring with task cards has been presented. The model encompasses peer tutoring as an instructional model, the learning process, and the peer tutoring outcomes. Significant variables have been highlighted and connections with the literature made. Special attention has been given to task card use and development, and organizational instruction. Also, the research model provides directions for future study. Continuing research in the area of peer tutoring with task cards is relevant, as this model has the potential to achieve motor, social, affective, and cognitive goals. These goals are the core business for every physical education teacher.

REFERENCES

d'Arripe-Longueville, F., Fleurance, P., & Winnykamen, F. (1995). Effects of the degree of competence symmetry-asymmetry in the acquisition of a motor skill in a dyad. *Journal of Human Movement Studies, 28*, pp.255-273.

d'Arripe-Longueville, F., Huet, M.L., Gernigon, C., Winnykamen, F., and Cadopi, M. (2002). Peer assisted learning in the physical activity domain: dyad type and gender differences. *Journal of Sport and Exercise Psychology. 24*, pp.219–238.

Barrett, T. (2000). *Effects of two cooperative learning strategies on academic learning time, student performance, and social behaviour of sixth grade physical education students.* Unpublished doctoral dissertation, University of Nebraska, Lincoln.

Barrett, T. (2005). Effects of cooperative learning on the performance of sixth-grade physical education students. *Journal of Teaching in Physical Education, 24*, pp.88-102.

Block, M.E., Oberweiser, B., & Bain, M. (1995). Using classwide peer tutoring to facilitate inclusion of students with disabilities in regular physical education. *Physical Educator, 52*(1), p.47.

Butler, S A., & Hodge, S. R. (2001). Enhancing student trust through peer assessment in physical education. *Physical Educator, 58* (1), pp.30-42.

Byra, M. (2006). Teaching styles and inclusive pedagogies. In: D. Kirk, D. Macdonald & M. O'Sullivan (Eds.), *The Handbook of Physical Education.* London, Sage Publications Ltd. pp.449-466.

Byra, M. (2004). Applying a task progression to the reciprocal style of teaching. *Journal of Physical Education, Recreation and Dance, 75*(2), pp.42-46.

Byra, M., & Marks, M.C. (1993). The effect of two pairing techniques on specific feedback and comfort levels of learners in the reciprocal style of teaching. *Journal of Teaching in Physical Education, 12*(3), pp.286-300.

Chandler, P., & Sweller, J. (1991). Cognitive load theory and the format of instruction. *Cognition and Instruction, 8*, pp.293-332.

Charlesworth, W.R., & Dzur, D. (1987). Gender comparisons of preschoolers' behavior and resource utilization in group problem solving. *Child Development, 58*, pp.191-200.

Cohen, E.G. (1994). *Designing groupwork: Strategies for the heterogeneous classroom* (2nd ed.). New York, Teachers College Press.

Cothran, D., & Kulinna, P.H. (2006). Students' perspectives on direct, peer, and inquiry teaching strategies. *Journal of Teaching in Physical Education, 25*(2), pp.166-181.

DeLeeuw, K.E., & Mayer, R.E. (2008). A comparison of three measures of cognitive load: Evidence for separable measures of intrinsic, extraneous, and germane load. *Journal of Educational Psychology, 100*(1), pp.223-234.

DePaepe, J.L. (1985). The influence of three last restrictive environments on the content motor-ALT and performance of moderately mentally retarded students. *Journal of Teaching in Physical Education, 5,* pp.34-41.

Dochy, F.J., & Alexander, P.A. (1995). Mapping prior knowledge: A framework for discussion among researchers. *European Journal of Psychology of Education, 10,* pp.225-242.

Dyson, B. (2002). The implementation of cooperative learning in an elementary physical education program. *Journal of Teaching in Physical Education, 22,* pp.69-85.

Dyson, B., & Rubin, A. (2003). Implementing cooperative learning in elementary physical education. *Journal of Physical Education Recreation and Dance, 74*(1), pp.48-54.

Ernst, M., & Byra, M. (1998). Pairing learners in the reciprocal style of teaching: Influence on student skill, knowledge and socialization. *Physical Educator, 55,* pp.24-37.

Fantuzzo, J.W., King, J.A., & Heller, L.R. (1992). Effects of reciprocal peer tutoring on mathematics and school adjustment: a component analysis. *Journal of Educational Psychology, 84,* pp.331-339.

Fantuzzo, J.W., Riggio, R.E., Connelly, S., & Dimeff, L.A. (1989). Effects of reciprocal peer tutoring on academic achievement and psychological adjustment: A component analysis. *Journal of Educational Psychology, 81,* pp.173-177.

Fuchs, L., Fuchs, D., Bentz, J., Phillips, N., & Hammlett, C. (1994). The nature of student interactions during peer tutoring with and without prior training and experience. *American Educational Research Journal, 31,* pp.75-103.

Fullan, M. (1999). *Change forces: The sequel.* London, Falmer Press.

Gillies, R.M. (2003). Structuring cooperative group work in classrooms. International *Journal of Educational Research, 39,* pp.35-49.

Hay, P.J. (2006). Assessment for learning in physical education. In: D. Kirk, D. Macdonald, & M. O'Sullivan (Eds.), *The Handbook of Physical Education.* London, Sage Publications Ltd. pp. 312-325.

Houston-Wilson, C., Dunn, J.M., van der Mars, H., & McCubbin, J. (1997). The effect of peer tutors on motor performance in integrated physical education classes. *Adapted Physical Activity Quarterly, 14,* pp.298-313.

Iserbyt, P. (2010). *Reciprocal peer tutoring with task cards. Fostering learning outcomes for learning psychomotor tasks.* Unpublished doctoral dissertation, Katholieke Universiteit Leuven, Belgium.

Iserbyt, P., Elen, J., Behets, D. (2010). Instructional guidance in reciprocal peer tutoring with task cards. *Journal of Teaching in Physical Education, 29*(1), pp.38-53.

Iserbyt, P., Elen, J., & Behets, D. (2009). Peer evaluation in reciprocal learning with task cards for acquiring Basic Life Support (BLS). *Resuscitation, 80*(12), pp.1394-1398.

Iserbyt, P., Madou, B., Vergauwen, L., & Behets, D. (2009). Effects of peer mediated instruction on motor skill acquisition in tennis. *Journal of Teaching in Physical Education* (in press).

Johnson, R. (2004). Peer assessments in physical education. *Journal of Physical Education, Recreation, and Dance, 75*(8), pp.33-40.

Johnson, M., & Ward, P. (2001). Effects of classwide peer tutoring on correct performance of striking skills in 3rd grade physical education. *Journal of Teaching in Physical Education, 20,* pp.247-263.

Johnson, D.W., & Johnson, R.T. (1994). *Learning together and alone. Cooperative, competitive, and individualistic learning* (4th ed.). Needham Heights, MA, Allyn and Bacon.

Johnson, D.W., & Johnson, R.T. (1999). Making cooperative learning work. *Theory into Practice, 38,* p.67.

Johnson, R.T., Bjorkland, R., & Krotee, M. (1984). The effects of cooperative, competitive, and individualistic student interaction patterns on the achievement and attitudes of students learning the golf skill of putting. *Research Quarterly for Exercise and Sport, 55,* pp.129-134.

Jonassen, D. (1991). Objectivism vs. constructivism. *Educational Technology Research and Development, 39*(3), pp.5-14.

Juell, C. (1996). Learning to learn from effective tutors. In: L. Schauble & R. Glaser (Eds.), *Innovations in learning: New environments for education.* Mahwah, NJ. Erlbaum. pp.49-74.

King, A. (1998). Transactive peer tutoring: Distributing cognition and metacognition. *Educational Psychology Review, 10,* pp.57-74.

King, A., Staffieri, A., & Adelgais, A. (1998). Mutual peer tutoring: Effects of structuring tutorial interaction to scaffold peer learning. *Journal of Educational Psychology, 90,* pp.134.

Kirschner, P.A., Sweller, J., & Clark, R.E. (2006). Why minimal guidance during instruction does not work: An analysis of the failure of constructivist, discovery, problem-based, experiential, and inquiry-based teaching. *Educational Psychologist, 41,* pp.75-86.

Lee, M., & Ward, P. (2002). Peer Tutoring: Student-centered learning in physical education for the 21st century. *Teaching Elementary Physical Education, 13*(4), pp.16-17.

Lirgg, C.D., & Feltz, D.L. (1991). Teacher versus peer models revisited: Effects on motor performance. *Research Quarterly for Exercise and Sport, 62,* pp.217-224.

Lou, Y., Abrami, P.C., Spence, J.C., Poulsen, C., Chambers, B., & d'Apollonia, S. (1996). Within-class grouping: A meta-analysis. *Review of Educational Research, 66,* pp.423-458.

Maheady, L. (1998). Advantages and disadvantages of peer-assisted learning strategies. In: K. Topping, & S. Ehly (Eds.), *Peer-assisted learning.* Mahwah, NJ, Erlbaum. pp.45-65.

Marzano, R.J. (2006). *Classroom assessment & grading that works.* Alexandria, VA: Association for Supervision and Curriculum Development.

Mayer, R.E. (2005). *The Cambridge handbook of multimedia learning.* New York, Cambridge University Press.

Mayer, R.E. (2004). Should there be a three-strikes rule against pure discovery learning? The case for guided methods of instruction. *American Psychologist, 59,* pp.14-19.

McCullagh, P., & Caird, J.K. (1990). Correct and learning models and the use of the model knowledge of results in the acquisition and retention of a motor skill. *Journal of Human Movement Studies, 18,* pp.107-116.

McCullagh, P., & Meyer, K.N. (1997). Learning versus correct models: Influence of model type on the learning of a free-weight squat lift. *Research Quarterly for Exercise and Sport, 68,* pp.56-61.

McCullagh, P., & Weiss, M.R. (2001). Modeling: Considerations for motor skill performance and psychological responses. In: R.N. Singer, H.A. Hausenblas, & C.M. Janelle (Eds.), *Handbook of research on sport psychology.* New York, Wiley. pp.205-238.

Metzler, M.W., Lund, J.L., & Gurvitch, R. (2008). Adoption of instructional innovation across teachers' career stages. *Journal of Teaching in Physical Education, 27*(4), pp.457-465.

Moreno, R., & Mayer, R.E. (2007). Interactive multimodal learning environments. *Educational Psychology Review, 19,* pp.309-326.

Mosston, M., & Ashworth, S. (2002). T*eaching physical education.* (5th ed.) San Francisco, Benjamin Cummings.

Olson, V. (1990). The revising processes of sixth-grade writers with and without peer feedback. *Journal of Educational Research, 84*(1), pp.22-29.

Pea, R.D. (1994). Seeing what we build together: Distributed multimedia learning environments for transformative communications. *Journal of the Learning Sciences, 3,* pp.285-299.

Person, N.K., & Graesser, A.C. (1999). Evolution of discourse in cross-age tutoring. In: A.M. O'Donnell & A. King (Eds.), *Cognitive perspectives on peer learning*. Mahwah, NJ, Erlbaum. pp. 69-86.

Putnam, J.W. (1998). *Cooperative learning and strategies for inclusion: Celebrating diversity in the classroom* (2nd ed.). Baltimore, Brookes.

Richard, J-F., Gotbout, P., Tousignant, M., & Grehaigne, J-F. (1999). The try-out of a team sport performance assessment procedure in elementary and junior high school physical education classes. *Journal of Teaching in Physical Education, 18*(3), pp.336-356.

Roscoe, R.D., & Chi, M.T.H. (2007). Understanding tutor learning: Knowledge-building and knowledge-telling in peer tutor's explanations and questions. *Review of Educational Research, 77*(4), pp.534-574.

Salomon, G., Perkins, D.N., & Globerson, T. (1991). Partners in cognition: Extending human intelligence with intelligent technologies. *Educational Researcher, 20*(3), pp.2-9.

Schunk, D.H., Hanson, A.R., & Cox, P.D. (1987). Peer-models attributes and achievement behaviours. *Journal of Educational Psychology, 79*, pp.54-61.

Schmidt, H.G. (2000). Assumptions underlying self-directed learning may be false. *Medical Education, 34*, pp.243-245.

Shepard L. (2001). The role of classroom assessment in teaching and learning. In: V. Richardson (Ed.), *Handbook of Research on Teaching* (4th ed.). Washington, D.C., American Educational Research Association. (pp.1066-1101).

Solmon, M. (2006). Learner cognition. In: D. Kirk, D. Macdonald & M. O'Sullivan (Eds.), *The Handbook of Physical Education*. London, Sage Publications Ltd. pp. 449-466.

Steffe, L., & Gale, J. (1995). *Constructivism in education*. Hillsdale, NJ, Lawrence Erlbaum Associates, Inc.

Sweller, J. (2005). Implications of cognitive load theory for multimedia learning. In: R.E. Mayer (Ed.), *The Cambridge handbook of multimedia learning*. New York, Cambridge University Press. pp.19-30.

Topping, K.J. (2005). Trends in peer learning. *Educational Psychology, 25*, pp.631-645.

Topping, K.J., & Ehly, S.W. (2001). Peer assisted learning: A framework for consultation. *Journal of Educational and Psychological Consultation, 12*, pp.113-132.

Ward, P. (1994). An experimental analysis of skill responding in physical education high school accountability. (Doctoral dissertation, Ohio State University, 1993). *Dissertation Abstracts International, 54*, 2950A.

Ward, P., & Lee, M.A. (2005). Peer-assisted learning in physical education: A review of theory and research. *Journal of Teaching in Physical Education, 24*, pp.205-225.

Ward, P., & Ward, M.C. (1996). The effects of classwide peer tutoring on correct cardiopulmonary resuscitation performance by physical education majors. *Journal of Behavioural Education, 6*(3), pp.331-342.

Webb, N.M. (1992). Testing a theoretical model of student interaction and learning in small groups. In: R. Hertz-Lazarowitz & N. Miller (Eds.), *Interaction in cooperative groups: The theoretical anatomy of group learning*. New York, Cambridge University Press. pp.102-119.

Weiss, M.R., McCullagh, P., Smith, A.L., & Berlant, A.R. (1998). Observational learning and the fearful child: Influence of peer models on swimming skill performance and psychological responses. *Research Quarterly for Exercise and Sport, 69*, pp.380-394.

CHAPTER 9

"TUNING UP" PHYSICAL EDUCATION FOR MULTI-CULTURAL NEEDS OF MODERN SCHOOLS

MALGORZATA BRONIKOWSKA

INTRODUCTION

The globalization of human communities bringing people closer together generates a propensity for both benefits and problems such as a disconnection between what people desire and realisation of that desire. Although people can touch almost anything (at least so it seems on the silver screens), they can scarcely experience it all. The process of global integration conceptualised as a form of "global village" has caused a shrinking and levelling of all spheres of human activity and endeavour and what was once regarded as stable, is now less so and arguably at a "tipping point", if not already over the edge, with a consequent loss of individual pride and feeling of national or cultural identification. In a broader sense, the "McDonaldization" of life may have transcended a wall of cultural re-actionism. Fundamental differences in understanding of universal values brought to multi-religious and multi-cultural "melting pots" of modern multi-national societies have resulted in a lack of "ludo-diversity" a concept which explains the mechanisms of extinction, survival and invention of movement cultures and to warn against modern sport mono-culture (Renson, 2004).

Cultures (for example, some Asian cultures) developed upon virtues based on doing good in one's moral life time differ from those (for example, some Western cultures) based on individual thriving for reward in one's immortal life, though in both cases not always necessarily following their own moral standards. But

> "cultural relativism does not imply normlessness for oneself, nor for one's society. It does call for suspending judgment when dealing with groups or societies different from one's own. One should think twice before applying the norms of one person, group, or society to another. Information about the nature of the cultural differences between societies, their roots, and their consequences should precede judgment and action" (Hofstede and Hofstede, 2005, p.6).

Therefore, the call for "back-to-basics" forms of physical education, conceptualizing physical education as the development of non-cognitive and narrowly sport-related fundamental motor skills and physical fitness is a cause for concern in its apparent lack of meaningfulness in many children's lives, the allegedly unauthentic ways in which physical education practices relate to other social practices, and by reports of children's alienation from physical activity, from their bodies and from themselves (Graham, 1995). Peters (1966) went even further when he observed that:

> "curriculum activities, on the other hand, such as science or history, literary appreciation, and poetry are 'serious' in that they illuminate other areas of life and contribute much to the quality of living. They have, secondly, a wide ranging cognitive content which distinguishes them from games. Skills, for instance, do

not have a wide ranging content. There is very little to know about riding a bicycle, swimming, or golf. It is largely a matter of 'knowing how' rather than of 'knowing that', of knack rather than of understanding" (p.159)

Part of what is at issue here is not only the role and function of sport and games, but the meanings attached to them. As already alluded to above, new technologies have radically altered participation in, and attitudes toward, physical activity. Front and centre in this regard has been the role played by television. The most typical viewpoint in this debate is the common refrain that an over-indulgence in watching TV has produced a sedentary society which, in turn, contributes to growing rates of obesity. Contrary to the readily prescribed assumptions, however, scholars such as Biddle et al. (2004) have noted how television viewing is largely uncorrelated with physical activity amongst children and youths, a feature borne out in other studies. Without wishing to revisit this debate, I would suggest that it serves to obscure how television has altered our relationship with physical activity in potentially more fundamental ways. This is particularly true of sport wherein we have increasingly become less as participants than as spectators, a situation that is more than merely suggesting that we are now more likely to watch rather than to play. It also serves to emphasize that it is now through the media coverage of sport that particular meanings and values associated with physical culture are produced and most widely disseminated. In and of itself, this is not necessarily dangerous, but it does pose a threat simply because what we value in sport on our screens, what keeps us glued to the set, is today more often than not likely to be forms of sport that Rowe (1995) has described as "the regulated expression of physical culture" (p.104). Put differently, the media only offer an increasingly limited view of the realm of sporting and physical experience. Tied to the market, the media offers little other than "achievement" or "Prolympic" Games as they strive to attract viewer attention.

Questions arise as such as how all this is reflected in the schooling process, and how this could be challenged and used in the process of formatting some universal principle like respect, peace and trust or love of others. My hypothesis is that this change provides a unique opportunity to reduce the potential tensions and broaden cultural understanding through traditional, playful activities and positive emotional engagement. Sports, many "traditional" sports in particular, have fallen by the wayside as legitimacy has been measured less by social value than media interest. This is, of course, a trend broader than the Olympics. Few children today probably know of sports other than those mainstream or standard ones practised in school or seen on television. Names like *kabbadi, gorodki, pelota, bocce* or *ring-ball* probably do not ring any bells for the vast majority of people. Television has enlarged the audience for sport while lowering the quality of the audience's understanding. There is a pressing need then to critically examine the measures by which sport is "valued". I do not wish to sound more mythical than historical here in suggesting that we are presently witnessing a decline in some kind of golden (sporting) age. Rather, I am suggesting that physical educators need to promote critical thinking and questioning about physical culture within society, part of which should be about understanding the ethos, rituals, traditions and internal goods of physical activities outside the usually recognized boundaries of "sport". Opening the minds of students to alternative forms of physical activity, near-forgotten traditional physical practices, and/or sports from other cultures could have a particular value – keeping children and tradition on the move. In the midst of the current dynamic changes, visible both in social relationships and daily habits, increasingly more often we hear calls for more extensive research of folk traditions in order to revive local sports and games. Renson (2004) commented that "ethnicity" (the cultural value of movement in play and traditional game) and "ludo-diversity" (the value of diversity in play and traditional game) provide new impulses to education through movement (p.165). Moreover, Reid (1997) believes that:

"In the context of games teaching, this reflects the traditional principle that fair play, sportsmanship and respect for one's opponent take precedence over the competitive objectives of winning and avoiding defeat [...] games and sports are forms of play, aimed essentially at promoting pleasure enjoyment, excitement, recreation, and the like, their primary value, in short, is hedonic. Winning from this point of view, is not, as is sometimes supposed, the ultimate goal of competitive games: enjoyment is, and competitive action, structured in highly specific ways by the operation of the norms, rules, codes, conventions and so on of the various particular sports and games, it the way in which the conditions of enjoyment are fulfilled, its possibilities realized" (p.12).

However, this matter is by no means new. In the 18th century, Joseph Strutt (1749-1802), an English ethnographer, anthropologist and historian, was probably the first to be seriously interested in describing English folk sports and recreational past-times. Hence, his work laid the foundations for future historical and ethnographic research in this area. In his most important book, *Sports and Pastimes of the People of England* (1801), he wrote:

"In order to form a just estimation of the character of any particular people, it is absolutely necessary to investigate the Sports and Pastimes most generally prevalent among them. War, policy, and other contingent circumstances, may effectually place men, at different times, in different points of view, but, when we follow them into their retirements, where no disguise is necessary, we are most likely to see them in their true state, and may best judge of their natural dispositions" (p.1).

A similar way of thinking about traditions in physical culture (the roots of plays[1], games and sports) was represented some time later by another leading British folklorist and a pioneer in the study of children's games, Alice Bertha Gomme (1853-1938), with her work *The Traditional Games of England, Scotland and Ireland* (1894). In Poland it was the researcher, Eugeniusz Piasecki (1872-1947), who took the matter seriously in his 1916 published work *Zabawy i gry ruchowe dzieci i młodzieży* ("Play and Games for Children and Youth"). He had argued earlier (Piasecki, 1911) that each man could only truly become himself through play, and only during play. Even Pierre de Coubertin (1863-1937), the French pedagogue and historian, advocated the promotion of traditional, national games as an idea to apply indigenous games and old sports. Indeed, this was the original idea behind his dreams of reviving the modern Olympic Games. The motto "All Games all Nations" was supposed to be the most important one among the values of neo-Olympism emphasised by de

---

1 Play here means a form of physical, playful activity, and a very first variety of game and sport. It refers to a range of spontaneous, voluntary, frivolous and non-serious activity.

Coubertin. At the 1904 Olympics in St Louis, USA, he unveiled an initiative, called "Anthropological Days", which were organized mainly for the participants from Africa, Asia and South America, who were supposed to present their regional games as a form of recognition of heritage of their unique cultures. Unfortunately the reality proved to be very different from de Coubertin's idea. The organizers arranged the days separately from the Olympic events, which marginalized the cultural festival and effectively reduced it to the "racial" games. The event was far removed from Coubertin's vision of presenting characteristic national events during the Olympic programme with the same respect to other culture, religion, political options or race. As a result, de Coubertin withdrew from pushing for the inclusion of traditional games as a part of the Olympic Games (Liponśki, 2003). More recently, Lorain Barbarash (1997), author of the book *Multicultural Games*, claimed that "a good way to explore other cultures and learn more about one's own is through play. […]. A multi-cultural, multi-ethnic approach to education provides children with information they can use to form opinions and practices for they own lives" (p.7).

These ideas have been integrated in regular research studies. The Flemish Catholic University of Leuven in Belgium was the first university which developed traditional games research, starting in the late 1970s. This academic enterprise had a background in the socio-cultural movement leading towards Flemish self-determination against the French (Wallon) supremacy of the Belgian state (Smulders, 1981). A similar situation brought attention to the rural games of Brittany in France (Floc'h & Fanch, 1987) and then in different parts of Spain as well. Folk sports became active manifestations of regional identity, particularly in the Basque Country (Aguirre, 1978), Catalonia (Lavega, 2003) and on the Canary Islands. All these initiatives influenced the foundation of *The European Traditional Sport and Games Association* (ETSGA) in 2001 (Jaouen, 2006). Additionally, in the late 1980s when former Soviet bloc regimes fell, central and eastern European folk sports were provided with an opportunity to be revitalized in many parts of the region (Liponśki, 1996). Totally different circumstances made Danish scholars aware of preserving traditional games: after becoming aware of the economic and political changes which inclined towards placing children in day-care institutions, they started to explore old games to make them usable for a new means of education through "the common heritage of humanity" (Eichberg & Nørgaard, 2005). Such concepts have potential for offering true value in school curricula but need to be revitalised and incorporated into today's physical education process. According to McNamee (2008)

> "While the argument is long on initiation into those practices that are partly definitive of a culture and its identity (-ies) it is short on the kinds of individualised, health-related activities. Historically, there have been two strands in what is called physical education: sport and health (in older times hygiene, posture and so forth). Health may seem socially 'valuable' but there are conceptualizing problems to turn it sufficiently into 'educational'. With sport it seems the other way round – this could be educational, but difficult to make it recognized as valuable" (p.23).

Thus, physical educators need to act sensibly about the base of its traditional roots to re-create new opportunities. Lack of these concepts in earlier physical education curricula has raised a number of complex and searching questions, the most obvious being the extent to which we ourselves as physical educators are part of the problem (our lack of appropriate knowledge) and what the best approach is to redressing our deficiencies on that subject. The basic problem is how the social and cultural imperatives of physical education have been increasingly disregarded. McNamee (2008) indicated that "where games are taught properly, ethical notions such as equality, fairness, honesty and rule-abiding action necessarily arise, but the problem is in the answer to the issue of the extent to which these notions are merely caught rather than taught is another matter" (p.18). Anyone can observe what has happened to traditional playful activities that once were the "core" of any human socializing processes.

THE VALUE OF TRADITIONAL GAMES

Johan Huizinga, a Dutch historian, cultural theorist and professor of anthropology, in his work *Homo Ludens* (1938, republished 1955), claimed that play is a prime source of man's culture. He argued that play is not a simple activity undertaken to entertain children, but it is also a universal social and cultural phenomenon enveloped by wider structures and processes of society. Furthermore play was considered an integral part of human social and cultural life. In recent times, Thomas Henricks (2006) has suggested adding a sociological and anthropological perspective to play because, as he claims, it provides yet another way of looking at it. In this sense, "play" means a form of physical, playful activity, in a way originating a variety of many present day games and sports. It refers to a range of spontaneous, voluntary, frivolous and non-serious activities. Some play exhibits neither goals nor rules and is considered to be "unstructured", yet it is still of educational value in the process of socializing oneself early on entering social structures and in this sense *playing* differs from *sporting*. Henricks (2006) points out that sport has increasingly become compartmentalized, rigid, and highly organized in its promotion of "sterile excellence" and, despite the fact that sport is based on a play, it has "stiffened into seriousness", and even though it has cultural prominence, it functions as a "profane diversion" at selected levels. Going even further and quoting Bronikowski (2000):

> "... It is in the capitalistic system that an individual strengthens his social position at the sacrifice of other members of the same society and this spinning circle demands more and more efficiency in such a rivalry. Success achieved at any costs explain it all – cruelty, aggression and cunning (various kinds of cheating and trickery). It leads to a 'rat race' in all life domains. Expansion of sport brought along mass popularity but values, once attached to the exclusively privileged elite, got mixed up with values of the lower social classes. Rapid development of communication only helped to spread more information and broadened its range. But it was the negative influences of every life that deformed the nature of sport, although it is difficult to say whether cheating, aggression or medial manipulation infiltrated sport or was it the other way round. Is therefore sport a mirror of the culture of the society or is it its culture pictured in sport?" (p.58).

However, this could all change if physical education teachers were to seek out a wide range of activities rooted in the cultures of their multi-national classes. The idea of re-introducing traditional sports and games could provide an interesting platform for multi-cultural integration, certainly refreshing the so-called standard teaching contents. Even in Ancient times, Greek philosopher, Plato, used to say that "one learns more about a human being by one hour of playing than by talking during a whole year". The idea hidden within traditional activities is not to organize yet another race (adding to the development of a "rat race"/materialistic generation) but to re-introduce universal values by arranging a playful context of traditional games. With the restoration of traditional games in schools, the usual stereotypes of the one-sidedness of sport (and physical education) could be challenged.

If the variety of play and games represents the commonwealth of the peoples of the world each reduction of their popularity is a threat against all of us/all of our cultures. That is why, if bio-diversity is the value for the survival of life, then ludo-diveristy is the value of play and games for the survival of culture (Eichberg 2005). According to UNESCO (2002), this is the common heritage of humanity and should be recognized and affirmed for future generations. Pierre Parlebas (2003), a French professor of humanistic and sociology science, expressed the cultural diversity of games noting that:

> "social group and people in general distinguish themselves as much by their games as they do by their languages and yet the Scottish *caber tossing*, American *baseball*, English *cricket*, Basque *pelote*, African dugout *races* or the Afghan *buzkashi* are practices that are as distinctive as their homes or the structure of their genetic heritage" (p.16).

Today, in order to create a healthy society, we need to reflect on its multi-cultural foundations, which should be taken seriously when planning long-term changes in education, including physical education. The inclusion of regional, traditional folk play and games (in the *ludic* sense believed to be valuable pieces of national cultural heritage) lead accordingly to a reassessment of pedagogical and psychological principles, which may be a refreshing concept. Traditional games can be the bearers of innovative, enriching ideas, the introduction of which can serve as an example to other regions, countries and continents seeking to launch similar action with regard to traditional games, understood as instruments for entertainment, socialization and education (Jaouen, 2006). This is what physical education ought to do to bring out the full value of this heritage and so help to create a space where people can truly live well, in harmony with different cultural expressions, building bridges between cultures and enhancing mutual understanding.

MULTI-CULTURALISM IN SCHOOL PHYSICAL EDUCATION CLASSES

McNamee (2008) argues that:

> "If we agree on the philosophical point that to be physically educated, what one knows must characterize the way one acts in the world, then as physical educators, it is our duty to both habitualise children into patterns of activity and engagement with social practices such as hockey and basketball, and to open up to our students the significant sporting inheritance of our cultures so that they too may come to savour its joys and frustrations and to know a little about the aspects

of the cultures which sporting practices instantiate (for no one would seriously deny their enormous significance in modern societies" (p.15)

As mentioned above, the realization and acceptance of importance of historical play and games, led to the establishment of the *European Traditional Sport and Games Association* in 2001. Long before that, during one of UNESCO's meetings in Paris, popularization of traditions of different cultures was considered one of the main objectives. Traditional games were recognized as a symbol of

"a cultural community, expressed by a group or individuals and recognized as reflecting the expectations of a community in so far as they reflect its cultural and social identity; its standards and values are transmitted orally, by imitation or by other means. Its forms are, among others, language, literature, music, dance, games, mythology, rituals, customs, handicrafts, architecture and other arts" (UNESCO 1990, p.254).

In short it was what Perlebas (2005) expressed in his work when he indicated that:

"... [Traditional] Games are the creation of a culture and the fruit of history.[...] [Their] are generally seen as community heritage; but we should not forget forms of enjoyment, of sharing the pleasure of acting together: we must not forget games! [...] they reflect the deep social roots of different ways of behaving, of communicating with others and entering into contact with the environment. Linked to secular beliefs, performed according to traditional rites and ceremonies, inspired by practices from everyday life, physical games from part of cultural heritage. [...] And this heritage is highly diverse and exuberant" (p.15).

Put simply, it is vital that traditional play and games should be included in modern physical education and sport curricula, in the range of settings within which they are practised. Opponents of legitimization of physical education in school curricula argue that physical education is not dealing adequately and systematically in facing the problem of differentiation of ethnic and cultural backgrounds among schools' pupils. Some (Taylor & Doherty, 2005) claim that pupils from ethnic minority groups are either less active in their new life situations or quite the opposite, are over-reacting. Communication among them is usually fraught and can be tense, and often causes emotional disorders, aggression or other behavioural problems. Without sufficient pedagogical help from school authorities, these pupils feel marginalised, lonely and helpless, and so do their teachers. There have been, however, some initiatives to introduce change in the situation through encouragement of involvement of both pupils and teachers, reflecting some recent trends in regionalism and ludo-diversity.

At present, in many European countries, national physical education curricula have been based mainly on mainstream sports such as basketball, football, handball, netball, gymnastics and track and field (Bronikowski, et al., 2008). Though it is true that some countries have included or try (or have tried) to introduce a small range of national sports (for example cricket or rugby in British schools), most of them provide only basic educational opportunities to learn more about local, regional games or national sports for their pupils.

An interesting idea emanating from two physical education teachers in Greece (A. Papathanasiou) and the Czech Republic (A. Mayova) respectively (e-twinning News, 2009) is worthy of the attention of education authorities, specialists and curricula designers to the increasing multi-cultural needs demanding development of e-learning methods. "Exchange of Games" is an e-twinning Project, which is grounded on traditional games taking place over the e-twinning web-site where teachers from all over the world can present their national games. It was developed out of an idea of searching for new methodological propositions to enhance traditional teaching content. It started with the game, *Beating Out,* and an old Greek game *Faininda*, which were compared with their Twin partner, after which pupils in the two schools played both games during physical education classes. In addition, the teachers also shared PowerPoint presentations that contained a number of pictures to help better understand the games. In the end, the pupils began to play the games on their own and introduce them to other pupils in their schools. It has now progressed further because the Project now involves not only physical education but also computer technology classes (as well as language and cultural exchanges) and other various subject teachers working in a network of schools. On the portal *Traditional Children's Games from Around the World* (www.topics-mag.com/edition11/games-section.htm) can be found a large number of ready to use traditional activities from different countries.

More examples of national traditional games from various cultures, which might appear on pupils' "culturgram" or simply as an activity in a physical education class are referred to below. The idea of "culturgram" was used by Courchene (2002), who described it as 4-sided handouts designed as briefings to aid understanding of, and communication with, people of other cultures (see also www.culturgram.com). The "culturgrams" refer to such things as:

(i) a map: indicating the continental location and principal cities;

(ii) customs and countries: greetings, visiting, eating, other social gestures;

(iii) lifestyles: the family, dating and marriage, social and economical levels, diet, work schedules, recreation, holidays; and

(iv) the nations; land and climate, history and government, economy, education, transportation, health.

Some ready-to-use examples of traditional games already in action in various physical education systems around the world are as follows:

1. Asia
a) Bangladesh: Kabaddi (Kabbadi or Kabadi)
Kabaddi is a team sport originally from the Indian subcontinent. It was probably invented to ward off group attacks. Buddhist literature notes that the Gautam Buddha played Kabaddi. There is also a legend that Indian princes use to play Kabaddi to display their strength. It is the national game of Bangladesh where it is known as **Hadudu**. It is popular throughout South Asia, and has also spread to Southeast Asia, Japan and Iran. Kabaddi was often played by British Army personnel for fun and to keep fit, but in addition as an

"invitation" to recruit soldiers from the British Asian community. The game has many forms and different names like Amar, Surjeevani or Gaminee.

Participants are divided into two teams of seven players and five substitutes; the teams are distinguished by sets of coloured bibs. The playing area (usually an outdoors grassy or sandy area, but can also be played in an indoor facility) comprises a court 12.5 metres long and 10 metres wide (roughly half the size of a basketball court). Each team occupies opposite halves of the court. The game is divided into two halves of 20 minutes each with a five-minute half-time break. After the break teams, switch sides of the court. Each team takes turns sending a "raider" into the other half, in order to win points by tagging or "wrestling" members of the opposing team. Meanwhile, defenders try to form a chain linking hands, and if the chain is broken, a member of the defending team is sent off. The object for the defenders is to halt the "raider" returning to the home side before taking a breath. The "raider", however, tries to return to his/her own half, holding his/her breath during the whole raid by uttering continuously "kabaddi, kabaddi, kabaddi...". If the "raider" takes a breath before returning he/she is sent off the field. Any tagged player is "out" and sent off the field. A player can also be deemed "out" by going over a limit line or any part of the body touches the ground outside the marked court (except during a struggle with an opposing team member). Each time a player is out, the opposing team scores a point. A two-point bonus ("*lona*") can be awarded when the entire opposing team is declared out. The team with the higher score wins.

b) Laos: Pick-up Sticks
Most of the traditional forms of recreational activities in Laos centre around religious holidays and festivals. There are many forms of strategic games played on a cardboards or chest boards. In "Pick-up Sticks", participants number 2 to 4 (or more but playing in pairs). The "game" can be played in- or out-of-doors. The class group is divided into pairs. Each pair of players has a bunch (10-15) of sticks and a small, round ball or large, round nut (such as a walnut). The sticks are held five to six inches above the floor and the whole bundle is dropped with the sticks falling in a random pattern. The ball is tossed up and the player has to pick up one stick before catching the ball. If a player successfully catches the ball in the hand holding the stick, the same player continues the next turn. On the next attempt two sticks have to be picked up, then three, and so on as long as the player is successful, each time emptying the hand before trying for more sticks. If a player picks up the wrong number of sticks or fails to catch the ball, the "turn" is over. The game continues until one player picks up all the sticks in one turn successfully.

2. Europe
a) England: "Anything Under the Sun"
This is an old street game (a variant of games like *Shop Windows, I sent my Son John'* etc.) and is known under many names such as *John Bull, Odds & Ends* or simply by the category name used to play it such as *Boys Names, Countries*. It is claimed to be an activity useful in reducing obesity and, according to category selection (e.g. countries, names of plants or animals etc), for increasing knowledge of geography, botany, zoology etc.

Any number of players can participate. No equipment is required and the activity can be "played" in either formal or informal (e.g. school backyard, park, street) area settings. For this activity, one "player" stands on the far side of the area setting (e.g. street); this player is the "caller". All other players remain where they were. The caller chooses a category and shouts out the challenge – e.g. a boys' name beginning with "M"! If a player wants to guess he/she must run to the caller then return to their place, then back to the caller once more and shout out their guess: "is it Mark?". If more than one player runs then only the one arriving first can make the guess. If correctly made then places are changed and the successful player becomes the new caller. Otherwise the game continues.

b) France (Provence): Pétanque

The Ancient Greeks and Romans played a game very much like pétanque. Greeks used round shaped rocks ("spheristics") and Romans used wooden balls covered with iron. They introduced the "jack" or "cochonnet" to play pétanque more for precision skills. The game was very popular in the Middle Ages, but in 14th century, it was forbidden by King Charles IV and then Charles V. In the 16th century, Pope Julius the II formed "a team", which was suppose to be invincible in pitching stones. During the Medieval wars the army often had fun playing with cannonballs as pastime activity. In modern times, "the ball game" became a common pastime activity for the nobility and aristocracy. At the turn of 19th century, a new form of "the ball game" known as a "jeu provençal" was introduced to the public and it became increasingly popular. Pétanque can be played individually (*tête-à-tête*/head to head) or in teams two on two, or three on three. Any flat area with a hardened surface, usually 15 metres long and 4 metres wide, can form the area of play; equipment comprises a set of steel balls (usually 6 balls plus 1 smaller one called the "jack" (*cochonnet, gari or lé*). This game involves throwing (underarm) the ball rather than rolling it. The players aim at the "jack", a significantly smaller ball. In individual and "two on two" games, each participant has 3 balls. In team games of 3 players on each side, everyone has 2 balls. The "round" (or "end") begins by the player who wins the toss of the coin and who starts by drawing a circle 35-50 cm in diameter, and then he/she throws the "jack", which should fall 6-10m from the perimeter of the circle. The participants throw their balls from a standing position with two feet within the circle. Only when the ball has fallen, may they leave the circle. This requirement of staying inside the circle is a feature distinguishing pétanque from "jeu provençal". Each player tries to aim the ball as close to the "jack" as is possible or to hit an/the opponent's ball, which is closest to this target ball. Thus, the opponent's ball is thrown aside and the new ball occupies its position. Each round is won by contestant or a team whose balls are closest to the "jack". One point is awarded for every ball closer to the target than the opponent's nearest ball. The score is accordingly from 1 to 6 points (in a team game). If there is more than one ball closest to the "jack" then it is a tie and no points are scored. The game lasts to 11, 13, 15, 18 or 21 points, depending on local tradition.

c) Poland: Pierścieniówka (Ring-net ball)

This game stems from the traditions of Polish fishermen who played it by throwing buoys through a holed fishing net. It was elaborated into a game in 1935 by a Polish physical education teacher, Wladyslaw Robakowski. Pierścieniówka developed its popularity up to World War II but then it was forgotten for years. In the 2000s, the game was revitalized by scholars from the University School of Physical Education in Poznan and is now growing in popularity again. Participants comprise two teams of 4 players with 2 substitute players for each team and play normally takes place on a volleyball size court (i.e. 9 metres x 18 metres) with a net with three rings (holes) set at a height as in regular volleyball at 224 centimetres for women). Each half of the court is divided into two playing areas: a back and a front. The back area extends from the rear court boundary of the court to within 1.5 meters of the net. The front boundary then extends from this line 1.5 meters to the net/centre line. Three players from each team stay in their rear area and may not move into the front area. One player (the play maker) stands in the front boundary. At the beginning of the game, a player serves the ball over the net. The aim is to pass the ball through one of the three rings in the net in such a way that the ball strikes the ground within the other team's boundary. Once on a team's side, the ball may not touch the ground and it can only be passed between team-mates, a maximum of three times. If the ball touches the ground/floor or goes out of bounds, the opposing team scores a point. The play maker's role is to pass the ball to one of the three players of his team in the back area to enable their team-mate to pass the ball through one of the three rings. The play maker may not throw the ball through the rings. All players can move during a game, but only without the ball. No player can move while holding the ball. There is a rotation of players after each change of service (as in volleyball). The team scoring the appointed number of points first (usually 15) wins the set of the game. The game ends after three sets.

d) Russia: Gorodki ("Little Towns")

Gorodki is a truly unique Russian street skittles game that has been played for centuries but the rules were only standardised in the 1920s. The game is famed for being a popular game of Lenin, Stalin, Tolstoy, Gorky and others. Any number of players can participate with the playing area quite flexible to include informal areas such as school yard, park, street; equipment is minimal – five cylindrical wooden blocks (about 6 inches in length), which form target skittles, set up in a series of 15 distinctive formations. These formations (the towns) are placed inside a chalked square area (the city) 13 metres away from the throwers. The throwers wield one metre long heavy wooden batons, which they hurl at the skittles in a sideways throw - the aim being to knock all sticks in the town outside of their containing square. Once all the skittles have been removed then the next formation is set up. The team that takes the fewest throws to destroy all 15 "towns" wins.

3. North America: Airplane

The origin of this game was in Alaska but it is known as well among other Native Americans. The English name was given to the game because of its resemblance to that of an airplane. It is one of the so-called "arctic sports" according to local sports terminology and it is one of the competitive events during Native American Indian folk games. Any number of players may participate but it is necessary to form groups of four. No equipment is needed to play this game and the playing area can be any indoor or outdoor area but with a safe surface. Each group of four finds an appropriate place for themselves to undertake the task. Then one of the four lies face down on the floor/ground with arms extended sideways and with straight legs held together. Thus, the "airplane" designation. The other three participants take the prone "player" by the arms and lower limbs and lift him/her up to about 1 metre above a ground and tries to carry him/her around as long as he/she can bear the rigid position. Those whose body sags below the shoulders or whose buttocks are above the level of the arms is swapped with the next member of their group. The group which lasts the longest is the winner.

4. Oceania (New Zealand): Tapu-Ae

Although most of the today's population of New Zealand originate from settlers from other countries, there are still some strong traces of Maori culture that remain and some rituals are still cultivated, including a lot of dancing and singing. One of the most interesting societal behaviours concerns greeting each other, which in Maori tradition is carried out by pressing noses together. The participating 24 players engage in this activity either indoors (e.g. sports hall) or on an outdoor recreational area. Equipment comprises two playground balls of different colours, and two skittles (pins) or Indian clubs. The teacher divides the class into two teams of 12 members each. Each team has six "shoots", three centres and one defender. The objective of the game is to knock down the opponent's skittle (club or pin) with a ball. A centre player from each team holds a ball and on the signal to begin, tries to throw the ball to the shoots on the same team. The shoots try to knock over the skittle as they and the "rovers" try to intercept the ball and pass it to someone on their own team. The ball must go to a centre as it is being passed across to the opposite court. Both balls can be in the same circle to make it more difficult for a defender to protect the skittle. Players must stay within their own area and there should be no running with the ball. Except for a step forward when throwing the ball, the player in possession of the ball must remain stationary. Players must pass the ball within five seconds. If a player breaks a rule, the ball goes to the closest player on the opposite team. A team scores one point for a knocking down the skittle with the team ball and two points for a knocking down the skittle with the opponent's ball. The first player to obtain 11 points wins.

CONCLUSIONS

It is time that physical educators started to use their cultural heritage and engage in exchange of the most valuable elements of various nations' physical culture traditions. But they do need to keep in mind that

> "cultural relativism affirms that one culture has no absolute criteria for judging the activities of another culture as 'low' or 'noble'. However, every culture can and should apply such judgment to its own activities, because its members are actors as well as observers" (Lévi-Strauss & Eribon, 1988, p.229).

Opportunities are opening up for including the above mentioned ideas in school physical education curricula as more sources and references have been, and are being, provided. There is international, well documented literature on rural and folk traditions in physical culture. To mention just two: (i) The *Encyclopaedia of Traditional British Rural Sports* (2005) provides a social, economic, and political revision of both field sports and other activities and customs labelled as rural sports from the past to the present across the United Kingdom and Ireland; it contains several hundred distinct varieties of traditional rural sports with a particular emphasis on the social history and traditional aspects; and (ii) Wojciech Liponski (2003) book, *The Encyclopedia of World Sport* (edited under the UNESCO logo) includes over 3,000 traditional sports and games and plays from most of the regions and cultures around the world and is an example of a cultural masterpiece on a unique scale. Each sport and each game and play comes with a carefully, ethnologically supported background, rooted in various historical sources from antique vases, through paintings, sculptures and literary sources (Bronikowska 2010).

A successful example of re-introducing traditional sporting or sports-related activity is the case of Polish *pierścieniówka* (ring-net ball), which has been reconstructed from literary sources dating from the 1930's and was recently introduced into the programme of the IVth World Traditional Games festival in Busan (South Korea) in 2008, since when it has been gaining more and more popularity all over Europe. Such initiatives confirm that now there is more attention paid to "old games". Using them in different ways in education not only seems a sensible way forward, but also considering the complex multi-cultural problems that appear or arise with the increases of multi-national/multi-ethnic classes, it is almost an essential imperative. Though it is true that it requires special efforts in the professional development of teachers, I believe in the cultural sensitivity of today's educationalists. In spite of Kelly's ruminations on

> "the question whether school should endeavour to promote a common culture or help diverse groups to develop their own different cultures is a vexed one, not least in relation to those minority ethnic groups that are to be found most societies. What concerns us more directly here, however is the implication that, even if we believe that the content of the curriculum should be based on the culture of the society, it will be impossible to assert with any real expectation of general acceptance what that culture is and therefore what the content of the curriculum should be"(p.60).

As educators, physical education practitioners should introduce, and teach pupils to respect, principles representative of other cultures, which are represented in local society. Of course, this does not mean resignation of their own traditions. They should search for a balance between educational demands in the context of physical education and each pupil with their cultural experiences, which they can, and should, apply to the school curriculum to help build mutual understanding. My idea then is to create a common platform for mutual understanding of the multi-cultures within an educational system and those that pupils "bring to school" with their experiences. Physical education, enriched by international plurality of traditional forms, can, and should, become a bonding link. The more that is learned and understood about school friends' cultures, the less strange they become.

REFERENCES

Barbarash, L. (1997). *Multicultural Games. Champaign*, Illinois, Human Kinetics.

Biddle, S.J., Gorely, T., Marshall, S.J., Murdey, I., & Cameron, N. (2004). Physical activity and sedentary behaviours in youth: issues and controversies. *The Journal of the Royal Society for the Promotion of Health, 124*(1), pp.29-33.

Bronikowska, M. (2010). Why Polish Sobótka, Palant and Jawor remained only local Polish traditions: Preserving national heritage through the traditional games, *Anthropology of Eastern Europe Review, 28*(1), pp.388-406.

Bronikowski, M. (2000). Development of various forms of physical culture as a determinant of broader social changes. *Studies in Physical Culture and Tourism, 7*, pp.53-61.

Bronikowski, M., González-Gross, M., Kleiner, K., Martinkowa, I., Stache, A., Kantanista, A., Cañada Lòpez, D., & Konlechner, A. (2008). Physical activity, obesity and health programmes in selected European countries. *Studies in Physical Culture and Tourism, 15*(1), pp.8-18.

Collins, T., Martin, J., & Vamplew, W. (2005). *The Encyclopedia of Traditional British Rural Sports*. London, Routledge.

Courchene, R. (2002) Preparing students to teach in theethnocultural/multicultural/antiracist/diverse/mainstream class-room. *Contact 28*(1), pp.2-12.

Eichberg, H., & Nørgaard, K. (2005). Education through Play and Game- Danish Experiences. *International Journal of Eastern Sports and Physical Education, 3*(1), pp.4-12.

Floc'h, M., & Fanch, P. (1987). *C'hoariou Breizh. Jeux traditionnels de Bretagne*. Rennes, Institut Culturel de Bretagne.

Graham, G. (Ed.) (1995). Physical education through students' eyes and in students' voices. *Journal of Teaching in Physical Education, 14*(4), pp.408-417.

Henricks, S. T. (2006). *Play reconsidered: sociological perspectives on human expression, Urbana and Chicago*, University of Illinois Press.

Huizinga, J. (1955). *Homo ludens*. Boston, Beacon Press.

Jaouen, G. (2006). An historic and innovative task. In: *Games and society in Europe, Cultura 2000*, Barcelona, Asociacion Europea de Juegos y Deportes Tradicionales, pp.7-12.

Kelly, A.V. (2007). *The curriculum. Theory and practice.* 6th edition. London, Sage.

McNamee, M. (2008). The nature and values of physical education. In: R. Bailey & D. Kirk (Eds.), *The Routledge Physical Education Reader*. London, Routledge, pp.9-28.

Lavega, B.P. (2003), *1000 juegos y deportes populars y tradicionales*. Spanien, Paidotribo.

Lévi-Strauss, C., & Eribon, D. (1988). *De près et de loin*. Paris, Editions Odile Jacob.

Liponśki, W. (1996). Still an unknown European tradition: Polish sport in the European cultural heritage. *The International Journal of the History of Sport, 13*(2), pp.1-41.

Liponśki, W. (2003). "All Games, All Nations?" Problems of cultural universality of the Olympic Movement. In: W. Liponśki (Ed.), *Studies in Physical Culture and Tourism* (Special Issue on Ethnology of Sport), X(1), pp.107-114.

Liponśki, W. (2003). *Encyclopedia of World Sport*. Poznaf, Atena.

Parlebas, P. (2003). The destiny of games heritage and lineage. In: W. Liponśki (Ed.), *Studies in Physical Culture and Tourism* (Special Issue on Ethnology of Sport), X(1), pp.15-26.

Peters, R.S. (1966). *Ethics and Education*. London, Allen and Unwin.

Piasecki, E. (1911). *Zabawa jako czynnik spoleczny*. In: Srebrna Ksiega Sokola Poznaśkiego, (Play as a Social Factor, In: Sylver Book of Poznańs Sokol Movement), Poznań, pp.116-117.

Piasecki, E. (1916). *Zabawy i gry ruchowe dzieci i mlodżiey – ze zródeł dziejowych i ludoznawczych, przeważnie rodzimych i tradycji ustnej,* (Play and games for children and youth – from the folk sources), Książnica Polska, Kijów.

Reid, A. (1997). Value pluralism and physical education. *European Physical Education Review, 3(*1), pp.6-20.

Renson, R. (2004). Ludodiversity: Extinction, Survival and Invention of Movement Culture. In: G. Pfister (Ed.), *Games of the Past – Sport for the Future?* (Ed.). Saint Augustin, Academia Verlag.

Rowe, D. (1995). *Popular Cultures: Rock Music, Sport and Politics of Pleasure,* London, Sage.

Smulders, H. (1981). Research methods and development of the Flemish Folk Games File. *International Review of Sport Sociology, 16*(1), pp.97-107.

Strutt, J. (1801). Sport and Pastimes of the People of England, London, Methuen.

Taylor, T., & Doherty, A. (2005). Adolescent sport, recreation and physical education; experiences of recent arrivals to Canada. S*port, Education and Society, 10*(2), pp.211-238.

UNESCO (2002). *UNESCO Universal Declaration on Cultural Diversity.* France.

http://www/unescocat.org. /ct/p6/diversitatcultural.pfd. accessed on 27.05.2009.

http://curriculum.qca.org.uk accessed on 20.05.2009.

http://www.etwinning.net/en/pub/news/interviews_/interview_with_kostas_papathan.ht m. accessed on 27.05.2009.

http://www.culturgram.com. accessed on 23.08.2009.

http://www.topics-mag.com/edition11/games-section.htm. accessed on 15.06.2010.

CHAPTER 10

PHYSICAL EDUCATION TEACHER EDUCATION:
HARMONISATION AND MODEL CURRICULUM DEVELOPMENT[1]

KEN HARDMAN

INTRODUCTION

The June 1999 European Union Bologna Declaration set in motion an agenda of policy reforms to make Higher Education in Europe more compatible, comparable and competitive, a feature of which was the pervasive principle of harmonization of provision. It is a principle that persists structurally, albeit with European Union-wide recognised acceptance of the importance of diversity in programme development. In Spring, 2000 in Lisbon, the European Council called for Europe's education and training systems to be modernized in response to becoming the most competitive and dynamic knowledge-based economy in the world, capable of sustainable economic growth with more and better jobs and greater social cohesion. The subsequent Council of Europe's Stockholm Meeting in March 2001 set three strategic goals encompassing the quality and effectiveness of the educational system and professional preparation, the creation of opportunities to study for all, and opening the education system and professional preparation worldwide. In the improvement of the quality and effectiveness of education and professional preparation, it was envisaged that curricula would need to focus on key competences, defined by the European Parliament and the Council Europe (2006) as a combination of knowledge, skills and attitudes appropriate to the context for lifelong learning.

As part of the process of harmonizing Higher Education provision, an ERASMUS Thematic Network project was initiated in October 2003 by the European Network of Sport Science, Education and Employment (ENSSEE) to *Align a European Higher Education Structure in Sport Science* (the AEHESIS Project), one sector of which is "Physical Education" (PE). Amongst other initial objectives, the sector's overarching aim "having in mind the necessity of enhancing the process of recognition and European integration of qualifications" was to formulate a model curriculum for Physical Education Teacher Education (PETE), which could have applicability across Higher Education Institutions (HEIs) in Europe involved with preparation of teachers and hence, represent a degree of harmonisation within the context of the intention and spirit of the Bologna Agreement and so accord with the 2001 Stockholm strategic goal of improving professional preparation. Of immediate pertinence here is that the recognition of "diversity" within the context of "harmonization" has particular resonance because historical antecedents, socio-

---

1 This chapter draws from the European Network of Sport Science, Education and Employment (ENSSEE)Aligning a European Higher Education Structure in Sport Science (AEHESIS) Project in the Area of Physical Education, the research group for which comprised Ken Hardman (University of Worcester, UK), Francisco Carreiro da Costa (Technical University of Lisbon), Gilles Klein (Paul Sabatier University of Toulouse, France), Göran Patriksson (University of Gothenburg, Sweden) and Antonín Rychteck. (Charles University, Prague, Czech Republic).

cultural-bound practices, politico-ideological settings and varying levels of state and/or regional legislation etc. have diversely shaped school physical education and PETE provision and practice across the world.

In many countries, PETE is generally well-regulated (usually at State or autonomous region level). The established political and legal contexts have consequences for development and acceptance of accredited, prescribed, harmonized continental region-wide PETE programmes. Prescriptions may not have the inherent propensity to cross boundaries and hence, may have restricted applicability. Relevant to the regulatory contexts within the settings of geo-political and socio-cultural diversity, is the identification of core general principles, which can frame PETE *Programmes of Study* and thus, serve as a guideline framework for providers. Whilst the AEHESIS Project was specifically focused on the European region, the "6-Step" methodological approach adopted in the pursuit of the over-arching aim of formulation of a PETE curriculum, has the propensity for universal applicability, as have the PETE curriculum model principles embracing Programmes of Study, Learning Outcomes and Competencies.

The content of this chapter provides an overview of the AEHESIS Project's methodological approach and progression of the 6-Step Model, prior to addressing contexts and issues, which collectively need to be taken into account when framing principles relevant to reference points to inform PETE Curriculum development. In turn, identity and quality characteristics of PE in schools and conceptual model of a PE Teacher reference points are presented prior to identification of Core General Principles underpinning PETE Programmes of Study, which are disaggregated into Fields of Study with respective credits' "weightings" within differentiated occupational programmes. Finally, sets of Programmes of Study Learning Outcomes and Occupational Competences are proposed along with suggestions on Assessments and Quality Assurance as points of convergence.

THE 6-STEP MODEL

The "6-Step" methodological approach (see Figure 1) to curriculum formulation was based on an adaptation (Klein, 2004) of the European Commission funded *Tuning Project* tool.

Step I	Definition of Professional Area
Step II	Definition of 3 major Standard Occupations
Step III	Definition of 4/5 Main Activities for the 3 Occupations
Step IV	Corresponding Competences for each activity listed in Step 3
Step V	Specification of Learning Outcomes expected at the end of the programme related to the agreed competences for the 3 Occupations
Step VI	Formulation of a Curriculum Model for one Occupation

Figure 1. The 6-Step Methodological Model Approach (adapted by Klein, 2004).

The *Tuning Educational Structures in Europe* Project began in 2000 as a means to link the political objectives of the *Bologna Process* and, later, the *Lisbon Strategy* to the Higher

Education sector. It aimed, and continues to do so, to identify points of convergence in education systems across Europe. By such "tuning" and locating common reference points, it is intended to make recognition of qualifications easier. The term *Tuning* reflects the idea that HEIs should not seek uniformity in degree programmes or prescriptive or definitive European curricula but rather look for points of reference (related to general and subject-specific competences acquired by students during a programme of study), convergence and common understanding.

PROGRESSION OF THE 6-STEP MODEL

Whilst the adapted methodological approach was arguably limited in its nature and scope, it provided a structural framework for purposeful pan-national and/or cross-cultural application. The 6-Step Model was progressed within the over-arching framework of the inter-relationships of key areas (refer Figure 2) to be considered for convergent Model PETE Curriculum formulation.

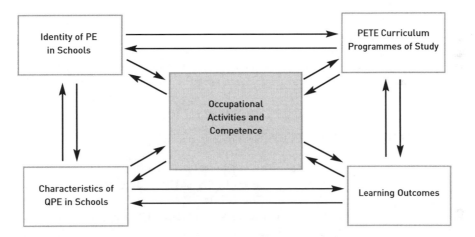

Figure 2. School PE, Occupational Competences and PETE Provider Programmes of Study and Learning Outcomes

Several procedural methods and research instruments were employed in data collection. These were characterised by a "bottom-up" approach to empirical data generation and research literature, analysis of current PETE provision and experts' considerations (academic/professional practices/ideals evidence). The research instruments comprised semi-structured and open questionnaires, and analysis of documentary and research evidence. For Steps I-V, data sets variously included samples of PETE providers, employees (teachers) and employers. Because of time and costs constraints, data generated from employers and employees were derived through national case studies and, therefore, were not cross-nationally representative; however, they provided illustrative examples and revealed patterns, which could be utilised in a cautionary way to inform Step VI, PETE Model Curriculum formulation.

STEP I. IDENTIFICATION OF PROFESSIONAL AREA

Physical Education Teacher was identified as the professional area. An immediate issue here is what constitutes a *Physical Education Teacher*. There is an assumption that a Physical Education Teacher is defined as a qualified teacher who has undertaken a programme of academic and professional training, over 50% of the study load of which (excluding general education or pedagogical study) has related to the subject known as *Physical Education* or its subject specific equivalent term. It is acknowledged that in some countries, PE teachers working in a "Basic School" may have undertaken study programmes, which comprise less than 50% of the total teacher education programme and, are, nevertheless, recognized as physical education teachers. In acknowledging the diversity in existing practice, it is necessary or may be pragmatically expedient to adopt a compromise, which recognizes or distinguishes between a "Specialist PE" teacher, a "PE" teacher and a "Generalist" teacher who teaches a full range of subjects in primary/elementary school settings. This notion of specialization in physical education is relevant to the various phases (or stages) of schooling, whether primary (elementary), basic (which tends to span primary and early/lower secondary education), or secondary (high).

(i) **Physical Education Teacher (One Subject Specialist)**
   Designation as a *Specialist Physical Education Teacher* assumes successful completion of a relevant PE-related Programme of Study including qualified teacher status with an accumulation of 240 ECTS[2]. The "Specialist PE Teacher" will have in-depth PE subject and related areas knowledge and understanding in the full range of required Fields of Study within an overall PE Programme of Study.

(ii) **Physical Education Teacher (2-3 Subjects)**
   Designation as a *Physical Education Teacher* assumes successful completion of a Programme of Study including qualified teacher status with an accumulation of 240 ECTS, in which a minimum of 35-50% (that is 84-120 ECTS) of content excluding professional training is PE-related. The "PE Teacher" will have extended PE subject and related areas foundation knowledge and understanding in all Fields of Study specified in a PE Programme of Study.

(iii) **Generalist Teacher**
   Designation as *Generalist Teacher* assumes successful completion of a Programme of Study including qualified teacher status with an accumulation of 240 ECTS, in which a minimum of 10% (that is 24 ECTS) of content is PE-related. The "Generalist Teacher" will have basic foundation PE subject knowledge in a sustainable range of Fields of Study including Practical Activities, Pedagogy/Didactics and School-based Teaching Practice indicated in the Programme of Study to facilitate proper delivery of a prescribed or framework guideline PE curriculum in early years of schooling (primary/elementary), (Hardman, 2006).

---

2 Under the European Credit Transfer and Accumulation System (ECTS), one credit generally corresponds to 25-30 work or study load hours with astudent workload ranging from 1500 to 1800 hours during an academic year. ECTS makes higher Education teaching and learning more transparent across Europe and facilitates the recognition of all studies. The system allows for the transfer of learning experiences between different institutions, greater student mobility and more flexible routes to acquire degrees.

A second issue related to terminological definition of the Professional Area is that of societal needs in evolving ideological and political settings within a dynamically changing world, which may impact on, and alter the functional roles of the designated professional area. With this scenario, occupational identity and associated functions and activities essentially need to be flexibly adaptable. With regard to flexible adaptation in a context of diverse accreditation practices, consideration should be given to different pathway routes (single subject, major/minor subject status and multiple subjects) to qualified PE teacher status at initial graduate (bachelor's) and post-graduate (master's) levels. Any such flexible adaptation could embrace traditions and recent developments of routes to teacher qualification and acknowledge the different career motivations/decisions of students entering provider HEI's.

STEP II. STANDARD OCCUPATION WITH 3 MAJOR FUNCTIONS

The ranked three major Standard Occupation (defined as *a set of tasks and duties executed, or meant to be executed, by one person*) functions derived from empirically generated data comprised:
(i) teaching physical education with emphasis on delivery of a broad and balanced curriculum fostering knowledge, skill and understanding;
(ii) teaching physical education including health and active lifestyle; and
(iii) teaching physical education including extra-curricular sport

STEP III. ACTIVITIES WITH LIST OF 4/5 OCCUPATIONAL ACTIVITIES (IN RANKED ORDER)

Five main Occupational Activities (defined as *the set of tasks and duties (i.e. functions) itself, relating to a specific occupation*) were determined:
(i) establishment of positive learning situations;
(ii) understanding and application of physical activity as a process;
(iii) fostering health and lifestyle perspectives;
(iv) planning, organising and teaching curricular/extra-curricular activities; and
(v) conception, implementation and assessment of PE and sport education processes/provision of advisory guidance and instruction.

STEP IV. COMPETENCES

Several competence frameworks embrace the provision of skills enabling learners to cope with increasing complexity in work tasks and are linked with the notion of "employability". Employability is associated with work-compatible values and attitudes, including a desire to learn, to apply that learning, to adapt and to respond proactively to change; basic skills, work needs' key skills, relevant up-to-date knowledge and understanding, up-to-date job specific skills, and the ability to manage one's own career (CBI, 1998, cited in Hoffman, 1999). A European Union survey in 2002 of "Key Competencies" found that all the then Member States included either explicit or implicit reference to the development of competencies, that identification was as much a matter of conceptualisation as terminology and that two motives fostered focus on key competencies: (i) quality in education, emanating from school to school variation in educational attainment; and (ii) internationalisation, scientific and technological progress and increasingly complex career paths (Scottish Qualifications Authority, 2003).

Over the last 20 years or so, there has been a marked shift in programme ethos and content of school subject curricula both in schools and in teacher training provider institutions. This shift is well illustrated in the domain of PE. Curricular aims are linked through subject content and pedagogical/didactical processes with ascribed and expected learning outcomes and competencies. Indeed, during this period, research into the issue of "professional competence", as defined by sets of competencies, has become a prolific enterprise across the world. Analysis of published research on PE teaching-related competencies reveals similarities in competences cited: group or class management, relational aspects (communication skills, motivation skills, team-work, inter-personal/interaction relations of teachers with pupils, colleagues, parents and local community), for which professional experience is seen as a determining factor, evaluation of pupils' progress, and planning, programming and realising curriculum content *inter alia*. At the same time, it is clear that competencies are accorded differentiated levels of importance, which more often than not reflect cultural and national contexts and traditions.

Research into PETE provider and school PE practitioner perceptions of competences, desired and/or required, held and lacking, reveals differences, which are variously embedded in socio-cultural traditions, experience and gendered features. The latter is epitomised in several European studies, in which female and male teachers showed differences in the self-perceptions of their actual levels of competence in general PE didactics, physical and motor development, analysis and planning, work with talented pupils, didactics of curricular sports, classroom management, organising sport activities, and assessment, evaluation and grading (see for example, Kovač, Sloan & Starc, 2008). From other research (Corke, 2008), generally employers, when recruiting, seek a combination of appropriate qualifications and experience (if and when relevant to the post to be filled), personal qualities and professional competencies to meet with job specification and description. Often sought after personal qualities include: levels of commitment (to subject and ethos and values of the teaching-learning community), dedication, enthusiasm, motivation, ambition, adaptability and flexibility, sense of humour, sensitivity to, and care for, others, personal and professional integrity, as well as those, which transcend the personal quality-competence divide or bridge such as communication including social, that is inter-personal and inter-action skills, self-organisation and time management etc.

The AEHESIS Project PE Area researchers adopted Tissot's (2003) working definition of competences, designated as the "ability to apply knowledge, know-how and skills in a habitual and/or changing work situation" with, according to the European Qualifications Framework[3], competences including:

---

3 Details of the background to the establishment of a Qualifications Framework are contained in the following chapter on Assessment and Qualifications (chapter 10).

"i) cognitive competence involving the use of theory and concepts, as well as informal tacit knowledge gained experientially; ii) functional competence (skills or know-how), those things that a person should be able to do when they are functioning in a given area of work, learning or social activity; iii) personal competence involving knowing how to conduct oneself in a specific situation; and iv) ethical competence involving the possession of certain personal and professional values".

The language of *competences* and *skills* refers to capacities demonstrated in action, which relates to working situations and the associated tasks and duties. Competences are distinguished between **generic and specific**. In PETE programmes of Study "generic" competences are related to general aspects of PE teacher training, common with other standard occupations; and "specific" competences are related to specific aspects of PE teacher occupation. In essence, generically and specifically "Standards" relate to what teachers should know and be able to do: the "know" relates to "Knowledge" learning outcomes and the "do" to "Competences". In the AEHESIS Project, PETE providers characterised the competent teacher by a) mastery of generic competences (instrumental, inter-personal and systemic) including subject knowledge, teaching organisation, team-work, critical abilities, adaptability to existing and new situations and ability to apply knowledge to practice, and b) by mastery of specific competences at the macro (the teacher and the agencies outside the school), meso (the teacher functioning in the school), micro (the teacher in the "classroom" with the students) levels in four areas, mainly regarding subject knowledge and pedagogical/didactical tools to adapt the subject-matter content to pupils and their developmental needs: academic/intellectual (subject skills); professional (teacher's functions/roles); personal practical activity performance; and transferable skills. Collectively, these imply capacity for planning, decision implementation analysis and modification according to context. Interestingly, competence for promotion or development of competitive sport, the aesthetic dimension, and the organisation of extra-curricular activities were not regarded as important professional competences; research was also similarly regarded.

In the everyday world, PE teachers face complex situations that require complex responses, and the more complex the work the more a combination of different competencies are required to work successfully. Competence needs to be contextualised because even within the same profession there are numerous differences between work places, environments and settings and, as revealed in the AEHESIS Project, between expectations of providers, employers and teachers; hence, a single set of competences may not work for all. The data generated from the three sets of "actors" revealed convergences and divergences. The greatest congruence between the three sample sets was related to knowledge of students, subject matter and pedagogy. Congruence was also found for other specific competences: reflective practice; inclusion and class heterogeneity; teaching a range of activities; and adaptability, team-work and capacity for analysis and synthesis. Divergences were most frequently apparent between employers and employees: the health education process, creativity, administrative aspects of curriculum development and knowledge of education systems and contexts were less favoured by employees and the cultural dimension of PE had little significance for the employers. Each actor category indicated some priorities.

Employers favoured curriculum planning and development, effective teaching and learning strategies, team-work and communication skills. There was a disposition amongst teachers in some countries to give some priority to extra-curricular sport whereas in others, priority was accorded to professional engagement, national curriculum teaching, didactical and pedagogical knowledge, and knowledge of pupils' ethical values. Some PETE providers accorded priority to scientific and pedagogical knowledge on teaching, subject-matter content, pupils' personality development, training processes, teaching skills and team-work, whilst others emphasised knowledge of pedagogical and didactical (including teaching styles) interventions, PE subject knowledge, skills and understanding, knowledge of students and their characteristics, knowledge of curriculum planning and development, and curriculum implementation (teaching activities). Armed with this research evidence-based information and model PE teacher concept (see below, Step VI c) together with contextualisation and as a basis for broadspread applicability in mind, the AEHESIS Project PE Area Research Team drew up sets of Knowledge Learning Outcomes and Competencies (for full details see Hardman, 2006; Hardman, Klein, Patriksson, Rychtecky & Carreiro da Costa, 2007), encompassing all the *Fields of Study* identified in the Step V section.

STEP V. LEARNING OUTCOMES AND PROGRAMMES OF STUDY

Information on Programmes of Study *Learning Outcomes*, defined as "the set of knowledge, skills and/or competences an individual has acquired and/or is able to demonstrate after completion of a learning process; learning outcomes are the competences seen from a "training" programme point of view" (Tissot, 2003), was derived from data provided by provider institutions. **Programmes of Study** were disaggregated into **Fields of Study**, recast (for simplification) to embrace *Practical Activities* (theory and practice in a sustainable range of areas, including valued national/local culturally traditional and "new lifestyle" activities), *Educational & Teaching Sciences* (Pedagogy and Didactics), *Natural and Biological Sciences* (General and Applied), *Social Sciences/Humanities* (General and Applied), *Scientific Work* (research related study such as dissertation or project), *School-based Teaching Practice* and *Specified Others*. Examples of Learning Outcomes listed most frequently for each Field of Study are as follows:

- *Practical Activities:* knowledge, understanding and analysis of (motor) skills and performance factors in range of activities and teach activities' skills/didactic competence connecting theory with practice
- *Pedagogy/Didactics:* knowledge of curriculum implementation and effective teaching theories
- *Natural/Biological Sciences*: knowledge of structure, function and control of physical systems and understanding and application of biomechanical principles to movement
- *Social Sciences/Humanities:* psychological/sociological knowledge of human movement and understand concept of culture and application to PE and sport
- *Research Studies:* preparation, conduct of and report on a PE project and ability to generate quantitative/qualitative data
- *Teaching Practica:* application of teaching skills and experience content, pedagogical and contextual knowledge
- *Other:* development of personal philosophy and use of new/multi-media technology

STEP VI. PETE CURRICULUM MODEL FORMULATION

The Model PETE Curriculum principles presented in this chapter took into account a number of issues including a) PE in school contexts, specifically its identity and characteristics of quality, for, as indicated earlier, they are important components of the inter-relationships of key areas of consideration PETE preparation and as such, they have resonance for PETE Curriculum formulation with significant consequences for PETE Programmes of Study and their Learning Outcomes, as well as associated Occupational Competences; b) structural elements that are central to PETE curriculum formulation, which frame reference points and level of convergence; and c) a concept of a model physical education teacher.

a) Identity and Characteristics of Quality Physical Education in Schools

In terms of identity, in recognising that PE makes a unique contribution to the education of all pupils, the European Physical Education Association (EUPEA) proposed (2006) that PE is principally concerned with learning, personal development and health, and essentially, is a means of teaching different types of physical activity as a part of pupil's overall educational experience with pupils having the right to experience a programme of PE that promotes at least the following:

- a broad base of physical competence and knowledge of physical activities
- growth and development
- insight and understanding of the importance of a healthy lifestyle
- a positive self-esteem within the context of physical activity
- interpersonal skills, such as the ability to solve problems and co-operate with others in the context of sport and physical activity
- the opportunity to develop oneself as an independent and responsible participant of sport-culture
- a lifelong interest and engagement in, and affinity for, physical activities

Quality Physical Education (QPE) has become a widely used term but there has been some apparent reticence to define the term, especially in the context of differentiated socio-cultural, economic and politico-ideological settings. Arguably, a set of characteristics indicative of QPE might resolve any such problem. By way of illustration, three from a set of characteristics are offered as a basis for such applicability:

- serves diverse needs of all pupils in schools; this implies a balanced and coherent curriculum, sufficiently challenging to all, delivered so as to ensure differentiated learning tasks and teaching styles or interventions appropriate both to the pupils and to the tasks
- provides opportunities and experiences for enhancement of knowledge, understanding and movement skills in a variety of physical activities
- promotes positive self-concepts and social interaction, a range of psycho-social qualities, and morally sound values and behaviours.

These characteristics instrumentally lead to positive outcomes of QPE programmes in schools. Three such outcomes suffice as illustrative exemplars:

- understanding of the essential role of physical education in contributing to personal well-being and to a balanced healthy, active lifestyle
- willingness and confidence to engage in different types of physical/sporting activity in a variety of capacities and settings as well as take initiative
- acquisition and application of a range of skills and techniques with good body control and movement[4].

The issue of QPE in schools also translates into a PETE context: the quality of physical education provided during "training" is critical to its effectiveness in shaping intending PE teachers' philosophy and attitudes. The provision of QPE rests at least upon a balanced, coherent and clearly defined curriculum, which covers a sustainable range of the many types of practical activities available, fosters knowledge and understanding of pedagogical and didactical processes and their application in school-related contexts including curriculum development, implementation and evaluation, effective communication and interaction in a variety of physical activity and safe learning environments, subject knowledge and understanding in relevant areas of the natural/biological (life sciences) and social sciences (including humanities), and which contributes to development of positive professional attitudes of reflective and research capable practitioners.

b) Model PETE Curriculum Structural Elements
Suggested main structural elements framing the Model PETE Curriculum and thus, providing common reference points and convergence, are as follows:

- units of study (modules) based on the ECTS 25-30 hours study load per credit system with an accumulation of 240 credits normally over four years for subject and qualified teacher status;
- a broad and balance curriculum to meet needs and trends in society, accord with cultural traditions, contribute to life-long learning and healthy active lifestyles;
- a balanced range of practical physical activities to accord with school PE curriculum practice and developments;
- a balance of applied bio-medical and social sciences (including humanities), which assumes integration of theory and practice;
- a full range of teaching methods suitably and appropriately selected to achieve learning outcomes and develop academic and professional competence;
- internal and external quality assurance procedures;
- a minimum of 10% (24 ECTS) of the total Programme of Study time allocated for school-based experiences appropriately distributed over the duration of the PETE programme;
- a Dissertation/Research Project (applied to PE);
- a time/credit allocation to education theory and applied education.

c) The Model PE Teacher
The concept of a PE teacher has undergone some reconstruction in recent years as the subject itself has absorbed the implications of a significant amount of curriculum development, and the changing context of schooling in the 21st century. Additionally,

---

4 For more detailed lists of QPE characteristics and outcomes of programmes, see Hardman, 2006. pp.216-217.

there have been new developments in what should be taught, why it should be taught and how it is most effectively taught and these have influenced the nature of the preparation of students trained to deliver PE in schools. Today, PE teachers are faced with a variety of tasks, which encompass overt and discrete contributions to young people's learning as well as facilitation, co-ordination and management of experiences available to young people in physical education through sources internal and external to the school. The need for more adaptable teachers is clear and PE teachers must be no less adaptable than others. It is evident that their roles are changing and if they are to be empowered to teach effectively, they will need to develop academic and professional competencies within a range of contexts, which may be subject to change.

The model of the PE teacher envisaged emphasises competence and professionalism and acknowledges the need for reflection on the complexities involved. The PE teacher is seen as a competent professional who is concerned to become more effective in facilitating and supporting children's learning and development within a variety of contexts through analysing, exploring and reflecting upon their own classroom practice. Any model of PE teacher competence should embrace both cognitive and attitudinal elements. This is demonstrated through knowledge and understanding of PE curriculum functions and by a command of subject knowledge and the ability to apply it at different levels of pupil ability. It requires the PE teacher to employ a variety of teaching styles so as to maximise pupil learning and progress. The teacher is expected to manage and control classes and to understand the organisation of the school and its place within the wider outside school community and is also required to have the knowledge, understanding and skills needed to assess, evaluate and report pupils' attainment and progress for formative and summative purposes.

As teachers are agents of change, they require not only subject and people knowledge and understanding but also the ability to manage change. One consequence is that PETE providers should be instrumental in developing and fostering such agents through programmes designed to produce the "model teacher" as: competently knowledgeable (e.g. familiar with the content of the requirements of the PE curriculum subject matter for the age-range studied; this includes acquisition of a subject content knowledge base, including key concepts and skills that provide the material to be taught and the ability to employ a range of teaching styles and methods within a variety of contexts); analytically reflective, that is critically thinking (e.g. able to critically evaluate own practice in relation to these issues and to synthesise and apply knowledge and understanding to the critical analysis and evaluation of physical education theory research and practice); and professionally effective (e.g. show an active commitment to the provision of equal opportunities for all pupils in physical education and able to communicate and work co-operatively with colleagues, parents and others in negotiating the curriculum and overall provision for, and care of, children in school). In summary, by the end of the study programme, successful trainee student teachers should be able to provide a reasoned rational argument for the enduring qualities of physical education whilst at the same time adopting an evolving critical approach to its place in the educational process. They should appreciate that their role in schools and teaching physical education will be a changing one (Chichester University, 2003).

MODEL PETE CURRICULUM: PROGRAMMES OF STUDY

The rationale of a PETE programme has at its core a model of the teacher who understands that pupils have individual needs and can respond to them, who is competent in curriculum areas and classroom practice and who, as an effective practitioner, is analytical, critically reflective, professional and as a continuing learner is receptive to new ideas with the ability to respond to, and manage change. Any model should build on recognised strengths of existing provision and should be based on the integration of theoretical, practical and professional work across the period of the programme. It should emphasise: sound subject knowledge; understanding of how children and young people learn and acquire skills; effective pedagogy; the contribution of Information Communication Technology; the development of trainee teachers' intellectual skills; a proactive and challenging approach to learning; and the development of trainee teachers' perspectives on life-long learning for personal and professional development (Hardman, 2006).

Study Programmes should establish a secure knowledge base to include an understanding of the knowledge, concepts, and skills of the subject as well as breadth and depth of subject knowledge, which extends beyond programmes. In the provision of a base for initial professional competence, elements that contribute to this are specific subject-based professional skills as well as recognition of the generic context of education across all class stages and the wider context of the community. For the development of intellectual and critical powers, throughout the study programme, students should be required to analyse, diagnose, select appropriate courses of action, report and evaluate within several contexts. In order to assist in the growth of personal qualities, attitudes and values, which are a necessary feature of the teacher of the future, teacher education should include elements of independent and cooperative learning, of self-appraisal and judgement of others, of reports and debates, of necessity and choice within a framework of challenge and sensitivity to others.

PETE Programmes of Study should be driven by clear conceptions and shared sets of institutional provider beliefs about what is valued in, and expected of, a prospective teacher, especially as teaching is not the only function that physical educators have in school contexts of societal change, cultural and ethnical diversity. The present day teacher is confronted with the need to demonstrate competence at three levels of professional activity: (i) tasks at the **micro** level concerning the teaching of Physical Education and School Sport; (ii) tasks at the **meso** level relating to school context; and (iii) tasks at the **macro** level in attaining relationships between School and community. Drawing from research (see for example, Bain, 1990; Behets, 2000; Hargreaves, 2000; O'Sullivan, 1996; O'Sullivan, 1998; and Hardman et al., 2008), and mirroring the characteristics of QPE in schools outlined earlier in the chapter, Core General Principles, which inform development of quality PETE Programmes of Study *inter alia* embrace:

- a balanced and coherent curriculum with sufficiency of width and depth to ensure professional and academic proficiency appropriate in teaching a progressive range of physical activities in physical education programmes in schools
- a curriculum that is formatively/developmentally based and progressively sequenced with clearly defined aims and learning outcomes and key concepts that provide a framework to assist in developing student perspective on learning to teach and commitment

- a curriculum that provides opportunities and experiences for enhancement of knowledge, understanding and movement skills in a variety of physical activities and related scientific areas of study
- a curriculum that leads to acquisition and application of a range of pedagogical, didactical and management techniques/skills that guarantee differentiation of learning tasks and teaching styles which are appropriate both to the tasks and to the students; these skills will include evaluation of student achievement and progress, reflective thinking, appropriate decision-making and initiative taking, and adaptive behaviours
- a curriculum that leads to understanding of the essential role of physical education in contributing to personal well-being and to a balanced healthy, active lifestyle
- a curriculum that develops ethically and professionally sound values and behaviours
- a curriculum that fosters safe behaviours (teaching and learning, physically and socially) and management of risk-taking
- there is a balance in the time and respect for learning content knowledge, learning about pedagogy, pedagogical knowledge, and experience in learning to teach
- supervision of teaching practice by appropriately professionally qualified/experienced provider staff and co-operating school teachers/mentors; induction of trainees into the professional cultures of schools is an imperative in teacher education
- positive internal (providers) and external (schools) institutional and individual/group networks; this is an essential key to the creation and dissemination of better pedagogical practice
- provision for research and development in teacher education
- a systematic plan in place for programme evaluation and quality assurance" (Hardman, 2006, pp.227-228).

Study Programmes might be structured to facilitate students passing through three broad phases: foundation (an introduction to the principles underpinning the study and teaching of PE; extension (greater depth of study); and synthesis (consideration of evolving experiences in the programme in general and PE and related areas in particular and integrating theory and practice in an independent dissertational or research project study). Units of study should combine experience in a range of activities with a thorough intellectual underpinning. The principal function of some units of study is the professional organisation of practical activities; they provide substantial opportunity for experience in physical activities that are currently part of the teaching of PE. Such units of study should include opportunities to experiment with a variety of teaching methods and approaches appropriate to the wide range of children they will serve. These units should ensure that students: increase their knowledge of individual development; develop an understanding of the rationale for individualised approaches to teaching and learning; realise that the activities engaged in provide an amplification of child-centred approaches in PE; learn to relate aims of PE to more general curricular objectives; and recognise that a central concern of PE is the development of personal capacities and that a pre-requisite of such an approach is the appreciation of the recipient as an active, evolving individual. Coherence and cohesion within, and between, these units of study are enhanced for students with the specific pedagogical reference points of school experience.

From PETE Programmes of Study curriculum content, it is logical to expect a set of *Learning Outcomes*. Illustrative exemplars[5] of learning outcomes (that is, standards relating to what teachers should know - knowledge), expected for trainee teachers, who successfully complete a PETE programme, are as follows:

- Specialist knowledge and understanding in PE to include acquisition of a subject content knowledge base, including key concepts and skills that provide the material to be taught and the ability to employ a range of teaching styles and methods within a variety of contexts;
- Acquired the necessary range of observational, analytical, interpretive and recording skills required for planning and implementation of programmes of study and competent organisation of the learning environment;
- An understanding of how children develop in a movement setting with particular attention to the more common learning difficulties experienced by some children;
- Knowledge and skills to support pupil's learning, progression and development within the school curriculum in an informed manner;
- A commitment to inclusion of and equal opportunities for all pupils in PE;
- A breadth of experience, knowledge and understanding of PE and its application in a range of contexts within the school's local community and regional/national cultural settings.

Learning Outcomes translate into Competences (that is, what teachers should be able to do) required for the occupation of a PE teacher in schools. The selected illustrative competences[6] are categorised into generic and specific.

Generic
- Curriculum planning and delivery competence with range of teaching interventions
- Effective classroom management with ability to respond to, and manage, change learners, and handle issues in an informed way so as to develop their practice in a changing world.
- Application of a range of pedagogical and didactical processes and management techniques/skills that guarantee differentiation of learning tasks and teaching styles, which are appropriate both to the tasks and to the students
- Planning and setting expectations (e.g. effectiveness of planning, identification of objectives, content, lesson structures relevant to students being taught; clear learning targets)
- Apply knowledge of teaching and managing student learning (e.g. technical competence in teaching; good standards of control and discipline; and use of appropriate teaching methods/interventions)
- Undertake assessment and evaluation (of learning outcomes; monitor formative progress; and provide constructive feedback)
- Establish relations with parents and wider community (preparation and presentation of reports to parents);

---

5 For a more detailed list of Study Programmes' Learning Outcomes, refer Hardman (2006, pp.224-225).

6 For a more detailed list of competences, refer Hardman, Klein, Patriksson, Rychtecky & Carreiro da Costa (2008, pp.76-77).

- Manage resources (selection and use of learning resources), and with experience demonstrate competence in policy formulation, strategic leadership etc.).

Specific
- Professional and practical proficiency appropriate in teaching a progressive and sustainable range of physical activities
- Ability to demonstrate competence in PE curriculum planning and review and appreciate the need for curriculum development
- Analyse (motor) skills and performance factors in range of activities
- Teach activities' skills/didactic competence connecting theory with practice
- Ability to synthesise and apply knowledge and understanding to the critical analysis and evaluation of physical education theory research and practice
- Prepare and conduct of PE-related project with ability to generate quantitative and qualitative data
- Actively commit to the provision of equal opportunities for all pupils in PE

For each dedicated category level of *PE Teacher* identified earlier in the chapter, it is important to define relevant functional activities and competencies required to deliver or contribute to quality PE curricula in the appropriate school phase/stage settings. Moreover, in order to "equip" each category level teacher with appropriate competencies to deliver PE curricula in schools, and demonstrate a degree of structural convergence, "weighting" of Fields of Study within PETE Programmes of Study should also be considered to ensure in-depth subject and related areas knowledge and understanding (the single subject specialist), extended subject and related areas knowledge and understanding (the 2-3 subject PE teacher), and foundation subject knowledge in a sustainable range of study fields (the "generalist" teacher). For an example of ECTS weightings of Fields of Study refer Figure 3 below.

Assessment modes should be sufficiently varied to enable students to give evidence of a range of knowledge, skills, understanding and competences developed by their programme of study and provide students with a clear idea of their progress as their programme of study unfolds. The safeguarding and enhancement of the standards of the teaching profession should be a central objective of an assessment scheme. Rigorous assessment ensures that students achieve expected standards of classroom practice and performance. The assessment of competency should be embedded in a profiling system that runs throughout the programme and across disciplines and areas of study. Semester by semester building of the profile would involve the students with an active process of self-appraisal, evaluation, and target setting.

Quality Assurance is a key factor in PETE provision and evaluation is an important component in the process. National evaluation models of higher education differ greatly throughout the world. Some countries have no centralised (i.e. national or autonomous region/state) evaluation systems and here responsibility tends to lie with each university and subject. The Bologna process calls for harmonisation alignment processes. In seeking harmonisation, the AEHESIS research team analysed several models of established, evolving and experimental, externally driven quality assurance practices.

Fields of Study	Single Subject Specialist: Min. 240 ECTS (100%) Weighting: ECTS & %	2/3 Subjects: Min. 80-120 ECTS (33-50%) Weighting: ECTS &%	Generalist: Min. 24 ECTS (10%) Weighting: ECTS & %
Practical Activities (Theory and Practice)	36-48 ECTS 15-20%	12-48 ECTS 10-20%	6 ECTS 25%
Balanced range to include valued national/local culturally traditional and new "lifestyle" activities	Full range	Extended range	Sustainable range
Educational & Teaching Sciences (Pedagogy/Didactics)	24-48 ECTS 10-20%	24-48 ECTS 10-20%	6 ECTS 25%
Natural and Biological Sciences (General and Applied)	36-48 ECTS 15-20%	12-48 ECTS 5-20%	1-3 ECTS up to 12.5%
Social Sciences/Humanities (General and Applied)	36-48 ECTS 15-20%	12-48 ECTS 5-20%	1-3 ECTS Up to 12.5%
Scientific Work (PE-related research study: dissertation or project)	12-24 ECTS 5-10%	12-24 ECTS 5-10%	1-3 ECTS Up to 12.5%
Teaching Practica (including school-based practice, theory, practice and professional)	24-48 ECTS 10-20%	24-48 ECTS 10-20%	6 ECTS 25%

Figure 3. Programmes of Study, ECTS and Total % Weighting

The motivations for evaluation include raising and maintaining quality of provision and delivery, enhancement of the quality of the student experience, public accountability and safeguarding the public interest in sound standards of higher education qualifications, informing policy and checking compliance with legal requirements. Systematic self-evaluation and associated report, peer review via site visit and report (to include institutional organisation details; staff and student profiles; programme structure, management, aims, contents including integration of theory and practice, learning outcomes and delivery of programmes; observation of trainees' teaching practices; use of information technology; quality assurance[7] measures; and student exit data etc.), and adherence to agreed academic/professional benchmark standards are central to the evaluation process on a regular basis. The final evaluation report, detailing strengths and weaknesses, providing examples of good practice and recommendations for improvement plans, should constructively contribute to the improvement of the educational process in a dialogue with the evaluated partner.

For quality assurance in PETE, it is recommended that monitoring and evaluation inspection is by independent non-ministerial agencies to provide impartial reports on

---

7 Quality assurance should be embedded in subject benchmark statements, which set out expectations about the standards of programmes of study.

management and quality assurance of provision, quality of training provided and standards achieved by trainees. These independent agencies should comprise vested interest groups' representatives, accountable to state authorities and carry out inspection on a regular basis, for example 4-6 year cycles.

CONCLUDING COMMENTS

The 1999 Bologna Declaration and subsequent process, significantly the 2001 Stockholm strategic agenda, mentioned in the introductory section, raised a number of key issues, not least of which was the meaning of notions of convergence, competence(s) and skills etc. Although such terms have become fashionable in scientific and policy domains, different meanings have led to conceptual confusion. Clarification of the significance of terms, identification of the issues at stake, and a common terminology are, therefore, a pre-requisite for communication in an inter-disciplinary and international context. It is important to ascertain the ideas that serve as a starting point for the identification of key competencies as well as the underlying normative criteria for defining key competences, and determine how different/various perspectives (e.g. pedagogue, PETE provider employer, teacher) can contribute to the construction of a set of indispensable competences in facing the challenges of a changing world. Futhermore, it is both necessary and relevant to clarify and establish the theoretical foundations, rationale, and selection processes behind sets of key competences, the political, social and economic factors that influence the definition and selection of key competencies in different socio-economic and cultural environments, and how this influence is exercised as well as the role of scientific findings and scientific methodology in these processes. The AEHESIS Project had a central concern with these issues. Additionally, it facilitated an opportunity to undertake an audit of PETE-related practices in Europe, from which it was readily clear that diversity in provision is prevalent across the region. The prevalence has evolved from a complex range of antecedent and contemporary variables including historical developments, geo-political and ideological settings, socio-cultural and economic influences and state-level interventions establishing legal frameworks, policy formulation and practice directions. The Bologna Declaration and subsequent inter-governmental EU policy Agreements and Commitments have provided an opportunity to harmonize provision in a concomitant context of respect for diversity. The AEHESIS Project PE Area Research Group adhered to harmonisation and diversity as well as the Bologna process inspired reference points, convergence and common understanding by formulating a PETE Curriculum based on sets of principles rather than specific prescriptions as guidelines. The proposals and framing are intended to cross cultural, national and institutional boundaries for they are deemed to have "universal applicability" in their flexibility and adaptability to suit "local" circumstances, conditions and traditions. Nevertheless, conceptually and contextually, they do also provide a reference point template for good practice(s) in PETE provision as well as a meaningful benchmark basis for European-wide, and perhaps, worldwide recognition.

The demands of PE in contemporary and ever changing school and wider community settings pose a challenge to teacher education institutions in equipping teachers, responsible for physical education, with the necessary competence to deliver relevant, quality PE programmes, which contribute to the development of the physically educated person. In the last decade, transformational and/or developmental changes have been introduced in many countries, especially in Europe: curriculum time allocation, curriculum content with cross-curricular, didactical innovations including negotiated learning etc., school organisational changes, shifting relationships between curricular, extra-curricular physical activity engagement, relationships with parents and other significant other wider community agencies.

Thus, teachers now face new situations, in which individual development, inclusion, evaluation as well as management of pupils raised in changed and changing socio-political environments, a significant number of whom have negative attitudes often connected with lifestyle trends in values and behaviours. Some changes have been met with teacher resistance, a form of defence mechanism triggered by insecurities of competence and in some cases exacerbated by slow responses of PETE providers to curricular developments and societal changes. The societal changes, developments and trends invoke demands for appropriate innovative approaches to teacher training. A pre-requisite for quality school PE is quality PETE programmes, relevant to the needs and requirements of individuals, the contemporary school and wider community environment. In this process, knowledge management is one important part of professional preparation; another is teachers as lifelong reflective learners, the seeds for which should be sown during initial training programmes and full accomplishment of which should be facilitated through quality continuing professional development programmes. Within teacher education programmes, some priority should be accorded to "changing minds and winning hearts and bodies". Associated changes in attitudes should emanate from development of knowledge and understanding, acquisition of appropriate pedagogical, didactical and managerial etc., competencies as well as critically analytical and reflective pedagogical and professional practice. Through accumulative experiences, teaching knowledge is incremental and competencies are appropriately adjustable but quality teaching is also defined by informed reflective practice attuned to ideals and values fostering true learning experiences in a dynamically changing world.

REFERENCES

Bain, L. (1990). Physical education teacher education. In: W. Robert Houston (Ed.). *Handbook of Research on Teacher Education.* New York, Macmillan Publishing Company, pp.758-781.

Behets, D. (2000). Physical education teachers' tasks and competencies.In: F. Carreiro da Costa, J. Diniz, M. Onofre, & L. Carvalho (Eds.), *Research on Teaching and Research on Teacher Education. Proceedings of the AIESEP International Seminar.* Lisboa, Edições FMH.

Chichester University (2003). *PETE Programme Handbook.* Chichester, School of Physical Education.

Corke, H. (2008). *An investigation into the qualities and competences that Employers look for in newly qualified physical education teachers.* Unpublished MA Education Dissertation, University of Worcester, Worcester, UK.

EUPEA (2006). *Issues of Quality.* Ghent, EUPEA.

Hardman, K. (2006). *PE Area Report.* In: K. Petry, K. Froberg and A. Madella (Eds.), *AEHESIS Thematic Network Project, Report of the Third Year.* Cologne, German Sports University. pp.201-238.

Hardman, K., Klein, G., Patrikkson, G., Rychtecky, A., & Carreiro da Costa, F. (2008). Implementation of the Bologna Process – Physical Education. In K. Petry, K. Froberg, A. Madella & W. Tokarksi (Eds.), *Higher Education in Sport in Europe. From Labour Market Demand to Training Supply.* Maidenhead, Meyer & Meyer Sport (UK) Ltd. pp.56-79.

Hargreaves, D. (2000). How to design and implement a revolution in teacher education and training: Some lessons from England. European Commission, *Teacher education policies in the European Union.* Lisbon: Portuguese Presidency of the Council of the European Union, pp.75-88.

Hoffmann, T. (1999). The Meanings of Competency. *Journal of European Industrial Training, 23*(6/7), pp.275-285.

Klein, G. (2004). A tool to build a curriculum model in the sport sector. *Communication to AEHEIS Project Management Group.* Brussels, November.

Kovač, M., Sloan, S., & Starc, G. (2008). Competencies in physical education teaching: Slovenian teachers' views and future perspectives. *European Physical Education Review, 14*(3), October. pp.299-323.

O'Sullivan, M. (1996). What do we know about the professional preparation of teachers? In: S. Silverman & C. Ennis (Eds.), *Student learning in physical education: Applying research to enhance instruction.* Champaign IL, Human Kinetics, pp. 315-338.

O'Sullivan, M. (1998). Education for an active lifestyle: challenges to teacher and coach preparation. In: R. Naul, K. Hardman, M. Piéron & B. Skirstad (Eds.), *Physical activity and active lifestyle of children and youth.* Schorndorf, Verlag Karl Hofmann, pp.131-149.

Scottish Qualifications Authority (2003). Key competencies – some international comparisons. *Policy and Research Bulletin, no.2.* Glasgow, Scottish Qualifications Authority

Tissot, P. (2003). *Terminology of vocational training policy, a multi-lingual glossary for an enlarged Europe.* Brussels, CEDEFOP, European Communities.

www.eupea.com, (2006). *EUPEA. About us.* November.

CHAPTER 11

ASSESSMENTS AND QUALIFICATIONS IN PHYSICAL EDUCATION

GEMMA VAN VUUREN-CASSAR

INTRODUCTION

Assessments of student learning and qualifications are an expanding world-wide phenomenon in education, training and on-going professional development. At the same time, the meaning and application of "assessment" and "qualification" in the education and employment domains need to being questioned in an attempt to inculcate clarity of use of these terms, as well as significance and appreciation of formal and informal assessments and qualifications. During the last 40 years, the shift towards more formal processes of conducting and recording assessments in physical education has been ongoing, yet the functions of formal and informal modes of assessment have not been interpreted equivocally by professionals and employers in teaching, coaching and training. Teachers and those involved in delivering courses in physical education and sport have been professionally challenged since they have been channelled to retain recreation, academic, examinations and vocational roles (Carroll, 1994) within physical education and sport (PE&S). For the purpose of this chapter, the domains of PE&S include areas of study leading to qualifications for jobs and professions in physical education, sport coaching, exercise, health and fitness and sports management.

The extraordinary increase of accreditations in PE&S (Stidder & Wallis, 2003; Green, 2008), and the greater opportunities in vocational courses and sport-related occupations (Stidder and Wallis, 2003) have contributed to the further development of qualifications in PE&S. Meanwhile, political influences and other factors (Piotriovski & Capel, 2000) have consolidated the infrastructure for more formalised assessments and qualifications' awards in physical education, sport, leisure, exercise and fitness. Therefore, assessments have become essential and integral to effective learning and training in PE&S at school levels and beyond (Carroll, 1994; Bailey, 2001; Green, 2008), especially for those keen to take up PE&S-related occupations. Assessments and qualifications are part of an ever evolving infrastructure stemming from teaching and learning and facilitating accreditation, certification, awards, official recognition, credentials and professionalization. Concurrently, significant changes have been taking place in European countries (Petry, Froberg & Madella, 2006) as well as in other regions of the world in an attempt to synchronise learning outcomes, content goals, curriculum standards, assessments, examinations, qualifications in the fields of higher education, training and employment in PE&S-related fields. The process of bringing together common understanding of learning structures, assessments and qualifications are typically explained within the European Qualifications Framework (EQF), which is discussed later in this chapter.

Commencing with an overview of European and other infrastructures of national qualifications frameworks, this chapter addresses a series of inter-related issues in qualifications and assessments and indicates how the task of implementing assessments and awarding qualifications may be approached. The focus of discussion including clarification of terms surrounding assessments and qualifications is the emergence, nature and role of assessment within national and European Qualifications Frameworks and the routes to academic, vocational and other qualifications in PE&S. The principles, purposes and modes of assessments are revisited with an emphasis on the implications for PE&S domains. It is argued that although assessment opportunities should be incorporated in learning experiences, particular attention should be paid to the planning, conducting and recording of assessments and the generation of qualifications. The intention is to identify areas of controversy and consensus regarding issues of assessment and qualifications worldwide, and in so doing, to provide knowledge and evidence for the formulation of improved applications of assessments and qualifications frameworks.

THE BOLOGNA DECLARATION, PROCESS
AND QUALIFICATIONS FRAMEWORKS

The 1999 Bologna Declaration currently with 46 European Cultural Convention of the Council of Europe signatory countries[1] (European Unit, 2010) led to the creation of the *European Higher Education Area* (EHEA) and as also indicated in chapter 10 was instrumental in instigating an on-going process of integration and harmonisation of higher education systems. The Bologna Process proposed that the EHEA be developed as a means of promoting mutual recognition of qualifications, demonstrating transparency of systems and easing the mobility of staff and students across higher education in Europe thus, committing countries to reform their higher education systems in order to generate European-wide convergence. One of the key features of the Process has involved the development of a National Qualifications Framework (NQF) in each country, and the development of criteria and procedures to verify that each national framework is compatible with an overarching Qualifications Framework for the EHEA. The EHEA Framework, representing the "face" of European Higher Education qualifications to the rest of the world, was adopted by European Ministers in May 2005.

The European Qualifications Framework for Lifelong Learning (EQF) was formally adopted by the European Union (EU) in April 2008. It covers all levels of education and is valid for EU countries, EU accession countries and countries of the European Economic Area. The EQF was developed after the EHEA framework and there is variation between them in wording, but there are no major differences between the two. It is possible for countries to construct NQFs that are compatible with the EQF as well as with the EHEA Framework, an aspect recognized by Ministers in their London Communiqué (2007): "We are satisfied that NQFs compatible with the overarching Framework for Qualifications of the EHEA will also be compatible with the proposal from the European Commission on a European

---

1 1999: Austria, Belgium, Bulgaria, Czech Republic, Denmark, Estonia, Finland, France, Germany, Greece, Hungary, Iceland, Ireland, Italy, Latvia, Lithuania, Luxembourg, Malta, Netherlands, Norway, Poland, Portugal, Romania, Slovakia, Slovenia, Spain, Sweden, Switzerland, United Kingdom
2001: Croatia, Cyprus, Liechtenstein, Turkey
2003: Albania, Andorra, Bosnia and Herzegovina, Holy See, Russia, Serbia, Macedonia
2005: Armenia, Azerbaijan, Georgia, Moldova , Ukraine
2007: Montenegro

Qualifications Framework for Lifelong Learning". The EQF initiative is closely related to the qualifications framework for the EHEA: the two frameworks are compatible and their implementation is coordinated (European Commission Education and Training, 2010a).

All countries have a qualifications system but a qualifications framework is a more systematic way of classifying qualifications, usually by a hierarchy of levels. The EQF, the development of which began in 2004 in response to compatibility requests from Member States, social partners and other stakeholders, is a common European transparent reference framework that enables European countries to link their qualifications systems to one another and assists learners and workers wishing to move between countries or change jobs or move educational institutions at home or across Europe. The key aim of the EQF is to contribute to creating a truly European workforce that is mobile and flexible. The EQF links countries' qualifications systems together, acting as a "translation" device to make academic degrees and vocational qualifications more readable and understandable across different countries and systems in Europe. The EQF applies to all types of education, training and qualifications, from school education to academic, professional and vocational. It encourages countries to relate their national qualifications systems to the EQF so that all new qualifications issued from 2012 on carry a reference to an appropriate EQF level. The European Commission Education and Training Unit (2010a) supported by the EQF for Lifelong Learning Expert Group proposed an 8-level framework based on learning outcomes aiming to facilitate the transparency and portability of qualifications and to support lifelong learning. This framework is now used by the EQF with the 8 reference levels based on learning outcomes defined in terms of knowledge, skills and competences. It provides details in terms of learning outcomes, which is "the set of knowledge, skills and/or competences an individual has acquired and/or is able to demonstrate after completion of a learning process, either formal, non-formal or informal" (Cedefop, 2008). Knowledge is described as theoretical and/or factual; skills are described as cognitive (involving the use of logical, intuitive and creative thinking) and practical (involving manual dexterity and the use of methods, materials, tools and instruments); and competencies are described in terms of responsibility and autonomy

> "to apply learning outcomes adequately in a defined context: education, work, personal or professional development... where competence is not limited to cognitive elements involving the use of theory, concepts or tacit knowledge; it also encompasses functional aspects (involving technical skills) as well as interpersonal attributes (e.g. social or organisational skills) and ethical values)" (Cedefop, 2008).

Tables 1 and 2 depict the knowledge outcomes and typical academic and vocational qualifications of the 8 levels.

Using the knowledge outcomes as a common reference point, the framework facilitates comparison and transfer of qualifications between countries, systems and institutions and is, therefore, relevant to a wide range of users at European as well as at national level. Most European countries have decided to develop NQFs reflecting, and responding

Table 1. The EQF levels 1-8 linked to the Bologna EHEA, and examples of knowledge learning outcomes and qualifications levels 1-3

Bologna EHEA	EQF level	Knowledge: Learning outcomes linked to levels	NQF level Examples of qualifications		FHEQ Examples of qualifications
			Entry[2] • Entry level certificates • English for Speakers of Other Languages (ESOL)		
-	1	Basic general knowledge • basic knowledge and skills • ability to apply learning in everyday situations • not geared towards specific occupations	• GCSEs grades D-G • BTEC Introductory Diplomas and Certificates • OCR Nationals	• Key Skills level 1 • NVQs at level 1 • Skills for Life	-
-	2	Basic factual knowledge of a field of work or study • basic knowledge and skills • ability to apply learning with guidance or supervision • may be linked to job competence	• GCSEs grades A*-C • BTEC First Diplomas and Certificates • OCR Nationals • Key Skills level 2	• NVQs at level 2 • Skills for Life • 16+ exams	-
-	3	Knowledge of facts, principles, processes and general concepts, in a field of work or study • good knowledge and understanding of a subject • ability to perform variety of tasks with some guidance or supervision • appropriate for many job roles	• A levels • Advanced Extension Awards • GCE in applied subjects • International Baccalaureate • Key Skills level 3	• NVQs at level 3 • BTEC Diplomas, Certificates and Awards • BTEC Nationals • OCR Nationals • 18+ exams	-

to, the EQF. These developments are important to ensure that the European-level cooperation process is properly anchored at national level. The rapid development of NQFs since 2004 demonstrates the need for increased transparency and comparability of qualifications at all levels and shows that the basic principles underpinning the EQF are broadly shared. There are 31 countries that are developing, introducing or already implementing a NQF for lifelong learning, including the 27 members of the EU (Pevec-Grm & Bjornavold, 2010). The majority of countries aim to develop and introduce a comprehensive NQF covering all levels and types of qualifications such as general education, vocational education and training, higher education and adult education and strive for stronger integration between sub-systems.

---

2 In the United Kingdom there are nine levels, with "entry" level preceding levels 1-8 of the EQF.

Table 2. The EQF levels 1-8 linked to the Bologna EHEA, and examples of knowledge learning outcomes and qualifications levels 4-8

Bologna EHEA	EQF level	Knowledge: Learning outcomes linked to levels	NQF level Examples of qualifications	FHEQ Examples of qualifications
	4	• Factual and theoretical knowledge in broad contexts within a field of work or study	• NVQs at level 4 • BTEC Professional Diplomas, Certificates and Awards	• certificates of higher education • higher national certificates
Short cycle within or linked to the 1st cycle	5	• Comprehensive, specialised, factual and theoretical knowledge within a field of work or study and an awareness of the boundaries of that knowledge	• HNCs and HNDs • NVQs • BTEC Professional Diplomas, Certificates and Awards	• diplomas of higher education • Foundation Degrees • higher national diplomas
1st cycle qualifications	6	• Advanced knowledge of a field of work or study, involving a critical understanding of theories and principles	• National Diploma in Professional Production Skills • BTEC Advanced Professional Diplomas, Certificates and Awards	• bachelors degrees • bachelors degrees with honours • graduate certificates and diplomas • Professional Graduate Certificate in Education
2nd cycle qualifications	7	• Highly specialised knowledge, some of which is at the forefront of knowledge in a field of work or study, as the basis for original thinking and/or research • Critical awareness of knowledge issues in a field and at the interface between different fields	• Diploma in Translation • BTEC Advanced Professional Diplomas, Certificates and Awards	• masters degrees • integrated masters degrees • postgraduate certificates • postgraduate diplomas
3rd cycle qualification	8	• Knowledge at the most advanced frontier of a field of work or study and at the interface between fields	• specialist awards	• doctoral degrees

LEARNING FROM EUROPEAN AND INTERNATIONAL EXPERIENCE

In the United Kingdom, the Framework for Higher Education Qualifications (FHEQ) has been designed by the higher education sector, and describes all the main higher education qualifications. It applies to degrees, diplomas, certificates and other academic awards granted by a university or higher education institution (apart from honorary degrees and higher doctorates). The FHEQ broadly corresponds with levels 4 to 8 of the NQF in terms of the demands the qualifications place on learners. On the other hand, the NQF sets out the level at which a vocational qualification can be recognised in each country. Only qualifications that have been accredited by the regulators can be included in the NQF. This ensures that all qualifications within the framework are of high quality, and meet the needs of learners and employers.

Countries differ markedly in the extent to which vocational qualifications are located in a single NQF with a single set of levels and common criteria. New Zealand has progressed furthest in this direction, although national qualification frameworks are in the process of being developed in Ireland, Scotland, South Africa, Australia and a number of other Commonwealth countries (Donn & Davies, 2003; Young, 2003). The arguments in favour of NQFs are endorsed by numerous countries: they are designed to promote flexibility, transparency and credit accumulation and so match many features of the new global economy. It is too early to assess whether they are achieving these ambitious goals. However, there are already some indications of inadvertent effects, which have escalated. For example, in practice, an NQF tends to downplay the specificity of different sectors and their demands for skill and knowledge, in order to draw attention and show partiality towards what is claimed to be common to all qualifications. Although there are common elements in qualifications for very different sectors, learners also have to acquire specific skills and knowledge in specific contexts. It is important to emphasize that while all NQFs have some features in common, countries have varied strikingly in how they have introduced them.

Some countries, like Scotland, emphasise enabling progression at crucial points such as between college and universities. Others, such as South Africa and New Zealand, have been more ambitious in bringing all qualifications into a single system. An academic/vocational divide is a feature of education and training systems that is found in all countries. In the cases of New Zealand and South Africa, attempts to abolish the distinction have led to severe conflicts and, in New Zealand, to dropping the attempt. Other countries have adopted quite different approaches to minimizing the negative effects of the academic/vocational divide. In France, it has been through a common "baccalaureate" framework, which ensures that even those following *vocational* baccalaureates are required to continue with their general education for a significant part of their studies (Powell, Coutrot, Graf, Bernhard & Kieffer, 2009). In Germany, there has been an attempt to develop a distinct form of vocational knowledge (work process knowledge), which, though general, is based on the knowledge demands of occupations, not academic disciplines (Boreham, 2004). The academic/vocational divide is not just a feature of either qualifications or educational provision; it is an expression of the division of labour and the occupational structure and as such is in a constant process of change. General and vocational qualifications have different purposes in all countries although both have an educational and an employment-related role. As many workplaces become more "knowledge intensive", the importance of the knowledge component associated with off the job learning relative to learning that takes place in workplaces increases. The balance and relationship between the two kinds of learning and, hence, the question of qualification design remains an issue in all systems.

The Australian Qualifications Framework (AQF) has been in place since 1995, making it one of the more long-established NQFs in operation. The AQF is a quality assured national framework of qualifications in the school, vocational education and training (VET), and higher education sectors. The framework links together all these qualifications and is a highly visible, quality-assured national system of educational recognition that promotes lifelong learning and a seamless and diverse education and training system.

"For example, a generalist Associate Degree program may be structured to articulate with an Advanced Diploma program delivering specialist industry competencies, to enhance employment opportunities or credit into a specialist

Bachelor Degree. The reverse pathway is also encouraged, where a program delivering an Advanced Diploma is articulated with a generalist Associate Degree program to enhance credit into a Bachelor Degree or broaden employment opportunities" (AQF, 2007, p.50).

The basis for equivalence and compatibility of qualifications in Europe, America, Canada, Great Britain and countries influenced by the British and Commonwealth educational tradition such as Australia, New Zealand and South Africa (Anglo/American education) is being facilitated through the transparency and parameters of accreditation processes explained through NQFs (DEST, 2006).

The issue of the value and currency of qualifications and certifications is debatable. On the one hand, society wants to safeguard its population by ensuring that those holding qualifications are indeed knowledgeable, competent and skilful to deliver a service of high standard for which they have been certified and qualified; on the other hand, in a world obsessed by qualifications, diplomas and credentials, it is important to remember that assessment and reporting have in the past been allowed to become one of the biggest barriers to learning for many young people.

> "Educational systems in virtually every country are to a greater or lesser extent being deflected from their true purpose of promoting education and developing the skills, abilities and potential of young people to meet the needs of their society into a punishing and more or less irrelevant paper chase in which few will win and many must fail" (Broadfoot, 1996, p.205).

The international outbreak of the so called "diploma syndrome", which has transformed so many educational systems, has shifted focus. The new focal point of European educational institutions is "harmonisation" within NQFs and the EQF. For many individuals, assessments and qualifications in academic and vocational routes of learning are becoming key authentic evidence of knowledge, skills and competencies. Qualifications harmonised within the EQF and NQFs are the currencies that show what one actually knows and is able to do, which is more relevant than the inputs of lengths of a learning experience, type of institution, qualification and so on. In so doing, the EQF

- supports a better match between the needs of the labour market (for knowledge, skills and competences) and education and training provision
- facilitates the transfer and use of qualifications across different countries and education and training systems
- facilitates the validation of non-formal and informal learning.

THE RELATIONSHIP BETWEEN VOCATIONAL AND GENERAL (ACADEMIC) QUALIFICATIONS

The growing demand for sports activities and the increasing mobility of sports professionals have led to new initiatives in the field of vocational education and training.

Sports professionals can benefit, where relevant, from the possibilities offered by instruments such as the European Qualifications Framework (EQF), the European Credit System for Vocational Education and Training (ECVET) or the Credit Transfer and Accumulation System (ECTS). ECVET is a European system of accumulation (capitalisation) and transfer of credits designed for vocational education and training in Europe. It enables the attesting and recording of the learning achievement/learning outcomes of an individual engaged in a learning pathway leading to a qualification, a vocational diploma or certificate. It enables the documentation, validation and recognition of achieved learning outcomes acquired abroad, in both formal VET or in non-formal contexts. It is centred on the individual, based on the validation and the accumulation of learning outcomes, defined in terms of the knowledge, skills and competences necessary for achieving a qualification. ECVET is a system designed to operate at the European level, interfacing with national systems and arrangements for credit accumulation and transfer (European Commission Education and Training, 2010b). By 2012, it should create a technical framework to describe qualifications in terms of units of learning outcomes, and it includes assessment, transfer, accumulation and recognition procedures. Each of the units is associated with a certain number of ECVET points developed on the basis of common standards: 60 ECVET points are allocated to the learning outcomes achieved in a year of full-time VET. The system also allows the possibility to develop common references for VET qualifications and is fully compatible with the European ECTS used in the EHEA, which also operate on 60 ECTS points per year on full-time study at undergraduate level.

In the 1980s, courses leading to qualifications in recreation and leisure were established by the City and Guilds of London Institute (C&G) and the Business and Technology Education Council (BTEC). These qualifications suffered from low status (Carroll, 1994). The Industry Lead Body in the UK commissioned research and established Technical Standards Working Groups to identity job competencies standards for the six occupational areas. These have created an infrastructure for vocational education and training (VET) such as the Level 3 BTEC Nationals in Table 3 below (BTEC, 2010). An interesting feature of VET is that the titles of the qualifications are strongly linked to specific occupations.

Table 3: Vocational Education and Training (VET): Occupational areas

Occupational areas	Level 3 BTEC Nationals
1. Coaching, teaching and instructions	1. Sport
2. Facility management	2. Sport (Development, Coaching and Fitness)
3. Operational services	3. Sport (Outdoor Adventure)
4. Outdoor Education	4. Sport (Performance and Excellence)
5. Play and play work	5. Sport and Exercise Sciences
6. Sports Development	

The vocational qualifications that fall under the umbrella of "sport" are all developed and placed within the qualifications and credit framework which "is the same as the national Qualifications Framework" (Directgov, 2010). Physical Education teachers in secondary schools and sport colleges in England are actively delivering courses leading to vocational and academic qualifications, with opportunities in practical areas such as coaching, instructing and leading outdoor and adventure activities, as well as in facility management and administration. Carroll, (1994), Stidder and Wallis, (2003), and Green (2008) have presented records of the growth and increase of students taking up courses leading to qualifications for 16 and 18 year olds in PE&S in England and Wales. The variety of qualifications in PE&S from 1990 to 2006 experienced a growth of 300% from 34,529 to 140,555 candidates for GCSE (16+); and a 3,000% growth for the same period with a humble beginning of 639 candidates to 21, 834 for the 18+ qualification (Green, 2008). In the UK, the Joint Qualifications Council publishes Annual Reports on the number of entrants and the grades awarded for various qualifications in PE&S for England, Wales and Northern Ireland. The candidates registered for PE certified courses leading to qualifications in 2009 for all of the UK numbered 185,530 (JCQ, 2009a) for all pupils aged 16+ (all PE GCSEs and Entry Certificate) and 52,764 (JCQ, 2009b) for 17-18+ aged pupils (all PE Advanced Subsidiary and Advanced levels) qualifications. For vocational qualifications, one of the providers (EDEXCEL, 2010) of the qualifications publishes benchmarks, percentage of students acquiring a particular grade and not the number of candidates. From the following table, it is evident that the levels of the EQF and the NQF are part of the title of the qualification. England has an "Entry" level in addition to the 8 levels.

Table 4: Vocational qualifications levels and titles

Edexcel **Level 2** BTEC First Diplomas:

Sport (Exercise and Fitness)

Sport (Outdoor Education)

Sport (Performance)

Edexcel **Level 3** BTEC National Certificates:

Sport and Exercise Sciences Sport (Development, Coaching and Fitness)

Sport (Outdoor Adventure)

Sport (Performance and Excellence)

Sport (Sports Development and Fitness)

Edexcel **Level 3** BTEC National Diplomas:

Sport and Exercise Sciences

Sport (Development, Coaching and Fitness)

Sport (Outdoor Adventure)

Sport (Performance and Excellence)

Sport (Sports Development and Fitness)

The PE&S courses offered in schools, which offer a platform for the acquisition of a qualification, has increased the academicisation, professionalistion and marketisation of PE (Green, 2008). These developments have further contributed to a shakeup in the management of PE in schools and in teacher training. A clear opportunity has emerged that has not only increased the status of the PE&S in schools and of the PE profession, but also has brought about an influx of resources for teaching, coaching, managing sport and exercise and fitness. The recipients of qualifications have also equipped themselves with certificates that have strong currency for further and higher education and the establishment of occupations in the sports sector. The expansion of sport-related programmes in higher education has also facilitated the development of assessments and qualifications in schools, and fostered the demand and interest in graduate qualifications in PE&S, thus contributing to the economic dimension of the labour market.

Talented and gifted students in PE&S, who go on to make successful careers in top-performance sports, also need to think of developing their career after top performance days are over. Conzelmann and Nagel (2003) found that German Olympic athletes take a course parallel to the period of educational and professional qualification whereby the engagement in sport rather favours the professional career in its course. The European Commission of Sport (2009) favours the "dual career" of young sports people, ensuring that they receive an education and/or professional training in addition to their sports training, so that they can prepare for a new career once they retire from professional sport. Evidence pertaining to how education and sports training is being developed suggests that the 27 member states of Europe have different structures in place Żyśko & Piàtkowska, 2009). In 19 countries, the development of elite level sports for able bodied and disabled young persons is taken into account by creating sports schools or specialised schools (INEUMconsulting, 2008). It remains to be seen what the impact is of the contribution of these infrastructures supporting "dual" careers of sports people.

THE CONTEXT OF ASSESSMENTS AND QUALIFICATIONS

The terms *assessment, test, exam(ination), measurement* and *evaluation* are often used interchangeably, however, it is important to distinguish between them so that some common understanding prevails. The same tendency is emerging for the terms *qualification, certification, credential, accreditation* and *licensure*. At a time when assessments take place in classrooms as well as while students are completing a work-related placement, an apprenticeship etc., or a worker is on a course of extending professional skills and development, this is not surprising. Simultaneously, professionals involved in the processes ought to appreciate that while these terms are related they are inherently different, as outlined below.

Assessment is a broad term defined as a course of action for generating and acquiring information that is used for making decisions about students, curricula, programmes, schools and educational policy *inter alia*. When a student is being assessed, the scope is usually limited to whether a learning target has been achieved. Typically, a variety of assessment techniques are usually used to collect such information (the modes of assessment are discussed in the next section). A *test* is an instrument or systematic procedure for generating, observing, describing and recording one or more characteristics, abilities, knowledge or other attributes of a student. An *exam(ination)* is a formally staged task or activity that is part of the testing procedure that produces information about how an individual student or an entity is progressing. The examination scores of all students can be pooled together to generate information about how a school, region or nation is performing with reference to national and international goals, standards or benchmarks of such testing procedures. Some examples of examination scores, familiarly known as "league tables" are published in England, Wales and Northern Ireland by the *Joint Council for Qualifications* (JCQ[3]). Other international examples are the *Trends in International Mathematics and Science Study* (TIMSS[4]) and Achievement and Attainment Tables[5]. Many national, regional and local education authorities use benchmarks for testing the success of individual schools at the various stages of schooling from entry to leaving. *Measurement* is defined as a procedure for awarding numbers (scores or levels) to a specified quality (e.g. knowledge, skill, competence) in a manner that the numbers/grades describe the degree to which the individual possesses the quality. For example, a university Bachelors degree holds level 4 status on the EQF scale of measurement. Likewise some schools use measures 1-100 for examinations while standardised tests use various forms of measurements. A numeric measurement is usually linked to a descriptive criterion or set of criteria expanding what that number stands for. Assessment is a broader term since the scope of a test or measurement is narrower; not all assessments yield measurements. *Evaluation* is defined as the course of action following the process of assessment. Evaluation of individuals can take place while they are still in the learning process, often referred to as formative or coursework assessment, whereas when evaluation occurs after the educational process has been completed, it is often called summative or terminal assessment (Rowntree, 1977; Nitko & Brookhart, 2011). Evaluation is a term which is typically used for schools, programmes and educational material. Formative evaluation is on-going and occurs after every session in a programme where amendments are often made to session notes. Summative evaluation of schools' programmes and educational materials tend to summarise the strengths and weakness, and describe whether the school implemented programme or educational materials have attained the stated goals. Summative evaluations are usually not aimed to provide suggestions for improvements, while formative evaluations are.

A *qualification* is a generic term that refers to the wide variety of higher education qualifications at different levels and across different countries. A qualification is typically manifested in an awarded so-called certificate (or licence in some countries) to an individual or an entity. A qualification is "formal certification, issued by a relevant

---

3 The JCQ (Joint Council for Qualifications) was established on 1st January 2004 and represents the major awarding bodies that serve England, Wales and Northern Ireland: AQA (Assessment and Qualifications Alliance), CCEA (Northern Ireland Council for the Curriculum, Examinations and Assessment), City & Guilds, Edexcel, OCR (Oxford, Cambridge and RSA Examinations) and WJEC (Welsh Joint Education Committee).

4 **The Trends in International Mathematics and Science Study** (TIMSS) is an international assessment of the mathematics and science knowledge of fourth- and eighth-grade students around the world. TIMSS was developed by the International Association for the Evaluation of Educational Achievement (IEA) to allow participating nations to compare students' educational achievement across borders. TIMSS was first administered in 1995, and every 4 years thereafter. In 1995, forty-one nations participated in the study; in 2007, 48 countries participated.

5 These tables provide information on the achievement and attainment of students of sixth-form age (17 and 18) in English secondary schools and further education sector colleges. They also show how these results compare with other schools and colleges in the area and in England as a whole.
These can be viewed on http://www.dcsf.gov.uk/performancetables.

approved body, in recognition that a person has achieved learning outcomes or competencies relevant to identified individual, professional, industry or community needs" (AQF, 2007). A *certificate* is usually issued as a printed document, which is used for many purposes and across all levels of education and training. Certificates are awarded to give recognition to participants in a diverse range of activities, including, for example, extra-curricular activity engagement, recognition of improved desirable behaviours, and on completion of a course or programme of study of a phase of education and/or training. The process of awarding a certificate for a degree, diploma or other certificate issued by a competent authority attesting the successful completion of a higher education programme is referred to as *certification*. For the purpose of this chapter, "certification" refers to an end of secondary school award of a certificate for individual or all subjects studied and assessed at school such as the school certificate (internal assessments), GCSE (General Certificate of Secondary Education, in England) and the IB (International Baccalaureate). *Credentials* usually refer to qualifications or evaluations or comparisons of "other" credentials to existing qualifications. Meanwhile, *accreditation* is the process by which one higher education institution or a professional body has acquired authority to award, and/or has acquired recognition of its qualifications from another senior competent authority; this might be the State, a government agency or another domestic or foreign higher education institution or training provider. The term has its origins in the American education system and is used in some European countries in the same way as "recognition" such as a university Ph.D. or a training provider Sports Leader Award in order to attest to the completion of specific training or education programmes by students. Accreditation attests to the successful completion of an assessed course or programme. *Licensure* refers to the granting of a license, which gives a "permission to practise". Licensing is a well-established and convenient method of activity regulation as exemplified in pilot and driving licenses, coaching licenses, adventure sports' licences and those required to work in the exercise and fitness industry. Thus, the process of assessments involves a variety of courses of action that can include the administration of tests, examinations, evaluations and the potential award of a certificate, a qualification or a licence over a period of time.

Assessments are variously used: provision of information about the progress of student learning of a student; decisions about areas that require further training, teaching and learning; and increasingly linked with certification of competence and the validation of skill' and tasks' performance related to specific jobs. Assessments feature in the prospectuses and policies of pre-primary, primary, secondary, high school, under-graduate and post-graduate educational entities as well as in commercial, leadership, management and vocational training thus, playing a significant role in certifying, accrediting and awarding qualifications to people in an age of qualifications' frameworks. Despite its significant role, it is a Programme Study area hitherto largely neglected: many are those who have acquired their assessment expertise on the job, through continuing professional development course attendance, the assistance of colleagues, personal interest and commitment to their job and chance at best. Knowledge of construction and implementation of assessments is valuable for practitioners because the results and outcomes of assessments are used widely for diagnosis, selection, certification, control, feedback, goal setting, accountability and maintaining standards in PE&S. Furthermore, tasks and strategies used for implementing assessments are an essential part of the teaching, learning and skill acquisition process. The ability for practitioners to develop useful, valid and reliable assessments contributing to qualifications does not happen by itself: knowledge understanding and application of assessments and their contribution to academic and vocational qualifications is an on-going evolution in the fields of education and training.

Those involved in constructing, implementing, validating, administering, processing and communicating assessment results and awarding certification and qualification should be concerned with the principles, purposes and modes of assessments; the assessment and qualifications frameworks and their implications for learning, employment and professional development as well as contemporary issues of assessment such as gender, talented and gifted individuals and the currency of qualifications in the age of lifelong professional development.

REVISITING THE PRINCIPLES, PURPOSES AND MODES OF ASSESSMENT

Principles of assessment such as *validity* and *reliability* in education (Popham, 2011; Reynolds, Livingston, Wilson, 2010; Osterlind, 2010) and physical education (Carroll, 1994) are discussed in this section with a focus on their use, importance and implications for teaching, coaching and training in PE&S.

Validity is the evaluation of the "adequacy and appropriateness of the interpretations and uses of assessment results" for a given group of individuals (Linn and Miller, 2005). Validity refers to whether an assessment, which could include a variety of examinations, tests and tasks; it measures what it is supposed to assess and is fit for purpose. Validity is measured in levels such as high, moderate, or low. The higher the validity of an assessment the more confidence can be placed on the measurements given. There are various types of validity.

Content-related Validity or Face Validity
The level of content validity refers to the extent to which the programme/learning objectives and the content and methods of teaching and learning are represented in the assessment. Content embraces knowledge, skills, competencies, attitudes and other relevant components. Content validity (or face validity) is aimed at appraising how well the sample of assessment tasks *represents* the domain of tasks to be measured. For example, for a PE teacher, an assessment high in content validity will include high representations of all the core content areas of knowledge of a course of study and all the key competencies of application experienced in the field.

Criterion-related Validity or Predictive Validity
Criterion validity is concerned with how well the test performance *predicts* future performance or *estimates* current performance on some valued measures such a descriptive criteria. Predictive validity assesses the *ability of a test to predict something it should theoretically be able to predict*. A battery of "proficiency" tests of a language, mathematics and physical education skills is often used for prospective PE teachers for the purpose of selection.

Construct-related Validity

Construct validity evidence is judged by determining how well an assessment can be interpreted as a meaningful measure of some quality or ability. For instance when performance of physical activity is assessed under highly competitive situations, teachers and coaches can help increase construct validity by trying to reduce factors that influence performance (stress, fatigue) but are irrelevant to the construct being assessed.

It is important for teachers, coaches and instructors to think about content validation when devising assessment tasks and one way to help do this is to devise a *Table of Specifications* (Linn and Miller, 2005). This table typically shows the relative emphasis in percentage marks and the number of test items or tasks for each learning outcome and the corresponding areas of content. Moreover, certain skills and competencies are more valid if assessed in the authentic environment (construct validity), as close as possible to the situation in which they occur, for example teaching and coaching physical activities and sport, and performing as an athlete. Since courses of professional education and training often include knowledge, skills, competencies, attitudes and other relevant factors, constructing assessments is now a more complex phenomenon.

An ultimate expected or desired outcome of PE lessons during compulsory schooling years is the physically educated individual, arguably defined as someone who

> "might be described as being physically literate, having acquired culturally normative skills enabling engagement in a variety of physical activities, which can help to maintain healthy well-being throughout the full life-span; they participate regularly in physical activity because it is enjoyable; and they understand and value physical activity and its contribution to a healthy lifestyle" (Hardman, 2007, p.iii).

The key issues here in PE&S are what assessments are implemented and what qualifications are awarded for every child to show a level of certification of being physically educated? When a series of tasks and questions are used at regular intervals to make up an assessment of a physically educated person, the assessment can usually be described as having a high level of validity. Some ways of assessing an individual could include personal oral or written reflection of on-going participation in physical activities, discussion of a diary of participation in physical activities with a peer, planning and executing a personal health, exercise and fitness plan, using information and communication technology in physical activities and sport ethically. Other tasks are: completing written and diagrammatic tasks to assess knowledge, understanding and synthesis, practical assessments to consolidate the application of knowledge, performance of techniques, tactics, and leadership of a sport and health related exercise activities, oral questioning on analysis of performance activities, the progress and activities of a particular role assigned to students using the Sport Education model (Siedentop, Hastie & van der Mars, 2006), an investigative project over a number of weeks and other relevant components for the individual such as a participation at a competitive level in sport or an advanced performer in a dance form as a gifted and talented child. Various PE programmes have tried to award recognition of levels of commitment by putting into place national policy documents with "levels of attainment" as in the case of the *Physical Education National Curriculum for England and Wales* (QCDA, 2010); and the *National Standards of Physical Education* (NASPE, 2004) in the United States of America. Additionally, there are National Sports Governing Bodies Awards often held in partnership with schools across various countries in Europe.

Reliability refers to the *consistency* of a measurement (Linn & Miller 2005) and is related to issues such as similarity of student scores if different test items are used, or if a different teacher, had graded the test. An assessment provides information about students by using a specific measure of performance at one particular time. Unless the results from the assessment are reasonably consistent over different occasions, different raters, or different tasks (in the same content domain), confidence in the results will be low and so cannot be useful in improving student learning. Reliability is measured statistically and more extensive discussion on these procedures is available in Popham (2011) and Osterlind (2010). Assessments with more tasks or questions more often than not have higher reliability. This means that assessments should have enough tasks included to reduce the influence of chance variations. Clear instructions for tasks help increase reliability. If the wording of specific tasks or questions is unclear, then students will not be able to answer the questions coherently because of lack of clarity of language. Clear marking criteria and a common understanding and application of the marking criteria (including training), usually ensure high reliability.

Carroll (1994) designated validity, reliability, objectivity and clear criteria in physical education as primary principles of assessments; he also argued for secondary principles in assessments such as variety of situations, balance of techniques and equality of opportunity. Bailey (2001) further suggested that assessments in PE should also be practical to implement. The principles of assessment provide a universal common understanding of the applications of assessment. The key questions related to "why" we assess become more meaningful when the purposes of assessments are taken into account. The main purposes of assessments as depicted by various authors over the last few decades are presented in the following table.

Table 5: The main purposes of assessment

Rowntree (1977)	Satterly (1989)	Gipps (1990)	Black *et al* (2003)	Reynolds *et al* (2010)
Maintain Standards Selection Motivation Feedback Preparation For Life	Accountability Certification Goal Setting Diagnosis Feedback	Control Certification Selection Diagnosis Screening	Accountability Certification Learning	Student Evaluation Instructional Decisions Selection, Placement, Classifications Policy Decisions Counselling and Guidance

Assessments serve a range of functions for the purpose of formal assessments for diagnosis, selection and certification, which are often seen as necessary and unproblematic, even when these are partly completed within the school setting.

Meanwhile, purposes of assessments that are shaped by school policy, education systems and take place "in the classroom" during a course of study often require further considerations and have generated questions related to the functional characteristics of the assessment, to whom the assessments are reported, what is assessed, how it is assessed and recorded, when assessments take place, and who moderates the work? Assessment forms such as observing, informal assessments that report directly to the pupil/individual serve a separate purpose from those assessments reporting to parents, employers and external examination bodies for instance. A clear distinction should be made between *assessment of learning* for the purposes of grading and reporting that has its own well-established procedures and *assessment for learning*, which refers daily classroom activities and calls for different priorities, new procedures and a new commitment (Black, 1999; Lockwood and Newton, 2004; and Frapwell, 2010). Spackman (2002) suggested strategies for applying assessment for learning in PE by sharing learning outcomes, feedback, questioning, and self and peer assessments by pupils. Assessments serve an important function in the process of learning and can be implemented in an enhancing and effective manner for the benefit of the learners. Assessment for learning is closely related to "formative" assessment and assessment of learning is often associated with "summative" assessment. These two terms are part of what Rowntree (1977) and Satterely (1981) have discussed extensively as bi-polar modes of assessments in education:

- Informal- Formal
- Continuous- Terminal
- Process-Product
- Convergent- Divergent
- Formative-Summative
- Coursework-examination
- Internal-External
- Idiographic-Nomethetic

These modes of assessments in PE have been discussed extensively by Carroll, (1994) and Piotrovski and Capel (2000) and there are numerous examples of how each of them is used on a regular basis in the fields of PE and sports coaching. The focus on formative assessment in current PE literature is relevant but the processes of assessments leading to qualifications and certification in PE and Sport furthermore include coursework, process, product, continuous, terminal and other modes of assessments on a regular basis. The function and purpose of the various modes of assessments should be considered more in PE&S since the variety of modes are the tools of assessment. Moreover, reference systems (Carroll, 1994; and Satterly, 1989) lend themselves to various philosophies of assessments in PE&S. There are several types of assessment or reference systems of assessments, for example

- criterion referenced
- ipsative referenced
- norm referenced
- domain referenced

Although it is educationally worthwhile to know how an individual is performing in an activity using criterion-referenced assessments and comparing the performance with pre-defined levels of performance, it is also useful to know how a learner has progressed in comparison with previous performances using ipsative referenced assessments. In team performance, selection and external assessments' results can show how an individual compares with others such as norm referenced systems, which has a meaningful purpose too. Domain referenced assessments are an outgrowth of criterion-referenced assessments where significance is attached to areas of content whether it is knowledge, skills and competencies related to a module of study. Educational assessment presumes that many achievements are attainable by all pupils, yet how and when they attain them varies from one to another. Since in criterion-referenced assessment, pupils' achievements are judged against explicit criteria, all pupils will have an opportunity to demonstrate a level of attainment hence, serving both formative and summative purposes.

The development of PE&S courses for school aged children also includes experiential engagements of formal apprenticeships, where knowledge and skills are experienced in an authentic environment and the reliance on a variety of modes of assessments is an effective way forward. At a time for change from a reliance on principles, and modes of assessments, more information on how to assess various modes is useful for teachers, instructors and those involved in constructing, completing and processing assessments. "Teachers engaged in the development and teaching examination courses must begin to reconcile the tensions that will inevitably emerge between the multiplicity of role definition and identity they are currently expected to fulfil" (Nutt & Clarke, 2002, p.162). Basic guidance on the construction, criteria and validation of oral type, project type, experiential/apprentice type and written type of formal and informal assessments, who will assess, and when to assess are necessary apart from "assessment for learning". Within any assessment framework, principles of assessments such validity and reliability will remain key to generate sound infrastructures of assessments and qualifications at all levels of education and training.

CONCLUSION

The acquisition of certification and accreditation leading to professional, vocational qualifications and employment is a cultural feature in European countries. The decade of the Bologna Process 1999-2010 has witnessed intensive reforms in higher education and vocational education structures. This was achievable because European governments have taken "a European approach to the modernisation of their national higher education systems" (European Union, 2010) and it is hoped that this momentum will be sustained and efforts will be maintained. The Bologna Process has established a strong EHEA, with coherent, transparent and outstanding Higher Education sector, which is essential for the cultural, economic and social development of Europe. The achievements of the Bologna process have to be consolidated and their sustainability at national and institutional level ensured within a logical European framework. In particular the on-going process of curricular renewal needs to be continued in Higher Education Institutions across Europe (EUA, 2008). Careful attention must be given to following up "unfinished business" to ensure that the qualitative changes required are embedded in institutional and also subject specific cultures, such as the sports sector. It is crucial to avoid the risk of achieving only superficial structural change across Europe. Moreover, in pursuing the common goal of a major shift to student centred learning, linking qualifications and credits with the introduction of learning outcomes, the continuing reform process needs to take account of different disciplinary cultures and also address the need for reform in the emerging sport sector, teacher training and regulated professions.

The development of compatible EHEA and EQF is a sound and promising strategy for the consolidation and recognition of education and qualifications and hence, education and employment opportunities across Europe. The NQF and educational systems across Europe support the development of standard occupations in the sport sector and opportunities for the development of a competent workforce are indeed in place. NQFs are facilitating the "harmonisation" of education and training, and are well underway with broad agreement on concept and aims, relevant policies and structures already in position. Europe has a highly diversified educational policy in the sport sector, made up of vocational, academic and non formal courses provided as a complement to field practice by governing bodies. The harmonisation for the education and training of "occupations" in the sport-related sector, needs further common language and understanding amongst training providers and employers to be further developed and applied across Europe. The existence of an EQF and NQF will underpin the standards and provide a sound support for the provision of assessments and qualifications.

The processes of assessments and the nature of qualifications undoubtedly shape the educational, vocational and employment future opportunities of many young persons and adults alike. Assessment and the award of qualifications through certification are increasingly widespread activities in education and training at every level throughout the world. Assessments and qualifications are used by learners and teachers to guide teaching and learning in the classroom, by employers and academics to help select employees or students and by local, national and international policy makers to evaluate the efficiency of their educational systems. Given the impact of assessment results on individuals and societies, it is important to try to ensure quality, compatibility, validity, reliability in assessment and wisdom in interpretation and consequent evaluation.

The challenges for education and training providers to revitalise their curricula and generate a culture of professionalisation of sport is a key institutional change that is inevitable for the success of "harmonisation", even though it will be met with "value laden" resistance. Employment of the sports sector in Europe can be enhanced through developing a better understanding of key aspects of the quality of "sport jobs" (Madella, 2003). The consolidation of sports professions will require a deal of work at grass root levels, particularly in schools, sports and health and fitness clubs and organised physical activities, where young individuals come across the professionals in an authentic scenario as well as through helping out voluntarily. PE teachers in schools and others involved in education and training at all levels have a key role in keeping themselves updated with the national and European policies and developments related to curricula, assessments and qualifications frameworks in the sport sector. Efforts need to be made for the dissemination of accurate and updated information about programmes and occupations in the sport sector through formal events and the use of channels of communications in education and training institutions such as intranet and dedicated web pages. The challenge of offering a wide selection of flexible qualifications requires in-depth planning for running programmes as well as conducting and recording assessments leading to the generation of certification and qualifications for life-long learning. The "European Sports Workforce Development Alliance", composed of key European stakeholders in education, training, employment and Olympic Committees, was set up in 2006 to "provide a mechanism to coordinate the development of the European sport's workforce to ensure a workforce with the "right skills at the right time in the right place" and develop an active partnership between the major decision makers of the sector" (Camy, Klein, Madella & Petry, 2006). Although the infrastructure for qualifications is in place, exciting and challenging times are awaiting the education, training, assessment and qualification stakeholders' and providers in every European nation.

REFERENCES

Australian Qualifications Framework (AQF), (2007). Australian Qualifications Framework Handbook (4th ed.) Available online:
http://www.aqf.edu.au/Portals/0/Documents/Handbook/AQF_Handbook_07.pdf
Accessed 30.3.2010.

Bailey, R. (2001). *Teaching Physical Education: A handbook for primary and secondary school teachers.* London, Kogan Page.

Black, P. (1999). 'Assessment, Learning Theories and Testing Systems' in P. Murphy (Ed.), *Learners, Learning and Assessment: OU Reader.* London, Paul Chapman.

Black, P., Harrison, C., Lee, C., Marshall, B. & Wiliam, D. (2003). *Assessment for learning: Putting it into practice.*, Maidenhead, Open University Press.

Boreham, N. (2004). Orienting the work-based curriculum towards work process knowledge: a rationale and a German case study. *Studies in Continuing Education, 26*(2), pp.209-227.

Broadfoot, P. (1996). Educational Assessment: The myth of measurement. In: P. Woods, *Contemporary issues in teaching and learning.* London, Routledge, pp.203-230

BTEC (2010). *BTEC Firsts Sport: Accreditation of BTEC Firsts and Nationals.* Available online at http://www.edexcel.com/quals/firsts/sport/pages/viewNotice.aspx?notice=1441 Accessed on 15.7.2010.

Camy, J., Klein, G., Madella, A., & Petry, K. (2006). Final conclusions and perspectives. In K. Petry, K. Froberg, & A. Madella, (Eds.), *Thematic Network Project Aligning a European Higher Education Structure in Sport Science: Report of the third year.* Cologne: Institute of European Sport Development and Leisure, pp.251-259.

Carroll, B. (1994). *Assessment in Physical Education: a teacher's guide to the issues.* London, Falmer Press.

Cedefop (2008). *Terminology of European education and training policy.* Available on line http://www.cedefop.europa.eu/EN/publications/13125.aspxat. Accessed on 23.7.2010

Conzelmann, A., & Nagel, S. (2003) Professional Careers of the German Olympic Athletes. International Review for the Sociology of Sport, 38(3), pp.259–280.

Department of Education, Science and Training (DEST- Australian government) (2006). The Bologna Process and Australia: Next Steps. Available online at http://www.dest.gov.au/nr/rdonlyres/d284e32f-98dd-4a67-a3c2-d5b6f3f41622/9998/bolognapaper.pdf Accessed on 23.7.2010.

Directgov (2010). *Education and learning: BTECs, OCR Nationals and other vocational qualifications.* Available on line at http://www.direct.gov.uk/en/EducationAndLearning/QualificationsExplained/DG_181 951. Accessed on 22.7.2010.

Donn, G., & Davies, T. (Eds.), (2003). *Promises and Problems for Commonwealth Qualifications Frameworks.* London and Wellington, Commonwealth Secretariat and NZQA.

EDEXCEL (2010). *BTEC Benchmarking* Available online at http://www.edexcel.com/quals/BTEC/Pages/benchmarking.aspx Accessed on 16.6.2010.

European Commission Education and Training (2010a). *European Qualifications Framework* Available online at http://ec.europa.eu/education/lifelong-learning-policy/doc44_en.htm. Accessed 10.07.2010.

European Commission Education and Training (2010b). *The European Credit system for Vocational Education and Training* (ECVET). Available online at http://ec.europa.eu/education/lifelong-learning-policy/doc50_en.htm Accessed 10.07.2010.

European Commission Sport (2009). *Education and training Sport can help in a number of ways in the education and training of children, young people and adults.* Available online at http://ec.europa.eu/sport/what-we-do/doc31_en.htm Accessed 26.7.2010.

European Union (2010). The EU contribution to European Higher Education Area. Available online at http://ec.europa.eu/education/pub/pdf/higher/ehea_en.pdf. Accessed 23.7.2010.

European Unit (2010). *Participating countries.* Available on line at http://www.europeunit.ac.uk/bologna_process/signatory_countries.cfm . Accessed on 24.7.2010.

European University Association (EUA), (2008). EUA policy position: The future of the Bologna Process post 2010.

Frapwell, A. (2010). Assessment for Learning. In: R. Bailey, (Ed.), *Physical Education for learning: a guide for the secondary school.* London, Kogan Press, pp.104-117.

Gipps, C. (1990). *Assessment: a teacher's guide to the issues.* London, Hodder and Stoughton.

Green, K., (2008). *Understanding Physical Education.* London, Sage.

Hardman, K. (2007). *Current Situation and Prospects for Physical Education in the European Union.* European Parliament, Brussels.

INEUMconsulting TAJ (2008). European Union Study on training of young sportsmen/women in Europe. Final Report: Study of the national and European legal and political frameworks preserving and promoting the training of young athletes. http://ec.europa.eu/sport/pdf/doc512_en.pdf. Accessed on 25.7.2010.

Joint Council for Qualifications (2009a). *GCSE, Applied GCSE and Entry level certificates Results 2009.* Available online at: http://www.jcq.org.uk/attachments/published/1129/JCQ-GCSE.pdf Accessed 15.6.2010.

Joint Council for Qualifications (2009b). *A, AS and AEA Results 2009.* Available online at http://www.jcq.org.uk/attachments/published/984/JCQ-A-Level.pdf Accessed 15.06.2010.

Linn, R., & Miller, M. (2005). *Measurement and assessment in teaching.* Columbus, OH, Pearson Education.

Lockwood, A., & Newton, A. (2004). Assessment in PE. In: S. Capel, *Learning to teach Physical Education in the secondary school: a companion to school experience.* (2nd ed.), Abingdon, Routledge.

Madella, A. (2003). Methods for analysing sports employment in Europe. *Managing Leisure, 8,* pp.56–69.

National Association for Sport and Physical Education (NASPE - USA) (2004). *Moving into the Future: National Standards for Physical Education,* (2nd ed.), Reston, VA, McGraw Hill.

Nitko, A.J., and Brookhart, S.M. (2011). *Education Assessment of Students: International Edition* (6th ed.). Boston, Pearson.

Nutt, G., & Clarke, G. (2002). 'The hidden curriculum and the changing nature of Teacher's work'. In: A. Laker, (Ed.), *The Sociology of Sport and Physical Education.* London, Falmer Routledge.

Osterlind, S.J. (2010). *Modern measurement: theory, principles and applications of mental appraisal.* (2nd ed.). Boston, Pearson.

Petry, K., Froberg, K., & Madella, A. (Eds.) (2006). *Thematic Network Project Aligning a European Higher Education Structure in Sport Science: Report of the third year.* Cologne: Institute of European Sport Development and Leisure. Available online at http://www.aehesis.de/images/FilesForDL/reports/aeh_report_3rd.pdf Accessed 15 June 2010.

Pevec-Grm, S., & Bjornavold, J. (2010). The Development of National Qualifications Frameworks in Europe: Cedefop Overview – EQFnewsletter, June.

Piotrovski, S., & Capel, S. (2000). Formal and informal modes of assessment in physical education. In: S. Capel & S. Piotrovski (Eds.), *Issues in Physical Education.* London and New York, Routledge, pp.99–114.

Popham, J.W. (2011). *Classroom Assessment: What teachers need to know.* (6th ed.) Boston, Pearson.

Powell, J.W., Coutrot, L., Graf, L., Bernhard, N., & Kieffer, A. (2009). Shifting tensions between General and vocational education in France and Germany: a neo-institutional approach. Equalsoc Working Paper 2009 / 6. Available online at http://www.equalsoc.org/uploaded_files/publications/Vocgene_Report1_Final200907 02.pdf. Accessed on 22.7.2010.

Qualifications and Curriculum Development Agency (QCDA-UK) (2010). *Physical Education National Curriculum: Level descriptions for physical education.* Available online at http://curriculum.qcda.gov.uk/key-stages-3-and-4/subjects/key-stage-3/physical-education/Level-descriptions/index.aspx Accessed on 12.6.2010.

Reynolds, C.R., Livingston, R.B., & Wilson, V. (2010). *Measurement and assessment in education: international edition* (2nd edn). Boston, Pearson.

Rowntree, D. (1977). *Assessing Students, how shall we know them?* London, Harper and Row.

Satterly, D. (1989). *Assessment in Schools.* Oxford, Basil Blackwell Ltd.

Siedentop, D., Hastie, P.A., & Van der Mars, H. (2006). *Complete Guide to Sport Education.* Champaign, Illinois, Human Kinetics.

Spackman, L. (2002). Assessment for learning: the lessons for physical education. *Bulletin of Physical Education, 38*(3), pp.179-193.

Stidder, G., & Wallis, J. (2003). Accreditation in Physical Education: Meeting the needs and interests of pupils in Key Stage Four. In: S. Hayes & G. Stidder (Eds.), *Equity and Inclusion in Physical Education and Sport*. London, Routledge, pp.185-210.

Young, M. (2003). National Qualifications Frameworks as a global phenomenon: a comparative perspective. *Journal of Education and Work, 16*(3), pp.223-237.

Żyśko, J., & Piàtkowska, M. (2009). Models of Organisation of Youth Elite Sports Training System in Europe. *Physical Culture and Sport Studies and Research, 47*, pp.64-72. Available online at http://versita.metapress.com/content/8l5m144104m36154/. Accessed on 26.7.2010.

CHAPTER 12

PHYSICAL EDUCATION TEACHERS' PROFESSION: CULTURES AND FRAMES

GÖRAN PATRIKSSON AND KONSTANTIN KOUGIOUMTZIS

INTRODUCTION

This chapter highlights institutional and organizational aspects of the profession of Physical Education teachers. More specifically, it focuses on relations with other teachers and depicts limitations connected with physical education provision utilizing the notions of a teacher culture and a frame factor respectively. Additionally, inter-relations between factors and frames are emphasized by applying the concept of code.

Educational systems in general and compulsory schools in particular refer to both an institution and an organization (Berg, 2003). As an institution, a school is obligated by State policy intentions in relation to the reproduction of legitimate knowledge, skills, values and norms. As an organization, a school is connected to a working milieu notably influenced by teachers' own professional traditions. In order to outline teacher cultures and frame factors as well as to capture inter-relations between the State and peripheral traditions, we draw on previous literature, Bernstein's (2000) code theory and nationwide surveys with in-service physical education teachers in Sweden and Greece.

A teacher's culture "comprises beliefs, values, habits and assumed ways of doing things among communities of teachers who had to deal with similar demands and constraints over many years" (Hargreaves, 1994, p.165). Fragmented individualistic teacher cultures promote discrete classroom management and isolated autonomous teaching practices. Collaborative teacher cultures reward internally developed professional communities with reflective dialogue among members as well as shared work responsibility and visions. So-called "Balkanized" collaboration and imposed or contrived collegiality can be connected to technicists' efforts to stress collegial milieux as part of the control of the process of teaching (Smyth, 2001).

A frame factor is a component that stays beyond the control of a teacher influencing the teaching process in the classroom. According to Lundgren (1979), three inter-connected categories of frame factors or frames are important. Constitutional frames indicate laws and policy documents, while organizational frames include the distribution of time allocation of various school subjects and physical frames consist of buildings, equipment and material necessary for instruction. School governance is often connected to the influence of laws and policies, though the impact of organizational and physical frames should not be under-estimated (Sandahl, 2005).

A code is "a regulative principle, tacitly acquired, which selects and integrates relevant meanings, the form of their realization and evoking contexts" (Bernstein, 2000, p.109).

The mode of a code depends upon the strength of classification and framing. Classification refers to boundaries between categories, while framing is connected to a degree of control. For example, strong classification between teachers indicates fragmented individualistic cultures and strong framing signifies resolute central governance steering. This combination reveals a "collection mode" of code, whereas weak classification combined with weak framing manifests an "integrated mode" of code.

In the following sections, the nature of teacher cultures and the impact of frame factors are emphasized with connections to previous literature and survey responses of physical education teachers in Swedish and Greek primary and lower secondary schools. Lundgren's frame factors and Hargreaves' teacher cultures correspond to modalities of framing and classification respectively. Thus, factors and cultures in the four contexts are described to help depict the modes of codes.

TEACHER CULTURES

In the literature, teachers' cultures appear to be predominantly fragmented individualistic with a low degree of collaboration, cooperation and sharing between teachers even in the same school (Stoll, Bolam, McMahon, Wallace & Thomas, 2006; Brook, Sawyer & Rimm-Kaufman, 2007). Moreover, the physical education teachers' profession is commonly addressed in terms of low subject status and occupational isolation or marginalization (Hardman, 2006; 2008a, 2008b). To refine descriptions of teachers' cultures in general as well as physical education teachers' position in schools and their relation to other teachers, we employed Hoyle's (2001) three-fold typology. According to this typology, teachers' positions in schools and relations to others can be addressed in terms of prestige, status and esteem revealing public perceptions, authority and dedication respectively.

Historically, teaching in general has been a low prestige job with mobility and turnover trends resulting in teacher shortage (Banville & Rikard, 2009). A teacher shortage occurs when demand exceeds supply of qualified or licensed personnel. According to Hardman and Marshall (2000), the shortage of qualified physical education is acute in Central and Eastern Europe. Furthermore, in many European countries and especially in primary schools, physical education classes are frequently taught by generalist teachers often not adequately trained to teach physical education. On other continents, the proportion of specialist or qualified personnel varies, ranging from about 80% in the United States to approximately 10% in some African and Asian countries. The supply of qualified physical education teachers might be a policy issue combined with matters related to initial teacher education. However, the prestige status of a job in terms of attraction and retention of effective individuals should not be overlooked.

The status of physical education and physical education teachers can be described in terms of a formal (legal) dimension and a semantic (informal or actual) dimension. Formal status is connected to legislation and curriculum while semantic status is associated with authentic school settings. Hardman (2008a, 2008b) and previously

Hardman and Marshall (2000) highlighted the status of physical education and physical education teachers worldwide. The findings of their studies point consistently to a formal status as high as that of other school subjects, especially in developed countries. However, the semantic status of physical education is low, indicated in practices inside schools as, for example, the frequency of cancellation of PE classes in favour of other school subjects. The questionable status of physical education teachers is highlighted elsewhere signifying strong boundaries between teachers in practical and theoretical school subjects (Van Deventer, 2009; Kardeliene, 2008).

Esteem forms a more personal aspect of physical education teachers' positions in schools as a general sense of professional competence. Shoval, Erlich and Fejgin (2010) found that physical education teachers describe themselves as ready to work hard and to face challenges. However, mistrust of colleagues is significant, driving professionals to lobbyism, pretending and hesitation to avoid feelings of collegial isolation. Moreover, the social structure of schools may result in professional isolation of physical education teachers (Ward & O'Sullivan, 1998). With impacts of teachers' professional work on making a difference in children's lives in mind, some researchers have focused on issues of career-long professional learning (for example, Armour, 2010; Cochran-Smith, 2005). It seems to be the case that the impact of continuing professional development on physical education teachers' identity, empowerment and sense of efficacy is variously supported by a number of studies (Martin, McCaughtry, Hodges-Kulinna & Cothran, 2008; Martin, McCaughtry, Kulinna-Hodges & Cothran, 2009; Shehu, 2009).

Emphasizing physical education teachers' low status and professional isolation or marginalization might result in a description of a strong classification between physical education teachers and teachers in other school subjects; yet by using Hoyle's typology, it seems that not only physical education teachers but also teachers in general face prestige problems. In addition, physical education teachers have to cope with issues of professional esteem but similar challenges for other subject teachers should not be under-estimated. Consequently, the classification between physical education teachers and teachers in other school subjects is a contested issue that needs to be further investigated.

THE IMPACT OF FRAME FACTORS

Frame factors correspond to organizational measures not only determining but also limiting educational processes in the classroom (Lundgren, 1989). In the physical education-related literature, issues of constitutional, organizational and physical frames have been addressed as curriculum implementation, time allocation as well as the quantity and quality of facilities, equipment and instruction materials respectively. The impact of constitutional frames on classroom teaching is a controversial issue as teachers' perceptions and the mode of school governance may interfere. On the one hand, Faucette (1987) suggests that only physical education teachers, who agree with innovation and work consciously to meet the requirements, can fully implement a new curriculum; on the other hand, Kirk and Macdonald (2001) argue that physical education teachers act as reproducers of State policy intentions. Instead, they should have a strong voice grounded in their knowledge of their students, available resources and the practicalities of the work. It seems though that minor or major discrepancies between State intentions and actual implementation exist in a global perspective. In Africa actual physical education provision corresponds to a very low extent with curricular requirements, while in Europe a clear majority of State requirements are implemented (Hardman & Marshall, 2000).

Discussions on organizational frames emphasize the gradual erosion of the prescribed time for physical education throughout the 20th century. According to Hardman (2008a, 2008b), weekly provision shrank in Denmark from 7 lessons to 4 in 1937, from 4 to 3 lessons in 1958 and from 3 to 2 lessons in 1970. Similar trends are reported in Sweden, France and Greece. During recent years, time allocated for physical education has largely remained the same in a majority of European countries (68%), increased in a few countries (16%) and actually decreased in some (16%). In some countries, time allocation is further squeezed by perceived more important school "academic" and/or new curricular subjects. The average delivered time for physical education in Europe was approximately 120 minutes per week in year 2000, while it was 110 minutes per week ten years later (Hardman, 2008b; Hardman & Marshall, 2000). Notably, the actual delivered time for PE varies significantly between schools even in the same school district (Hardman, 2008a; Hardman & Marshall, 2000).

Issues of physical frames as the quality and quantity of facilities, equipment and instruction materials have been reported both in a global perspective and within the European Union (Hardman, 2006, 2008a, 2008b; Hardman & Marshall, 2000). Whilst nation-specific situations are obvious (in Sweden, for example, physical education teachers report few constraints (Lundvall & Meckbach, 2008) in the region, less than half of European schools have excellent or good facility quality; additionally, less than half have excellent or good quality equipment. Inappropriate facilities, inadequate equipment and insufficient material can inhibit curriculum implementation (Frazer-Thomas & Beaudoin, 2002; MacPhail & Hallbert, 2005; Van Deventer, 2009) and teachers' sense of autonomy (Carson & Chase, 2009). Furthermore, lack of facilities and equipment can contribute to discrepancies between curricular expectations and actual provision (Shehu, 2009).

The impact of constitutional, organizational and physical frames highlighted above does not make clear the inter-connection patterns between the various frame categories as expressions of the modalities of educational governance, which have hitherto been under-estimated. To give an example, limitations connected to a lack of facilities are not purely an economic issue but should be analyzed within a broader agenda of governance. In the case of physical education, it seems that existing organizational and physical frames inhibit quality provision and teachers' sense of autonomy giving signs of strong framing procedures. However, the strength of, and inter-connection patterns between, various categories of frames should be addressed more holistically.

THE CASES OF SWEDEN AND GREECE

Governance of schools in Greece has a centralized bureaucratic character with the Ministry of Education at the head of the administration hierarchy constraining initiatives at the local school level (Stylianidou, Bagakis, & Stamovlasis, 2004). In Sweden, municipal authorities and school units have a great deal of latitude for decisions based on local circumstances (Regeringskansliet, 2003). The Swedish curriculum for compulsory schooling consists of general guidelines (Utbildningsdepartement, 1994/1998), whilst the Greek curriculum is characterized by a significant degree of prescription (YPEPTH, 1995/1997, 1995/2007). Pupils in both Sweden and Greece participate in approximately 6,650 teaching hours (i.e. 60 minute "hours" as opposed to some countries, where "hours" can mean, for example, lessons varying in time from 30 to 50 minutes) during their first nine years of education (OECD, 2005). The warranted time for physical education is 400 teaching "hours" in Sweden and 495 "hours" in Greece. However, available teaching time in Sweden is not fully determined centrally and can vary depending on local circumstances connected to the profile of the school and pupils' choices. Bodily (that is physical) practices form the basis of the physical education in both countries with special attention devoted to socialization. However, a change towards a more theoretical approach to physical education can be observed in the latest Swedish physical education syllabi.

The physical education syllabus in Sweden outlines two categories of aims (Utbildningsdepartementet, 1994/1998). The "aims striving towards" describe the overall purpose of the subject. The "must be reached aims" guarantee the minimum amount of physical education that pupils receive. Physical education teachers in Sweden can influence the formation of local projects at schools. These projects can be seen as concrete formulations of the central physical education syllabus. In Greece, physical education teachers follow the instructions of a central curriculum (YPEPTH, 1995/1997, 1995/2007). The Greek curriculum promotes a transition towards subject fusion through inter-disciplinarity and cross-thematic integration (Matsaggouras, 2005). Inter-disciplinarity implies within-subject efforts to grasp content with a scientific pluralism, while cross-thematic integration refers to teaching and learning associated with areas of mutual interest among school subjects.

According to previous studies, Greek physical education teachers (Koustelios & Tsigilis, 2005) seem to be more marginalized than their Swedish counterparts (Larsson & Redelius, 2008). Furthermore, physical education teachers encounter restrictions caused by lack of facilities and insufficient teaching time. In Sweden, research suggests that lesson formation is mainly influenced by organizational and physical frames (Larsson & Redelius, 2004; Sandahl, 2005). Similar studies in Greece are rare, but it appears that physical education teachers depend upon directives from central syllabuses (Katsikadelli, 1990; Kossiva, 2005). In Sweden the prescribed time allocation has decreased during recent decades (Utbildningsdepartement, 1994/1998). Some researchers indicate a radical time reduction (Allert & Bergh, 2000), while others argue that the decreases have only occurred in some schools (Sandahl, 2005). In Greece, prescribed time allocation increased at the beginning of the 1990's (Karadaidu, 2000). In terms of school sport facilities, there is high variability in Sweden (Sandahl, 2005). However, the standard in sport equipment provision is quite good across the country. In Greece, PE teachers' working conditions are associated not only with the absence of sport facilities but also with a lack of equipment (Kossiva, 2005). It seems that classification between physical education teachers and teachers in other school subjects is stronger in Greece than in

Sweden, whereas, constitutional frames are obviously stronger in the centralized Greek system than they are in the decentralized form of Swedish governance. Physical frames are stronger in Greece because of the relative lack of facilities and equipment. It would seem that organizational frames should be strong in some Swedish schools because of the recent curriculum time reduction.

A COMPARATIVE SURVEY

Previous national accounts on the impact of frame factors and the nature of teacher cultures in Sweden and Greece incorporate a great deal of prescription and there are difficulties in generalizing the findings. To avoid prescribed norms related to the strength of classification and framing and to ground the generalization of the findings, a comparative study was undertaken in the two countries. The double nation-wide survey was based on a specially constructed and previously pilot-tested questionnaire (5-Likert-scaled) administered in stratified random samples of In-service physical education teachers in each country. The final sample consisted of physical education teachers divided into four groups working in Swedish primary schools (293 teachers), Swedish lower secondary schools (414 teachers), Greek primary schools (214 teachers) and Greek lower secondary schools (237 teachers).

The findings of the study are presented in two sections. The first section highlights teacher cultures and the classification between physical education teachers and other teachers in terms of formal cooperation, de-privatized practices and personalized inter-action. The second section focuses on framing as perceived by physical education teachers regarding the impact of constitutional, organizational and physical frames. The various batteries of questions showed very good reliability and internal consistency estimates (Kougioumtzis & Patriksson, 2007, 2008, 2009; Patriksson & Kougioumtzis, 2006, 2008).

The presentation of the findings is based on analysis of variance to establish statistically significant differences between the means of the four groups. Non-significant differences with a p-value above .001 are not included, a feature that provides a degree of confidence in drawing conclusions on the basis of the established differences. Data presentation has been modified in order to make it easier for the reader to grasp the information. This means that the various tables contain verbal approximation on the basis of the statistics. For numerical expressions and detailed statistics, the reader can refer to the original studies (Kougioumtzis & Patriksson, 2007, 2008, 2009; Patriksson & Kougioumtzis, 2006, 2008).

CLASSIFICATION

Classification between physical education teachers and other teachers were looked at through three batteries of four questions each, focusing on formal cooperation, de-privatized practices and personalized interaction respectively. Formal cooperation refers to scheduled school meetings with teachers from several or all school subjects as participants; de-privatized practices embrace joint efforts to plan and conduct each teacher's classes, shared lessons or common projects; and personal interaction indicates a degree of professional intimacy, as it is associated with sharing and working together on a personal level.

Formal cooperation (see Table 1) has been indicated by frequency of meetings, physical education teachers' own participation pattern (degree of activity), perceived climate (degree of positive reception from other teachers) and absence of power misuse among teachers, that is, lack of decisions not in the physical education teachers' interests.

Table 1. Formal Cooperation

| | Sweden | | Greece | |
	Primary Schools	Secondary schools	Primary schools	Secondary schools
Meeting frequency	Often	Very often	Rarely	Rarely
Degree of own activity	High	High	High	High
Positive reception	Good	Good	Not so good	Not so good
Absence of power misuse	Clear	Very clear	Not so clear	Not so clear

As can be seen in Table 1, the frequency of meetings in general is higher in the Swedish context than in the Greek one. The verbal approximations correspond to statistically significant established differences. In Greece, differences between primary and lower secondary schools cannot be established. However, Swedish physical education teachers meet more frequently with other teachers than their counterparts in primary schools.

The absence of power misuse (decisions contrary to physical education teachers' interests due to the lower status of the subject in comparison with other perceived more academic subjects) is stated more clearly by Swedish physical educators than by Greek physical educators. Differences between the two groups of physical education teachers could not be established in Greece. On the contrary, lower secondary school teachers in Sweden more clearly reported an absence of power misuse than teachers in primary schools. These results are in line with previous research indicating the lower status of "practical" school subjects. However, it seems that physical education in Sweden occupies a rather good semantic or actual status.

In matters of a positive reception by colleagues in other school subjects, Swedish physical education teachers reported a better climate than did their Greek counterparts. Furthermore, there were no differences between the four groups of teachers in aspects of the degree of their own activity showing a rather elevated dedication.

De-privatized practices (see Table 2) were measured utilizing frequency of collaboration on subject matters with other physical education teachers, teachers in "academic" school subjects, teachers in other "practical" school subjects and jointly carrying out activities and events like sport days, exhibitions etc.

Table 2. Deprivatized Practices

	Sweden		Greece	
	Primary Schools	Secondary schools	Primary schools	Secondary schools
With other PE teachers	Often	Very often	Often	Very often
With teachers in "theoretical" subjects	Often	Often	Rarely	Rarely
With teachers in other "practical" subjects	Rarely	Rarely	Rarely	Rarely
Jointly carrying out events	Often	Often	Rarely	Rarely

According to the findings, physical education teachers collaborate with other physical education teachers more intensively in lower secondary schools than in primary schools. This is to be rather expected as lower secondary schools are large units with several physical education teachers, while primary schools are smaller units with one or few physical education teachers. Collaboration between physical education teachers and teachers in "academic" school subjects occur more frequently in Sweden than in Greece, without any differences between groups from the same country. Moreover, Swedish physical education teachers jointly carry out activities/events with other teachers more often than Greek physical education teachers do. However, the four groups showed reduced collaboration with teachers who teach other "practical" subjects like music etc.

Despite the fact that the curriculum supports inter-disciplinarity and cross-thematic subject integration in Greece, it is obvious that such practices are rather limited in authentic school settings. On the contrary, de-privatized practices are more common in Sweden without detailed central directives.

Personalized inter-action (see Table 3) was studied through the degree of sharing individual problems, supporting colleagues, and joint dialogues with colleagues generally and with other physical education teachers particularly.

Table 3. Personalized Interaction

	Sweden		Greece	
	Primary Schools	Secondary schools	Primary schools	Secondary schools
Sharing individual problems	Rarely	Rarely	Rarely	Often
Supporting colleagues	Rarely	Rarely	Rarely	Often
Joint dialogues with colleagues in general	Rarely	Rarely	Rarely	Often
Joint dialogues with other PE teachers	Rarely	Rarely	Rarely	Often

The analysis of findings reveals the highest degree of individual practice sharing in lower secondary schools in Greece. The same pattern is apparent not only for supporting colleagues generally, but in dialoguing with colleagues in "practical" school subjects specifically. The position of Greek lower secondary schools is stronger in matters of joint dialogues with colleagues regardless of subject. For this issue, Greek lower secondary teachers reported significantly more interaction than their colleagues in the other three groups. It seems that the intensification of the educational processes in Sweden limits individual professional possibility to inter-act with colleagues on an informal level.

Summarizing the findings, formal cooperation and de-privatized practices are more common in Swedish schools in general and especially so in lower secondary schools. However, personalized inter-action is more frequent in Greek lower secondary schools. On the basis of the findings, classification seems to be very weak in Swedish lower secondary schools, weak in Swedish primary school and overwhelmingly strong in Greek schools in general.

FRAMING

Framing as constitutional, organizational and physical frames was measured through three batteries of four questions. More specifically, the strength of each frame factor was obtained through questions related to the perceived impact on semester content, activity sequencing, difficulty of exercises and forms of work. These four dimensions represent Bernstein's (1977) selection, timing, pacing and organization respectively. More specifically, semester content has been used to study sources that restrict content selection over a semester period. Activity sequencing shows the order of appearance of the various activities during a semester and hence, can be connected to the content of individual lessons. Difficulty of exercises has been used to focus on sources that influence the ways that teachers progress the lesson content offering more difficult or more meaningful subject content. Finally, the form of work is indicative of methodological aspects.

Constitutional frames refer to influences from the central State curriculum in Greece and to both central State curriculum and local syllabus in Sweden. Physical education teachers' responses related to the impact of constitutional frames are featured in Table 4.

Table 4. Constitutional Frames

	Sweden		Greece	
	Primary Schools	Secondary schools	Primary schools	Secondary schools
Semester content	Often	Always	Often	Often
Activity sequencing	Often	Often	Often	Often
Difficulty of exercises	Often	Often	Rarely	Sometimes
Forms of work	Often	Often	Often	Often

As seen in Table 4, there are no differences between the four groups regarding activity sequencing and forms of work. In relation to semester content, physical education teachers in Swedish lower secondary schools reported the highest impact compared with the other three groups. In matters of the degree of difficulty of exercises, Swedish teachers in general reported a higher impact than did their Greek counterparts.

Table 5 depicts restrictions connected to organizational frames (e.g. available teaching time) as perceived by physical education teachers in aspects of semester content, activity sequencing, difficulty of exercises and forms of work.

Table 5. Organizational Frames

	Sweden		Greece	
	Primary Schools	Secondary schools	Primary schools	Secondary schools
Semester content	Rarely	Often	Rarely	Sometimes
Activity sequencing	Rarely	Often	Rarely	Sometimes
Difficulty of exercises	Rarely	Often	Rarely	Sometimes
Forms of work	Rarely	Often	Rarely	Sometimes

According to the information obtained, organizational frames mostly restrict physical education teachers in Swedish lower secondary schools as the other groups reported fewer restrictions, especially in primary schools. The gradual erosion of time available to physical education teachers internationally has been discussed intensively in the literature. It seems that even physical education teachers in Swedish lower secondary schools suffer from the restricted curriculum time allocation, for in our comparative study, lower secondary school physical education teachers reported more restrictions. This is seemingly in contrast with earlier research (Allert & Bergh, 2000; Sandahl, 2005), which suggested that the available teaching time is more adequate in lower secondary schools than in primary schools. The difference in the respective research findings might be explained by a broader curriculum content that physical education teachers have to cover within the given time.

Physical framing concerns restrictions caused by inappropriate facilities, inadequate equipment and insufficient instruction materials.

Table 6. Physical Frames

	Sweden		Greece	
	Primary Schools	Secondary schools	Primary schools	Secondary schools
Semester content	Rarely	Rarely	Often	Often
Activity sequencing	Rarely	Rarely	Often	Often
Difficulty of exercises	Rarely	Rarely	Often	Often
Forms of work	Rarely	Rarely	Often	Often

According to Table 6, differences between Greece and Sweden are evident as Greek physical education teachers reported a higher degree of limitations connected to physical frames related to semester content, activity sequencing, difficulty of exercises and forms of work. It seems that the quality and quantity of facilities and equipment in Sweden are in line with the needs and requirements of physical education teachers.

In summary, constitutional frames seem to be strongest in Swedish lower secondary schools. Constraints connected to organizational frames are also obvious in this group, while physical frames in Greece clearly restrict physical education provision.

MODES OF CODES

A code is a composite of classification and framing, while the mode of a code depends upon the strength of classification and framing. On the one hand, a strong classification indicates boundaries between physical education teachers and other teachers, while a weak classification signifies collaborative practices; on the other hand, a strong framing shows more restrictions connected to constitutional, organizational and physical frames, while weaker framing implies more freedom for a physical education teacher to form selected aspects of instruction.

Interpretation of physical education teachers' responses in terms of the strength of classification and framing the modalities of codes is represented in Table 7. It needs to be emphasized that the adjectives "weak" and "strong" do not represent absolute values but are based on comparisons between groups taking into account the significant differences (for statistics see Kougioumtzis & Patriksson, 2007, 2008, 2009; Patriksson & Kougioumtzis, 2006, 2008).

Table 7. Classification, framing and mode of code

| | Sweden | | Greece | |
	Primary Schools	Secondary schools	Primary schools	Secondary schools
Formal Cooperation	Weak	Very weak	Strong	Strong
Deprivatized Practices	Weak	Weak	Strong	Strong
Personalized Interaction	Strong	Strong	Strong	Weak
Classification	**Weak**	**Weak**	**Strong**	**Strong**
Constitutional Frames	Strong	Very strong	Strong	Strong
Organizational frames	Weak	Strong	Weak	Weak
Physical Frames	Weak	Weak	Strong	Strong
Framing	**Weak**	**Strong**	**Strong**	**Strong**
Mode of code	Integrated	*Nuanced*	Collection	Collection

As Table 7 shows, both classification and framing as perceived by physical education teachers in Swedish primary schools are overwhelmingly weak giving signs of an integrated code, collaborative teacher cultures and decentralized school governance. The two Greek groups represent a collection code as overwhelmingly strong in both classification and framing. It seems that Greek physical education teachers are part of fragmented individualistic teacher cultures with resolute centralized governance. The code of mode in Swedish lower secondary schools implies a nuanced mode as the combination of weak classification and strong framing is uncommonly reported in previous studies.

CONCLUDING COMMENTS

The aim of this chapter was to describe not only relations between physical education teachers and teachers in other school subjects but to delineate limitations connected to frame factors as well. Additionally, inter-connection patterns between cultures and frames have been pictured utilizing the notions of classification, framing and code. Previous literature has focused on constitutional, organizational and physical frames as well as the position of physical education teachers in schools. However, inter-connection patterns have been somewhat under-estimated. Highlighting these patterns incorporates the potential opportunity to picture the mechanism through which frames and cultures are part of broader educational phenomena.

Lindensjö and Lundgren (2000) discussed a bureaucratic mode of central State control and a mode of governance through professionals focusing on the function and not the structure of a centralized versus a decentralized school governance system. A bureaucratic control of a school system means that the central State is defining teacher's work on the basis of a vertical hierarchy. On the contrary, more professional governance is connected to strong professions to adapt in complex social and educational situations and to make decisions on the basis of local circumstances. The strong classification and framing procedures in Greek primary and lower secondary schools can be clearly understood within a bureaucratic control of schooling. The weak classification and framing in Swedish primary schools signifies a mode of educational governance that characterized the Swedish model during the 1970's and 1980's (Bernstein, 1977).

The weak classification associated with overwhelmingly strong framing in the Swedish lower secondary school can be seen with the novel developments on educational control in mind and a mode of professional governance. On the one hand, the partial deregulation of the school timetable in favour of students' and schools' local choices as well as the potential to construct local syllabi seem to have increased the level of these teachers' professional autonomy. On the other hand, the weakening of boundaries between traditional teacher categories through the addition of two or three main subject teachers might have had an impact on traditional teacher cultures in Sweden. This impact is connected to a move from a marginal and peripheral role of physical education teachers in schools towards a more professional standing.

To sum up, we argue that constitutional, organizational and physical frames as well as the boundaries between various categories of teachers are part of broader educational processes. On the basis of our findings, we have clearly demonstrated inter-connection patterns between the way that physical education teachers perceive limitations connected to policy documents, available teaching time, quality of facilities and equipment as well as their relations to teachers in other school subjects and their position at schools in four educational contexts. This means that efforts to upgrade physical education teachers' position at schools and to manipulate factors that limit physical education quality provision should be seen as part of a broader professional agenda. We suggest more holistic approaches instead of influencing distinct aspects of physical education teachers' professional situation, as educational milieux are remarkably interactive.

Physical education teachers in Sweden and Greece as well as in other countries play a central role laying the foundations of pupils' physical health and lifelong active lifestyle. However, scientists, professionals and laymen internationally focus predominantly on didactical aspects of physical education provision. Without neglecting the importance of teachers' didactical competence, we call upon an intensification of efforts connected to issues of the professional standing of physical education teachers. An upgraded competency can contribute to an elevated status for physical education teachers. Notwithstanding this, several non-didactical matters that remain beyond the control of a physical education teacher might jeopardize quality provision as for example constitutional, organizational and physical frames. These frames have a strong impact on physical education teachers' position within the school. We believe that physical education teachers' prestige, status and professional esteem in the community might interconnect with various frames and not solely with the declined status of perceived "non intellectual" school subjects.

REFERENCES

Allert, L., & Bergh, S. (2000). *Idrotten i grundskolan* [Physical Education in Grundskola]. Stockholm, Riksidrottsförbundet.

Armour, K. (2010). The physical education profession and its professional responsibility … or … why '12 weeks paid holiday' will never be enough. *Physical Education and Sport Pedagogy, 15*(1), pp.1-13.

Banville, D., & Rikard, G. L. (2009). Teacher Induction - Implications for Physical Education Teacher Development and Retention. *Quest 61*(2), pp.237-256.

Berg, G. (2003). *Att förstå skolan. En teori om skolan som institution och skolor som organisationer* [Understanding schools. A theory on schools as institutions and organizations]. Lund, Studentlitteratur.

Bernstein, B. (1975). *Class, Codes and Control. Towards a Theory of Educational Transmissions.* London, Routledge & Keagan Paul.

Bernstein, B. (2000). *Class, Codes and Control. Pedagogy, symbolic control and identity.* Theory, research, critique. Lanham, GB, Rowman & Littlefield.

Brook, L., Sawyer, E., & Rimm-Kaufman, S. (2007). Teacher collaboration in the context of the Responsive Classroom approach, *Teachers and Teaching: Theory and Practice, 13*(3), pp.211-245.

Carson, R. L., & Chase, M.A. (2009). An examination of physical education teacher motivation from a self-determination theoretical framework. *Physical Education and Sport Pedagogy, 14*(4), pp.335-353.

Cochran-Smith, M. (2005). The New Teacher Education: For Better or For Worse? 2005 Presidential Address. *Educational Researcher, 34*(7), p.3-17.

Faucette, N. (1987). Teachers' concerns and participation styles during in-service education. *Journal of Teaching in Physical Education, 6*(4), pp.425-440.

Frazer-Thomas, J., & Beaudoin, C. (2002). Implementing a Physical Education Curriculum: Two Teachers' Experiences. *Canadian Journal of Education, 27*(2), pp.249-268.

Hardman, K. (2006). Promise or Reality? Physical Education in Schools in Europe. *Compare: A Journal of Comparative Education, 36*(2), pp.163-179.

Hardman, K. (2008a). Physical Education in schools: a global perspective. *Kinesiology 40*(1), pp.5-28.

Hardman, K. (2008b). The situation of physical education in schools: a European perspective. *Human Movement 9*(1), pp.5-18.

Hardman, K., & Marshall, J.J. (2000). The state and status of physical education in schools in international context. *European Physical Education Review, 6*(3), pp.203–229.

Hargreaves, A. (1994). *Changing Teachers, Changing Time. Teachers' Work and Culture in the Postmodern* Age. London, Cassell.

Hargreaves, A. (2000). Four ages of professionalism and professional learning. *Teachers and Teaching: History and Practice, 6*(2), pp.151-182.

Hoyle, E. (2001). Teaching. Prestige, Status and Esteem. *Educational Management and Administration, 29*(2), pp.139-152.

Karadaidu, M. (2000). I fysiki agogi stin elliniki mesi ekpedefsi (1862–1990) kai idrimata ekpedefsis gymnaston (1882–1982). Thessaloniki, Kyriakides.

Kardeliene, L. (2008). Attitudes of teachers of physical education and other subjects towards social communication. *Education, Physical Training Sport, 71*, pp.43-48.

Katsikadelli, A. (1990). *Sistimatiki meleti ton dedomenon tis Fysikis Agogis kai idikotera tis Petosferisis sti horra mas stin Protovathmia kai Deftero-vathmia ekpedefsi.* Athina, Ethniko kai Kapodistriako Panepistimio, Tmima Epistimis Fysikis Agogis kai Athlitismou.

Kirk, D., & Macdonald, D. (2001). Teacher voice and ownership of curriculum change. *Journal of Curriculum Studies, 33*(5), pp.551-567.

Kossiva, I. (2005). *Paragontes pou diaforopioun ta epipeda drastiriotitas ton mathiton-trion, ti siberifora ton kathigiton kai to periehomeno tis fysikis agogis sto gymnasio.* Athina, Ethniko kai Kapodistriako Panepistimio, Tmima Epistimis Fysikis Agogis kai Athlitismou.

Kougioumtzis, K., & Patriksson, G. (2007). Framing physical education in Greek and Swedish schools. *International Journal of Physical Education, 44*(3), pp.106–116.

Kougioumtzis, K., & Patriksson, G. (2008). PE teachers' school based collaboration in Greek and Swedish Schools. *Proceedings of the 2008 Biennial Conference of the International Society for Comparative Physical Education and Sports.* Macau, China.

Kougioumtzis, K., & Patriksson, G. (2009). School-based teacher collaboration in Sweden and Greece. Formal co-operation, deprivatized practices and personalized interaction. *Teachers and teaching: theory and practice, 15*(1), pp.131–154.

Koustelios, A., & Tsigilis, N. (2005). The relationship between burnout and job satisfaction among physical education teachers: a multivariate approach. *European Physical Education Review, 11*(2), pp.189–203.

Larsson, H., & Redelius, K. (Eds.) (2004). *Mellan nytta och nöje. Bilder av ämnet idrott och hälsa* (Rapport nr 2 i serien Skola-Idrott-Hälsa). Stockholm, Idrottshögskolan.

Larsson, H., & Redelius, K. (2008). Swedish physical education research questioned - current situation and future directions. *Physical Education and Sport Pedagogy, 13*(4), pp.381-398.

Lindensjö, B., & Lundgren, U.P. (2000). *Utbildningsreformer och politisk styrning* [Educational reforms and political steering]. Stockholm, HLS.

Lundgren, U.P. (1979). Background; the Conceptual Framework. In U. P. Lundgren & S. Pettersson (Eds.), Code, Context and Curriculum Processes. Stockholm, CWK Gleerup.

Lundgren, U.P. (1987). Frame Factors. In M.J. Dunkin (Ed.), *The International Encyclopedia of Teaching and Teacher Educationa*. Oxford, Pergamon Press.

Lundvall, S., & Meckbach, J. (2008). Mind the gap: physical education and health and the frame factor theory as a tool for analysing educational settings. *Physical Education and Sport Pedagogy, 13*(4), pp.345-364.

MacPhail, A., & Halbert, J. (2005). The implementation of a revised syllabus in Ireland: circumstances, rewards, costs. *European Physical Education Review, 11*(3), pp.287-308.

Martin, J. J., McCaughtry, N., Hodges-Kulinna, P., & Cothran, D. (2008). The influences of professional development on teachers' self-efficacy toward educational change. *Physical Education and Sport Pedagogy, 13*(2), pp.171-190.

Martin, J. J., McCaughtry, N., Kulinna-Hodges, P., & Cothran, D. (2009). The Impact of a Social Cognitive Theory-Based Intervention on Physical Education Teacher Self-Efficacy. *Professional Development in Education, 35*(4), pp.511-529.

Matsaggouras, I. (2005). Diepistimonikotita, diathematikotita kai eniaiopoiisi sta nea Programmata Spoudon: Tropoi organosis tis sholikis gnosis [Inter-disciplinarity cross-thematic integration and the new Syllabus: Structuring educational knowledge], *Epitheorisi Ekpaideftikon thematon* [Educational Issues Review], 7, pp.19-36.

OECD (2005). *Education at a Glance. OECD Indicators 2005. Executive Summary.* Paris, OECD.

Patriksson, G., & Kougioumtzis, K. (2006). PE-teachers in Greek and Swedish schools: Cooperation with teachers teaching other school subjects. In I. Warren, Abstracts, *Bulletin of Sport and Culture, 25.*

Patriksson, G., & Kougioumtzis, K. (2008). Within physical education classification in Greek and Swedish Schools. *Proceedings of the 2008 Biennial Conference of the International Society for Comparative Physical Education and Sports.* Macau, China.

Regeringskansliet (2003). Attracting, Developing and Retaining Effective Teachers. *Background Report prepared for the OECD Thematic Review of Attracting, Developing and Retaining Effective Teachers.* Stockholm, Regeringskansliet.

Sandahl, B. (2005). *Ett ämne för alla? Normer och praktik i grundskolan idrottsundervisning 1962–2002* [A school subject for all?. Norms and praxis in Physical Education in Grundskola 1962-2002]. Stockholm, Carlssons.

Shehu, J. (2009). Professional Development Experiences of Physical Education Teachers in Botswana: Epistemological Implications. *Teacher Development, 13*(3), pp.267-283.

Shoval, E., Erlich, I., & Fejgin, N. (2010). Mapping and interpreting novice physical education teachers' self-perceptions of strengths and difficulties. *Physical Education and Sport Pedagogy, 15*(1), pp.85-101.

Smyth, J. (2001). *Critical Politics of Teachers' Work. An Australian Perspective.* New York, Peter Lang.

Stoll, L., Bolam, R., McMahon, A., Wallace, M., & Thomas, S. (2006). Professional Learning Communities: A review of the literature, *Journal of Educational Change, 7*(4), pp.221-258.

Stylianidou, F., Bagakis, G., & Stamovlasis, D. (2004). Attracting, developing and retaining effective teacher. OECD Activity. *Country background Report for Greece.* Aten, Education Research Centre.

Utbildningsdepartementet (1994/1998). *Läroplan för det obligatoriska skolväsendet, förskoleklassen och fritidshemmet* [Curriculum for the compulsory schools ...]. Stockholm, Fritzes.

Van Deventer, K. (2009). Perspectives of teachers on the implementation of Life Orientation in Grades R-1 1 from selected Western Cape schools. South African *Journal of Education, 29*(1), pp.127-145.

Ward, P. & O'Sullivan, M. (1998). Similarities and differences in pedagogy and content: 5 years later. *Journal of Teaching in Physical Education, 17*(2), pp.195-213.

YPEPTH (1995/1997). *I fysiki agogi sto dimotiko sholio* [Physical Education in primary schools]. Athina, OEDB.

YPEPTH (1995/2007). *Idigies gia ti didaktea ili kai ti didaskalia sto gymnasio kata to sxoliko etos 2007-2008* [Instructions related to lesson content and teaching in lower secondary schools for the school year 2007-2008]. Athina, OEDB.

CHAPTER 13
SCHOOL AGE CHILDREN, PHYSICAL ACTIVITY AND FITNESS AND HEALTH

KARSTEN FROBERG AND LARS BO ANDERSEN

INTRODUCTION

A sedentary lifestyle is common among adults and is associated with a higher mortality rate and rates of common diseases such as cardiovascular disease (CVD), diabetes and some cancers. These diseases are not usually manifest in children, but for those who lead relatively inactive lives, predictably it may become increasingly difficult to change to a more physically active lifestyle in later years. Thus, it is necessary to promote a healthy lifestyle during the early life years with preference always accorded to primary prevention as early as possible rather than prevention at a time when irreversible pathological changes have occurred. The latter may be particularly related to metabolic diseases such as cardiovascular disease and type 2 diabetes.

There is a rationale for primary prevention in relation to health promotion in children if the following hypotheses are valid:

A sedentary lifestyle causes increased levels in disease risk factors, which are known to increase risk of premature death.

A large percentage of European children have a sedentary lifestyle to a degree that it may increase the risk of developing atherosclerosis and lifestyle diseases such as CVD and type II diabetes prematurely.

Risk factors or sedentary behaviour track during childhood and into adulthood.

Interventions including increased physical activity in children at risk are efficient in decreasing risk factor levels and changing behaviour to a more physically active lifestyle.

In this chapter, we argue that the above hypotheses are true. The chapter focuses on: i) physical activity in children and youth: recommendations and determinants; ii) key mechanisms, which link physical activity to the biological CVD risk factors including the atherosclerotic process; iii) associations between physical activity/fitness and CVD risk factors; iv) tracking of physical activity, fitness and CVD risk factors; v) what can be done; and vi) concluding remarks.

PHYSICAL ACTIVITY IN CHILDREN AND YOUTH: RECOMMENDATIONS AND DETERMINANTS

Physical activity should be a normal part of daily living habits for young people. Throughout the lifespan, physical activity plays a key part in young people's physical, social and mental development. All forms of activity have a part to play over the years, whether they be informal play, "free range" activity and games, physical education, sport, walking and cycling as transport, or more formal "exercise". Babies learn and develop physical capabilities through play; toddlers develop key social skills through games with others; and young people develop basic skills and an understanding of rules and team membership through sport and physical education (PE). Therefore, physical educators frequently allege that "the pre-eminence of skill should be regarded as a main educational objective in physical education" (Arnold, 1991, p.73) and that "... Physical education should seek the development of reasonably skilful movers who have access to, participate in and enjoy participating in physical activity" (O'Sullivan, 2001, p.38). Another important reason for supporting an increase in the amount of physical activity, PE and sport in childhood is proffered by Trudeau & Shephard (2008). In their review of quasi-experimental and cross-sectional studies, they found that additional emphasis on PE may result in small absolute gains in academic grade point average as well as a positive association between academic performance and physical activity. They also found a positive influence of physical activity on concentration, memory and classroom behaviour as well as a positive relationship between physical activity and intellectual performance, a relationship verified by Åberg, Pedersen, Toren et al., (2009) in relation to male youngsters. In a cohort study following Swedish men born in the period 1950-1976, who were enlisted for military service at age 18 (n =1.221.727 including 1432 monozygotic twin pairs), they found a positive association between cardiovascular fitness and intelligence after adjusting for relevant confounders, and of crucial importance, this was also obtained by the monozygotic twin pairs. The association was primarily explained by individual specific, non-shared environmental influences (>80%), whereas heritability explained less than 15% of the co-variation. It was also demonstrated that cardiovascular fitness level at age 18 years predicted educational achievements later in life. The data substantiate that physical exercise can be an important instrument in public health initiatives to optimise educational achievements and cognitive performance at societal level.

A physically active lifestyle has direct and indirect health benefits for young people, particularly through the possible prevention of overweight and obesity, the promotion of good mental health and the establishment of healthy lifestyles that may be continued into adulthood. Many young people do take part in regular physical activity and sport. However, there is increasing evidence to suggest that large numbers of young people across the European Union region are not taking part in physical activity to a recommended level to benefit their health. The provision of PE in schools appears to be declining, and opportunities to be active in daily life are tending to be marginalized because of the increasingly popularity of the car as a mode of transport, and the computer and/or TV screen as a mode of recreation (Dietz, 2001). Separately and collectively these factors are sufficient to justify recommendations to address the key issue: physical inactivity harms current and future health. There is now strong evidence to support the relationship between physical activity and many aspects of adult health. Physical activity reduces morbidity and mortality from many of the leading causes of ill health, notably coronary heart disease, as well as having positive effects on aspects of health including body fat and weight control, and depression and anxiety (Paffenbarger, Hyde, Wing et al., 1993; and Blair, Kampert, Kohl et al., 1996).

The established causal links between health status and CVD risk factors have not yet been confirmed in children, but behavioural, physiological and genetic risk factors for CVD can be identified in children and young people. Lifestyle related risk factors such as low physical activity (PA) and physical fitness (PF) has been independently linked to risk factors for CVD mortality in men and women, and furthermore related to CVD risk factors such as elevated blood pressure and unfavourable blood lipids at an early stage in children (Katzmarzyk, Malina & Bouchard, 1999). It is biologically plausible that PA improves the metabolic health profile - also in children, and it has been shown that objectively measured PA is inversely related to clustering of risk factors related to the metabolic syndrome (Andersen, Harro, Sardinha et al., 2006).

In young people the main morbidities, which affect adults, and which are caused at least in part by a sedentary lifestyle, have not had sufficient time to develop. The main exception to this is childhood obesity, which has been referred to as a global epidemic, and can be considered a health problem in its own right (Calim & Caprio, 2008). But exposure to physical inactivity through childhood can serve, as previously mentioned, as a critical risk factor for the early origin of CVD in adulthood. Several prospective cohort studies have documented that sedentary adults, as compared with their physically active counterparts, are at considerable risk for various CVD (Haskell, Lee, Pate et al., 2007). These studies have laid the foundation for physical activity recommendations presented by public health authorities. In contrast, very limited evidence exists based on prospective research for the current physical activity recommendations in children and adolescents. Thus, little is known about the long term negative effects of physical inactivity during the period of childhood.

RECOMMENDATIONS

According to expert opinion and empirical evidence, current recommendations suggest that children and adolescents should participate in physical activity of at least moderate intensity for at least one hour per day with 20 minutes of physical activity being more intensive a couple of times per week (Strong, Malina, Blimkie et al., 2005). This recommendation is primarily based on intervention studies of highly selected participants (such as obese children) and cross-sectional studies associating self-reported physical activity to various health parameters.

The Canadian Society for Exercise Physiology, in partnership with the Public Health Agency of Canada, has recently initiated a review of their physical activity guidelines to promote healthy active living for Canadian children, youth, adults and older adults. Comprehensive systematic reviews were completed to ensure a rigorous evaluation of evidence informing the revision of physical activity guidelines for the different populations. Using an independent expert panel to review the background materials and systematic reviews, a paper has been published representing their interpretation of the evidence (Kesaniemi, Riddoch, Reeder et al., 2010). The paper includes recommendations for evidence-informed physical activity guidelines. The Panel made three recommendations for school-age children and youth, which should stimulate sound growth and development and confer protection against known risk factors for adult chronic disease.

Recommendation 1: Children and youth aged 5-19 years of age should accumulate at least one hour and up to several hours of at least moderate-intensity Physical Activity on a daily basis to achieve most of the health benefits associated with Physical Activity. Some health benefits can be achieved through 30 minutes/day of moderate-intensity Physical Activity, and this should be used as a "stepping stone" for currently sedentary children.

Recommendation 2: Vigorous-intensity activities should be incorporated or added when possible, including activities that strengthen muscle and bone.

Recommendation 3: Aerobic activities should make up the majority of the daily Physical Activity. Muscle- and bone-strengthening activities should be incorporated on at least three days of the week.

Recently, cross-sectional data based on objective measures of physical activity from the European Youth Heart Study (EYHS) has been published showing that physical activity levels should be higher than the current international guidelines of at least one hour per day of physical activity of at least moderate intensity to prevent clustering of CVD risk factors (Andersen, Harro & Sardinha, 2006). But clearly, further research is needed to validate and qualify the current recommendations for children and adolescents.

Principally, the difficulty in elucidating the influence of physical activity during youth on the risk of CVD in adulthood is inherent to the difficulty of estimating habitual physical activity in children and adolescents and to the considerable lag time between exposure to a risk factor and manifestation of a cardiovascular event. In recent years, a deal of resources have been investigated in developing methods to measure physical activity objectively by utilizing accelerometry and software development to quantify habitual physical activity objectively (Brage, Brage, Franks et al., 2004; and Ekelund, Sjöström, Yngve et al., 2001). Furthermore, methods have been developed analyzing CVD risk factors as a composite risk score without dichotomizing their continuous nature rendering it a better measure of cardiovascular health in younger populations (Andersen, Harro & Sardinha, 2006; and Brage, Wedderkopp, Ekelund et al., 2004). Now it is also possible to measure early structural and functional changes of large vessels using non-invasive measurement techniques and this represents a novel means of studying the initiation and progress of arterial disease during the important early years of life. Thus, arterial properties such as carotid intima-media thickness (IMT), arterial stiffness and endothelial function can be determined by high-resolution ultrasound imaging. Both IMT, arterial stiffness and endothelial function predicts the development of CVD independent of conventional risk factors and clustering of conventional risk factors is a very strong condition predicting future CVD (Conroy, Pyorala, Fitzgerald et al., 2003). Together with obesity measures, these measures serve as attractive end-points in epidemiological studies of the early origins of CVD.

So for sure, the importance of physical activity during childhood is accepted and additionally as well because obesity rates escalate and the onset of chronic disease appears at earlier stages of the life course. However, more research using randomized trials as well as the newest methods regarding both activity and the manifestation of a cardiovascular event are essential before any concluding evidence can be made for physical activity recommendations for children and youth.

DETERMINANTS

From a societal point of view, a lifelong high level of Physical Activity is a commendable goal to obtain and its determinants must be examined in order improve physical activity levels in the population. Several studies have investigated potential determinants and have discovered a number of factors with different degrees of influence on the level of adult Physical Activity (Seefeldt, Malina & Clark, 2002; and Trost, Owen, Bauman et al., 2002. Most of these studies are based on cross-sectional designs both because of the concurrency (and hence, the close association) and the availability of data and thus, hinders the possibility of concluding cause and effect. Only a few studies have used longitudinal data to search for indications of adult Physical Activity level and thereby investigated potential determinants earlier in life. The success of interventions depends on many complex factors of different degree of influence and not least on age. The younger an individual is the more impressionable he/she is to changes (Seefeldt, Malina & Clark, 2002; and Malina, 2001). Furthermore, an extensive drop out of sports participation and Physical Activity during the late teen years has been observed (Brown & Trost, 2003). Therefore, it is of great value to investigate the determinants in order to enhance the hours and intensity of Physical Activity in adulthood.

Better understanding of the correlates of physical activity and sedentary behaviours in children and adolescents will support the development of efficient interventions promoting physically active lifestyle. A review by Van der Horst, Paw, Twisk et al., (2007) of 60 studies dealing with children and youngsters in the age group of 4 to 18 years of age shows the following: for children (age range 4-12 years), gender (male), self-efficacy, parental physical activity (for boys) and parent support were positively associated with Physical Activity; for adolescents (age range 13–18 years), positive associations with physical activity were found for gender (male), parental education, attitude, self-efficacy, goal orientation/motivation, physical education/school sports, family influences, and friend support; for adolescents, a positive association was found between gender (male) and sedentary behaviour, whereas an inverse association was found between gender and insufficient physical activity; Caucasian ethnicity, socio-economic status, and parental education were found to be inversely associated with adolescents' sedentary behaviours; but they concluded that more prospective studies are needed examining the correlates of insufficient Physical Activity and sedentary behaviour.

In recent years the Ecological Systems Theory (EST) has been used as a model, when examining the strength of neighbourhood factors as outlined in EST. This includes factors related to the family, the environment and the school, which are embedded in larger social contexts of the community and society. These factors are referred to in the literature as the "built environment", which encompasses the entire range of structural elements in a residential setting including, for example, housing mix, transportation networks, public resources, and presence of sidewalks or trails. Whereas progress has been made with respect to the body of evidence supporting the role of neighbourhood factors on childhood activity and obesity-related behaviours, much work remains to be done to enhance our understanding of neighbourhood level factors. Nevertheless, as the body of evidence grows, these studies will inform multi-level interventions, which are urgently needed to tackle the growing epidemic of childhood inactivity and obesity (Galvez, Pearl & Yen, 2010).

Research into the link between the built environment and childhood obesity is still in its infancy. Analysts do not know whether changes in the built environment have increased rates of obesity or whether improvements to the built environment will decrease them. Nonetheless, the policy implications are clear: people who have access to safe places to be active, neighbourhoods that are walkable and local markets that offer healthful food are likely to be more active and to eat more healthful food - two types of behaviour that can lead to good health and may help in avoiding obesity (Sallis & Granz, 2006).

The findings of determinants can be summarized as follows, elucidating the broad scope of both generic and behaviour specific factors, which are influencing activity habits in youth.

GENERIC FACTORS AND THE BUILT ENVIRONMENT

They can be separated into *Objective built environments such* as housing density, land use, crime, traffic flow and transport links and green space.

Perceived built environment such as play space, aesthetics, accessibility, safety and traffic in local area.

Social environment such as income, education, car ownership, housing, childcare, family support and rules, friend support and social network

BEHAVIOUR SPECIFIC FACTORS

Behaviour specific factors are *psychological factors* such as efficacy, enjoyment, preference, attitudes, beliefs, intention, motivation, knowledge and readiness to change.

Physiological factors such as age, gender, pubertal status and body build (lean, overweight, tall etc.).

Activity can be divided into: *Activity patterns* such as unstructured leisure, structured exercise/sport and active transport; *Leisure patterns* such as TV viewing, computer and internet use and reading; and *Meal patterns* such as fast food, drinks, fruit and vegetables and high calorie snacks.

As demonstrated, the determinants influencing behaviour are complex. They can be divided into environmental factors (built and social environment – objective and perceptional) and specific factors, which again are influenced by psychological and physiological factors. All of them influence the pattern of activity, leisure and eating habits. This again is very much related to age, gender and obesity, which is the reason for the necessity of making interventions very specific, if they are to have any chance of success and influence physical activity behaviour.

KEY MECHANISMS LINKING PHYSICAL ACTIVITY TO THE BIOLOGICAL CVD RISK FACTORS INCLUDING THE ATHEROSCLEROTIC PROCESS

The most convincing evidence, which is normally used when causal conclusions are drawn between an exposure and a disease, comes from randomised controlled trials. This type of study has not been performed with respect to any of the major life style risk factors where hard end-points are considered. Knowledge of biological mechanisms is, therefore, important in the evaluation of possible causal relationships between physical activity and CVD risk factors, and in the understanding of type, frequency and intensity of the physical activity beneficial for health. Benefits of physical activity can be separated into acute changes caused by the activity itself and more long term physiological changes caused by the training effects of physical activity on the muscle and fat tissues, the heart, and the action of enzymes and hormones. Most of the biological CVD risk factors are linked to the metabolism, which are regulated by enzymes and hormones, mainly the oxidative enzymes, insulin and noradrenalin/adrenalin. Clustering of CVD risk factors is closely linked to high levels of fasting insulin (Andersen, Boreham, Young et al., 2006). It is, therefore, important to understand the relationship between physical activity and insulin sensitivity and level, and how insulin affects CVD levels, but it is also important to understand that physical activity has beneficial effects through different independent mechanisms, which all change risk factor levels in a positive direction.

Acute physical activity and exercise training cause different physiological changes, which influence CVD risk factors. Some of these mechanisms are shared with the changes caused by overweight while others are unique for physical activity, but may affect fat accumulation. The most important physiological change is probably insulin and adrenaline sensitivity, and both of these hormones can double their action after a few months of exercise training. At least for insulin, the change is located to the training muscle, and if only one leg is trained, the increased glucose clearance will be limited to the trained leg (Dela, Larsen, Mikines et al., 1995). Training increases adrenaline sensitivity and decreases adrenaline release, leading to increased glucose clearance since adrenaline blocks insulin-mediated glucose uptake. Besides this effect of training, glucose can enter the muscle cell when it contracts without the presence of insulin (Franch, Aslesen & Jensen, 1999). This glucose transport is an important mechanism related to all intensities of activity. It causes 24-h insulin levels to decrease in the physically active, and may affect lipid storage in the fat cells, and indirectly appetite regulation. The contraction-mediated glucose uptake in the muscle cell is increased when the stored glycogen is used during prolonged exercise. Further, the contraction-mediated glucose uptake is not blocked by adrenaline. Even during periods of stress, physical activity may help to maintain low levels of insulin. Other acute effects are a lowering of triglyceride level and increased HDL (Hicks, MacDougall & Muckle, 1987). In contrast to these mechanisms located in the muscle cells, fat tissue releases cytokines such as tumour necrosis factor alpha (TNF-α) into the circulation, which can decrease insulin sensitivity systemically (Hotamisligil, Shargill & Spiegelman, 1993). Most of the common CVD risk factors are made worse by the action of insulin, which affects both metabolic pathways (blood lipids) and sympathetic nervous system (blood pressure). The insulin sensitivity of the muscle cells is, therefore, extremely important because 80-90% of the glucose will enter the muscle cell as insulin-mediated under normal conditions.

Other mechanisms related to prolonged training are increased lipoprotein lipase (LPL) activity and increased oxidative enzymes in the trained muscles. LPL is situated on the inner wall of the capillaries, and the number of capillaries increases in proportion to the training state of the muscle (Shono, Mizuno, Nishida et al., 1999). LPL catalyzes triglyceride transported from LDL or VLDL cholesterol into the muscle cell, where it is burned, thereby improving the ratio of total cholesterol/HDL. Changes in oxidative enzymes related to training are substantial. After only eight weeks of training of untrained young subjects, key enzymes such as SDH (succinate dehydrogenase) and HAD (hydroxyl acyl dehydrogenase) have been shown to increase by 30-40% (Klausen, Andersen & Pelle, 1981). This change improves the metabolism of triglycerides, which in turn improves glucose uptake. However, the effect of training on oxidative enzyme levels disappear as fast as it develops after the cessation of training.

ASSOCIATIONS BETWEEN PHYSICAL ACTIVITY/FITNESS AND CVD RISK FACTOR

As mentioned above, physical activity works through many different physiological mechanisms. This means that CVD risk factors change in the same direction in an individual during training no matter what the causes of the changes are. High levels in many CVD risk factors simultaneously have been observed in children not more than 9 years of age (Andersen, Wedderkopp & Hansen, 2003). This condition was first described by Reaven (1993). A suggestion has been made to define the metabolic syndrome in children from the fact that CVD risk factors are not independently distributed, and a continuous composite score of the risk factors may define the condition better (Anderssen, Cooper, Riddoch et al., 2007). A major problem related to research of the health effects of physical activity has been quite weak associations between physical activity (or fitness) and CVD risk factors. This is partly caused by methodological problems, because both physical activity and most CVD risk factors fluctuate widely from day to day. This fluctuation is caused by both measurement error and true changes. Analyzing a composite score of many CVD risk factors can solve part of this problem, because physical activity mediated true changes in CVD risk factors occur in the same direction, and fluctuations in the single CVD risk factors are by and large independent, for example, blood pressure may change within minutes in an arousal stage while cholesterol may change 1 mmol/l over a week. A composite score for the risk factors is especially useful in children because health is difficult to define in the absence of hard end-points amongst children, who are free from disease, but still have higher risk factor levels than their peers. Many studies have reported increased levels of individual CVD risk factors in overweight or sedentary children, though few have analyzed clustering of risk factors.

No matter what mechanisms are responsible, clustering of risk factors is an unhealthy condition, and it makes sense to analyze a composite score of risk factors. We have recently analyzed such clustering of risk factors in relation to objectively measured physical activity (refer Andersen, Harro & Sardinha, 2006), physical fitness (Anderssen, Cooper & Riddoch, 2007), and combinations of physical activity, fitness and obesity (Andersen, Sardinha, Froberg et al., 2008). We found around 13 times increased risk for clustering of CVD risk factors for the lower quartile of fitness compared with the upper quartile, and around 10 times increased risk for the upper quartile of fatness compared with the lower. Odds ratios depend on which CVD risk factors are included in the composite score, and the fact that one exposure shows a higher odds ratio than another does not mean that it is more important. The different exposures are measured with different amounts of error variation, and physical activity variables will always give weaker associations than the more precisely assessed fitness and fatness variables even if physical activity may be just as important. However, skin-fold thickness predicted clustering of risk factors as strongly as waist circumference or Body Mass Index (BMI). Physical activity exhibited a protective effect even after adjustment for both fitness and fatness in the *European Youth Heart Study* (EYHS). Some studies have observed that the association between CVD risk factors and physical fitness or activity has disappeared after adjustment for fatness (Christou, Gentile, DeSouza et al., 2005. This has wrongly been interpreted as avoiding getting fat being more important than keeping fit. It is not possible from observational studies to make such conclusions, because we do not know how these parameters interact. If fitness and fatness are part of the same causal pathway and both are entered into the analysis, only the intermediate variable will be significant and the real cause will statistically disappear. However, if fitness and fatness are competing exposures, we should make adjustments for the other one as a confounder. The available mechanistic knowledge suggests that fitness and fatness both are inter-related and have independent effects on CVD risk factors. Studies have consistently reported higher levels in all the risk factors related to the metabolic syndrome in obese versus non-obese children and adolescents (Nielsen & Andersen, 2003); the same is true for the association between fitness and CVD risk factors. Blood pressure was 10 mmHg higher in the upper 10% of BMI compared with the lower 10% in 17-year old adolescents, and the association between blood pressure and BMI became stronger when only the least fit part of the population was analyzed. Fitness and BMI were independently associated with blood pressure, but also to each other. Gutin, Johnson, Humphries et al., (2007) analyzed the association between blood lipids, fasting insulin, fitness and fatness in black and white 14-18 year olds. Both fitness and fatness were associated with blood lipids, but when they were both entered into regression models, only fatness was significant despite a moderately strong correlation between fitness and fatness (r=0.69). The authors concluded that interventions to improve lipid profile should be designed primarily to minimize fatness. But the conclusion is based on an assumption of competing risk factors, which may not be true (see above).

Recently, we analyzed clustering of CVD risk factors in pre-school children 6-7 years of age, and surprisingly we did not find any sign of clustering. It was surprising because children included individuals who were unfit, fat and showed low insulin sensitivity (International Journal of Paediatric Obesity, in press). Also, there was no association between fatness or fitness and CVD risk factors. The children were tracked until the age of 9 years, and at this time clustering had developed in around 14% of the children. Further, we found that the lowest quartile of fitness had a 35 times increased risk of having clustering of risk factors. It would seem that the metabolic syndrome develops after the children start school, and one suggestion could be that the decrease in physical activity that occurs when children are seated could be important. Further studies are needed before firm conclusions can be drawn. CVD risk factors cluster in children, and clustering is associated independently with obesity, low physical activity and fitness. These observations can be accounted for by defined physiological mechanisms that are thought to be at the origin of the risk factor clustering.

TRACKING OF PHYSICAL ACTIVITY, FITNESS AND CVD RISK FACTORS

Tracking is a measure of how well subjects keep rank order within a variable. It can be expressed as a correlation calculated over the whole distribution or as an odds ratio of staying at risk from one point of time to another. The former is a good way to express stability in a variable if risk increases linearly, which it does in many CVD risk factors, and there is no well defined cut off point in the different risk factors for children above which risk increases. Odds ratio of staying at risk or staying above a defined level in a risk factor may be a better way to analyse relationships if they are not linear or to analyse clustered risk. It may be of less importance if a subject changes from the lower part of the distribution to the middle than a change from the middle to the top. However, many CVD risk factors are linearly associated to CVD. A high tracking coefficient gives a high predictive value of the risk factor measured later in life, but a low value does not necessarily mean the opposite, because it may be caused by measurement error or short time fluctuations, i.e. total cholesterol is precisely measured in a particular blood sample, but day to day fluctuations are great. A tracking co-efficient can never be better than the error variation in the risk factor and it is, therefore, difficult to compare tracking coefficient between risk factors. Assessment of physical activity is difficult and both accelerometer measurements and self-reported activity have a low reproducibility, so tracking coefficients are always low, which does not necessarily mean that the activity level in childhood is not a determinant of adult activity. Fitness is more stable and changes gradually if physical activity is changed, and a precise assessment is possible. The tracking coefficient normally decreases with increasing time span between the measurements.

TRACKING OF PHYSICAL ACTIVITY

Low tracking coefficients are found in studies where self-reported physical activity has been analysed. Part of the explanation may be assessment problems related to self-reported activity, but some studies have found that childhood participation in sports, educational level, other life experiences and fitness level are predictors of adult physical activity level (Telema, Laakso & Yang, 1994). Only few large population studies have reported tracking of physical activity measured with accelerometers, and in one of them data was corrected for error variation (Kristensen, Moller, Korsholm et al., (2008). In this study, which included longitudinal data from the EYHS study, moderately tracking in Physical Activity from childhood to adolescence (stability coefficients of 0.53 and 0.48 for boys and girls respectively) was found when analyses were corrected for seasonal variation, within-week variation, activity registration during night time sleep, within instrumental measurement error and day-to-day variation. The *Danish Youth and Sport Study* followed subjects for eight years from adolescence to young adulthood and found correlations of 0.31 for men (p<0.01) and 0.20 for women (non significant) (Andersen &

Haraldsdóttir, 1993). The risk for a sedentary man to stay inactive was 2.2 times higher than expected, but for women, more sedentary women than expected from a random distribution became active. Similar results were found in the *Young Finns Study* (Raitakari, Porkka, Taimela et al., 1994) and in the *Amsterdam Growth and Health Study* (Twisk, Kemper & van Mechelen, 2000).

TRACKING OF PHYSICAL FITNESS

Physical fitness is assessed as aerobic fitness or as different measures of strength, flexibility, and motor coordination often assessed by field test batteries. When tracking of aerobic fitness is analysed, the results depend on the assessment method, because indirect methods include measurement error. Only few studies have used direct measurements of VO_2max. Aerobic fitness tracks moderately with a correlation coefficient around 0.5 (Twisk, Kemper & van Mechelen, 2000; and Andersen, 1995). Somewhat higher coefficients are found when isometric strength is assessed (r=0.7), but if strength is expressed relative to body size values similar to aerobic fitness are found. Even higher coefficients were found in the Leuven *Longitudinal Study* (Maia, Beunen, Lefevre et., 2003).

TRACKING OF CVD RISK FACTORS

Only a few studies have measured tracking of CVD risk factors from adolescence to young adulthood, and they found similar results (Andersen, 1996). Both blood lipids and blood pressure (BP) track in children, but higher correlation coefficients are usually found in cholesterol fractions (0.5-0.7) compared with BP and to triglyceride (0.3-0.4). Tracking of BP was assessed in an American study, which followed 211 subjects from childhood (3-11 years) to adulthood (30 years and 50 years of age) (Nelson, Ragland & Syme, 1992. Correlations between juvenile blood pressure and adult blood pressure were low, but lower for measurements at age 50 years compared with measurements at age 30 years. Tracking in systolic blood pressure was higher than in diastolic blood pressure. However, more hypertensive subjects dropped out, which could influence tracking coefficients. Also, many subjects at age 50 years use drugs for hypertension, which is an additional bias. Correlations for blood pressure vary between 0.2 and 0.5. Associations between blood pressures measured with years interval are weakened by large intra-subjects' variability from day to day and even within minutes. Part of this variation could be diminished by more measurements before the follow-up and after the follow-up, but such data are not available.

Blood lipids and lipoproteins are more stable than physical activity and blood pressure from childhood to adulthood except for triglyceride (Twisk, Kemper & van Mechelen, 1997). Most correlations are between 0.5 and 0.7 for total cholesterol and LDL cholesterol, and somewhat lower for triglyceride and other lipoproteins. This is quite high because big fluctuations occur from day to day in total cholesterol. Subjects in the highest quintile of total cholesterol as children have a 2-3 fold increased risk of being in the highest quintile after 8 years of follow-up (Andersen & Haraldsdóttir, 1993) and a doubled risk after 15 years of follow-up (Bao, Srinivasan & Wattigney, 1996).

TRACKING OF CLUSTERED RISK

In the *Danish Youth and Sport Study*, a total risk score was calculated as the sum of scores in the single risk factors (ranked into 1 to 6) (Andersen, 1996). A high correlation coefficient was found from adolescence to adulthood in men (r=0.67, p<0.001) but not in women (r=0.33, p<0.01). Recently, a Report analysing tracking of clustered risk was published from this cohort, and those who had clustered risk such as teenagers had a six fold increased risk of having clustered risk as young adults (Andersen, Hasselstrøm, Grønfeldt et al., 2004). In conclusion on CVD risk factors and physical fitness tracks, blood pressure, triglyceride and physical activity only show weak tracking, which in part could be related to difficulties in assessing these variables, but clustered risk tracks strongly.

WHAT CAN BE DONE?

Increase in physical activity may be achieved in different ways, and the most effective way in a specific population may depend on the culture. A key issue is how sedentary children are reached. Increasing physical activity in the most active children may reveal limited health gain while an increase among the sedentary children may be much more important in the prevention of future disease. Some arenas where sedentary children could be targeted are schools and in interventions targeting everyday living such as active transport. In many countries, there are strong Associations promoting organized sport. These Associations may have the resources to promote sport, but as their main goal is to improve performance and develop elite athletes, they very often lack initiatives to include children who are not successful in sport.

In countries where PE is compulsory, school based interventions are a possible way to reach sedentary children. Dobbins, De, Robeson et al., (2009) recently reviewed the effects of school-based intervention to increase physical activity and improve health. Studies showed positive effects of interventions on physical activity behaviour and a number of health outcomes. It is possible to improve physical fitness and blood lipid profile, but most studies did not find any effect on blood pressure and only few found an effect on BMI. However, an effect of increased physical activity may be increased muscle mass, and studies where only BMI and not body composition is assessed, may not be able to detect an improvement in fat mass. An interesting analysis was undertaken by Resaland, Andersen, Mamen et al., (2009), when they carried out a two-year intervention in a rural city in Norway. They found a substantial increase of 9% in cardio-respiratory fitness in the intervention group compared to the control group. However, in a *post hoc* analysis, where they stratified subjects into quartiles according to their baseline fitness level, they found a 13% increase in the least fit quartile and a 3% increase in the most fit quartile compared with the corresponding quartiles in the control group. This is interesting from a health perspective, because metabolic risk factors tend to cluster in the least fit children (Anderssen, Cooper Riddoch et al., 2007). In general, it is necessary that the intervention includes a substantial increase in physical activity if health gains are to be achieved. Small effect sizes have been found with an increase from two to four PE lessons, but studies including 60 minutes of physical activity every school day have shown substantial health effects. The 60 minutes need not be PE lessons, but can be arranged as play in the school yard as long as some intensity is achieved.

Another setting which may be promising is active transport. There are no randomized trials looking at the effect of walking or cycling to school in children, but some observational studies have shown that cycling to school may result in improved health. The *European Youth Heart Study* analyzed changes in fitness in children aged 9-15 years, who did not cycle at baseline. Some of these children changed to cycling while others were non-cyclists at the age of 15 years; in children starting cycling, a 9% a higher fitness level was observed at the age of 15 years (Cooper, Wedderkopp, Jago et al., 2008); beside improved fitness, an improvement was found in metabolic risk factors (Andersen, Wedderkopp, Kristensen et al., 2010).

Potentially, interventions can be targeted at the general population of children or at children at risk such as overweight and obese children. Intervention studies in obese youths show that favourable changes in insulin sensitivity, lipid profile, indices of inflammation, endothelial function, cardiac parasympathetic activity and carotid IMT are produced by moderate-vigorous physical activity doses of 150-180 minutes/week (Balagopal, George, Patton et al., 2005; Kang, Gutin, Barbeau et al., 2002; and Meyer, Kundt, Steiner et al., 2006). However, for non-obese youths, intervention studies suggest that such doses are not effective; higher moderate-vigorous physical activity doses of 300 minutes/week seem necessary (Barbeau, Johnson, Howe et al., 2007).

CONCLUSIONS

A sedentary lifestyle in children is associated with increased levels in disease risk factors, which are known to increase risk of premature death, and the prevalence of clustered cardiovascular risk is more common in sedentary children. Further, a large percentage of European children have a lifestyle sedentary to a degree that it may increase the risk of developing atherosclerosis and lifestyle diseases such as CVD and type II diabetes prematurely. It has also been verified that both risk factors and sedentary behaviour track during childhood and into adulthood, and there is, therefore, a rationale for early prevention. Interventions including increased physical activity in children and especially in children at risk are efficient to decrease risk factor levels and change behaviour to a more physically active lifestyle. An important setting for this is the school, where through PE lessons, activities in breaks, active commuting to the school as well as in after-school sports, there is the opportunity to reach all children as well as children at risk through specific activity programmes.

REFERENCES

Aberg, M.A., Pedersen, N.L., & Toren K., et al. (2009) Cardiovascular fitness is associated with cognition in young adulthood. *Proceedings of the National Academy of Sciences of the United State of America* (PNAS).

Andersen, L.B., Boreham, C.A., & Young, I.S., et al. (2006) Insulin sensitivity and clustering of coronary heart disease risk factors in young adults. The Northern Ireland Young Hearts Study. *Preventive Medicine, 42,* pp.73-7.

Andersen, L.B. (1995) Tracking of VO$_2$max, strength and physical activity from teenage to adulthood. *Pediatric Exercise Science.*

Andersen, L.B. (1996) Tracking of risk factors for coronary heart disease from adolescence to young adulthood with special emphasis on physical activity and fitness. *Danish Medical Bulletin, 43,* pp.407-18.

Andersen, L.B., & Haraldsdóttir, J. (1993) Tracking of cardiovascular disease risk factors including maximal oxygen uptake and physical activity from late teenage to adulthood. An 8-year follow-up study. *Journal of Internal Medicine, 234,* pp.309-15.

Andersen, L.B., & Haraldsdóttir, J. (1994) Changes in physical activity, maximal isometric strength and maximal oxygen uptake from late teenage to adulthood: an eight-year follow-up study of asdolescents in Denmark. *Scandinavian Journal of Medicine and Science in Sports, 4,* pp.19-25.

Andersen, L.B., Harro, M., & Sardinha, L.B., et al. (2006) Physical activity and clustered cardiovascular risk in children: a cross-sectional study (The European Youth Heart Study). *Lancet, 368,* pp.299-304.

Andersen, L.B., Hasselstrøm, H., & Grønfeldt, V., et al. (2004) The relationship between physical fitness and clustered risk, and tracking of clustered risk from adolescence to young adulthood: eight years follow-up in the Danish Youth and Sport Study. *International Journal of Behavioural Nutrition and Physical Activity, 1, 6.*

Andersen, L.B., Sardinha, L.B., & Froberg, K., et al. (2008) Fitness, fatness and clustering of cardiovascular risk factors in children from Denmark, Estonia and Portugal: the European Youth Heart Study. *International Journal of Pediatric Obesity,* 3 Suppl 1, pp.58-66.

Andersen, L.B., Wedderkopp, N., & Hansen, H.S., et al. (2003) Biological cardiovascular risk factors cluster in Danish children and adolescents. Danish part of the European Heart Study. *Preventive Medicine, 37,* pp.363-7.

Andersen L.B, Wedderkopp, N., & Kristensen, P.L. et al. (2010) Cycling to school and cardiovascular risk factors: A longitudinal study. *Journal of Physical Activity and Health,* (in press)

Anderssen, S.A., Cooper, A.R., & Riddoch, C., et al. (2007) Low cardiorespiratory fitness is a strong predictor for clustering of cardiovascular disease risk factors in children independent of country, age and sex. *European Journal of Cardiovascular Preventive Rehabilitation, 14,* pp.526-31

Arnold, P. (1991) The pre-eminence of skill as an educational value in the movement curriculum. *Quest, 43,* pp.66-77.

Balagopal, P., George, D., & Patton, N., et al. (2005) Lifestyle-only intervention attenuates the inflammatory state associated with obesity: a randomized controlled study in adolescents. *Journal of Pediatrics,146,* pp.342-8.

Barbeau, P., Johnson, M.H., & Howe, C.A., et al. (2007) Ten months of exercise improves general and visceral adiposity, bone, and fitness in black girls. *Obesity (Silver Spring)*, *15*, pp.2077-85.

Blair, S.N., Kampert, J.B., & Kohl, H.W., et al. (1996) Influences of cardiorespiratory fitness and other precursors on cardiovascular disease and all-cause mortality in men and women. *JAMA, 276*, pp.205-10.

Brage, S., Brage, N., & Franks, P.W., et al. (2004) Branched equation modeling of simultaneous accelerometry and heart rate monitoring improves estimate of directly measured physical activity energy expenditure. *Journal of Applied Physiology, 96*, pp.343-51.

Brage, S., Wedderkopp, N., & Ekelund, U., et al. (2004) Features of the metabolic syndrome are associated with objectively measured physical activity and fitness in Danish children: the European Youth Heart Study (EYHS). *Diabetes Care, 27*, pp.2141-8.

Brown, W.J., & Trost, S.G. (2003) Life transitions and changing physical activity patterns in young women. *American Journal of Preventive Medicine, 25*, pp.140-3.

Cali, A.M., & Caprio, S. (2008) Obesity in children and adolescents. *Journal of Clinical Endocrinological Metabolism, 93*, pp.31-36.

Christou, D.D., Gentile, C.L., & DeSouza, C.A., et al. (2005) Fatness is a better predictor of cardiovascular disease risk factor profile than aerobic fitness in healthy men. *Circulation, 111*, pp.1904-14.

Conroy, R.M., Pyorala, K., & Fitzgerald, A.P., et al. (2003) Estimation of ten-year risk of fatal cardiovascular disease in Europe: the SCORE project. *European Heart Journal, 24*, pp.987-1003.

Cooper, A.R., Wedderkopp, N., & Jago, R., et al. (2008) Longitudinal associations of cycling to school with adolescent fitness. *Preventive Medicine, 47*, pp.324-8.

Dela, F., Larsen, J.J., & Mikines, K.J., et al. (1995) Insulin-Stimulated Muscle Glucose Clearance in Patients with Niddm - Effects of One-Legged Physical-Training. *Diabetes, 44*, pp.1010-20.

Dietz, W.H. (2001) The obesity epidemic in young children. Reduce television viewing and promote playing. *British Medical Journal, 322*, pp.313-4.

Dobbins, M., De, C.K., & Robeson, P., et al. (2009) School-based physical activity programs for promoting physical activity and fitness in children and adolescents aged 6-18. *Cochrane Database Systematic Review*, CD007651.

Ekelund, U., Sjöström, M., & Yngve, A., et al. (2001) Physical activity assessed by activity monitor and doubly labeled water in children. *Medicine and Science in Sports and Exercise, 33*, pp.275-81.

Franch, J., Aslesen, R., & Jensen, J. (1999) Regulation of glycogen synthesis in rat skeletal muscle after glycogen-depleting contractile activity: effects of adrenaline on glycogen synthesis and activation of glycogen synthase and glycogen phosphorylase. *Biochemical Journal, 344*, pp.231-5.

Galvez, M.P., Pearl, M., & Yen, I.H. (2010) Childhood obesity and the built environment. *Current Opinion in Pediatrics, 22*, 202-7.

Gutin, B., Johnson, M.H., & Humphries, M.C., et al. (2007) Relationship of visceral adiposity to cardiovascular disease risk factors in black and white teens. *Obesity (Silver Spring), 15*, pp.1029-35.

Haskell, W.L., Lee, I.M., & Pate, R.R., et al. (2007) Physical activity and public health: updated recommendation for adults from the American College of Sports Medicine and the American Heart Association. *Circulation, 116*, pp.1081-93.

Hicks, A.L., MacDougall, J.D., & Muckle, T.J. (1987) Acute changes in high-density lipoprotein cholesterol with exercise of different intensities. *Journal of Applied Physiology, 63*, pp.1956-60.

Hotamisligil, G.S., Shargill, N.S., & Spiegelman, B.M. (1993) Adipose expression of tumor necrosis factor-alpha: direct role in obesity-linked insulin resistance. *Science, 259*, pp.87-91.

Kang, H-S., Gutin, B. & Barbeau, P., et al. (2002) Physical training improves insulin resistance syndrome markers in obese adolescents. *Medicine in Science of Sports and Exercise, 34*, pp.1920-7.

Katzmarzyk, P.T., Malina, R.M., & Bouchard, C. (1999) Physical activity, physical fitness, and coronary heart disease risk factors in youth: the Québec Family Study. *Preventive Medicine, 29*, pp.555-62.

Kesaniemi, A., Riddoch, C.J., & Reeder, B., et al. (2010) Advancing the future of physical activity guidelines in Canada: an independent expert panel interpretation of the evidence. *International Journal of Behavioural Nutrition and Physical Activity, 7*, p.41.

Klausen, K., Andersen, L.B., & Pelle, I. (1981) Adaptive changes in work capacity, skeletal muscle capillarization and enzyme levels during training and detraining. *Acta Physiologica Scandinavia, 113*, pp.9-16.

Kristensen, P.L., Moller, N.C., & Korsholm, L., et al. (2008) Tracking of objectively measured physical activity from childhood to adolescence: the European youth heart study. *Scandinavian Journal of Medicine and Science in Sports, 18*, pp.171-8.

Maia, J.A., Beunen, G., & Lefevre, J., et al. (2003) Modelling stability and change in strength development: a study in adolescent boys. *American Journal of Human Biology, 15*, pp.579-91.

Malina, R.M. (2001) Physical activity and fitness: pathways from childhood to adulthood. *American Journal of Human Biology, 13*, pp.162-72.

Meyer, A.A., Kundt, G., & Steiner, M., et al. (2006) Impaired flow-mediated vasodilation, carotid artery intima-media thickening, and elevated endothelial plasma markers in obese children: the impact of cardiovascular risk factors. *Pediatrics, 117*, pp.1560-7.

Nelson, M.J., Ragland, D.R., & Syme, S.L. (1992) Longitudinal prediction of adult blood pressure from juvenile blood pressure levels. *American Journal of Epidemiology, 136*, pp.633-45.

Nielsen, G.A., & Andersen, L.B. (2003) The association between high blood pressure, physical fitness, and body mass index. *Preventive Medicine, 36*, nr. 2, pp.229-34.

O'Sullivan M. (2001). Looking outward to the future: a reaction to Locke's looking backward: 2100-2000. In: P. Ward & P. Doutis (Eds.), Physical education for the 24th century. *Proceedings of the Janus Conference*. Lincoln, NE: University of Nebraska, Lincoln, pp.35-49.

Paffenbarger, R.S.Jr., Hyde, R.T., & Wing, A.L., et al. (1993) The association of changes in physical-activity level and other lifestyle characteristics with mortality among men. *New England Journal of Medicine, 328*, pp.538-545.

Raitakari, O.T., Porkka, K.V.K., & Taimela, S., et al. (1994) Effects of persistent physical activity and inactivity on coronary risk factors in children and young adults. *American Journal of Epidemiology, 140*, pp.195-205.

Reaven, G.M. (1993) Role of insulin resistance in human disease (syndrome X): an expanded definition. *Annual Review of Medicine, 44*, pp.121-31.

Resaland, G.K., Andersen, L.B., & Mamen, A., et al. (2009) Effects of a 2-year school-based daily physical activity intervention on cardiorespiratory fitness: the Sogndal school-intervention study. *Scandinavian Journal of Medicine and Science of Sports*, Nov 5. [Epub ahead of print].

Sallis, J.F., & Glanz, K. (2006) The role of built environments in physical activity, eating, and obesity in childhood. *Future Child, 16,* pp.89-108.

Seefeldt, V., Malina, R.M., & Clark, M.A. (2002) Factors affecting levels of physical activity in adults. *Sports Medicine, 32,* pp.143-68.

Shono, N., Mizuno, M., & Nishida, H., et al. (1999) Decreased skeletal muscle capillary density is related to higher serum levels of low-density lipoprotein cholesterol and apolipoprotein B in men. *Metabolism, 48,* pp.1267-71.

Strong, W.B., Malina, R.M., & Blimkie, C.J., et al. (2005) Evidence Based Physical Activity for School-age Youth. *Journal of Pediatrics, 146,* pp.732-7.

Telema, T.R., Laakso, L., & Yang, X. (1994) Physical activity and participation in sports of young people in Finland. *Scandinavian Journal of Medicine in Science of Sports, 4,* pp.65-74.

Trost, S.G., Owen, N., & Bauman, A.E., et al. (2002) Correlates of adults' participation in physical activity: review and update. *Medicine and Science in Sports and Exercise, 34,* pp.1996-2001.

Trudeau, F., & Shephard, R.J. (2008) Physical education, school physical activity, school sports and academic performance. *International Journal of Behavioural Nutrition and Physical Activity, 5,* p.10.

Twisk, J.W.R., Kemper, H.C.G., & van Mechelen, W., et al. (1997) Tracking of risk factors for coronary heart disease over a 14-year period: a comparison between lifestyle and biologic risk factors with data from the Amsterdam Growth and Health Study. *American Journal of Epidemiology, 145,* pp.888-98.

Twisk, J.W.R., Kemper, H.C.G., & van Mechelen, W. (2000) Tracking of activity and fitness and the relationship with cardiovascular disease risk factors. *Medicine and Science in Sports and Exercise, 32*(1), pp.455-61.

Van Der Horst, H.K., Paw, M.J., & Twisk, J.W., et al. (2007) A brief review on correlates of physical activity and sedentariness in youth. *Medicine and Science in Sports and Exercise, 39,* pp.1241-50.

CHAPTER 14

PROMOTING ACTIVE AND HEALTHY LIFESTYLES AT SCHOOL: VIEWS OF STUDENTS, TEACHERS, AND PARENTS IN PORTUGAL

FRANCISCO CARREIRO DA COSTA AND ADILSON MARQUES

INTRODUCTION

In recognition that the majority of children and young people attend school and because of the considerable amount of time they spend there, the fundamental role schools and Physical Education (PE) can assume in the promotion of active and healthy lifestyles has been largely accepted both by researchers (Bidddle & Chatzisarantis, 1999; Pate, Davis, Robinson, Stone, McKenzie & Young, 2006; Sallis & McKenzie, 1991; Trudeau & Shepard, 2005) and by numerous organizations (e.g. National Association for Sport and PE, 2004; WHO, 2000). Through inclusive, enjoyable and motivating physical activities, PE has the propensity for developing motor skills, knowledge, attitudes and competencies necessary for an active lifestyle over the life span and the benefits of regular physical participation throughout childhood, youth, and adulthood are well documented (Campbell, Crews, & Sinclair, 2002; Rimmer, 2008; Whitt-Glover, O'Neill & Stettler, 2006).

The proportion of young children and adolescents showing low levels of Physical Activity (PA) is a cause of some concern (Currie et al. 2004). The problem is particularly marked among girls (Kimm et al., 2002; WHO, 2009), disabled students (Fitzgerald, 2006) and those from lower socio-economic groups (WHO, 2009). Moreover, because PA habits developed early in life may persist into childhood (Malina, 2001; Telama & Yang, 2000), adequate participation in PA during childhood and adolescence may also be critical in the prevention of obesity and chronic disease in later life. It should also be emphasized that children and adolescents with physical and cognitive disabilities have a higher prevalence of overweight compared with their non-disabled peers (Rimmer, Rowland, & Yamaki, 2007).

Low levels of PA are a cause of the rapid rise of over-weightness and obesity among young people (Berkley et al., 2000), together with poor dietary choices (Lee, Wechsler & Balling, 2006). These behaviours are influenced by many sectors of society, including families, community organizations, health care providers, faith-based institutions, government agencies, the media and schools. None of these sectors can alone solve the childhood obesity epidemic; whatever, it is unlikely to be solved without strong school-based policies and programmes (Lee et al., 2006). The issue here is whether schools have built up an educational climate able to promote the practise of PA, in and through PE, for all students.

Research examining PE classes, has consistently shown that students spend a limited amount of time engaged in moderate-to-vigorous PA (MVPA) (McKenzie et al., 1995; Fairclourgh & Stratton, 2006). Moreover, studies concerned with the impact of PE on the practice of PA show that the former is not especially successful in PA facilitation (Portman, 2003; Piéron, Ruiz & Montes, 2009; Rikard & Banville, 2006). Additionally, studies evaluating what students are learning in PE, suggest that students lack knowledge about the relationship between PA and health, and how to self-manage their own PA. Knowledge and conceptions of fitness concepts were found to be narrow, vague, and often inaccurate among students at all educational levels, (i.e., in elementary and secondary schools and further education) (Hernandez et al., 2007; Keating et al., 2009; Stewart & Mitchell, 2003). Furthermore, PE teachers demonstrate a limited knowledge about how to achieve the objectives of health-related PE (Castelli & Williams, 2007; Miller & Housner, 1998). The congruence of these findings strongly supports the opinion of those who argue that many PE programmes are inadequate in educating young people physically. It is important to ascertain what students know and what they can do on completion of their education. Part of being a "physically educated person" includes being physically fit, as well as knowing and valuing the benefits of a physically active lifestyle. While knowledge *per se* is probably not enough to change behaviours, improving and developing mastery of health-related fitness knowledge might be a first step in the establishment of healthy PA behaviours.

Counter to the negative PE scenario outlined above, there are indications of a more positive state of affairs. Carreiro da Costa et al. (2008) taking into account that schools that form collaborative teams (inter-disciplinary and cross-grade level) are more effective (Bernauer & Cress, 1997), have carried out a case study focused on a secondary school PE department, members of which work as a team in scheduling the students' curriculum for the entire school year. The main purpose of the study was to analyse the relationship between PE teachers' value orientations and the amount of PA provided for students. Even though teachers of the PE school department, as expected, share different PE value orientations, nine out of ten teachers engaged their students in MVPA for more than 50% of the available time during the three lessons observed; and six of the teachers reached more than 60% of MVPA.

In a very recent study, Van Acker et al. (2010) investigated the potential of modified game forms to promote sex equity in 13-year-old pupils' PA engagement during co-educational lessons. Findings showed that the proportion of MVPA was significantly higher among girls (69.9%) when compared with boys (56.8%); this was the case for all lesson contexts (co-educational and single sex). They concluded that using modified game forms with simplified rules has the potential as a co-educational instrument to produce MVPA levels that correspond with PA guidelines among both sexes, independently of lesson context. In particular, these findings offer a promising means of stimulating girls' PA levels during PE lessons.

Several PE interventions aiming to improve students' activity levels or to learn to be lifelong PA consumers have been successful (Fairclough & Stratton, 2006; Jamner, Spruit-Metz, Bassin & Cooper, 2004; McKenzie, 2003). Therefore, it may be that the failure of PE in promoting PA out of schools and aiming to facilitate lifelong active living is *inter alia* a consequence of the prevailing conditions (constraints on achievement of aims) within schools (Tyson, 1996) or how PE classes are organized and how teaching is delivered.

In accordance with the ecological model (Cale & Harris, 2006; Sallis et al., 2006), school-based interventions to promote young people's PA will only be successful if a change occurs in perceptions and attitudes of politicians, school principals, teachers, and parents towards the value of PE and PA. One of the strongest lines of research on school change is work related to teacher perceptions of reform effort. Research suggests that teacher values and perceptions will influence how a reform is interpreted and implemented (Carreiro da Costa, 2005; Hall & Hord, 2001). Parents also play health related roles, including PA, for their children as models of appropriate behaviours, as gatekeepers to opportunities and barriers, and as a major source of reinforcement in most children's lives (Cleland et al., 2005; Ornelas et al., 2007; Welk et al., 2003). Finally, Graham's study (1995) on student voice highlighted that getting to know how children perceive, feel, and subsequently evaluate attitude is the key to improving children's disposition towards PE.

Recognizing, on the one hand, that to obtain the support and adherence of all educational agents is crucial to obtain success in school interventions aiming to promote the practise of PA, and on the other, that this intervention needs to be built and implemented based on a profound knowledge about subjects and processes involved, a study, focused on teachers (from all subjects), students and their parents in six Lisbon Metropolitan Region' Basic and Secondary schools, was undertaken.

THE STUDY

Purpose
The specific purposes of this study were:

1. To determine the lifestyle of children and youths from different socio-economic groups, as well as their attitudes toward school, PE, and the practise of PA; their personal perceptions of health and competency, practise of PA, and achievement goal orientation; and students' perceptions of the practise of PA of their parents (father and mother).
2. To determine the lifestyle of teachers of all school subjects, and their perceptions about both the value of PE and the aims of PE in the school curriculum; to describe teachers' perceptions about health, past experiences in PE, and about the amount of PA they practise.
3. To determine parents' lifestyle (father and mother) and their perceptions of health, past experience in PE, the value of PE in the school curriculum and the aims of PE; to know parents' perceptions about the quantity of PA they perform and about the quantity of PA their sons/daughters practise.
4. To analyse (and characterise) the relationships between students' attitudes towards PE, the students' and parents' lifestyle concerning physical activities, the parents' past experience in PE, and the students' and parents' views regarding PE.
5. To characterise teachers' views regarding PE taking into account their past experience in PE.

Methods: Participants and Procedures
One thousand and six hundred and forty two students (835 male, 807 female) from fifth to twelve grade levels (ages ranging from 10 to 18 years old) of six "Basic" and Secondary schools participated in the study (170 in grade 5; 349 in grade 6; 308 in grade 7; 121 in

grade 8; 177 in grade 9; 203 in grade 10; 132 in grade 11; and 182 in grade 12). Parents of the students (n=2462; 1056 fathers and 1406 mothers) participated as did the students' teachers (n=294; 75 male; 219 female; and comprising 40 PE teachers and 254 other subject teachers).

Questionnaires, (see Marques, 2010), were used to collect data from students, teachers and parents. Students' participation and the importance of leisure time activities were "measured" using a list of activities selected from Telama et al. (2002), and a series of questions related to physical activities during leisure time concerning the frequency and intensity of PA, participation in organized sport and informal PA, participation in competitions, and the kinds of sports the subject had participated in. Students' hygienic and dietary habits were "measured" using a question from the European Network HBSC questionnaire (Matos et al., 2000). Lintunen's (1990) scale was used to measure students' perceived physical competence. Students' goal orientation was measured using Duda's (1992) scale. The questions concerning students' attitudes toward school and PE were: "What do you think about going to school?" and "What do you think about your PE lessons at school?" These were the same as the questions in the World Health Organisation Study (Aaro et al., 1986). Responses were given on a five-point scale ranging from "I dislike them very much" to "I like them very much". Students' perceptions about their parents' PA were measured using the following question: "Do your parents practise sport or physical activities?"; responses were categorized: "Never"; "Time to Times or only during holidays"; "Once a week during all year as minimum"; and "I don't know".

Teachers' and parents' participation and the importance of leisure time activities were measured using a list of activities adapted from Telama et al. (2002). The item concerning their past experience in PE was: "Taking into account your past experience in PE in the schools you have attended, how do you classify it?" Responses were given on a five-point scale ranging from "Very bad" to "Very good". Teachers' and parents' opinions about both the value and aims of PE in the school curriculum were measured using questions from Carreiro da Costa et al's (1998) questionnaire. Items concerning teachers' and parents' self-perceptions of PA as well parents' perceptions about son/daughter lifestyle were measured using a five-point scale ranging from "Sedentary" to "Very active".

Parental educational level was derived from a closed question, grouped as follows: primary school level; secondary level; university level; and without identification of educational level. Parents' occupations were obtained through an open question and classified according to the INE (the Portuguese Institute of Statistics) list of occupations.

The students' questionnaire was administered at the beginning of the PE lesson by a researcher with the collaboration of the PE class teacher. The researcher made clear to the students that there were no right or wrong answers, and that the best answer was the one that corresponded most closely to their views and to their perceptions. Informed written consent was obtained from the students and their parents before the study began. Teachers' and parents' questionnaires were completed by self-administration. Each teacher received an envelope containing a questionnaire and a letter explaining the objectives of the study and asking for return of the completed questionnaire within two days. Parents received (delivered by the son/daughter) sealed envelopes containing two questionnaires and a letter explaining the objectives of the study and how to complete the questionnaire. Parents' completed questionnaires were returned by the children.

Data analysis
Data were processed using the SPAD 3.5 (Système Portable pour l'Analise des Donnés). Descriptive statistics were computed for all three questionnaires responses. The use of cluster analysis displayed different analyses: (a) distinguish groups of students by attitudes towards PE; (b) distinguish each group of parents with distinct views about the education process in PE; and c) distinguish teachers' perceptions taking into account the past experience in PE and the subject they teach.

FINDINGS

The findings are presented in two different steps: (i) "global" frequencies from all the items of the students', teachers' and parents' questionnaires concerning the practise of physical activities and their views regarding the value and aims of PE; and (ii) data from the cluster analysis portray the characteristics of the students, parents and teachers.

Global frequencies
Tables 1 to 8 present the global frequencies observed in all categories in the three groups of participants (students, parents and teachers). In some variables, the sum of the categories is not equal to 100% because a few participants did not respond to some questions.

Table 1. Students' lifestyle concerning physical activities

Category	Informal practise of PA				Formal practise of PA			
	Boys		Girls		Boys		Girls	
	n	%	n	%	n	%	n	%
Never practise	98	14.1	128	18.0	321	46.1	443	62.4
Practise PA less than once a week	64	9.2	89	12.5	16	2.3	15	2.1
Once a week	104	14.9	173	24.4	41	5.9	69	9.7
From 2 to 3 times a week	197	28.3	187	26.3	201	28.9	135	19.0
More than 4 times a week	326	32.5	128	18.0	106	15.2	38	5.4
Total	689	99.0	705	99.2	685	98.4	700	98.6

Table 2. Students' attitudes toward school, Physical Education and Physical Activity

Category	School				PE				PA			
	Boys		Girls		Boys		Girls		Boys		Girls	
	n	%	n	%	n	%	n	%	n	%	N	%
I like very much	55	6.6	57	7.1	321	38.3	201	24.9	367	43.8	173	1.4
I like	328	39.1	393	48.6	351	41.9	358	44.3	344	41.1	395	48.9
Indifference	276	32.9	225	27.9	95	11.3	136	16.8	98	11.7	172	21.4
I don't like	119	14.2	110	13.6	46	5.5	87	10.8	16	1.9	56	7.0
I dislike very much	54	6.4	19	2.4	23	2.7	21	2.6	9	1.1	9	1.1
Total	832	99.3	804	99.5	836	99.8	803	99.4	834	99.5	805	99.6

Table 3. Students' perceptions about their parents' lifestyle

Category	Father		Mother	
	n	%	n	%
Never practise	386	36.6	650	46.2
Time to times or only during holidays	289	27.4	360	25.6
Once a week as minimum	242	22.9	249	17.7
I don't know	112	10.6	129	9.2
Total	1030	97.5	1388	98.7

Table 4. Teachers' and parents' self-perceptions of Physical Activity

Category	PE teachers		Other teachers		Fathers		Mothers	
	n	%	n	%	n	%	n	%
Active or very active	17	45.0	52	20.4	484	45.8	697	49.5
Active enough	14	35.0	85	33.4	468	44.3	577	41.0
Insufficient active or sedentary	8	20.0	116	45.6	88	8.0	103	7.3
Total	40	100.0	253	99.4	1040	98.1	1377	97.8

Table 5. Teachers' and parents' past experience in Physical Education

Category	PE teachers		Other teachers		Fathers		Mothers	
	n	%	n	%	N	%	n	%
Good or very good	30	75.0	143	56.3	451	42.7	653	46.4
Neither good nor bad	6	15.0	71	27.9	272	25.7	368	26.1
Bad or very bad	4	10.0	30	11.8	115	10.8	101	7.1
Total	40	100.0	244	96	838	79.2	1122	79.6

Table 6. Teachers' and parents' perceptions about Physical Education's status in the curriculum

Category	PE teachers		Other teachers		Fathers		Mothers	
	n	%	n	%	n	%	n	%
Compulsory and examinable	39	97.5	209	82.2	578	54.7	773	54.9
Compulsory and non examinable	1	2.5	38	14.9	374	35.4	467	33.2
An optional subject			4	1.5	53	5.0	74	5.2
No PE in the curriculum			2	0.7	14	1.3	10	0.7
Without opinion					20	1.8	52	3.7
Total	40	100.0	253	99.3	1039	98.2	1376	97.7

Table 7. Teachers' and parents' perceptions about the aims of Physical Education at school

Category	PE teachers		Other teachers		Fathers		Mothers	
	n	%	n	%	n	%	n	%
Catharsis			9	3.5	83	7.8	137	9.7
To promote learning and to improve techniques	7	17.5	27	10.6	238	22.5	267	18.9
To promote citizenship			9	3.5	31	2.9	20	1.4
To promote active and healthy lifestyles	32	80.0	196	77.1	603	57.1	839	59.6
To promote enjoyment			3	1.1	58	5.4	57	4.0
Without opinion		0		0	9	0.8	24	1.7
Total	39	97.5	244	95.8	1022	96.5	1344	95.3

Table 8. Parents' perceptions regarding their children lifestyle

Category	Father		Mother	
	n	%	n	%
Very active	243	23.0	328	23.3
Active	400	37.8	531	37.7
Active enough	272	25.7	334	23.7
Insufficient active	112	10.6	173	12.3
Sedentary	11	1.0	15	1.0
Total	1038	98.1	1381	98.0

Cluster analysis
Characterization of students with different attitudes toward PE (refer Table 9 below)
The students were set into three distinctive groups:
1. Students liking or liking PE very much;
2. Students with an indifferent attitude toward PE;
3. Students disliking or disliking PE very much.

The results of the analysis revealed nine different variables in which the differentiation between the student groups lies. These variables are: gender, age; grade, attitudes toward school and PA, perceptions of competence and fitness, goal orientation, lifestyle, and parental profession and perceptions.

As can be seen below in Table 9, the group of students' with a positive attitude toward PE is characterized by 78.7% of them being males (52.5% of all boys that constitute the sample). The group of students with a negative attitude toward PE is characterized by being females (61% of them). As for school grade, the group of students showing a positive attitude is characterized by the students from the 5th grade (12% of them, 87.4% of all students within the category) and 6th grade (22.7% and 82.9% respectively). The 12th grade students are characteristic not only of the group of students with a negative attitude (37.7% of them, 39.5% within the category) but also the group sharing an attitude of indifference toward PE (19.9% of them, 25.7% within the category). In accordance with the characteristics of each group when the students' grade is taken into account, the older students (16-18 years old) characterize the group of students with a negative attitude (50.9% of them, 22.8% of all students with that age). On the contrary, the younger students (10-12 and 13-15 years old) characterize the group of students with a positive attitude toward PE (40.1% of them, 80.1% of all students with 10-12 years, and 39.5% of them, 78.2% of all students with 13-15 years).

The group of students' with a positive attitude toward PE are also characterized by having a positive attitude toward PA (38.4% like it very much, corresponding to 88.5% of all students within this category, and 48% like it, the equivalent to 78.7% of all students within the category). In contrast, the group of students' with an indifferent attitude toward PE is characterized by 40.8% of them having an indifferent attitude toward PA (34.3% within in the category), while 16.4% of the students' of the group with a negative attitude toward PE also dislike PA (43.3% of all students with the same response).

As for students' self-perceptions of motor competence and fitness, those who have a positive attitude toward PE are characterized by showing a high perception of competence (20.2% of them, equivalent to 91% of all students that indicate this category), and 23.5% of them also reveal a high perception of fitness (88.1% in the category). Low perception of competence and low perception of fitness are categories that characterize the group of students with a negative attitude toward PE (28.3% and 23.3% of them, respectively) and the group with an indifferent attitude (25% and 23%).

Table 9. Characterization of students with different attitudes toward Physical Education

	Variable	Category	% Group/ Cat	% Cat/ Group	Global	Prob
Positive	Attitude toward PE	Positive	100.0	100.0	74.3	0.000
	Attitude toward PA	I like it very much	38.4	88.5	32.22	0.000
	Perception of competence	High level	20.2	91.0	16.5	0.000
	Practise of school sport	I practice	24.1	88.4	20.3	0.000
	Perception of fitness	I am very fit	23.5	88.1	19.8	0.000
	Practise of sport informally	Every day	18.0	85.1	15.7	0.000
	Practise PA under guidance of a coach	I do	57.1	79.4	53.5	0.000
	Weekly practise of school sport	2 times a week	8.1	93.3	6.4	0.000
	Do you practise PA informally	I do	51.9	79.1	48.7	0.000
	Grade	5th	12.0	87.4	10.2	0.000
	Age	10-12 years old	40.1	80.1	37.2	0.000
	Grade	6th	22.7	82.9	20.3	0.000
	Gender	Male	78.7	52.5	49.5	0.000
	Attitude toward PA	I like it	48.0	78.7	45.3	0.000
	PE status according to mothers	Compulsory and examinable	62.7	41.7	55.3	0.000
	Profession of their fathers	Workers	16.0	83.5	14.2	0.001
	Profession of their mothers	Non-qualified workers	11.9	84.4	10.5	0.001
	Fathers' perceptions about the aims of PE	To promote learning	28.1	45.2	22.9	0.002
	Age	13-15 years old	39.5	78.2	37.5	0.005
	Weekly practise of school sport	3 times a week	2.8	93.6	2.2	0.006
	Practise of sport informally	2 or 3 times a week	29.0	78.9	27.3	0.008
	Mothers' perceptions about the aims of PE	To promote learning	23.1	44.4	19.2	0.010
Indifference	Attitude toward PE	Indifference	100.0	100.0	13.9	0.000
	Attitude toward PA	Indifference	40.8	34.3	16.6	0.000
	Perception of competence	Low level	25.0	25.1	13.9	0.000
	Grade	12th	19.9	25.7	10.8	0.000
	Perception of fitness	I am not fit	23.0	24.2	13.2	0.000
	PE status according to mothers	Compulsory without examination	43.6	16.5	33.9	0.008
Negative	Attitude toward PE	Negative	100.0	100.0	11.3	0.000
	Attitude toward PA	I dislike it	16.4	43.3	4.27	0.000
	Grade	12th	37.7	39.5	10.8	0.000
	Age	16-18 years old	50.9	22.8	25.3	0.000
	Perception of competence	Low level	28.3	23.1	13.9	0.000
	Perception of fitness	I am not fit	23.3	19.9	13.2	0.000
	Profession of their mothers	Experts	28.3	17.4	18.4	0.001
	Profession of their fathers	Senior executive	10.1	25.0	4.6	0.001
	Gender	Female	61.0	13.7	50.5	0.003
	Statute of PE according to fathers	Compulsory without examination	50.7	10.2	35.9	0.005

On the matter of students' lifestyle, those with a positive attitude toward PE are characterized not only for practice of school sport 2-3 times a week (24.1% of them, 88.4% within the category), but also for sports practice outside school, in a sport club, under the guidance of a coach (57.1% of them, 79.4% of all students that responded the same). The informal practice of sport (51.9%) or PA (29%, practice 2-3 times a week, and 18% every day) also characterizes the students' with a positive attitude.

These three groups can be distinguished by parental profession and perceptions. Of the students with a negative attitude toward PE, 10.1% of their fathers have senior executive positions, and 28.3% of the mothers are categorized as "experts". In contrast, the 16% of fathers of the group of students with a positive attitude are "blue-collar" (83.5% of all fathers within this category) and 11.9% of the mothers do not have any qualification. Regarding parents' perceptions about the aims of PE, the group of students with a positive attitude is characterized by their parents indicating the promotion of learning as the main aim of PE (28.1% of their fathers, corresponding to 45.2% of all fathers within the category, and 23.1% of mothers, 44.4% of them within the category). The mothers of students with a positive perception are of the opinion that school PE should be compulsory and examinable (62.7% of them, 41.7% of all mothers within the category). The mothers (43.6%) of the group of students with an indifferent attitude and the fathers (50.7%) of the group of students with a negative attitude are of the opinion that PE should be compulsory but not examinable.

Characterization of the teachers according to past experience in PE (Table 10)

The teachers were divided into three distinctive groups:
1. Teachers with a positive experience (evaluating as good or very good their past experience in PE);
2. Teachers with a neutral experience (evaluating as neither good nor bad their past experience in PE);
3. Teachers with a negative experience (evaluating as bad or very bad their past experience in PE).

The group of teachers with a neutral past experience in PE are not discussed here because the group was not characterized by any variable. Only variables related to the teaching-learning process distinguished the groups of teachers, namely: contents, how the PE classes were organized, PE teacher competency, facilities and learning outcomes. The teachers, who evaluated their past experience in PE as positive, are characterized by indication in their response of "very important" for the characteristics of the PE classes (for 66.5% of them, comprising 69.3% of all teachers that indicate this category), relationships with peers (for 64.2%), learning benefits (for 65.3% of them), contents (64.7%), and the competency of the PE teachers (for 72.8% of them, 66.3% of all teachers with the same response). In contrast, the group of teachers who had a bad or very bad experience in PE mentioned the characteristics of the PE classes (38.2% of them), and contents (29.4%) as variables totally important in forming their opinion. Facilities were deemed to have no importance in the formation of their perception (11.8% of them, comprising 57.1% of all teachers that indicate this category).

Table 10. Characterization of the teachers according to past experience in Physical Education

	Variable	Category	% Group/ Cat	% Cat/ Group	Global	Prob
Positive	Past experience in PE - Relationship with peers	Very important	64.2	69.3	51.4	0.000
	Past experience in PE - Characteristics of the PE classes	Very important	66.5	69.3	56.5	0.000
	Past experience in PE - Learning benefits	Very important	65.3	68.9	55.8	0.000
	Past experience in PE – Contents	Very important	64.7	68.3	55.8	0.000
	Past experience in PE - Competence of the PE teachers	Very important	72.8	66.3	64.6	0.000
Negative	Past experience in PE - Experience in PE	Negative	100.0	100.0	11.6	0.000
	Past experience in PE - Characteristics of the PE classes	Totally important	38.2	25.5	17.4	0.002
	Past experience in PE – Contents	Totally important	29.4	28.6	11.9	0.003
	Past experience in PE – Facilities	Not important	11.8	57.1	2.4	0.004

CHARACTERIZATION OF PARENTS WITH DIFFERENT PERCEPTIONS ABOUT PE STATUS IN THE CURRICULUM (REFER TABLE 11)

The results of the analysis revealed that the three groups of parents are distinguished by the following variables: past experience in PE, aims of PE, perception about their children's lifestyle, self-perception of PA, reasons used to classify their past experience in PE, and parents' level of education and occupation.

As for past experience in PE, the group of parents that share the opinion that PE should be compulsory and examinable is the only group characterized by having a good experience as past students of PE in Basic and Secondary schools (49.4% of them, 60.4% of all parents within the category). Their perceptions are based on the importance of learning outcomes (49.2% of them, 58.2%, within the category) and the characteristics of PE classes (49.4% and 57.6% respectively) in forming their opinions. In contrast, the group of parents believing that PE should be compulsory but non- examinable, is characterized by 11.3% of them referring to a negative experience in their Basic and Secondary PE (44% of parents within the category), and 29.5% having an indifferent attitude (38.8% within the category). Facilities were not considered an important factor by 5.1% of them (46.2% within the category) in explaining their negative experience in past PE. An indifferent attitude toward past experience in PE is also a characteristic of the group of parents believing that PE should be an optional subject in the school curriculum (36.2% of them, 7.2% within the category).

With regard to the aims of PE, the parents who share the view that PE must be compulsory and examinable indicate promotion of learning as the main aim of PE in the curriculum (23.6% of them, 63.2% of fathers with the same answer). Interestingly, the group of parents responding that PE should not feature in the school curriculum, shares the same opinion (54.2% of them, 2.6% within the category). The group of parents with the view that PE should be compulsory but non-examinable considers that the main aim of PE should be the promotion of enjoyment. However, 63.5% of them intimate that how exercise and sport relate to health is an important aspect to be learned by students in PE.

Table 11. Characterization of parents with different perceptions about Physical Education status in the curriculum

	Variable	Category	% Group/ Cat	% Cat/ Group	Global	Prob
Compulsory and examinable	PE status in the curriculum	Compulsory and examinable	100.0	100.0	54.9	0.000
	Past experience of PE	Good experience	49.4	60.4	44.8	0.000
	To appraise critically reports of sports	Do not select the option	99.0	55.4	98.1	0.000
	Children lifestyle	Very active	26.1	61.7	23.2	0.000
	Aims of PE	To promote learning	23.6	63.2	20.5	0.000
	Past experience in PE - Learning outcomes	Very important	49.2	58.2	46.4	0.001
	Past experience in PE - Characteristics of the classes	Very important	49.4	57.6	47.1	0.005
Compulsory but not examinable	PE status in the curriculum	Compulsory but non examinable	100.0	100.0	34.2	0.000
	Profession	Administrative Services	17.1	43.6	13.4	0.000
	PE exercise related to health	Important	63.5	36.8	58.9	0.000
	Past experience of PE	Negative	11.3	44.0	8.8	0.001
	Level of education	Secondary school	26.2	39.6	22.5	0.001
	Children lifestyle	Insufficient active	14.4	42.5	11.6	0.001
	Aims of PE	Enjoyment	6.4	47.0	4.7	0.002
	Past experience of PE	Indifference	29.5	38.8	26.0	0.003
	Profession	Seniors executive	3.1	51.0	2.1	0.009
	Past experience in PE – Facilities	Not very important	5.1	46.2	3.8	0.009
a)	PE status in the curriculum	Optional	100.0	100.0	5.2	0.000
	Past experience of PE	Indifferent	36.2	7.2	26.0	0.006
b)	Aims of PE	To promote learning	54.2	2.6	20.5	0.000

a) Optional
b) Should not exist

It should also be emphasized that 99% of the parents, who think that PE should be compulsory and examinable, did not critically appraise reports of sport events as an important part of learning content.

As for parents' perceptions about their children's lifestyle, 26.1% of those who observe that PE should be compulsory and examinable indicate that their children are very active (61.7% within the category). In contrast, only 14.4% of the parents who state that PE should be compulsory but non-examinable point out that their children are insufficiently active (42.5% within the category). The other two groups are not characterised neither by parents' perceptions about their children lifestyle nor by their self perceptions of PA.

Differences between groups in parents' perceptions about PE status are evident and appear to relate to parents' level of education and occupation. The group of parents of the opinion that PE should be compulsory and examinable is not characterized by those variables, whereas 26.2% of the parents with the view that PE should be compulsory but non-examinable indicate secondary school level education (39.6% of all parents with this level of education) and are employed in administrative services (17.1% of them, 43.6% of all within the category) and senior executive positions (3.1% and 51%, respectively).

DISCUSSION AND IMPLICATIONS

The purpose of this study was to obtain an overview of students', teachers' and parents' sport and PA participation and to characterize their views towards PE and PA. The information gathered will serve not only to furnish future school interventions but also enhance PE teacher education programmes and in-service staff-development programmes in the proper preparation of teachers, i.e., contribute to the development of required competences to promote active lifestyles in schools. Without adequate teacher preparation, it is very difficult, if not impossible, to create physically educated youngsters (McKenzie, 2007).

From a summary of the results, in global terms, our data confirm previously reported results concerning students' lifestyles and attitudes toward school and PE. Many children and adolescents are physically inactive and become even less active as they age (Aarnio et al., 2002). It is evident that only a small proportion of students are exposed to regular PA outside PE. As expected, our study reports lower level of activity in girls with boys 15%-20% more physically active than girls, with age appearing to be a decisive factor for PA during childhood.

As for the practice of school sport, 79.4% of the students are not involved in it (78.9% of the girls; and 80% of the boys). Only 19.6% of the students practise sport at school as an optional subject (20% of the girls; 19.2% of the boys). It should be emphasized that 47.6% of the students who refer to being involved in the practice of school sport, only practise once a week or less and 46.9% practise for one hour or less. These data are alarming because school sport is an elective subject designed to supplement the regular PE programme by providing opportunities for students to participate in a variety of activities that allow for exploration of individual skills and talents in an inclusive student-centred environment.

The data regarding students' PA inside and outside school are consistent with previous studies carried out in Portugal (Esculcas & Mota, 2005; Matos & Diniz, 2005; Matos et al., 2000). The persistence of high levels of inactivity in Portuguese schools provides a case for an urgent need to increase our understanding of motivational determinants associated with PA in youth, particularly among girls, who, in this study, do not show any real commitment to PE as observed in other studies (Daley, 2002).

A comparative study of eight countries, including Portugal (Delfosse et al., 1997), revealed a very high proportion of students who expressed feelings of indifference towards school. However, Portugal had a high proportion of students expressing a very favourable opinion towards school. Although an important proportion of students shows a low level of dissatisfaction toward school in this study, with girls indicating a higher level of satisfaction than boys, the proportion of students with feelings of indifference and dissatisfaction is clearly higher than those verified in Portugal in the 1990s (Duarte, 1992; Gonçalves, 1998). There seems to be an emerging attitude of indifference concerning school among Portuguese students.

The results characterizing the group of students with a positive attitude towards PE confirm the results obtained in previous studies in Portugal (Gonçalves, 1998; Pereira,

Carreiro da Costa & Diniz, 2009; Shigunov, 1991), and elsewhere (Trudeau & Shephard, 2005). Boys, mainly the younger ones, like more PE and PA than girls, have a higher self-perception of competence and are more active. There is, however, evidence to suggest that pupils who show negative feelings toward PE also may refrain from engaging in PA outside school (Carlson, 1995). The relationship between a positive attitude toward PE and sport and PA practices are very clear in the group of students with a positive attitude: 24.1% of them are involved in school sport; 57.1% practise sport outside school under the guidance of a coach; and 51.9% practise PA informally.

Higher incomes and educational levels of parents have been shown to correlate with positive attitudes about the value of PA during leisure time by youth (Stephens, Jacobs & White, 1985). From results of a study carried out with students in grades 5 and 6, Carreiro da Costa et al. (1998) verified that sport participation outside school, the students' views, and participation in school PE were related to their parents' beliefs and attitudes towards PE, as well their parents' sporting lifestyle and level of education. Contrary to what was expected, in this present study, the group of students with a positive attitude toward PE are characterized by fathers of a low social level (workers and unqualified workers), while the group of students with a negative attitude are characterized by parents of a high social level (experts – mother; senior executives – father). These results may be linked to a narrow view about the value of PE in favour of the defence of the "core", vocationally orientated components of the curriculum (Sibley & Etnier, 2003) from parents with a high social level. On the other hand, only mother's perceptions toward PE distinguish the groups of students, with mothers of the students showing a positive attitude in indicating that PE should be a compulsory and examinable subject and the mothers of the group sharing an indifferent attitude by saying that PE must be a compulsory but non-examinable subject in the school curriculum. These data seem to imply that mothers have a greater influence in socializing their children for schooling.

It is known that teachers' beliefs play an important part in judgements, understanding, and interpretations they make every day, impacting on their perceptions and on what teachers do and say (Carreiro da Costa, 2005; Tsangaridou, 2006). Thus, to understand the status that PE has in the school setting, it is important to hear what all teachers in the school settings think about the physical education process. Assuming an attitude of optimism, it is encouraging to note that 56% of other subjects' teachers share the vision that PE should be compulsory and examinable. However, the proportion of them viewing PE as a non-examinable subject is still high and could be an institutional constraint to the promotion of PA at schools. Teachers' opinions may be being influenced by their past experience in PE. A significant number of teachers (37.8%) responded that they had not had a positive experience in PE as a student. Taking into account that the majority of other subjects' teachers are female, together with the importance given by them to contents and class organization to justify their evaluation, the influence of a negative past experience assumes relevance. The "contents" delivered in PE classes and "class organization" are areas of girls' criticism when justifying their negative attitude toward PE (Daley, 2002; Trost, 2006).

When asking teachers if the amount of PA aiming to promote health benefits in the students provided by school is enough, 45.9% responded "Yes" (47% of PE; and 45.6% of others teachers) and 50.7% "No" (52.5% of PE; 50.4% of others teachers). There is no difference between the groups of teachers regarding that question. Considering both time allocated to PE and the proportions of students participating in school sport, the PE teachers' perception is quite surprising. How should this be interpreted? Castelli & Williams (2007) maintained that PE teachers show limited knowledge about achieving the objectives of health-related PE. Thus, there is a need to analyse what is going on among the Portuguese PE teachers regarding this issue.

The two groups of teachers (PE teachers and other subjects' teachers) indicated that the promotion of active and healthy lifestyles is the main aim of PE at school. It will be necessary to verify the consistency of this view by comparing it with the real value assigned to PE by action for students' education and development. In fact, taking into account that the proportion of the total weekly curricular time that a School Board allocates to PE is a major determinant of overall student PA, Marques (2010) enquired of a Secondary School Principal why the School Board did not meet the request of the PE department that time prescribed in the National Programme be allocated. The Principal responded: "I cannot sacrifice the whole school to favour one subject". However, before answering the question, the Principal had commented that PE was a very important subject for the students' personal and integral development.

One notable result of this study concerns the mismatch between parents' perceptions about the PA of their off springs and the PA reported by their children. In fact, 86.5% of the fathers and 84.7% of the mothers intimated that their sons or daughters are very active, active or enough active, while 41.3% of the students refer to not practising sport under the guidance of a coach, and 25% of them allege they practise PA informally from four days a week to everyday. It is clear that parents do not know the amount and frequency of PA that their children and themselves should practise to derive health benefits. Parents also over-estimate the PA they undertake. In the Pan-EU *Survey on Consumer Attitudes to PA, Body-weight and Health* (European Commission, 1999), 50% of the Portuguese aged 35-54 years, and 67% of those aged 55+ years responded: "I do not need to do more PA/exercise than I already do". It should be emphasised that at that time, according to official statistics, 23% was the proportion of participation in PA (including sporting activities) of the Portuguese from 15 to 74 years of age (Marivoet, 2001). As can be seen in Table 4 above, 90% of the parents indicated they were active or sufficiently enough active. It could be argued that some parents have occupations, which necessitate exercise but this is not the case for the majority of them. A strategy encouraging people to be more physically active will only be effective if they actually perceive this need. The same applies to interventions in schools. To persuade students to become more active involves changing misconceptions that parents, teachers and Principals share about the amount, intensity and frequency of PA their children and students need.

Carreiro da Costa et al. (1996) studied parents' perceptions about the status of PE in the school curriculum. The Study verified that although most parents regard PE as a compulsory subject, few think of it as an examinable subject. The parents' views do not appear to have changed since then. Indeed, Table 6 above shows that 35.4% of fathers and 33.2% of mothers share the opinion that PE should be a compulsory but non-examinable subject, and about 6% of parents assert that PE should be optional or even be eliminated from the curriculum.

Although there were some differences between the four groups of parents with different views about PE status in the curriculum, a close look at Table 12 makes clear that past experience seems to play an important role distinguishing those parents who think that PE must be examinable and those who consider that PE should be non-examinable. A past positive experience characterizes the group of parents that are in favour of PE as an examinable subject. On the other hand, a negative or indifferent past experience characterizes the group of parents asserting that PE should be non-examinable. These findings indicate the importance of past experiences in PE for the development of habits, beliefs and attitudes that valorise the practice of PA (Trudeau & Shephard, 2005).

CONCLUDING COMMENTS

The findings of the study reported in this chapter suggest that many fathers and mothers do not have an adequate idea and perception about the real needs of their children's PA engagement. The same perspective is shared by the majority of the teachers. The findings also suggest that a dominant socio-cultural view of PE as peripheral to the accomplishment of the central functions of schooling remains among the Portuguese parents, and among many teachers. It is important to stress that this dominant form of thinking about school, curriculum and PE, were, and are, socially reproduced in face-to-face relations involving the actors of classroom, school and family settings. Thus, parents build their views on a social-cultural context in which PE is valueless as a subject matter relevant to fulfil both symbolic and material expectations related to schooling. However, those views are also constructed through a dialectical socialisation process, which plays an important role in their experiences as students, their current perceptions and images of PE (based on their children' portraits of PE activities and PE teachers' practices), and their own commitment to PA.

Thus, PE teacher education programmes and all those who are involved in initial and in-service teacher education processes should be more concerned about the necessity to reflect on the efficacy of their work, and the responsibility to permanently assess knowledge and teaching competences they are developing in present and future PE teachers regarding the promotion of health-related PE.

It is necessary to revise the expectations and roles that physical educators play as school staff members, assuming that to teach a class is not the only function of a PE teacher at school. It is also important to recognize the need for preparing PE teachers able to deal at the meso level (teacher functioning in the school mainly with other subject teachers), as well as at the macro level (the teacher able to interact with parents and with structures outside of the school) (Behets, 2000; Carreiro da Costa, 2007). To fulfill these new roles requires that physical educators learn new skills, and in turn, initial teacher preparation and continuing in-service staff-development programmes need to be modified to ensure teachers are well prepared for them.

REFERENCES

Aaro, L., Wol, B., Kannas, L., & Rimpela, M. (1986). Health behavior in schoolchildren. A WHO cross national survey. *Health Promotion, 1,* pp.17-33.

Aarnio, M., Winter, T., Peltonen, J., Kujala, U., & Kaprio, J. (2002). Stability of leisure-time physical activity during adolescence – a longitudinal study among 16, 17 and 18-years-old Finnish youth. *Scandinavian Journal of Medicine & Science in Sports, 12,* pp.179-185.

Behets, D. (2000). Physical Education teachers' tasks and competences. In: F. Carreiro da Cost, J. Diniz, L. Carvalho & M. Onofre (Eds.), *Research on Teaching and Research on Teacher Education*. Lisboa, Edições FMH. pp.208-212.

Berkley, C., Rockett, H., Field, A., Gillman, M., Frazier, L., Camargo, C., & Coldizt, G. (2000). Activity, dietary, and weight changes in a longitudinal study of pre-adolescent and adolescent boys and girls. *Pediatrics, 105*(4), pp.56-65.

Bernauer, J., & Cress, K. (1997). How school communities can help redefine accountability assessment . *Phi Delta Kappan, 79,* pp.71-75.

Biddle, S., & Chatzisarantis N. (1999). Motivation for a physically active lifestyle through Physical Education. In: Y. Auweele, F. Bakker, S. Biddle, M. Durand and R. Seiler (Eds.), *Psychology for Physical Educators*. Champaign, IL, Human Kinetics. pp.5-26.

Cale, L., & Harris, J. (2006). School-based physical activity interventions: effectiveness, trends, issues, implications and recommendations for practice. *Sport, Education and Society, 11,* pp.401-420.

Campbell, V., Crews, J., & Sinclair, L. (2002). State-specific prevalence of obesity among adults with disabilities. Eight states and the District of Columbia, 1998–1999. *Morbidity and Mortality Weekly Report, 51,* pp.805–808.

Carlson, T. (1995). We hate gym: student alienation from Physical Education, *Journal of Teaching in Physical Education, 14,* pp.467-477.

Carreiro da Costa, F. (2007). La enseñanza de la Educación Física ante la implantación del espacio Europeo de educación superior. In: P. Palou Sampol, F. Ponseti, P. Borràs & J. Vidal (Eds.), Educación Física en el Siglo XXI. *Nuevas Perspectivas Nuevos Retos*. Baleares, Universitat de les Illes Balears. pp.19-31.

Carreiro da Costa, F. (2005). Changing the curriculum does not mean changing practices at school: the impact of teachers' beliefs on curriculum implementation. In: F. Carreiro da Costa, M. Cloes, & M. González Valeiro (Eds.), *The Art and Science of Teaching in Physical Education and Sport*. Lisboa, Edições FMH. pp.257-278.

Carreiro da Costa, F., Carvalho, L., Diniz, J., & Onofre, M. (1998). School Physical Education views: parents' and students' connections. In: R. Naul, K. Hardman, M. Piéron & B. Skirstad (Eds.), *Physical Activity and Active Lifestyle of children and Youth*. Schorndorf, Verlag Karl Hofmann. pp.152-163.

Carreiro da Costa, F., Dinis, J., Carvalho, L., & Onofre, M. (1996). School Physical Education purpose – the parents' view. In: R. Lidar, E. Eldar, I. Harari (Eds.), Bridging the Gaps between Disciplines, Curriculum and Instruction. *Proceedings of the 1995 AEISEP Word Conference*. Israel, Wingate Institute. pp.181-187.

Carreiro da Costa, F., Marques, A., & Diniz, J. (2008). Physical Education teachers' value orientation and students' health-related fitness. A PE school department case study. In: H-P. Brandl-Bredenbeck (Ed.), *Bewegung, Spiel und Sport in Kindheit und Jugend*. Aachen, Meyer & Meyer Verlag. pp.49-62.

Castelli, D., & Williams, L. (2007). Health-related fitness and Physical Education teachers' content knowledge. *Journal of Teaching in Physical Education, 26*, pp.3-19.

Cleland, V., Venn, A., Fryer, J., Dwyer, T., & Blizzard, L. (2005). Parental exercise is associated with Australian children's extracurricular sports participation and cardio-respiratory fitness: a cross-sectional study. *International Journal of Behavioral Nutrition and Physical Activity. 2* (3), pp.1-9.

Currie, C., Roberts, C., Morgan, A., Smith, R., Settertobulte, W., Samdal, O., & Rasmussen, V. (2004). *Young people's health in context. Health behaviour in school-age children (HBSC) study: International report from the 2001/2002 survey.* Copenhagen, WHO.

Daley, A. (2002). School based physical activity in the United Kingdom: can it create physically active adults? *Quest, 54*, pp.21-33.

Delfosse, C., Ledent, M., Carreiro da Costa, F., Telama, R., Almond, L., Cloes, M. & Piéron, M. (1997). Les attitudes de jeunes européens à l'égard de l'école et du cours d'Éducation Physique. *Sport, 159/160*, pp.96-105.

Duarte, A. (1992). *Contributo para o estudo das atitudes dos alunos do ensino secundário face à disciplina de Educação Física.* PhD Dissertation. University of Porto.

Duda, J. (1992). Motivation in sport settings: a goal perspective approach. In: G. Roberts (Ed.), *Motivation in Sport and Exercise.* Champaign, IL, Human Kinetics. pp.57-91.

Esculcas, C., & Mota, J. (2005). Actividade física e práticas de lazer em adolescentes. *Revista Portuguesa de Ciências do Desporto, 5* (1), pp.69–76.

European Commission (1999). *A pan-EU survey on consumer attitudes to physical activity, body-weight and health.* Luxembourg, Office for Official Publications of the European Communities.

Fairclough, S., & Stratton, G. (2006). A review of physical activity levels during elementary school Physical Education. *Journal of Teaching in Physical Education, 25*, pp.239-257.

Fitzgerald, H. (2006). Disability and Physical Education. In: D. Kirk, D. Macdonald & M. O'Sullivan (Eds.), *The Handbook of Physical Education.* London, Sage Publications. pp.752-766.

Gonçalves, C. (1998). *Relações entre as Características, Significados e Acções dos Alunos e os seus Comportamentos de Aprendizagem nas Aulas de Educação Física.* PhD Dissertation. Technical University of Lisbon.

Graham, G. (1995) Physical Education through students' eyes and in students' voices: Introduction, *Journal of Teaching in Physical Education, 14*, pp.364-371.

Hernandez-Álvarez, J., Velázquez-Buendía, R., Alfonso-Curiel, D., Garoz-Puerta, I., López-Rodríguez, A., & Maldonado-Rico, A. (2005). The conceptual knowledge in PE and health: what do our students know? A research on Spanish school population. In: J. Diniz, F. Carreiro da Costa & M. Onofre (Eds.), *Active Lifestyles: The Impact of Education and Sport, Proceedings of the AIESEP* 2005 World Congress. Lisboa, Edições FMH. pp.293-305.

Hall, G., & Hord, S. (2001). *Implementing change: patterns, principles, and potholes.* Boston, Allyn & Bacon.

Jamner, M., Spruijt-Metz, D., Bassin, S., & Cooper, D. (2004). A controlled evaluation of a school-based intervention to promote physical activity among sedentary adolescent females: Project FAB. *Journal of Adolescent Health, 34*, pp.279-289.

Keating, X., Harrison, L., Chen, L., Xiang, P., Lambdin, D., Dauenhauer, Rotich, W., & Piñero, J. (2009). An analysis of research on student health-related fitness knowledge in K-16 Physical Education programs. *Journal of Teaching in Physical Education, 28*, pp.333-349.

Kimm, S., Glynn, N., Kriska, A., Barton, B., Kronsberg, S., Daniells, S., Crawford, P., Sabry. Z., & Liu, K. (2002). Decline in physical activity in black girls and white girls during adolescence. *New England Journal of Medicine, 347*, pp.709-715.

Lee, S., Wechsler, H., & Balling, A. (2006). The role of schools in preventing childhood obesity. President's Council on Physical Fitness and Sports. *Research Digest, 7*(3), pp.1-8.

Lintunen, T. (1990). Perceived physical competence scale for children. In: A. Ostrow (Ed.), *Directory of Psychological Tests in the Sport and Exercise Sciences*. Morgantown, WV, Fitness Information Technology. p. 40.

Malina, R. (2001). Adherence to physical activity from childhood to adulthood: a perspective from tracking studies. *Quest, 53*, pp.346-355.

Marivoet, S. (2001). *Hábitos desportivos da população portuguesa*. Lisboa, Instituto de Formação e Estudos do Desporto.

Marques, A. (2010). *A Escola, a Educação Física e a Promoção de Estilos de Vida Activos e Saudáveis: Estudo de um Caso*. PhD Dissertation, Technical University of Lisbon.

Matos, M., & Diniz, J. (2005). Portuguese adolescents: active lifestyles and health. In: J. Diniz, F. Carreiro da Costa & M. Onofre (Eds.), *Active Lifestyles: the Impact of Education and Sport*. Lisboa, Edições FMH. pp.57-68.

Matos, M., Simões, C., Canha, L., & Fonseca, S. (2000). *Saúde e estilos de vida nos jovens portugueses*. Lisboa, Edições FMH.

McKenzie, T. (2003). Assessing physical activity innovations in schools. In: L. Sena Lino, R. Ornelas, F. Carreiro da Costa & M. Piéron (Eds.), *Innovation and New Technologies in Physical Education, Sport, Research and/on Teacher and Coach Preparation*. Proceedings of the Madeira AIESEP Congress, CD –ROM.

McKenzie, T. (2007). The preparation of Physical Educators: A public health perspective. *Quest, 59*, pp.346-357.

McKenzie, T., & Sallis, J. (1996). Physical activity, fitness, and health-related Physical Education. In: S. Silverman and C. Ennis (Eds.), *Student Learning in Physical Education. Applying Research to Enhance Instruction*. Champaign, IL, Human Kinetics. pp.223-246.

McKenzie, T., Feldman, H., Woods, S., Romero, K., Dahlstrom, V., Stone, E., Strikmiller, P, Williston, J., & Harsha, D. (1995). Children's activity levels and lesson context during third-grade Physical Education. *Research Quarterly and Sport, 66*, pp.184-193.

Miller, M., & Housner, L. (1998). A survey of health-related physical fitness knowledge among preservice and inservice physical educators. *Physical Educator, 55*, pp.176-186.

National Association for Sport and Physical Education (2004). *Moving into the future national standards for Physical Education*. Reston, VA, NASPE Publication.

Ornelas, I., Perreira, K., & Ayala, G. (2007). Parental influences on adolescent physical activity: a longitudinal study. *International Journal of Behavioral Nutrition and Physical Activity, 4* (3). http://www.ijbnpa.org/content/pdf/1479-5868-4-3.pdf.

Pate, R., Davis, M., Robinson, T., Stone, E., McKenzie, T., & Young, J. (2006). Circulation. *Journal of the American Heart Association, 114*, August, pp.1214-1224.

Pereira, P., Carreiro da Costa, F., & Diniz, J. (2009). As atitudes dos alunos face à disciplina de Educação Física: um estudo plurimetodológico. *Boletim SPEF, 34*, pp.83-94.

Piéron, M., Ruiz, F.M., & García Montes, H. (2009). La opinión del alumnado de enseñanza seundaria sobre las clases de Educación Física: Un desafío para los profesores y los formadores en la Educación Física y el Deporte. In: La Educación Física y el Deporte en la Universidad, Investigación e Inivación, *Fuentes, 8*, pp.197-217.

Portman, P. (2003). Are Physical Education classes encouraging students to be physically active?: experiences of ninth graders in their last semester of required Physical Education. *Physical Educator, 22*, pp.150-160.

Rikard, L., & Banville, D. (2006). High school student attitudes about Physical Education. *Sport, Education and Society, 11*, pp.385-400.

Rimmer, J. (2008). Health promotion for people with disabilities: implications for empowering the person and promoting disability-friendly environments. *American Journal of Lifestyle Medicine, 2*, pp.409-420.

Rimmer, J., Rowland, J., & Yamaki, K. (2007). Obesity and secondary conditions in adolescents with disabilities: addressing the needs of an underserved population. *Journal of Adolescent Health, 41*, pp.224–229.

Sallis, J., Cervero, R., Ascher, W., Henderson, K., Kraft, M., & Kerr, J. (2006). An ecological approach to creating active living communities. *Annual Review of Public Health, 27*, pp.297-322.

Sallis, J., & McKenzie, T. (1991). Physical Education's role in public health. *Research Quarterly and Sport, 62*, pp.124-137.

Shigunov, V. (1991). *A relação pedagógica em Educação Física. Estudo da influência das intervenções de instrução e afectividade no grau de satisfação dos alunos.* PhD Dissertation, Technical University of Lisbon.

Sibley, B., & Etnier, J. (2003). The relationship between physical activity and cognition in children: a meta-analysis. *Pediatric Exercise Science 15*, pp.243–56.

Stephens, T., Jacobs, D., & White, C. (1985). A descriptive epidemology of leisure-time activity. *Public Health Reports. 100*, pp.147-158.

Stewart, S., & Mitchell, M. (2003). Instructional variables and student knowledge and conceptions of fitness. *Journal of Teaching in Physical Education, 22*, pp.533-551.

Telama, R., Naul, R., Nupponen, H., Rychtecky, A., & Vuolle, P. (2002). Physical fitness, sporting lifestyles, and Olympic ideals: cross-cultural studies on youth sport in Europe. ICSSPE, *Sport Science Studies, 11.* Schorndorf, Verlag Karl Hofmann.

Telama, R., & Yang, X. (2000). Decline of physical activity from youth to young adulthood in Finland. *Medicine & Science in Sport & Exercise, 32*, pp.1617-1622.

Trost, S. (2006). Public health and Physical Education. In: D. Kirk, D. Macdonald & M. O'Sullivan (Eds.), T*he Handbook of Physical Education.* London, Sage Publications. pp. 163-184.

Trudeau, F., & Shephard, R. (2005). Contribution of school programmes to physical activity levels and attitudes in children and adults. *Sports Medicine, 35*, pp.89-105.

Tsangaridou, N. (2006). Teachers' beliefs. In: D. Kirk, D. Macdonald & M. O'Sullivan (Eds.), *The Handbook of Physical Education.* London, Sage Publications. pp. 486-501.

Tyson, L. (1996). Context of schools. In: S. Silverman & C. Ennis (Eds.), *Student Learning in Physical Education. Applying Research to Enhance Instruction.* Champaign, IL, Human Kinetics. pp. 55-79.

Van Acker, R., Carreiro da Costa, F., De Bourdeaudhuij, I., Cardon, G., & Haerens, L. (2010). Sex equity and physical activity levels in coeducational Physical Education: exploring the potential of modified game forms. *Physical Education and Sport Pedagogy, 15*, pp.159-173.

Welk, G., Wood, K., & Morss, G. (2003). Parental influences on physical activity in children: an exploration of potential mechanisms. *Pediatric Exercise Science, 15*, pp.19-33.

Whitt-Glover, M., O'Neill, K., & Stettler, N. (2006). Physical activity patterns in children with and without Down syndrome. *Pediatric Rehabilitation, 9*, pp.158-164.

World Health Organization (2000). *Promoting active living in and through schools. Policy statement and guidelines for action*. Geneva, World Health Organization.

World Health Organization (2009). *A Snapshot of the Health of Young People in Europe*. Compenhagen, WHO Regional Office for Europe.

CHAPTER 15
SOCIAL CHANGE AND THE FUTURE FOR PHYSICAL EDUCATION AND SPORT
RICHARD FISHER

INTRODUCTION

Examining the impact of socio-economic change on the structure and delivery of educational systems and attempting to plan for the future is nothing new. What is new is the pace of that change over the last two decades, fuelled by ever increasing levels of technological sophistication that has ensured that the effects are truly global. From the provision of schools to the curriculum on offer, the system of teacher education and the school-community interface, policy makers are aware of the importance of being sensitive to the nature of that change and the pace and scale at which it happens. What the global financial crisis of 2009 taught us was that the economic and political drivers of change are significantly more powerful and volatile than many had previously assumed and that the impact could actually threaten sovereign stability, even in countries in the supposedly secure Eurozone. In Physical Education (PE) Klein (2004) pointed out that while the subject has been vigorously and justifiably addressing risks to its position in the educational system, it is advisable to move beyond debates such as the gap between political promises and professional reality and grasp the significance of the bigger picture. He argued that the evolution of the political, economic and institutional contexts that frame those debates has created a different dynamic that is changing the fundamental structure of education and how it will be delivered. Public services globally were already in a parlous condition before the latest financial crisis, whether it was admitted officially or not, and together with a widespread pensions' crisis were fuelling the disengagement of the state from welfare policy. The Organisation for Economic Co-operation and Development's (2001) project about the school of tomorrow has been one of the more significant international initiatives seeking to come to terms with this change and explore the need for new and more appropriate strategies to deal with it. The immediate force of the latest economic tsunami may have abated somewhat but the implications for public institutions have only begun to unfold and the need for PE to understand the nature of socio-political change remains a key element of professional debate. Indeed, this chapter assumes that social and cultural change give value and meaning to PE, sport and health provision, and shape the forms in which they exist.

However, whilst it is important to understand the nature of change and both exciting and challenging to consider options for the future, history is replete with examples of predicted trends that never materialised or plans that were derailed by unforeseen circumstances, so a degree of caution is appropriate. In recent years England and Wales *(Building Schools for the Future)* and other European countries such as Portugal initiated the largest school re-building reforms in their history. Plans for what the future might look like, how schools will function, what building designs are appropriate, what parents will require and pupils engage with, not to mention how teacher education will adapt have been more than just academic debates. However, as a Seminar to explore the implications for PE of the *Building Schools for the Future* programme demonstrated (Pro-Active South London, 2007), some schools and local government authorities in the first phase of that initiative were already reporting that their plans had not been radical enough to deal with the pace of change and the increasing unpredictability of the future. In any case, 2010 brought about the dismantling of the programme as the new UK Coalition government deemed it unaffordable in the face of a large public finance deficit. Notwithstanding this note of caution, a central theme of this chapter is the notion that such an unprecedented pace of change demands different ways of thinking and more flexible approaches that are sensitive to the shifting social demand. However, it must be acknowledged that this is a demanding task especially when taking an international perspective of such issues and it is necessary to be selective, in spite of the obvious risks of doing so. Indubitably, crossing national cultures is problematic in itself not least because culture is itself a *slippery and contested concept* according to Curtis and Pettigrew (2009). The nature of social change and some implications for education and sport are used here as a platform for interpreting the current and future context of PE and school sport and for proposing some examples of what might be deemed to be good practice.

In concluding this section it is important to acknowledge Martin and Segal's (2004) fundamental point that changing behaviour and practice is problematic, since the essential driver for many societies is to maintain stability and create a safe, coherent and, as far as possible, predictable environment. Hence, the desire to maintain the *status quo* and reduce the possibility of chaos actually militates against change, for example in attempting to cope with such phenomena as so-called *change overload* resulting from the unprecedented speed of technological development. They argue also that one of the effects of this technological wave could well be generation separation as the young become *de facto* the teachers of their elders in this particular regard. In an international context it is useful to refer to the International Council of Sport Science and Physical Education's Directory of Sport Science (Borms, 2008) for a good overview of definitions of PE and sport.

SOCIAL CHANGE, EDUCATION AND PHYSICAL EDUCATION

According to Apple (2001), the essential nature of social change is embedded in the global dynamics that flow from the influential discourses of so called neo-liberal capitalism. These have impacted significantly on the public sector in recent years and involve at least the following features: the increasing influence of the private sector in public provision; the impact of the "market" and a competitive approach to the provision of services; the growth in systems of accountability and reporting on performance, and an increasing focus on developing enterprising people who will make the most of the opportunities available in this new world, rather than slotting into mostly pedestrian state systems. To this analysis can be added escalating technological innovation, changes to so-called traditional family relations and loss of confidence both in moral and scientific certainties (Curtis & Pettigrew, 2009).

The fragmentation and multiplicity of cultures that has accompanied these phenomena, which include in particular the emergence of new youth movements, is well rehearsed elsewhere and is not explored in detail here. What is important to note is the complexity that is distinctive of modern society and the fluidity of modern culture, summed up by Bauman (2000) as *liquid modernity*. Even so, Curtis and Pettigrew (2009) propose that it is possible to identify common characteristics of contemporary modern industrial societies and these provide a useful framework for the purposes of this analysis. These characteristics embrace:

- *Individualism:* the dominance of individual interests and the fragmentation of social groups and community bonds;
- *Consumerism:* buying for "need" is supplanted by buying for "want";
- *Globalisation:* huge increase in movement and co-operation between nations;
- *Technophilia:* the influence of, and reliance on, technology; it took radio 38 years to reach an audience of 50 million people, whereas it was 13 years for television and only 4 years for the internet;
- *Internet hegemony:* the web as an embedded part of culture; it started in 1993 and by 2007 there were 2.7 billion searches on "Google" and "MySpace"; with circa 25,000 new users per day it had become the 10th largest nation in the world;
- *Democracy of Fame:* easier than ever before to become famous through internet sites like "YouTube" and reality TV shows;
- *An emphasis on youth:* young people have become much closer to the centre of culture and their "voice" has strengthened considerably;
- *The prevalence and significance of the media:* hand in hand with the internet the media as a dominant source of information and knowledge.

The rapid pace of change associated with these characteristics clearly demands a re-thinking of where education is, what opportunities it provides and where it might be going. Framing this process are the core questions raised by OECD (2001) in their international analysis of education in the future:

> "What will schools look like in the future? What big trends are most influential in shaping education and how might these unfold in coming years? What policy questions need to be tackled today for desirable pathways into the future to become more likely?" (p.3).

In this context, we can turn to the *Teaching 2020* initiative in the UK, which was part of the *Futures Project* designed to take a sustained look at what type of schooling would be appropriate in the future. It evolved out of the OECD *Schooling for Tomorrow* Project and following seminars with teachers all over the country became *Teaching 2012* as the profession sought to find a more manageable timescale. Newby (2005) concluded a review of this initiative with some core assumptions for education in the future, including the following:

- Governments will continue developing public/private partnerships in education to create more capacity to service the pensions deficit;

- Private enterprise and the commercial sector will increasingly provide more of the resources and play a leading role in educational provision so that the balance of power in education will shift;
- Uniform, centralised provision will decline and a wider range of local agencies and organisations will emerge to provide a wider range of learning opportunities for a broader mix of ages – in and out of the school;
- Teachers will link up with other providers and operate at the centre of new learning networks, whilst the workforce itself will be trained in many different places, not just universities;
- The curriculum will change to prepare young people for increasingly disorganised environments with more emphasis on ways of knowing rather than subject knowledge.

It is worth noting that the OECD (2001) Project that raised global awareness of many of these issues arose from an invitation from Ministers of Education to assess alternative visions of the school of tomorrow. Significantly the main focus was on lifelong learning and the ways in which schools can make their contribution as one part of a whole process; the rather precise and tightly constrained education processes typical of many national systems need to embrace a greater variety of joined up approaches in more fluid arrangements between school, home and community. In this way it could be possible to prepare and sustain individuals more effectively for an increasingly uncertain future.

"Many lament the stubborn persistence of 'industrial age' bureaucratic models of schools and systems as inappropriate for 21st century knowledge societies. To what extent can educational networks replace cumbersome bureaucracies as sources of innovation, decision-making and professionalism?" (p.3).

Curtis and Pettigrew (2009) pursue much the same line and claim that the overall impact on learning in contemporary culture is to be seen in a number of developments. These include personalised learning and the increasing redundancy of "one size fits all" approaches, an increasing purchaser-provider context in education, the growth of the citizenship agenda, internet based learning and assessment, a demand for more interactive and stimulating learning environments and a much stronger policy focus on children's wellbeing and social development. To some extent at least there is sufficient evidence now of all these agendas in operation, which begs the question about how education systems in general and PE in particular are responding to this new world and indeed their capacity or willingness to do so.

It should be acknowledged at this point that notwithstanding the effects of globalisation the various cultures and social contexts involved are by no means universally similar. Nevertheless, it is clear from the circumstances of the last two years that for large parts of the globe major socio-economic transitions are under way, as Miller (2001) observed at the turn of the millenium:

"Will daily life by the third decade of the 21st Century seem radically different for large parts of the world's population when compared with the last decades of the 21st Century? On all counts the striking answer to this question is 'yes'"(p.147).

In the UK, the new coalition government of 2010 used its early days and its first budget to mirror initiatives that were already evident, or clearly emerging, in a number of other countries such as Canada and Sweden. The principle is the reduction of the role of the state and the pruning of public sector provision to what can be afforded, with a consequentially increased reliance on the private sector to fill the gaps. In so doing, the new government moved quickly to signal a markedly reduced role for local authorities in school provision, an increase in private sector engagement and much greater flexibility regarding who can be allowed to open and run schools, thereby creating a much wider range of educational opportunities.

The need to respond to the sort of challenges outlined above by reviewing core educational principles in a new context and ensuring that schools evolve rapidly and effectively in this new era has been flagged in a UK House of Commons Report (2010). The core of the debate contained in the Report was around central or local control of schools, with the latter clearly favoured and government's role seen as providing broad frameworks rather than seeking to micro-manage the day to day work of teachers. Lower levels of prescription in the curriculum, expansion of the increased freedom enjoyed by the more independently run so-called "Academies" to all remaining state schools, increased self-regulation and teacher assessment becoming a significant part of the national assessment regime were some of the main recommendations. Subsequently the new Secretary of State for Education in the UK Coalition government, the Rt. Hon. Michael Gove (2010), has outlined policy objectives for the future to the National College Annual Conference. Based on evidence from Scandinavia, Singapore, Canada and Australia and in the context of accelerating global change, he emphasised the lessons to be learned from these various systems. These encompass the importance of the autonomy of individual schools to innovate and drive up standards, national frameworks of accountability, transparency of performance on a school by school basis that is externally moderated and a culture of high expectations for all pupils.

In relation to the general position of PE in these debates, Klein (2004) draws attention to what he describes as the contamination of education by neo-liberal opinions rooted in new European and global discourses that have compromised humanist education. He suggests that the impact of these influences is evident in a more prominent focus on lifelong learning for the wage earner, the transmission of operative knowledge and the slide from cultural values to economic values on a large scale. Furthermore, Klein highlighted the need for PE to acknowledge the state's increasing disengagement with the public sector as the financial burden of sustaining the range of services becomes too great. In this context, the particular ramifications for PE can be seen to include such things as increased provision for the subject outside of the school, the strengthening of education through sport and a more flexible approach to who actually teaches the subject, or supports those who teach it. PE, he argues, is at the centre of a tension between new opportunities to reinforce its position in the curriculum and the risk of being excluded. In this regard, Evans and Penney (2008) caution us to acknowledge the ongoing struggles that exist between competing and often changing political ideologies about desirable forms of schooling and the associated message systems regarding curriculum, pedagogy and assessment.

Furthermore, in relation to what she refers to as the learning area of health and physical education (HPE) and in the context of the relationship between contemporary education discourses and policy and curriculum development, Penney (2008) suggests that the subject is in a crowded and openly congested policy space. Policy itself is often a matter of expediency and a by-product of other policies or particular social agendas such as increasing obesity or the national sporting context. O'Donovan and Kirk (2008) reinforce the presence and influence of powerful discourses outside the school and societal expectations that privilege traditional approaches to PE and school sport. They criticise the pervasive influence of popular and physical culture that maintains a focus on fitness and skill at the expense of more inclusive approaches that touch base with youth culture and lifestyles. This continues to occur in spite of seemingly widespread acknowledgement that young people no less than the societies they live in have changed, and are changing, in significant ways. Brettschneider (2001) highlighted the increasing sophistication of young people who have become writers of their own biographies, in a world where they occupy an increasingly influential position as indicated above. Furthermore, Fisher (2004) flagged ongoing levels of pupil dissatisfaction with school PE in as far as it is bore insufficient relation to youth lifestyles and activity preferences, which is consistent with Hardman and Marshall's (2009) findings in their follow up world-wide study of the state and status of PE. They record the persistence in many nations of relatively restricted conceptions of PE that continue to privilege traditional competitive sports and achievement oriented approaches to pedagogy and participation. Whilst identifying a number of global issues to do with facilities and resources, they also note problems such as:

- the relevance and quality of the PE curriculum, especially where there is a sustained pre-disposition towards sports competition and performance-related activities dominated by Games, Gymnastics and Track and Field Athletics
- barriers to full gender and disability inclusion
- the failure of society to attach value to school PE and sport

It has to be acknowledged that Hardman and Marshall were aware that much of the evidence emerging on PE in schools was negative and they did encourage the identification of examples of best practice. However, relatively few respondents to their questionnaire took the opportunity to provide examples of good practice and of those that did the most frequent references were to sporting competitions. Typically progression in PE and school sport was linked to various competition structures up to national level and these were usually related to televised events involving Olympic sports. Theoretically, opportunities were open to all young people but the highlights were about those who reached the top and it could be argued that it was more about talent development than high quality provision in curriculum PE for all pupils. However, Smith et al's (2007) study of pupils' participation in the National Curriculum in the UK revealed that the portfolio of sports and physical activities available to young people in some schools has embraced newer team and individual games and so-called lifestyle activities. Whilst the data was variable between contexts and circumscribed by gender and the type of school attended, there was progress in providing what might be described as a youth relevant curriculum. Furthermore, notwithstanding Hardman and Marshall's reflections on the predominance of competitive sport, the world survey did record examples of programmes to promote lifelong physical activity and certainly in Europe there were examples of innovative curriculum developments. These included green tourism, dance teaching, daily sport programmes to encourage activity, the creation of links between schools and community sports clubs and a number of initiatives making increased use of the environment. There were also projects to promote social integration between different ethnic groups and encouragingly some that focused on improving the quality of PE programmes.

A particularly important period of schooling in relation to efforts to ensure an engagement in active lifestyles as well as building capacity to engage in a wide range of activities is the primary age range, typically up to 11/12yrs of age. Much has been written about the significance of ensuring a high quality programme for this age range and indeed the lack of success in making it happen in many countries but one of the key issues remains progression to the next level of schooling. Dismore and Bailey (2010) examined the important period in the English national curriculum of transition between Key Stage 2 (7-11yrs) to Key Stage 3 (11-14yrs) and its impact on attitudes to, and interest in, PE. The pupils in their study maintained a generally positive attitude to PE during this process and the pattern was fairly consistent whether they were in primary/secondary schools or middle schools. Important aspects of young people's perspectives of PE revolved around fun and enjoyment, social relations and the facilities available. Unsurprisingly, the shaping of these attitudes was confirmed as a complex matter revolving around the nature of the system itself through to such things as the curriculum and the nature of the activities on offer. Dismore and Bailey observe that during this transition pupils were aware of the progression from fun and games to more serious preparation for competitive sport. Such a curriculum they point out raises the possibility of the formation of elite groups with attendant issues about who is included or excluded on the basis of a relatively narrow range of experiences and in many respects could be viewed as a form of apprenticeship (Penney, 2004). In similar vein, Evans and Penney (2008) identified "competency" and "performance" codes in the PE curriculum and the practice associated with those approaches, for example in relation to the assessment of ability. Competency codes recognise diverse, adaptable and malleable abilities with weaker teacher-pupil boundaries, whilst performance codes recognise and accept relatively fixed ability hierarchies and tighter boundaries between teacher and those taught. Without privileging either of these codes, they do identify the current emphasis on performance codes and in so doing regret the apparent erosion of qualitative dimensions of learning such as fun, risk and spontaneity as well as sociability and interdependency. PE and school sport are also important arenas for social development (Dismore & Bailey, 2010) and such restricted curricula can mean that the subject actually touches base with only a small selection of the broad range of social experiences and interactions to be found in the larger community.

In concluding this section perhaps the central point lies in Penney's (2008) argument that the essential purposes and value of education can easily become eroded and the subject sidetracked in order to meet the rather complicated agendas discussed above: "... Amidst a sustained dominance of discourses of sport and health, it is as if we have become afraid to reaffirm education as the essence and indisputable 'core business' of HPE" (p.37).

This is not to dismiss these discourses and to do so would be naive since they flow from important social and political agendas that reflect the interests of powerful communities of practice. However, it is to argue for reaffirming the essentially educational nature of the subject and ensuring that it serves a variety of public and social purposes, not only the traditional high profile agendas. She argues further that the significant discourses for which HPE needs to have a clear educational agenda are lifelong learning, the development of learning communities and learning networks, personalised learning and promoting both inclusion and excellence, some of which are addressed below.

LOOKING TO THE FUTURE

Any view of the future is framed within the context outlined above with its inherent complexity and the associated challenges it offers to education systems, notably the ever increasing demand to offer learners more flexible and forward looking programmes. In a world of multiple agendas and ever increasing connections between different types of learning, there is merit in identifying with Penney's (2008) view that the subject could present itself as a key component of the core educational agenda of tomorrow. The argument is that the great advantage of HPE, as she refers to it, is that the very nature of its subject area carries opportunities to become a so-called *connective specialism*. The attempt to capture the picture of those policy connections can be seen in Figure 1.

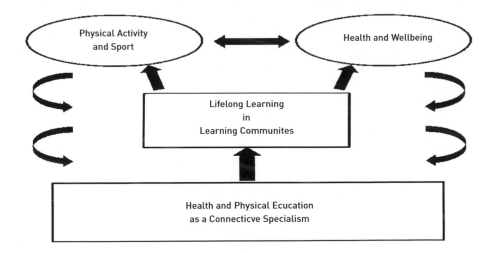

Figure 1: HPE as a "Connective Specialism". (Source: Penny, 2008, p.39).

Lifelong learning is at the centre of the contemporary social endeavour as an ongoing process to develop the skills that enable us to deal competently with the world as it confronts us, to have the personal and social skills and knowledge to have an effect on that world and in turn to shape our own place within it. Rooted in the discourses of learning networks and communities as indicated above, HPE, it is argued, has the advantage of occupying a central position in these multiple lifelong learning agendas and, therefore, in this context becoming an important part of the educational "gel" enabling young people to engage effectively with the challenges of the day. The potential for the subject to offer connections between different facets of learning is one that has been recognised also by the Association for Physical Education Scotland (2010), which has identified a number of structural and delivery issues central to building a forward looking PE curriculum for the 21st Century. These include the provision of experiential and active learning experiences that connect to young people's lives outside school. However, whilst pupil centred, individually relevant teaching-learning approaches sit at the heart of this agenda and they need contributions from effective local partnerships as well as those from other areas of the curriculum.

In a related vein, Wild (2010) reports on several opportunities that have been taken to change the PE curriculum and in so doing reflect a growing trend to create a school environment that is more learner relevant. Schools that demonstrated the sort of traditional programme balance referred to above reflected on their current practice in the light of what young people needed and the sort of individual challenges and personalised approaches most appropriate to meeting those needs. At the heart of the process were strategies to de-emphasise teacher led, skills based activities and allow pupils to manage more of their own learning. One of the strategies employed was to recognise and build on the cross-curricular potential of PE as a means of encouraging pupils to become more independent and better at problem solving. Lessons that emphasised learning intentions and thinking objectives encouraged pupils to a better understanding of the principles of activities and moved the focus away from a pre-occupation with skill development. The resultant shift from a prescriptive to a more dynamic and enterprising curriculum appears to have found favour with the pupils who reported higher levels of enjoyment, perceived themselves to be progressing more effectively and demonstrated higher participation.

Another significant element of these school-based projects was greater use of multi-skill, multi-activity and pathway approaches that reflects the emergence of a multi-skills agenda in PE in recent years. Of course it has long been recognised that a rich movement experience at a young age is critical to the emergence of an individual's later competence to participate in a range of activities and indeed to the development of high ability and the emergence of talent in a range of fields (Fisher & Bailey, 2009). However, the potential of multi-skill programmes is seen not only in the platform it can provide for future skill development but equally importantly it has the great advantage of being readily accessible to all pupils regardless of background or ability. However, whilst the development of a rich repertoire of movement potential in young people has been recognised as important for many years a number of factors have constrained efforts to bring it about. The persistence of a poor quality PE offer in primary schools has been the identified across the world by numerous writers and professional organisations (e.g. Hardman & Marshall, 2009) and to this can be added factors such as the sport and health dominated curricula identified already. The rapid rise of programmes to offer multi-skills opportunities is regarded as an important contribution to promoting fundamental movement skills (Morley 2009a) and, in turn, it is easy to locate such work within the notion of talent development pathways. Whilst there are dangers that it takes on a life of its own, indeed a business opportunity as multi-skill coaches emerge apace, the notion of establishing a foundation for personal development and opening up a wider range of future participation opportunities remains sound.

However, Morley (2009b) reminds us that moving policy into practice is contextualised by a process of interpretation and reinterpretation that impinges on most initiatives in education as they progress from what ought to be happening to what actually happens as teachers and pupils interact. Both Penny and Evans (1999) and Fisher (2004) have identified the many and complex networks that influence this process and result in multiple variants of the original intention, also referred to as policy slippage. There is the ongoing influence of the comfort of existing practice identified above (Martin & Segal, 2004), the norms of influential stakeholders and the extent to which there is ownership of any proposed change. Morley (2009b) raises important questions concerning the extent to which the agencies promoting and developing the multi-skills agenda are coming to terms with these underlying constraints. Wild stressed the importance of ensuring clarity as to how these programmes equate to children's development as well as the need to ensure a consistent delivery pattern across a variety of contexts. He also identified the importance of securing the engagement of senior managers in driving change, as did Goodwin (2007) in the context of the inclusion of pupils with physical disabilities in PE. Whilst she stressed the need to better understand the personal experience of children with learning difficulties and for better, more coherent structures to support them, she identified the engagement of senior staff teams as critical to providing focus and meaning to curriculum change without which teachers felt more isolated and uncertain of their practice.

However we construe the future, we have to be clear about what type of professionals are required at the heart of a new more expansive approach to education, as well as who will provide them and what qualifications they will possess. In reflecting on teacher education in our new world, Newby (2005) summarised some important signposts for the future. Acknowledging the shift in the public-private balance in education provision, increasingly global access to education, a broader more community oriented role for schools and the need for education to work in partnerships, he identifies some important issues for teacher education:

- The education, training and development of the teaching workforce will be located in many places, not only higher education, but business, schools, industry, community, faith and cultural organisations.
- Higher education will work in partnership with schools to provide initial and continuing teacher education – those courses and programmes that will flourish will be those that remain sensitive to the consumer's needs for *premium quality* provision. Schools, with their greater power and autonomy will determine what they need and when, rather than universities deciding what they will offer.
- Educational research, the conceptual dynamo for innovation and development, will increasingly be undertaken in consortia and funding (from a variety of sources) will go to those who demonstrate a clear connection to practice.

- The content of teacher education will come to reflect the needs of schools in the 21st century – what does it mean for a student to be literate in the 21st Century and how do we deliver it?
- Teacher education and development is a lifelong process and Continuing Professional Development (CPD) has to evolve in different, more flexible ways that go far beyond the traditional offering.

At the heart of this agenda is the clarification and definition of what constitutes the most appropriate process of preparing somebody to teach. Whilst these issues cannot be addressed in any depth here, it is informative to consider again some of the reflections contained in the UK House of Commons Report (2010). Consistent with their thoughts on the nature of the education system itself and in the context of rolling back the influence of the state, the Committee concluded that centrally prescribed requirements for initial teacher training are having a *deadening effect* on the process as a whole. They encourage the government "to take urgent steps to minimise the regulatory burden on providers [of teacher training] and to encourage genuine local autonomy to respond to wider policy change" (p.28).

Equally interesting in the same Report is the encouragement to explore the potential for increasing the opportunities for employment based routes into teaching based in schools. This route to becoming a teacher currently accounts for some 15% of national provision and it is suggested could usefully be expanded to around 30%. The subsequent policy proposals of the Secretary of State for teacher education build on this philosophy of apprenticeship style training working alongside fellow professionals. Other aspects of the agenda identified by Newby can be seen in the disappointment expressed in the Report at the lack of contribution made by research active staff to training provision and the emphasis placed on viewing teaching as a learning profession - teachers constantly reviewing and reflecting on their practice and supporting colleagues.

International efforts to develop a high quality profession have inevitably drawn on the idea of a career long development process and there has been considerable progress in many countries in developing more flexible, practice-based models of continuing professional development (CPD). An initial qualification followed by a diet of short in-service courses and further qualifications may or may not have relevance to teachers' everyday lives and, therefore, have more or less impact on teaching and learning in the classroom. Since Armour and Yelling (2004) suggested that CPD for teachers lacked coherence and relevance, newer models have emerged that take place within the school day, involve the collective participation of teachers from a school or clusters of schools in a community of practice. Such models mirror the emergence of personalised learning agendas for pupils by placing greater emphasis on small group work- and practice-based interaction with colleagues designed to generate greater impact on practice. In terms of the future, Goodwin and Askew (2010) highlight the importance of transformational leadership in driving innovation and change in schools. In a project to promote a culture of challenge and encouragement in schools, they argue for the value of shared knowledge constructions between school leaders and teachers and between teachers and learners. Through what might be viewed as a triangulation of voices, there are more opportunities to challenge and reflect on practice and thus to generate the sort of complex cultural shifts necessary for change.

More practice-based models of teacher education and development demand different, more flexible and personalised approaches to learning and as indicated above more effective use of research in practice. Cordingley (2010) draws attention to the lack of attention paid to the processes involved in using evidence and research in practical contexts and the importance of the role of CPD in doing so. Central to that process are coaching and mentoring as important means of helping to make the research practice connections. A simplified version of the national framework for mentoring and coaching can be seen in Figure 2 and is founded on an interface between three main elements:

- Mentoring – a structured approach for supporting professional learners through career transitions
- Specialist Coaching – a structured process for developing specific aspects of a learner's practice
- Co-coaching – a structured, sustained process to enable two or more professional learners to explore and embed new knowledge and skills

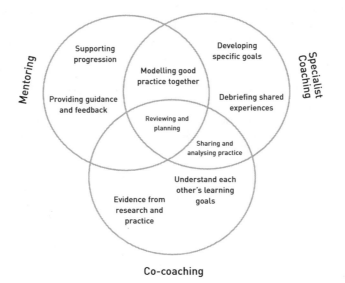

Figure 2: Mentoring and Coaching
Source: Adapted from Centre for the Use of Research and Evidence in Education (www.curee.co.uk).

Mentoring and coaching are in effect mediating processes helping to provide a rich environment in which research supports teachers to sharpen their focus on particular developments, test their theories on practice behaviour and evaluate their research based strategies in the context of pupils' learning. Cordingley (2010) highlights the rather generic nature of this work thus far and urges the development of more specific approaches focusing on particular fields such as mathematics and science, to which we can add PE.

In the context of professional collaboration to keep pace with change and in view of benefits to be gained by interacting with colleagues, it is useful to look outside the education profession for examples of good practice. Barr (2007) reported on a project looking at the value of Inter-professional Education (IPE) in pre-registration courses (initial training) in the health sector and its relevance for other professional sectors including education, sport science and health for example. Based on related developments in the UK, Australasia, North America and the Nordic countries, it pursued a collaborative approach to professional education and practice through so called *common learning programmes* shared with related but different professions in the health sector, that is, collaborative professional training that spans related but different disciplines. In one of the four case studies in the Report, there were trainees from nursing, medicine, physiotherapy, speech and language therapy, occupational therapy, medical imaging, and social work. The aim was to develop, implement and embed innovative work-based practice placements to promote a new type of collaborative learning across the professions. The purpose was to highlight for trainees how their roles interface with other related professions and the importance of providing a coherent experience and support systems for patients, or in our case learners. The argument is that reconfiguring professional training into a collaborative enterprise between different professions promotes the following:

- Teamwork;
- Collaboration between professions, organisations and patients;
- A good skill mix and flexible working between professions;
- Opportunities to switch training pathways for career progression;
- New types of workers;

It should be acknowledged that the project was not without its problems including resistance from some of the trainees who just wanted to focus on their chosen discipline, so further development is necessary since change can be, and often is, unsettling. Even so, Barr (2007) suggested that one of the values of IPE in the health sector is its increasing relevance in other fields such as education.

CONCLUSION

Any attempt to understand the future in education is framed not only by ongoing patterns of socio-economic change but also the challenge of attempting to move often quite cumbersome systems forward in appropriate ways within reasonable timescales. This chapter has sought to identify the nature of rapidly changing socio-economic circumstances, to look at what the implications might be for education in general and PE in particular and then to highlight some of the approaches that have been adopted to cope effectively with these new circumstances. There has been little attempt to deal with the process of change *per se* since that is worthy of a chapter on its own. Clearly there is an appreciation in the profession of the need to understand the future shape of "education" and the circumstances that shape it. Rix and Twining (2007) suggest that the diversity of provision required to cope effectively with the needs of tomorrow's learner reflects three core agendas for schooling: standards, choice and inclusion, which in turn go together with extensive growth in information communication technologies, thus reflecting core neo-liberal thinking. In this context, their examination of different forms of educational provision identifies a new type of learner programme, one that:

> "would be short or long term, rooted in creativity and involving high learner choice. It would allow all learners the opportunity to engage with learning opportunities at all points in their life, and in all possible learning settings, while at the same time providing them with a systematic arena (regulation) that could support and formally acknowledge their learning" (p.340).

However, there have been a large number of policy shifts and curriculum renewal initiatives over the last two decades but the predominant view of the state of PE (Green, 2008; Hardman & Marshall, 2009) confirms that in spite of this activity PE has retained a relatively consistent and traditional offer. There is evidence of curriculum renewal and innovation as indicated above but the most common features of the PE curriculum are continuity, stability and the centrality of the agendas of sport and health. As Green (2008) points out this is not necessarily a criticism but it does raise questions about the extent to which the subject is meeting the needs of technologically sophisticated and more independent learners. Local, national and international initiatives such as those identified above have focused on preparing for an increasingly complex future and have delivered some exciting possibilities that may assist in future proofing the educational experiences offered in PE. However, the impact on practice appears to have some way to go; systems and curricula have changed but in relation to the reality of the classroom it is tempting to recall Sparkes' (1991, p.1) reference to Evans' (1985) view of several educational initiatives at the time as representing *innovation without change and change without innovation*, which probably remains more relevant today than might be hoped.

PE does have a number of tensions to deal with both from a general systemic point of view as Klein (2004) pointed out, as well as trying to meet the demands of strong established communities of practice such as sport, not to mention fighting for a place in the crowded and congested place that the curriculum has become (Penney, 2008; Green, 2008). In dealing with these tensions the lessons from initiatives that appear to have been successful in transforming practice are evident in the UK House of Commons Report (2010). Moving away from central control and the micro-management of teachers, thereby allowing much greater freedom to interpret the national curriculum rather than being tied to it, is a key principle, accompanied by the notion of meaningful self assessment by schools and genuine self evaluation. This chimes well with a number of successful curriculum initiatives such as those highlighted above and including evolving patterns of CPD for teachers. Essentially it involves building capacity at local level to review classroom practice and devise strategies for development, thus giving greater ownership of projects to teachers and engaging school communities in a different, more effective way. As Goodwin and Askew (2010) point out, driving innovation and change is not a management tool and a much more complex cultural shift is required that engages learners and leaders alike and offers more control of the learning environment to those who inhabit it. It is salutary, however, to note politicians' view of their own practice as indicated in the Report above:

"Our only concern – and one which we voiced in our report on School Accountability – is whether actions will match rhetoric. We found ample evidence in that enquiry that the government, contrary to the statement in the recent White Paper that each school was responsible for its own improvement, was trying to drive improvement through central programmes and targets, some of which had a distorting effect and were perceived as harmful" (p.5).

A conservative and relatively inflexible culture at all levels of education has remained largely intact in spite of official rhetoric to the contrary and is perhaps at the heart of a seeming inability to innovate sufficiently quickly or deeply enough. The extent to which local solutions and real ownership of the curriculum become a reality, therefore, would appear to be an important determinant of schools' capacity to deal effectively with the future.

REFERENCES

Apple, M.W. (2001). Comparing Neo-Liberal Projects and Inequality in Education. *Comparative Education Review, 37*(4), pp.409-423.

Armour K.M. & Yelling, M.R. (2004). Continuing professional development for experienced teachers in physical education. *Sport, Education and Society, 9*(1), pp.95-114.

Association for PE Scotland (2010). Physical Education in Scotland in the 21st Century. *Physical Education Matters, 5*(1), pp.11-14.

Barr, H. (Ed.) (2007). *Piloting Interprofessional Education: Four English Case Studies.* London, the Higher Education Academy.

Baumann, Z. (2000). *Liquid Modernity.* Cambridge, Polity Press.

Borms, J. (2008). *Directory of Sport Science.* Berlin, International Council of Sport Science and Physical Education.

Brettschneider, W-D. (2001). Psychological outcomes and social benefits of sport involvement and physical activity implications for physical education. In G. Doll-Tepper & D. Scoretz, *Proceedings of the World Summit on Physical Education*, Berlin, ICSSPE, pp.77-82.

Cordingley, P. (2010). *Stepping Stones, Bridges and Scaffolding*, CUREE, www.curee-paccts.com/resorces/publications/stepping-stones-bridges-scaffolding.

Curtis, W., & Pettigrew, A. (2009). *Learning in Contemporary Culture.* Exeter, Learning Matters.

Dismore, H., & Bailey, R. (2010). 'It's been a bit of a rocky start': attitudes toward physical education following transition. *Physical Education and Sport Pedagogy, 15*(2), pp.175–192.

Evans, J., & Penney, D. (2008). Levels on the playing field: the social construction of physical 'ability' in the physical education curriculum. *Physical Education and Sport Pedagogy, 13*(1), pp.31-47.

Fisher, R.J. (2004). Physical Education: Current Trends and Future Perspectives. Presentation, *World Sport for All Congress*, Rome, November 11–14.

Fisher, R.J., & Bailey, R. (Eds.) (2009). *Talent Identification and Development – The Search for Sporting Excellence.* Perspectives Series, Berlin, International Council of Sport Science and Physical Education.

Goodwin, L.J. (2007). *The inclusion of children with disabilities in physical education,* Ph.D. Thesis, Guildford, University of Surrey.

Goodwin, L.J., & Askew, P. (2010). *Leading Innovation and Change.* Paper presented to the 6th International Symposium on Educational Reform, Kempton Park, South Africa, July 19-23.

Gove, M. Rt. Hon. (2010). Speech to the Annual Conference of the National College, 17th June, www.michaelgove/content/national-college-annual-speech.

Green, K. (2002). Physical Education and 'The Couch Potato Society'. *European Journal of Physical Education, 7*(2), pp.95-107.

Green, K. (2008). U*nderstanding Physical Education*, London, Sage.

Hardman, K., & Marshall, J.J. (2009). *Second World-Wide Survey of School Physical Education*, Berlin, International Council of Sport Science and Physical Education.

House of Commons Children, Schools and Families Committee (2010). *From Baker to Balls: the foundations of the education system.* London, The Stationery Office HC422.

Klein, G. (2004). Opportunities and Risks for School Physical Education in a Post-Welfarist Context. Unpublished paper presented to *Portuguese Society of Physical Education,* Lisbon, November, 13-16.

Martin, P., & Segal, R. (2004). *Learning from Innovations: Reflections on the Innovations Initiative.* Milton Keynes, The Open University.

Miller, R. (2001). 21st Century Transitions: Opportunities, Risks and Strategies for Governments and Schools. In: OECD, *What Schools for the Future?* Paris, OECD, pp.147-156.

Morley, D. (2009a). Multi-skills: Contexts and Constraints, *Physical Education Matters, 4*(3), pp.19-23.

Morley, D. (2009b). Multi-skills: The Competence and Confidence Constraints, *Primary Physical Education Matters, 5*(1), pp.vii-viii.

Newby, M. (2005). Some Conclusions, *Journal of Education for Teaching, 31*(4), November, pp.311-317.

O'Donovan, T., & Kirk, D. (2008). Re-conceptualizing student motivation in physical education: an examination of what resources are valued by pre-adolescent girls in contemporary society. *European Physical Education Review, 14*(1), pp.71-91.

Organisation for Economic Co-operation and Development (2001). *What Schools for the Future*, Paris, OECD.

Penney, D. (2004). Physical Education. In J. White, (Ed.), *Rethinking the school curriculum: values, aims and purposes.* London, Routledge Falmer, pp.138-152.

Penney, D. (2008). Playing a political game and playing for position. Policy and curriculum development in health and physical education. *European Physical Education Review, 14*(1), pp.33-39.

Penney, D., & Evans, J. (1999). *Policy, politics and practice in physical education and sport.*, London, E & FN Spon.

Pro-Active South London (2007). *Building Schools for the Future*, Fairfield Hall, Croydon, 26 November, www.pro-activesouthlondon.org.

Rix, R., & Twining P. (2007). Exploring education systems: towards a typology for future learning? *Educational Research, 49*(4), pp.329-341.

Smith, A., Thurston, M., Lamb, K., & Green, K. (2007). Young people's participation in National Curriculum Physical Education: a study of 15-16 year olds in North-West England and North-East Wales. *European Physical Education Review, 13*(2), pp.165-194.

Sparkes, A. (1991). Curriculum Change: On Gaining a Sense of Perspective. In N. Armstrong & A. Sparkes (Eds.), *Issues in Physical Education*, London, Cassell Educational Limited, pp.1-19.

Wild, A. (2009). Implementation of the new Secondary Curriculum. *Physical Education Matters, 4*(3), pp.15-18.

CONTRIBUTORS

Lars Bo Andersen, Centre of Research in Childhood Health (RICH), Institute of Sports Science and Clinical Biomechanics, University of Southern Denmark, Odense.

Daniël Behets, Professor, Research Centre for Movement Education and Sport Pedagogy, Faculty of Physical Education and Rehabilitation Sciences, Catholic University Leuven, Leuven, Belgium

Hans Peter Brandl-Bredenbeck, Professor, Department of Sport and Health, University of Paderborn, Paderborn, Germany.

Wolf-Dietrich Brettschneider, Professor Emeritus, Department of Sport and Health/Faculty of Natural Sciences, University of Paderborn, Paderborn, Germany.

Malgorzata Bronikowska, Lecturer, Department of Olympism and Ethnology of Sport, University School of Physical Education, Pozna*f*, Poland.

Michal Bronikowski, Associate Professor, Head of Department of Methodology of Teaching Physical Education (Head of Department), Faculty of Physical Education, Sport and Rehabilitation, University School of Physical Education, Pozna*f*, Poland

Ed Cope, Graduate Teaching Assistant, Institute of Sport & Exercise Science, University of Worcester, Worcester, UK.

Francisco Carreiro da Costa, Professor, Faculty of Human Kinetics, Technical University of Lisbon, Lisbon, Portugal.

José Alves Diniz, Professor, Faculty of Human Movement, Technical University of Lisbon, Lisbon, Portugal.

Richard Fisher, Professor, Head of 2012 Preparations and Sport Strategy, St Mary's University College, Twickenham, United Kingdom

Karsten Froberg, Associate Professor, Head of Centre of Research in Childhood Health (RICH), Institute of Sports Science and Clinical Biomechanics, University of Southern Denmark, Odense, Denmark.

Ken Hardman, Visiting Professor, Institute of Sport and Exercise Science, University of Worcester, UK.

Peter Iserbyt, Research fellow, Research Centre for Movement Education and Sport Pedagogy/Faculty of Physical Education and Rehabilitation Sciences, Catholic University Leuven, Leuven, Belgium

Ruan Jones, Senior Lecturer in Physical Education, Department of Childhood Studies, Faculty of Education, Canterbury Christ Church University, Canterbury, UK.

Gregor Jurak, Associate Professor, Department for Physical Education, Faculty of Sport, University of Ljubljana, Ljubljana, Slovenia.

Konstantin Kougioumtzis, Senior Lecturer, Department of Nutrition and Sport Science, Faculty of Education, University of Gothenburg, Gothenburg, Sweden.

Marjeta Kovač, Associate Professor, Head of Department for Physical Education, Faculty of Sport, University of Ljubljana, Ljubljana, Slovenia.

Adilson Marques, Assistant Professor, Faculty of Human Kinetics, Technical University of Lisbon, Lisbon, Portugal

Richard Medcalf, Senior Lecturer, HE Business and Applied Sports Sciences, University of West England Hartpury, Hartpury, UK.

Göran Patriksson, Professor, Department of Nutrition and Sport Science, Faculty of Education, University of Gothenburg, Gothenburg, Sweden

Rose-Marie Repond, EUPEA President, HES Professor, Federal Institute of Sport, Bern University of Applied Sciences, Macolin, Switzerland.

Gregor Starc, Associate Professor, Department for Physical Education, Faculty of Sport, University of Ljubljana, Ljubljana, Slovenia.

Janko Strel, Professor, Department for Physical Education, Faculty of Sport, University of Ljubljana, Ljubljana, Slovenia.

Gemma van Vuuren-Cassar, Senior Lecturer, Department of Childhood Studies, Faculty of Education, Canterbury Christ Church University, Canterbury, UK.